Simca 1100 & 1204 Owners Workshop Manual

by J H Haynes
Member of the Guild of Motoring Writers

and P G Strasman
MISTC

Models covered:

Simca 1100 Saloon, Estate, Van & Pick-up, 1118 cc (68.2 cu in)
Simca 1204 Saloon, 1204 cc (73.4 cu in)
Simca 1100 Special & 1100 TI Saloon, 1294 cc (79 cu in)
Dodge 1100 Van & Pick-up, 1118 cc (68.2 cu in)

ISBN 0 85696 507 3

ABCDE
FGHIJ
KLMNO
PQRS

Printed in England *(088 - 4E2)*

HAYNES PUBLISHING GROUP
SPARKFORD YEOVIL SOMERSET ENGLAND
distributed in the USA by
HAYNES PUBLICATIONS INC
861 LAWRENCE DRIVE
NEWBURY PARK
CALIFORNIA 91320
USA

Acknowledgements

Our extended thanks must go first to F.W.B. Saunders Limited of Sherborne, Dorset who were very patient with the supply of technical information and with the loan of a model of the marque; and to Chrysler (UK) Limited for the use of some of their illustrations.

Lubrication data was supplied by Castrol Limited, and the Champion Sparking Plug Company supplied the illustrations showing the various spark plug conditions. The bodywork repair photographs used in this manual were provided by Lloyds Industries Limited who supply 'Turtle Wax', 'Dupli-Color Holts' and other Holts range products.

Bill Kinchin must not be forgotten for his stalwart efforts in laying out the text of the book, and thanks are also due to all those members of the Haynes organisation who helped in its production.

Last but not least, thanks must go to Peter Strasman, who compiled the Supplement, and to Robin Wager who edited it.

About this manual

Its aims

The aim of this Manual is to help you get the best value from your car. It can do so in several ways. It can help you decide what work must be done (even should you choose to get it done by a garage), provide information on routine maintenance and servicing, and give a logical course of action and diagnosis when random faults occur. However, it is hoped that you will use the Manual by tackling the work yourself. On simpler jobs it may even be quicker than booking the car into a garage, and going there twice to leave and collect it. Perhaps most important, a lot of money can be saved by avoiding the costs the garage must charge to cover its labour and overheads.

The Manual has drawings and descriptions to show the function of the various components so that their layout can be understood. Then the tasks are described and photographed in a step-by-step sequence so that even a novice can do the work.

Its arrangement

The Manual is divided into thirteen Chapters, each covering a logical sub-division of the vehicle. The Chapters are each divided into Sections, numbered with single figures, eg 5; and the Sections into paragraphs (or sub-sections), with decimal numbers following on from the Section they are in, eg 5.1, 5.2, 5.3 etc.

It is freely illustrated, especially in those parts where there is a detailed sequence of operations to be carried out. There are two forms of illustration: figures and photographs. The figures are numbered in sequence with decimal numbers, according to their position in the Chapter: eg Fig. 6.4 is the 4th drawing/illustration in Chapter 6. Photographs are numbered (either individually or in related groups) the same as the Section or sub-section of the text where the operation they show is described.

There is an alphabetical index at the back of the Manual as well as a contents list at the front.

References to the 'left' or 'right' of the vehicle are in the sense of a person in the driver's seat facing forwards.

Whilst every care is taken to ensure that the information in this manual is correct no liability can be accepted by the authors or publishers for loss, damage or injury caused by any errors in, or omissions from, the information given.

Introduction to the Simca 1100

Early 1967 saw the introduction of the SIMCA 1100 in France. The English motoring press who were invited across to its launch came away ecstatic about its roadholding and brisk performance. In 1973 such has been the general advancement in these two areas that this range of front wheel drive cars hardly features in any comparisons and it has mellowed into the background to some extent. Whilst still available in a number of forms in the United Kingdom they are no longer exported to America.

The SIMCA 1100 was the French company's launch into the front wheel drive '1100-1300' market. Whilst certainly nothing startling to look at they were fairly sophisticated, even complicated, mechanically, even though they were designed around the very familiar SIMCA 1000 engine fitted to the rear of that car. The engine was mounted 'east-west' but had a separate gearbox which is removable from the engine as a unit.

Many versions have been available but their dissimilarities are few in concept. Three body styles, a saloon, estate and van, have been available even though the saloon has a rear opening door at the back. Two (or three) and four (or five) door saloons have been available as with the estate versions. A semi-automatic gearbox has been offered on some versions but these are not very common. The SIMCA 1100 not called a SIMCA 1100 was the SIMCA 1204; and this has been rather confusing. The 1204 was a 'stroked' version of the 1100 saloon to give the appropriate increase in engine size and with some other modifications, some increase in performance. This nomenclature was later dropped when the engine was increased further in size to 1294 cc and the car re-named the 1100 Special or TI.

They are a relatively cheap and economic car with much in their favour with regard to comfort and all round performance but apart from in their native France they have not been constantly successful in the UK and almost unsuccessful in America. However this is probably not so much due to the car but more to problems associated with buying an imported car.

Contents

4

SIMCA 1100 GLS TO UK SPECIFICATION

(Other versions of the saloon differ very little in their appearance from the car shown here. The estate and van have an extended rear bodywork so that the rear door is nearly vertical)

Ordering spare parts

Always buy genuine SIMCA spares from a Chrysler/Simca dealer. Most parts are immediately available and components not in stock at a dealership can usually be supplied within a day or two.

When ordering spare parts, it is essential to give full details of your vehicle to the storeman. He will need to know the type, the serial number and where the engine or gearbox is concerned, the serial numbers of these units as well.

The vehicle serial number, body number, paint code and other details will be found either on a single plate (early models) located within the engine compartment (photo) or on separate index strips as shown in Fig.RM.9.

The engine number is found on the side of the engine block, Fig.RM.10.

The gearbox number is located as shown in Fig.RM.11.

It is always helpful to take along the component which is to be renewed as an additional safeguard against modifications which may have taken place to the particular component since the vehicle was built. Many of the vehicle manufacturers original parts can no longer be exchanged on a factory reconditioned basis. New components can only be purchased outright.

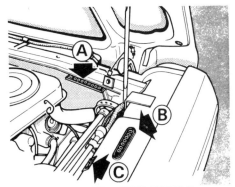

RM.9. DATA PLATE, LATER MODELS

(A)   *Type number*   *(B)*   *Body number*
                    (C)   *Paint code*

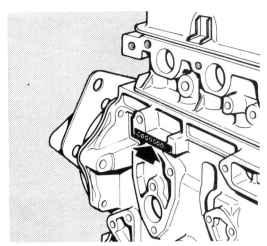

RM.10. Engine serial number

Single plate serial numbers

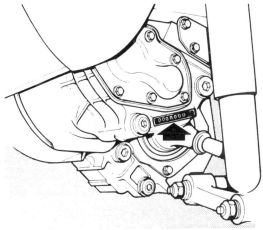

RM.11. Gearbox number

Tools and working facilities

Introduction

A selection of good tools is a fundamental requirement for anyone contemplating the maintenance and repair of a motor vehicle. For the owner who does not possess any, their purchase will prove a considerable expense, offsetting some of the savings made by doing-it-yourself. However, provided that the tools purchased are of good quality, they will last for many years and prove an extremely worthwhile investment.

To help the average owner to decide which tools are needed to carry out the various tasks detailed in this manual, we have compiled three lists of tools under the following headings: *Maintenance and minor repair, Repair and overhaul,* and *Special.* The newcomer to practical mechanics should start off with the *Maintenance and minor repair* tool kit and confine himself to the simpler jobs around the vehicle. Then, as his confidence and experience grows, he can undertake more difficult tasks, buying extra tools as, and when, they are needed. In this way, a *Maintenance and minor repair* tool kit can be built-up into a *Repair and overhaul* tool kit over a considerable period of time without any major cash outlays. The experienced do-it-yourselfer will have a tool kit good enough for most repair and overhaul procedures and will add tools from the *Special* category when he feels the expense is justified by the amount of use these tools will be put to.

It is obviously not possible to cover the subject of tools fully here. For those who wish to learn more about tools and their use there is a book entitled *How to Choose and Use Car Tools* available from the publishers of this manual.

Maintenance and minor repair tool kit

The tools given in this list should be considered as a minimum requirement if routine maintenance, servicing and minor repair operations are to be undertaken. We recommend the purchase of combination spanners (ring one end, open-ended the other); although more expensive than open-ended ones, they do give the advantages of both types of spanner.

Combination spanners to cover the range 10 to 18 mm
Adjustable spanner — 9 inch
12 mm AF Allen key for drain plugs
Spark plug spanner (with rubber insert)
Spark plug gap adjustment tool
Set of feeler gauges
Brake adjuster spanner
Brake bleed nipple spanner
Screwdriver — 4 in long x ¼ in dia (flat blade)
Screwdriver — 4 in long x ¼ in dia (cross blade)
Combination pliers — 6 inch
Hacksaw, junior
Tyre pump
Tyre pressure gauge
Oil can
Fine emery cloth (1 sheet)
Wire brush (small)
Funnel (medium size)

Repair and overhaul tool kit

These tools are virtually essential for anyone undertaking any major repairs to a motor vehicle, and are additional to those given in the *Maintenance and minor repair* list. Included in this list is a comprehensive set of sockets. Although these are expensive they will be found invaluable as they are so versatile — particularly if various drives are included in the set. We recommend the ½ in square-drive type, as this can be used with most proprietary torque wrenches. If you cannot afford a socket set, even bought piecemeal, then inexpensive tubular box spanners are a useful alternative.

The tools in this list will occasionally need to be supplemented by tools from the *Special* list.

Sockets (or box spanners) to cover range in previous list
Reversible ratchet drive (for use with sockets)
Extension piece, 10 inch (for use with sockets)
Universal joint (for use with sockets)
Torque wrench (for use with sockets)
'Mole' wrench — 8 inch
Ball pein hammer
Soft-faced hammer, plastic or rubber
Screwdriver — 6 in long x 5/16 in dia (flat blade)
Screwdriver — 2 in long x 5/16 in square (flat blade)
Screwdriver — 1½ in long x ¼ in dia (cross-blade)
Screwdriver — 3 in long x 1/8 in dia (electricians)
Pliers — electrician side-cutters
Pliers — needle nosed
Pliers — circlip (internal and external)
Cold chisel — ½ inch
Scriber (this can be made by grinding the end of a broken hacksaw blade)
Scraper (this can be made by flattening and sharpening one end of a piece of copper pipe)
Centre punch
Pin punch
Hacksaw
Valve grinding tool
Steel rule/straight edge
Allen keys
Selection of files
Wire brush (large)
Axle stands
Jack (strong scissor or hydraulic type)

Special tools

The tools in this list are those which are not used regularly, are expensive to buy, or which need to be used in accordance with their manufacturers' instructions. Unless relatively difficult mechanical jobs are undertaken frequently, it will not be economic to buy many of these tools. Where this is the case, you could consider clubbing together with friends (or a motorists' club) to make a joint purchase, or borrowing the tools against a deposit from a local garage or tool hire specialist.

The following list contains only those tools and instruments freely available to the public, and not those special tools produced by the vehicle manufacturer specifically for its dealer network. You will find occasional references to these manufacturers' special tools in the text of this manual. Generally, an alternative method of doing the job without the vehicle manufacturers' special tool is given. However, sometimes, there is no alternative to using them. Where this is the case and the relevant tool cannot be bought or borrowed you will have to entrust the work to a franchised garage.

Valve spring compressor
Piston ring compressor
Balljoint separator
Universal hub/bearing puller
Impact screwdriver
Micrometer and/or vernier gauge
Carburettor flow balancing device (where applicable)
Dial gauge
Stroboscopic timing light
Dwell angle meter/tachometer
Universal electrical multi-meter
Cylinder compression gauge
Lifting tackle
Trolley jack
Light with extension lead

Buying tools

For practically all tools, a tool factor is the best source since he will have a very comprehensive range compared with the average garage or accessory shop. Having said that, accessory shops often offer excellent quality tools at discount prices, so it pays to shop around.

Remember, you don't have to buy the most expensive items on the shelf, but it is always advisable to steer clear of the very cheap tools. There are plenty of good tools around at reasonable prices, so ask the proprietor or manager of the shop for advice before making a purchase.

Care and maintenance of tools

Having purchased a reasonable tool kit, it is necessary to keep the tools in a clean serviceable condition. After use, always wipe off any dirt, grease and metal particles using a clean, dry cloth, before putting the tools away. Never leave them lying around after they have been used. A simple tool rack on the garage or workshop wall, for items such as screwdrivers and pliers is a good idea. Store all normal spanners and sockets in a metal box. Any measuring instruments, gauges, meters, etc., must be carefully stored where they cannot be damaged or become rusty.

Take a little care when tools are used. Hammer heads inevitably become marked and screwdrivers lose the keen edge on their blades from time-to-time. A little timely attention with emery cloth or a file will soon restore items like this to a good serviceable finish.

Working facilities

Not to be forgotten when discussing tools, is the workshop itself. If anything more than routine maintenance is to be carried out, some form of suitable working area becomes essential.

It is appreciated that many an owner mechanic is forced by circumstances to remove an engine or similar item, without the benefit of a garage or workshop. Having done this, any repairs should always be done under the cover of a roof.

Wherever possible, any dismantling should be done on a clean flat workbench or table at a suitable working height.

Any workbench needs a vice: one with a jaw opening of 4 in (100 mm) is suitable for most jobs. As mentioned previously, some clean dry storage space is also required for tools, as well as the lubricants, cleaning fluids, touch-up paints and so on which become necessary.

Another item which may be required, and which has a much more general usage, is an electric drill with a chuck capacity of at least 5/16 in (8 mm). This, together with a good range of twist drills, is virtually essential for fitting accessories such as wing mirrors and reversing lights.

Last, but not least, always keep a supply of old newspapers and clean, lint-free rags available, and try to keep any working area as clean as possible.

Spanner jaw gap comparison table

Jaw gap (in)	Spanner size
0.250	¼ in AF
0.275	7 mm AF
0.312	5/16 in AF
0.315	8 mm AF
0.340	11/32 in AF; 1/8 in Whitworth
0.354	9 mm AF
0.375	3/8 in AF
0.393	10 mm AF
0.433	11 mm AF
0.437	7/16 in AF
0.445	3/16 in Whitworth; ¼ in BSF
0.472	12 mm AF
0.500	½ in AF
0.512	13 mm AF
0.525	¼ in Whitworth; 5/16 in BSF
0.551	14 mm AF
0.562	9/16 in AF
0.590	15 mm AF
0.600	5/16 in Whitworth; 3/8 in BSF
0.625	5/8 in AF
0.629	16 mm AF
0.669	17 mm AF
0.687	11/16 in AF
0.708	18 mm AF
0.710	3/8 in Whitworth; 7/16 in BSF
0.748	19 mm AF
0.750	¾ in AF
0.812	13/16 in AF
0.820	7/16 in Whitworth; ½ in BSF
0.866	22 mm AF
0.875	7/8 in AF
0.920	½ in Whitworth; 9/16 in BSF
0.937	15/16 in AF
0.944	24 mm AF
1.000	1 in AF
1.010	9/16 in Whitworth; 5/8 in BSF
1.023	26 mm AF
1.062	1.1/16 in AF; 27 mm AF
1.100	5/8 in Whitworth; 11/16 in BSF
1.125	1.1/8 in AF
1.181	30 mm AF
1.200	11/16 in Whitworth; ¾ in BSF
1.250	1¼ in AF
1.259	32 mm AF
1.300	¾ in Whitworth; 7/8 in BSF
1.312	1.5/16 in AF
1.390	13/16 in Whitworth; 15/16 in BSF
1.417	36 mm AF
1.437	1.7/16 in AF
1.480	7/8 in Whitworth; 1 in BSF
1.500	1½ in AF
1.574	40 mm AF; 15/16 in Whitworth
1.614	41 mm AF
1.625	1.5/8 in AF
1.670	1 in Whitworth; 1.1/8 in BSF
1.687	1.11/16 in AF
1.811	46 mm AF
1.812	1.13/16 in AF
1.860	1.1/8 in Whitworth; 1¼ in BSF
1.875	1.7/8 in AF
1.968	50 mm AF
2.000	2 in AF
2.050	1¼ in Whitworth; 1.3/8 in BSF
2.165	55 mm AF
2.362	60 mm AF

Routine maintenance

The maintenance instructions listed are basically those recommended by the manufacturer. They are supplemented by additional maintenance tasks proven to be necessary.

The additional tasks are primarily of a preventative nature in that they will assist in eliminating the unexpected failure of a component due to fair wear and tear.

Weekly, or every 250 miles

1 Check the level of the engine oil by removing the dipstick, Fig.RM.1.

2 Check that the level is kept between the minimum and maximum marks on the dipstick. If topping up is required, add Castrol GTX through the filler cap (A) on the rocker box, Fig.RM.2.

3 When checking the oil level, always ensure that the vehicle is standing on level ground and that the engine has been switched off for at least ten minutes to allow the oil to drain back to the sump.

4 With the engine cold, check that the coolant level in the expansion chamber is maintained between the minimum and maximum marks, Fig.RM.3.

5 Check the tyre pressures, including the spare and inflate them if required to the recommended pressures.

6 Examine the treads and tyre walls for cuts and damage and if the tread pattern is showing a depth of 1 mm or less, the tyre must be renewed.

7 Check the battery electrolyte level and top up with distilled water if necessary to just above the top of the plate separators.

8 Refill the windscreen washer bottle to the correct level, using a proprietary fluid in the washer to facilitate cleaning and to prevent freezing of the solution.

9 Check the security of the road wheel nuts.

10 With automatic transmission, the fluid reservoir is located on the left hand wheel housing within the engine compartment, Fig.RM.4.

11 The level within the reservoir must be maintained between the maximum and minimum marks with the engine and transmission cold.

12 Check the level of the brake and clutch fluid in the reservoir and top up as necessary. The need for continued or excessive topping up must be immediately investigated as it probably indicates a leak in the hydraulic circuit.

When a new car is delivered the engine contains sufficient running-in oil for the running-in period. Providing the level is maintained between the low and high marks on the dipstick during this period topping up is unnecessary. At the first 'Free Service' the running-in oil is drained and the sump replenished to the level of the high mark on the dipstick.

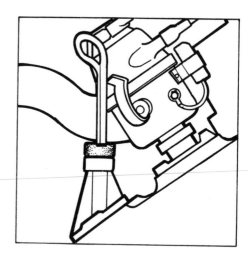

RM.1. Location of the engine oil dipstick

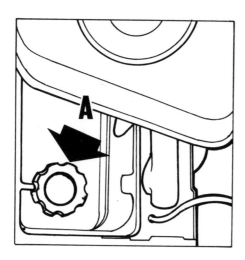

RM.2. Rocker box, engine oil filler cap

RM.3. Cooling system expansion bottle

Every 3000 miles (or 3 months)

1 Run the engine until it is at full operating temperature and then drain the oil into a suitable container placed beneath the sump. This is accomplished by unscrewing and removing the socket drain plug (12 mm hexagonal) Fig. RM.5.

2 Refill the sump through the rocker cover filler cap with 3 litres of Castrol GTX (photo).

3 Remove the distributor cap and withdraw the rotor from its shaft. Apply two or three drops of engine oil to the felt pad located in the top of the distributor shaft. Refit the rotor and the cap.

4 Check the tension of the water pump drive belt and adjust if necessary after reference to Chapter 2 or 11.

5 Check and adjust the clutch pedal free movement as described in Chapter 5.

6 Remove, clean, check and adjust the spark plugs and check the distributor points gap as described in Chapter 4.

7 At the beginning of spring and autumn, check the position of the air filter intake pipe. The lever positioned below the air cleaner body should be moved to the ETE (summer) or HIVER (winter) position as appropriate, Fig.RM.6.

Filling the engine with oil

Every 6000 miles (or 6 months)

1 Drain and refill the engine oil as described for the 3000 mile service.

2 Renew the oil filter. The filter is a disposable cartridge type, located below the exhaust manifold. Unscrew the old filter and catch the oil which will be released, in a suitable container. Grease the rubber sealing gasket of the new filter and screw it into position by HAND ONLY. Run the engine and check for oil leaks. Top up the oil level to replace that absorbed by the new filter.

3 Remove the air filter element from within the air cleaner body as described in Chapter 3. Tap the element on a piece of wood to remove any surface dust and refit it in a different position to that originally occupied within the cleaner body, in order to present a fresh surface to the intake airflow.

4 After a run when the transmission oils are warm, drain the gearbox and the final drive (differential) units Fig.RM.7 and Fig.RM.8. Refill with the correct quantity of Castrol EP 90 oil, (photo).

5 Lubricate all door hinges, locks and handles with engine oil (photo).

6 Repeat the operations described in paragraphs 3,4,5 and 6 of the 3000 mile service schedule.

7 Check the thickness of the front disc brake friction pads as described in Chapter 10.

8 Check all water, brake , fuel and vacuum pipe unions for security.

Oiling a door hinge

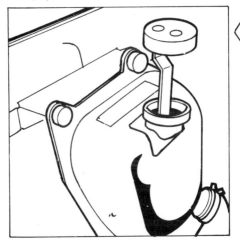

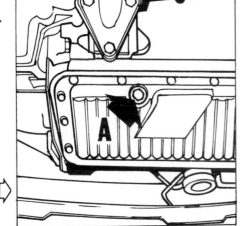

RM.4. Automatic transmission, fluid reservoir and dipstick

RM.5. Engine oil drain plug

Every 12000 miles (or 12 months)

1   Repeat the operations from the 3000 or 6000 mile services which are appropriate and carry out the following additional work.

2   Dismantle, repack with grease and adjust the rear hubs as described in Chapter 9.

3   Renew the air cleaner element.

4   Adjust the valve rocker clearances as described in Chapter 1.

5   Bleed all old hydraulic fluid from the braking and clutch circuits and refill the reservoir with fresh fluid of the recommended type. The bleeding procedure is described in Chapter 10.

6   Remove the rear brake drums, clean the dust from the shoes and drums and check the friction linings for wear, (Chapter 10).

7   Adjust the handbrake (Chapter 10).

8   Check the steering rack and pinion unit rubber bellows for deterioration. Renew if necessary as described in Chapter 8.

9   Check the drive shaft rubber bellows for deterioration and renew if necessary as described in Chapter 7.

10 Check the ball joint rubber covers for deterioration and renew as appropriate (Chapter 7 and 8).

11 Examine all steering and suspension components for wear. Push and pull the linkage and operating rods in order to detect wear in the swivels, ball joints bushes and bearings.

12 Examine the underside of the bodyframe and wings and make good any under seal which has been chipped off. Where a more general deterioration of the under vehicle protection is evident, it will be advantageous to have the underside steam cleaned and a new application of protective coating made.

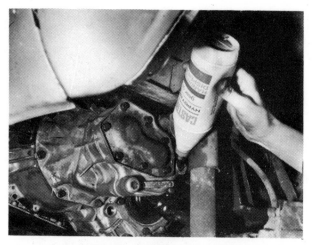

Filling the gearbox with oil

Filling the final drive with oil

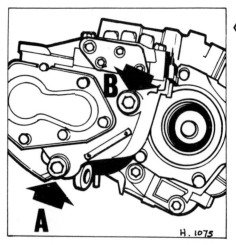

RM.6. Air intake control lever (Winter and Summer)

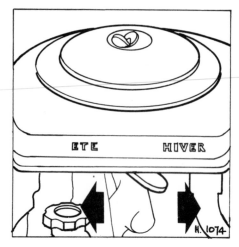

RM.7. Gearbox,
(A) drain plug (B) filler plug

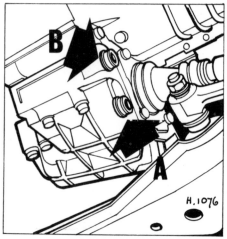

RM.8. Final drive unit,
(A) drain plug (B) filler plug

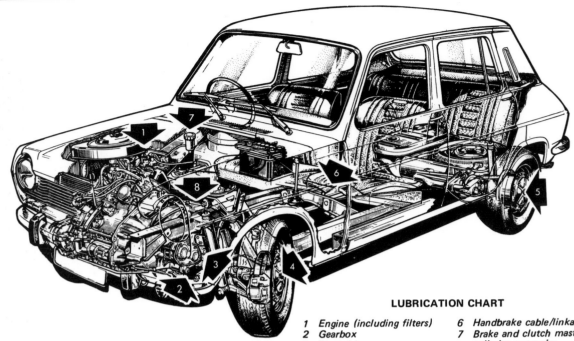

LUBRICATION CHART

1 Engine (including filters)
2 Gearbox
3 Final drive
4 Front hubs
5 Rear hubs
6 Handbrake cable/linkages
7 Brake and clutch master cylinder reservoirs
8 Steering rack

Recommended lubricants and fluids

COMPONENT	TYPE OF LUBRICANT OR FLUID	CORRECT CASTROL PRODUCTS	NOMINAL REFILL CAPACITIES
ENGINE	Multi-grade engine oil 20W/50	Castrol GTX	5.75 pints (3.3 litres)
GEARBOX AND FINAL DRIVE	Gear oil SAE 90EP	Castrol Hypoy - Gearbox (manual)	0.9 pint (0.6 litre) Gearbox (semi-auto) 0.8 pint (0.5 litre) Final drive 0.8 pint (0.5 litre)
AUTOMATIC TRANSMISSION CONVERTOR		Castrol TQF	7.5 pints (4.3 litres)
FRONT AND REAR WHEEL BEARINGS	Medium grade multi-purpose grease	Castrol LM Grease	
STEERING RACK	Medium grade Molybdenum Grease	Castrol MS3 Grease	
DISTRIBUTOR & GENERATOR BEARINGS	Engine or light oil	Castrol GTX or 'Everyman'	
BRAKE AND CLUTCH MASTER CYLINDERS	Hydraulic fluid	Castrol/Girling Universal Brake and Clutch Fluid	
ANTI-FREEZE	GLYCOL ANTIFREEZE	Castrol Antifreeze	10.4 pints (6 litres)
CONTACT BREAKER CAM	Petroleum jelly (vaseline)		
BATTERY TERMINALS	Petroleum jelly (vaseline)		

Additional Castrol GTX can be used to lubricate locks, hinges, cable linkages and latch mechanisms.

Chapter 1 Engine

Contents

Specifications

Engine type	ohv, four cylinder in-line, crossflow head
Location	Transverse, inclined to rear 41°
Material	Crankcase - cast iron
	Cylinder head - aluminium alloy
Firing order	1 3 4 2
Direction of crankshaft location	Anti clockwise viewed from flywheel end

Engine type	350/350S	353/353S North American models	366/366TT
Bore	2.9134 in (74 mm)	2.9134 in (74 mm)	3.0156 in (76.7 mm)
Stroke	2.5591 in (65 mm)	2.7559 in (70 mm)	2.7559 in (70 mm)
Capacity	1118 cc	1204 cc	1294 cc
Compression ratios (low)	(350) 8.2:1	(353) 8.7:1	(366) 9.6:1
(high)	(350S) 9.6:1	(353S) 9.5:1	(366TT) 10:1
Max. power output (DIN) BHP at rev/min	54 at 6000 (350) 60 at 6000 (350S)	70 at 6000 (353) 75 at 6000 (353S)	75 at 5800
Max. torque (DIN) lb ft at rev/min	60 at 3200 (350) 62 at 3200 (350S)	67 at 3600 (353) 70 at 3600 (353S)	72 at 3400

Crankshaft and connecting rods

Main bearing, journal diameter (red)	2.0463 - 2.0467 in	(51.975 - 51.985 mm)
Main bearing, journal diameter (blue)	2.0459 - 2.0463 in	(51.966 - 51.976 mm)
Shell thickness (red)	0.075 - 0.076 in	(1.915 - 1.924 mm)
Shell thickness (blue)	0.076 - 0.077 in	(1.924 - 1.933 mm)

Running clearance	0.00158 - 0.00307 in	(0.040 - 0.078 mm)	
Big end crankpin diameter (red)	1.6125 - 1.6128 in	(40.957 - 40.965 mm)	
Big end crankpin diameter (blue)	1.6122 - 1.6125 in	(40.949 - 40.958 mm)	
Shell thickness (red)	0.059 - 0.060 in	(1.492 - 1.501 mm)	
Shell thickness (blue)	0.060 - 0.061 in	(1.500 - 1.509 mm)	
Running clearance	0.00118 - 0.00252 in	(0.030 - 0.064 mm)	
End-float of crankshaft	0.0016 - 0.0031 in	(0.040 - 0.078 mm)	
Connecting rod side play	0.0012 - 0.0025 in	(0.030 - 0.065 mm)	
Crankshaft undersizes	0.004 - 0.008 - 0.020 in	(0.1 - 0.2 - 0.5 mm)	
Width of centre main bearing journal	1.237 - 1.239 in	(31.43 - 31.47 mm)	
Small end bore diameter	0.8648 - 0.8652 in	(21.965 - 21.976 mm)	
Crankshaft thrust washer thickness	0.091 - 0.093 in	(2.31 - 2.36 mm)	

Pistons

Material	Aluminium alloy
Rings	2 compression 1 oil control

Standard piston diameters

Engine type		Piston diameter	To fit cylinder bore
350, 350S, 353, 353S	A	2.9116 - 2.9128 in (73.955 - 73.985 mm)	2.9131 - 2.9135 in (73.992 - 74.002 mm)
	B	2.9120 - 2.9132 in (73.965 - 73.995 mm)	2.9135 - 2.9139 in (74.002 - 74.012 mm)
	C	2.9124 - 2.9136 in (73.975 - 74.005 mm)	2.9139 - 2.9143 in (74.012 - 74.022 mm)
366, 366TT	A	3.0179 - 3.0183 in (76.655 - 76.665 mm)	3.0194 - 3.0198 in (76.692 - 76.702 mm)
	B	3.0183 - 3.0187 in (76.665 - 76.675 mm)	3.0198 - 3.0202 in (76.702 - 76.712 mm)
	C	3.0187 - 3.0191 in (76.675 - 76.685 mm)	3.0202 - 3.0276 in (76.712 - 76.722 mm)

Oversize pistons available	0.00394 - 0.01575 in (0.1 - 0.4 mm)
Piston clearance in bore	0.0010 - 0.0018 in (0.027 - 0.047 mm)

Piston rings (350/353 series engines)

Ring width (top compression)	0.06890 in (1.75 mm)
(lower compression)	0.07874 in (2.00 mm)
(oil control)	0.15748 in (4.00 mm)
Ring clearance in groove (compression)	0.0018 - 0.0028 in (0.045 - 0.072 mm)
(oil control)	0.0010 - 0.0022 in (0.025 - 0.057 mm)
Ring end gap (compression)	0.008 - 0.016 in (0.20 - 0.40 mm)
(oil control)	0.010 - 0.018 in (0.25 - 0.45 mm)

Gudgeon pins

Material	Steel
Length	2.5197 in (64 mm)
Outside diameter	0.8658 - 0.8659 in (21.991 - 21.995 mm)
Clearance in piston	0.0004 - 0.0007 in (0.010 - 0.019 mm)
Interference fit in con rod small end	0.0006 - 0.0012 in (0.016 - 0.030 mm)

Camshaft

Bearing journal diameter (numbered from flywheel end)	
(No 1)	1.39495 - 1.39595 in (35.444 - 35.459 mm)
(No 2)	1.61195 - 1.61255 in (40,944 - 40.959 mm)
(No 3)	1.63165 - 1.63224 in (41.444 - 41.459 mm)
Bearing clearance	0.00098 - 0.00299 in (0.025 - 0.076 mm)
End-float	0.004 - 0.008 in (0.10 - 0.20 mm)
Cam lift (inlet)	0.2252 in (5.72 mm)
(exhaust)	0.2415 in (5.416 mm)

Tappets (Cam followers)

Diameter	0.90551 - 0.90654 in (23.0 - 23.026 mm)
Height	1.57480 - 1.57583 in (40.0 - 40.026 mm)

Valves and guides

	Prior to 1970	After 1970
Inlet valves		
Head diameter	1.29921 in (33 mm)	1.33858 in (34 mm)
Stem diameter	0.31005 - 0.31456 in (7.875 - 7.990 mm)	
Stem to guide clearance	0.0013 - 0.0022 in (0.032 - 0.056 mm)	
Face angle	45°	
Valve lift	0.338 in (8.58 mm)	

Exhaust valves	
Head diameter	1.10 in (28 mm)
Stem diameter	0.313 - 0.314 in (7.950 - 7.965 mm)
Stem to guide clearance	0.0022 - 0.0035 in (0.057 - 0.090 mm)
Face angle	45°

Valve lift	0.33780 in (8.118 mm)

Valve guides

Inside diameter	0.31583 - 0.31653 in (8.022 - 8.040 mm)
Outside diameter	0.55071 - 0.55130 in (13.988 - 14.003 mm)
Length	2.04725 in (52 mm)
Seat angle	44º - 44º 30'

Valve clearances

Inlet - COLD	0.012 in (0.30 mm)
Inlet - HOT	0.014 in (0.35 mm)
Exhaust - COLD	0.014 in (0.35 mm)
Exhaust - HOT	0.016 in (0.40 mm)

Lubrication system

Oil pump	Externally mounted, camshaft driven
Oil filter	Full flow, disposable cartridge type
Oil pump shaft side play	0.002 - 0.020 in (0.05 - 0.50 mm)
Sump capacity	5.28 imperial pints, 3.0 litres

TORQUE WRENCH SETTINGS

	lb ft
Cylinder head bolts	45
Main bearing cap bolts	47
Connecting rod cap bolts	26
Oil relief valve cap	20
Flywheel to crankshaft bolts	40
Drive plate to crankshaft (auto. gearbox)	40
Drive plate to torque convertor (auto. gearbox) ...	26
Crankshaft pulley bolt	96
Oil pressure switch	22
Inlet manifold nuts	10
Exhaust manifold nuts	14.5
Spark plugs	20
Crankshaft oil seal housing to cylinder block	8.5
Camshaft retaining plate	10.5
Camshaft sprocket bolts	10.5
Timing gear cover bolts	14.5
Sump to block bolts	8.5
Sump pan bolts	6.5
Oil pump retaining bolts	8.5

1 General description

1 The SIMCA range includes saloons, vans and estate cars fitted with either high or low compression engines and offered with three or five doors according to model.

2 The standard engine is of 1118 cc capacity and in its low compression form (8.2 : 1) is designated the 350 while in high compression form (9.6 : 1) is designated the 350S. Certain vehicles are fitted with a smaller 944 cc engine (352) but these are only distributed in a few territories. Although not specifically mentioned here they are basically similar.

3 The 1100 special is fitted with a 1294 cc engine (366) which is an uprated version of the 1204 cc power unit (353S) previously fitted to the 1204 Special car.

4 All engine types are basically similar and are of four stroke, four cylinder, overhead valve type.

5 The engine is constructed of cast iron with a light alloy cylinder head. It is transverse mounted and inclined at 41º from the vertical within the engine compartment.

6 The power unit transmits motion to the front road wheels through a unitary gearbox/differential (mounted ahead of and below left of the engine) and open drive shafts.

7 A forged steel crankshaft is fitted, supported on five bearings with replaceable shells.

8 The valves are operated by push rods and the pistons are of aluminium alloy with two compression and one oil control ring. Piston assemblies are removed through the top of the block.

9 Lubrication is by means of an externally mounted, camshaft driven pump. A full flow oil filter is incorporated in the system and closed circuit type of crankcase breathing is employed.

10 Cooling is by sealed system and the radiator is cooled by an electrically driven, thermostatically controlled fan.

11 Ignition is by conventional battery, coil and distributor.

12 Full specifications of all engine types and vehicle model applications are to be found in 'Specifications'. Certain modifications made to engines fitted to vehicles destined for the U.S.A. market are dealt with in a later section of this Chapter.

2 Major operations with engine in position in vehicle

1 The following operations may be carried out with the power unit in position in the vehicle.

2 Removal and replacement of the cylinder head assembly.

3 Removal and replacement of the oil pump.

4 Removal and replacement of the engine and gearbox mountings.

5 Removal of the gearbox/differential for access to clutch and flywheel.

6 Removal and renewal of the major engine ancillaries, starter motor, water pump, distributor, alternator, oil filter.

3 Major operations with engine/gearbox removed from vehicle

1 Renewal of engine main bearings.

2 Removal of crankshaft.

3 Removal of piston assemblies.

4 Removal of camshaft.

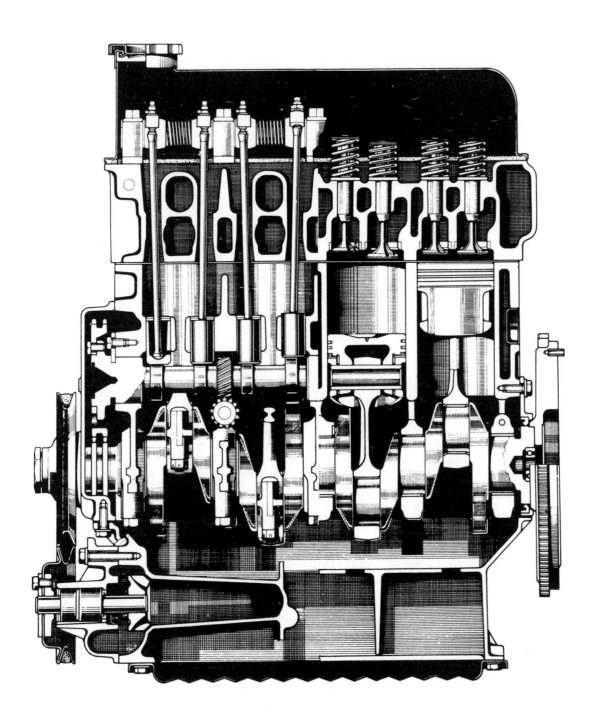

Fig. 1.1. Sectional view of engine (Sec. 1)

4 Engine/gearbox/differential (single unit) - removal

1 There is no point in removing the gearbox/differential unit separately from the engine when major servicing operations are to be carried out on the engine but the combined engine/gearbox/differential should be removed as a single unit for later separation.

2 Before commencing operations, hire or borrow a hoist or lifting tackle and a trolley onto which the engine unit can be lowered after removal from **below** the vehicle.

3 Jacking up the car securely and at a sufficient height is essential to enable the power unit to be withdrawn forwards from below the car after it has been lowered from the engine compartment. Suitable jacks, stands and chocks should therefore be acquired. Alternatively, an inspection pit may be used but this method will present difficulties in moving the car after engine removal and hoisting the engine from the pit floor.

4 The inclined angle of the engine within the engine compartment will necessitate using lifting slings of different lengths so that the inclination of the unit will be maintained during removal. The slings should be made up from suitably strong steel or terylene rope. The length of one of them should be 44½ inch terminating in S hooks, and the other 28½ inch terminating at one end in a loop 13½ inch long, and at the other end in a 2 inch diameter ring.

5 Disconnect the battery terminals.

6 Disconnect the bonnet hinges and remove the bonnet lid. The hinge bolts are accessible after removal of the front grille (four screws). Photo.

7 Remove the radiator filler cap and unscrew the drain plug located below the water pump.

8 Retain the coolant if required for re-use.

9 Raise the front of the vehicle by placing the front road wheels on ramps or blocks.

10 Remove the water pump/alternator driving belt cover.

11 Loosen the alternator mounting bolts, push the unit towards the engine block and remove the driving belt.

12 Disconnect the electrical leads from the alternator, remove the mounting bolts and lift the unit away.

13 Disconnect the wires from the starter solenoid.

14 Disconnect the hydraulic clutch slave cylinder from the clutch withdrawal lever and tie it out of the way. By not disconnecting the hydraulic components of the clutch actuating mechanism, the system will not have to be bled on reassembly.

15 Disconnect the exhaust pipe at its connection with the manifold.

16 Detach the gearchange mechanism (rods or rod and cable according to fitment) from the gearbox and disconnect the speedometer cable from the differential housing.

17 Remove the protective guard from the right hand inner drive shaft joint.

18 Unbolt and remove the engine rear mounting.

19 Detach the two front telescopic dampers and in their place fit two rods which should be made up to the following pattern. Steel rod ½ inch (12.7 mm) diameter, 16 inch (406 mm) in length with lower eye fittings to match those of the dampers and the upper ends of the rods to be threaded with nuts and washers fitted. The substitution of these rods is to avoid strain of the dampers by the reaction of the torsion bars when at a later stage the suspension is hanging free with the vehicle frame supported on jacks.

20 Drain the differential, and the gearbox. (photo)

21 Support the vehicle on jacks or stands placed under the jacking points.

22 Remove the two front road wheels and remove the blocks or ramps upon which they were suported.

23 Disconnect both front disc calipers and support them so that the hydraulic flexible hoses are not strained (Chapter 9).

24 Disconnect the steering link ball joints using an extractor or wedges.

25 In a similar manner disconnect the swivel ball joints from the lower suspension links.

26 Remove the threaded keys from the upper ends of the stub axle carriers, and disconnect the joints.

27 Carefully supporting the driveshafts, withdraw them from their connection with the differential by pulling outwards on the stub axle and brake discs.

28 Take care not to damage the seals or rubber bellows round the inner driveshaft joint during this operation.

29 Remove the air cleaner.

30 Disconnect all cooling system and heater hoses. Special hose clips are fitted and if the correct tool is not available for removal, they should be removed with a pair of pliers or cut off and renewed with worm-drive type. (photo)

31 On the GLS and Special versions, disconnect the brake servo hose and remove the servo unit (see Chapter 8).

32 Disconnect the accelerator linkage and remove the portion located between the upper suspension transverse member and the carburettor.

33 Disconnect the choke control.

34 Disconnect the fuel feed hose from the fuel pump. Plug the hose and tie it back out of the way.

35 Disconnect the earthing strap from the cylinder head.

36 Disconnect all electrical leads from the engine. Tie them back out of the way and mark them for ease of reconnection.

37 Unscrew the radiator cooling fan securing bolts and remove the assembly.

38 Remove the distributor cover and rotor arm.

39 Fit the prepared lifting slings to the engine.

40 Take the weight of the engine on a hoist and then unscrew and remove the engine side mounting bolts to leave the bonded rubber blocks still secured to the vehicle frame.

41 Lower the engine carefully onto a trolley jack taking care not to damage the oil filter assembly.

42 Remove the lifting slings and withdraw the engine/gearbox/transmission unit forward from beneath the car. Adjust the height of the supporting jacks if necessary to accomplish this.

5 Engine dismantling - general

1 It is best to mount the engine on a dismantling stand but if one is not available, then stand the engine on a strong bench so as to be at a comfortable working height. Failing this, the engine can be stripped down on the floor.

2 During the dismantling process the greatest care should be taken to keep the exposed parts free from dirt. As an aid to achieving this, it is a sound scheme to clean down the outside of the engine, removing all traces of oil and congealed dirt.

3 Use paraffin or a good grease solvent such as 'Gunk'. The latter compound will make the job much easier, as, after the solvent has been applied and allowed to stand for a time, a vigorous jet of water will wash off the solvent and all the grease and filth. If the dirt is thick and deeply embedded, work the solvent into it with a stiff paint brush.

4 Finally wipe down the exterior of the engine with a rag and only then, when it is quite clean should the dismantling process begin. As the engine is stripped, clean each part in a bath of paraffin or petrol.

5 Never immerse parts with oilways in paraffin, i.e. the crankshaft, but to clean wipe down carefully with a petrol dampened rag. Oilways can be cleaned out with wire. If an air line is present all parts can be blown dry and the oilways blown through as an added precaution.

6 Re-use of old engine gaskets is a false economy and can give rise to oil and water leaks, if nothing worse. To avoid the possibility of trouble after the engine has been reassembled ALWAYS use new gaskets throughout.

7 Do not throw the old gaskets away as it sometimes happens that an immediate replacement cannot be found and the old gasket is then very useful as a template. Hang up the old gaskets as they are removed on a suitable hook or nail.

8 To strip the engine it is best to work from the top down. The sump provides a firm base on which the engine can be supported in an upright position. When the stage where the sump must be

Fig.1.2 Location of cooling system drain plug (Sec 4)

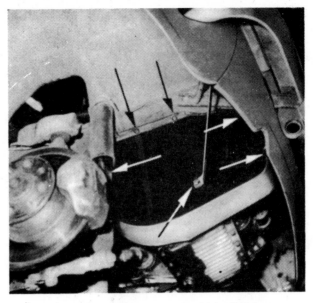

Fig. 1.3. Attachment points of the pulley driving belt cover (Sec. 4)

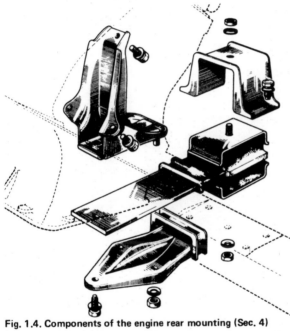

Fig. 1.4. Components of the engine rear mounting (Sec. 4)

4.6 Removing bonnet hinge bolts

4.20a Differential drain plug

4.20b Gearbox drain plug

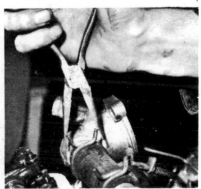

4.30 Method of hose clip removal

Fig. 1.5. Disconnecting a steering link ball joint with an extractor (Sec. 4)

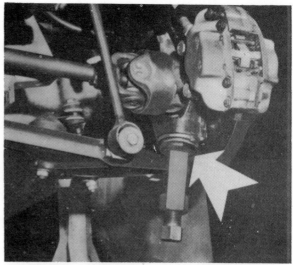

Fig. 1.6. Using an extractor to disconnect a lower suspension swivel joint (Sec. 4)

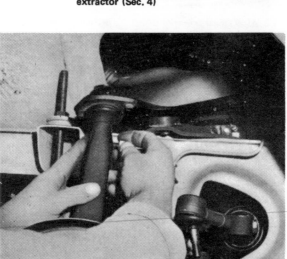

Fig. 1.7. Removing a threaded key from an upper suspension wishbone to stub axle carrier joint (Sec. 4)

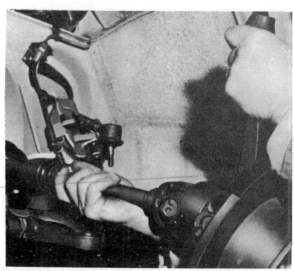

Fig. 1.8. Disconnecting a drive shaft from the differential unit (Sec. 4)

Fig. 1.9. Radiator cooling fan assembly mounting bolts (Sec. 4)

Fig. 1.10. Attachment points for engine hoisting slings (Sec. 4)

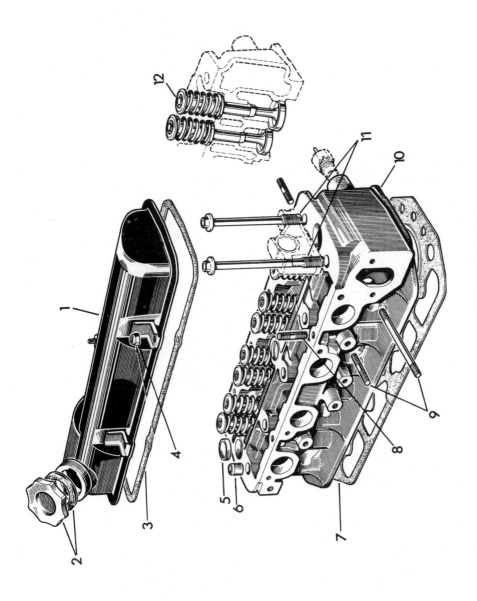

FIG. 1.11. COMPONENTS OF THE CYLINDER HEAD (SEC. 8)

1 Rocker cover	5 Core plug	9 Manifold studs
2 Oil filler cap and washer	6 Positioning dowel	10 Cylinder head
3 Gasket	7 Cylinder head gasket	11 Cylinder head bolts
4 Rocker cover nut	8 Stud	12 Valve assemblies

removed is reached, the engine can be turned on its side and all other work carried out with it in this position.

9   Wherever possible, replace nuts, bolts and washers finger-tight from wherever they were removed. This helps avoid later loss and muddle. If they cannot be replaced then lay them out in such a fashion that it is clear from where they came.

6   Engine/gearbox/differential - separation

1   The gearbox/differential unit should now be removed from the engine. First remove the starter motor.
2   Unscrew the securing bolts and remove the flywheel cover plates. There are two of these, one adjacent to the starter motor and the other near the differential.
3   Remove the bolts which secure the differential unit to the clutch housing, noting their differing lengths.
4   Remove the bolts which secure the clutch housing to the cylinder block and withdraw the gearbox. During this operation do NOT allow the weight of the gearbox to hang upon the primary shaft while it is still engaged with the splined hub of the clutch friction disc or damage to the clutch components may result.

7   Ancillary engine components - removal

1   Before basic engine dismantling begins the engine should be stripped of all its ancillary components. These items should also be removed if a factory exchange reconditioned unit is being purchased. The items comprise:-

   Warm air intake
   Rocker cover
   Spark plugs
   Distributor and attachment plate,
   vacuum pipe and HT cables
   Fuel pump (retain the thick insulating washer)
   Carburettor
   Inlet and exhaust manifolds
   Sump breather plug and pipe
   Thermostat housing on cylinder head
   Temperature sender unit
   Water inlet pipe on the crankcase
   Water manifold
   Oil dipstick and bracket
   Pulley and belt on the water pump
   Water pump
   Oil filter element

2   Drain the oil from the sump by removing the drain plug at the lowest point of the sump.
3   Remove the oil pressure relief valve assembly, body, (11) spring (10), and ball (9). Fig. 1.12 page 21.
4   Remove the oil pump cover (6) and then withdraw the oil pump body (4).
5   Ancillary components have now been removed and dismantling and stripping of the engine unit may now commence as described in the next Section.

8   Cylinder head - removal

1   This operation may be carried out with the engine still in position in the car but of course the cooling system must first be drained.
2   Unscrew each cylinder head bolt, a turn at a time, starting at number 10 and following in reverse to the order shown in Fig. 1.14 page 21.
3   When all the bolts have been withdrawn, lift off the rocker assembly.
4   Withdraw the pushrods from the tappet blocks (cam followers) by using a twisting motion to break the sealing effect of the oil and prevent displacement of the tappet blocks. Keep the pushrods in exact order for replacement.
5   Remove the cylinder head. Should it be stuck to the block, strike it in several places with a wooden or plastic faced mallet or refit the spark plugs and turn the engine over to enable compression to assist its removal. Never insert a chisel in the gasket joint or attempt to prise the head from the block.
6   Withdraw the tappet blocks and keep them in strict order for exact replacement.

9   Valves and rocker gear - dismantling

1   The valves should be removed from the cylinder head with the aid of a conventional valve spring compressor. Take great care to protect the alloy surfaces of the head from damage during these operations.
2   Compress the valve springs and remove the split cotters, cups and valve springs, seals and washers.
3   Place each valve and its components in strict order so that they may be refitted in their original positions.
4   Where necessary, the rocker shaft assembly may be dismantled by drifting the pins (1) from their locations as shown in Fig. 1.17 page 22. .

10   Lubrication system and oil sump - removal

1   The engine lubrication system is shown in diagrammatic form in Fig. 1.18 page 23.).
2   Oil contained in the sump is drawn through a strainer and delivered under pressure by the action of a camshaft-driven pump mounted on the rear face of the cylinder block.
3   The oil passes through a full-flow type filter and is fed to the connecting rod, camshaft and crankshaft bearings, the rocker assembly and the distributor and oil pump drive shafts. The cylinder bores, gudgeon pins and valve stems are splash lubricated.
4   The engine should be turned upside down and the sump retaining bolts unscrewed in a diametrically opposite sequence a few turns at a time.
5   Remove the oil strainer and gauze.

11   Clutch assembly - removal

1   Unscrew and remove the securing bolts which retain the clutch pressure plate cover to the flywheel. Unscrew them a few turns at a time in alternate sequence and mark the position of the cover relative to the flywheel for exact replacement.
2   Lift the cover away and catch the driven plate. Do not let it fall to the ground or it may fracture. Damage could also occur to the friction linings.

12   Crankshaft pulley and timing gear - removal

1   Lock the engine to prevent rotation by inserting a lever or large screwdriver blade in the flywheel ring gear.
2   Unscrew the crankshaft pulley. Several sharp blows on the arm of the spanner will loosen the retaining bolt where leverage will fail.
3   Remove the securing bolts from the timing cover.
4   Unscrew and remove the three bolts which secure the camshaft sprocket to the camshaft flange.
5   Remove the camshaft sprocket complete with chain which should be detached from the crankshaft sprocket.
6   Remove the crankshaft sprocket which may require the use of a puller or two levers placed behind it. Withdraw the key.

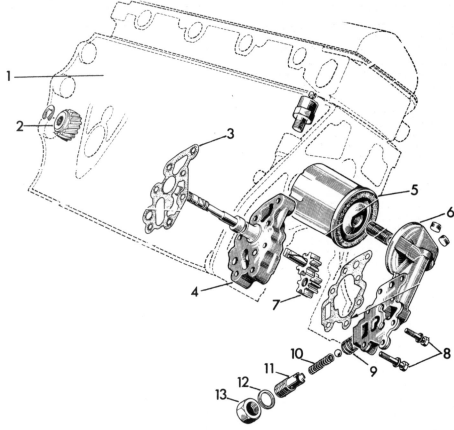

FIG. 1.12. COMPONENTS OF THE OIL PUMP, DRIVE AND FILTER LOCATED ON THE REAR FACE OF THE ENGINE BLOCK (SEC. 7)

Key

1 Circlip	4 Body	7 Pump gears	10 Relief valve spring
2 Drive gear	5 Filter	8 Securing bolts	11 Relief valve body
3 Gasket	6 Pump cover	9 Relief valve ball	12 Washer
			13 Locknut

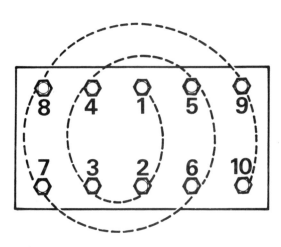

Fig. 1.13. Cylinder head bolt tightening sequence (Sec. 8)

Fig. 1.14. Location of the engine side mounting bolts (Sec. 4)

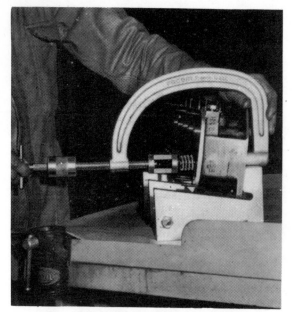

Fig. 1.15. Compressing a valve spring (Sec. 9)

Fig. 1.17. Drifting the rocker shaft locating pins from their positions (Sec. 9)

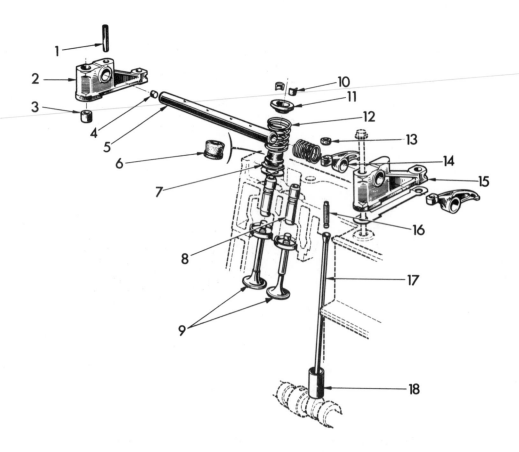

FIG. 1.16. COMPONENTS OF THE VALVE AND ROCKER GEAR (SEC. 9)

1 Pin	5 Rocker shaft	9 Valve	14 Rocker arm
2 Rocker shaft pillar	6 Seal	10 Split cotters	15 Rocker shaft pillar
3 Positioning dowel	7 Washers	11 Cup	16 Adjuster screw
4 Plug	8 Valve guide	12 Spring	17 Push-rod
		13 Locknut	18 Tappet (cam follower)

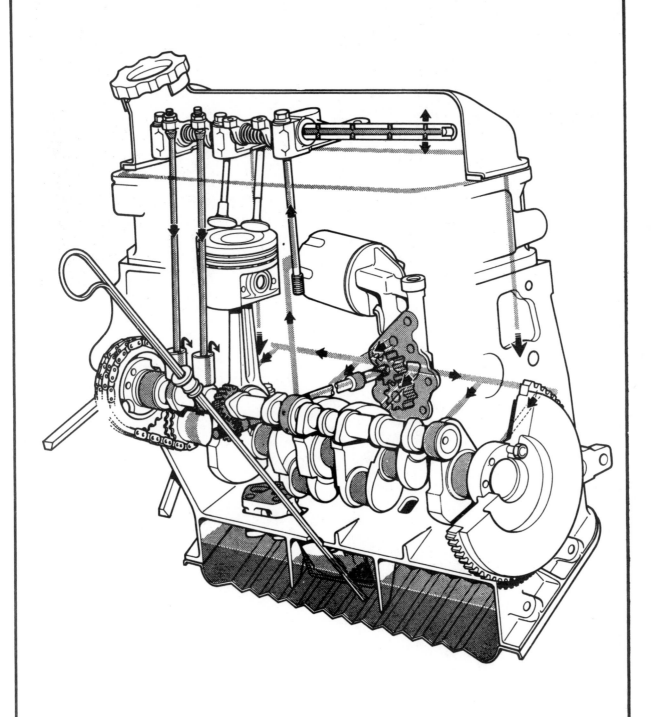

Fig. 1.18. Diagrammatic view of the engine lubrication system (Sec. 10)

24

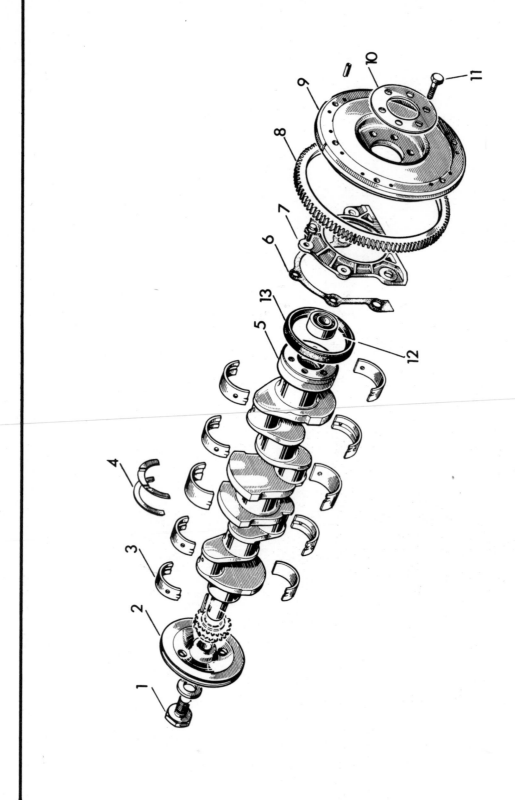

FIG. 1.19. COMPONENTS OF THE CRANKSHAFT, MAIN BEARINGS AND FLYWHEEL (SEC. 12)

1 Pulley retaining bolt
2 Pulley
3 Shell bearing
4 Thrust washers
5 Crankshaft
6 Gasket
7 Oil seal cover
8 Starter ring gear
9 Flywheel
10 Locking plate
11 Flywheel bolt
12 Spigot bush
13 Crankshaft rear flange seal

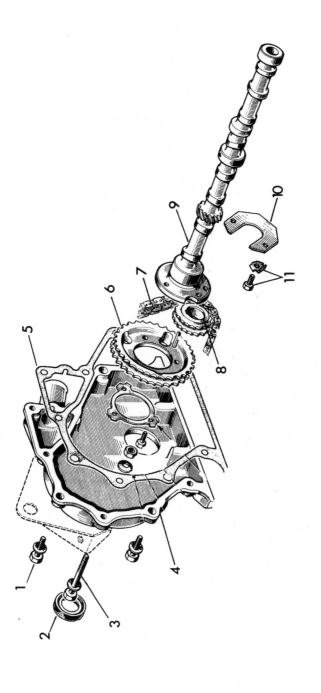

FIG. 1.20. COMPONENTS OF THE CAMSHAFT AND TIMING GEAR (SEC. 12)

1 Bolt	3 Timing cover bolt	5 Gasket
2 Crankshaft pulley oil seal	4 Timing cover	6 Camshaft sprocket

7 Timing chain	9 Camshaft	11 Thrust plate bolt
8 Crankshaft sprocket	10 Camshaft thrust plate	

13 Camshaft and oil pump drive shaft - removal

1   The tappet blocks having already been removed after withdrawal of the cylinder head, the camshaft may now be extracted.
2   From the hole vacated by the distributor, extract the circlip from the oil pump drive shaft which retains the gear and remove the shaft and gear.
3   Unbolt and remove the camshaft thrust plate.
4   Withdraw the camshaft carefully from the cylinder block so that the bearings are not knocked or damaged by the passage of the cams through them.

14 Piston/connecting rod assemblies - removal

1   Rotate the crankshaft by turning the flywheel so that each piston is (approximately) positioned half way down each bore.
2   Taking extreme care, scrape off the carbon ring which will be found to have formed at the top of each cylinder bore. Where the engine has seen considerable service, a 'wear' ring will also have been formed due to the lower portion of the cylinder bore having worn away. It is essential not to score the lower surfaces of the cylinder bore during the scraping operation. Removal of the carbon and 'wear' rings is necessary to permit the pistons and rings to pass out through the top of the block during withdrawal without fracturing the rings.
3   Invert the cylinder block and turn the flywheel until number one piston is either at TDC or alternatively the big-end is at its lowest point.
4   Unscrew and remove the big-end bearing cap nuts.
5   Remove the big-end bearing cap and extract the shells.
6   Push the piston/rod assembly out through the top of the cylinder block but restraining the outward expansion of the piston rings as they emerge from the bore to prevent them breaking.
7   Ensure that the big-end bolt threads do not score the inside of the bore as they travel upwards.
8   Refit the bearing cap to the connecting rod by screwing on the securing nuts a few turns. Mark the bearing cap with the bore location number and note particularly the correct orientation of the connecting rod for refitting.
9   Repeat the operations on the remaining three piston/connecting rod assemblies.

15 Flywheel, crankshaft and main bearings - removal

1   Unscrew and remove the six securing bolts, from the flywheel.
2   Pull off the flywheel and inset plate.
3   Unscrew and remove the cover plate and gasket and extract the oil seal.
4   Unbolt the five main bearing caps and remove them, noting carefully their orientation and sequence.
5   Lift the crankshaft from the crankcase bearings.
use of a solvent cleaner such as 'Gunk' is to be recommended,
6   Remove the shells from the crankshaft main bearing caps and from the crankcase locations. Temporarily refit the main bearing caps.
7   Retain the thrust washers (two) noting their location.
8   The engine is now completely dismantled and checking examination and renovation of the components should commence as described in the following Sections.

16 Engine components - examination for wear

Before any detailed examination of the dismantled components can be carried out, they must be thoroughly cleaned. A paraffin bath and stiff brush is an ideal method for the removal of grease, oil and grit. Where heavy deposits of grease and dirt have to be cleaned from the exterior of the engine casting,

this should have been done before dismantling the engine.

17 Crankcase and cylinder block - examination and renovation

1   Thoroughly clean the interior and exterior surfaces of the casting and inspect for cracks. Should any be apparent then the cost of repairing by a specialist welder must be compared with the purchase of a new or secondhand unit.
2   Check the security of studs and for stripped threads in all tapped holes. If necessary have thread inserts fitted such as 'Helicoil' or examine the possibility of fitting oversize bolts and studs.
3   Where there is evidence of water or oil leakage from the various core plugs these should be renewed. Remove the cap or plug by either drilling a central hole and levering out or tapping a thread and using a bolt and bridge piece as an extractor. With the smaller plugs or caps, they may be tapped inwards on one side and levered out. Protect the edge of the hole with a piece of wood as shown in Fig. 1.23 page 27. When driving in a new plug or cap, do not knock it harder than is required to effect a good seating.
4   Examine the camshaft and if the bearing bushes are worn, scored or chipped, renew them as described in Section 21.
5   Examine the oil pump drive shaft bearings and renew them if necessary as described in Section 26.
6   Examine the cylinder bores for scoring and wear. This operation is undertaken in conjunction with the examination of the pistons and by consideration of the previous history of oil consumption and smoke emission. Reference should be made to Section 24.

18 Crankshaft - examination and renovation

1   A rough visual check for wear in the crankshaft main bearings and big-end bearings may be carried out before removal of the crankshaft from the crankcase. If movement can be felt by pushing and pulling it and also slackness observed in the big-ends, then almost certainly the crankshaft will have to be reground.
2   With the crankshaft removed, all journals should be measured at two or three different points for ovality with a micrometer. If the measurements taken at one journal differ by more than 0.011 inch (0.03 mm) then the crankshaft must be reground.
3   Regrinding must be undertaken by a specialist firm who will regrind to the permitted tolerances and supply matching oversize shell bearings (see Specifications).

19 Main and big-end shell bearings - examination and renewal

1   When connecting rods are removed from the crankshaft the bearing shells will be released and even though the crankshaft journals are in good condition the bearings may need renewal. Certainly if their bearing surfaces are anything other than an even, matt grey colour they should be renewed. Any scores, pitting or discolouration is an indication of damage by metal particles or the top bearing surface wearing away. If there are any doubt it is always a good idea to replace them anyway unless there is a definite record that they have only been fitted for a small mileage. The backs of the shells are marked with serial numbers and an indication of whether or not they are undersized due to the crankshaft having been reground previously. If in doubt take them to your supplier who will be able to ensure that you are sold new ones of the correct type. If the crankshaft is being reground new bearings will be required anyhow and these are always available from the firm which does the regrinding.

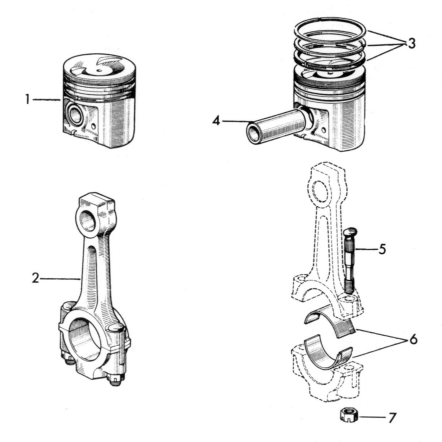

FIG. 1.22. COMPONENTS OF THE CONNECTING ROD/PISTON ASSEMBLIES (SEC. 14)

1 Piston	3 Piston rings	5 Big-end bolt	7 Big-end bolt nut
2 Connecting rod	4 Gudgeon pin	6 Big-end shell bearings	

Fig. 1.21. Extracting the oil pump drive securing circlip (Sec. 13)

Fig. 1.23. Levering out a core plug (Sec. 17)

20 Tappets - examination and renovation

1 The tappets should be checked in their respective bores in the crankcase and no excessive side-play should be apparent. The faces of the tappets which bear against the camshaft lobes should also have a clear, smooth shiny surface. If they show signs of pitting or serious wear they should be renewed. Re-facing is possible with proper grinding facilities but the economics of this need investigating first.

21 Camshaft and bearings - examination and renovation

1 The lobes of the camshaft should be examined for any indications of flat spots, pitting or extreme wear on the bearing surfaces. If in doubt get the profiles checked against specification dimensions with a micrometer. Minor blemishes may be smoothed down with a 120 grain oil stone and polished with one of 300 grain. The bearing journals also should be checked in the same way as those on the crankshaft. The camshaft bearings are renewable.
2 Drive out the camshaft front bearing (flywheel end) sealing cap. To do this, insert a rod or tube from the other end of the crankcase.
3 Removal of the front, rear and centre camshaft bushes is best accomplished by the use of a length of threaded rod and nuts with suitable tubular distance pieces.
4 Note the precise positioning of each bearing bush before removal and ensure that the bearing seats are not damaged during the removal operation.
5 Fit the new bearing bushes using the same method as for removal, starting with the centre one. It is essential that the bearing oil hole is in exact alignment with the one drilled in the bearing seat and marks should be made on the edge of the bearing bush and seat before pulling into position.
6 Fit a new camshaft front bearing sealing cap.

22 Connecting rods and small end bushes - examination and renovation

1 It is unlikely that a connecting rod will be bent except in cases of severe piston damage and seizure. It is not normally within the scope of the owner to check the alignment of a connecting rod with the necessary accuracy so if in doubt have it checked by someone with the proper facilities. It is in order to have slight bent connecting rods straightened - the manufacturers provide special jigs for the purpose. If a rod needs replacement, care should be taken to ensure that it is within 10 grams in weight of the others. If too heavy, connecting rods may be lightened by removing metal from the shoulders near the big end of the wider parts where the bearing cap mates up to it.
2 The small end bushes, if worn, will have to be renewed by exchanging the connecting rod assembly. If this procedure is followed, then it will be preferable to leave the removal and refitting of the piston and gudgeon pin to the agent from whom the component is obtained.
3 Removal of the gudgeon pin and piston for other reasons may be carried out as described in the following Section.

23 Pistons and piston rings - removal and refitting

1 A piston ring should be removed by prising the open ends of the ring just sufficiently far to enable three feeler blades or strips of tin to be slid round behind it. Position the strips at equidistant points to provide guides so that the piston ring may be slid over the other grooves and removed.
2 The gudgeon pin is a press fit in the connecting rod small end bearing and it must be removed on a press using suitable distance pieces to prevent damage to the soft alloy of the piston body. (It is too difficult to do at home!).
3 Refitting of the gudgeon pin is carried out on a press but the small end bearing must be expanded by placing the connecting rod in an oven (220-250º C) or immersing it in hot oil.
4 Note that the piston/connecting rod assembly should be as shown in Fig. 1.26 page 29 (in relation to the camshaft), before inserting the gudgeon pin.

5 Check that the protrusion of the gudgeon pin is equal either side of the piston body and adjust if necessary by further minor pressing.
6 Refit the piston rings in a manner similar to that described for removal but check their gapping in the cylinder bores as described in the next Section. Three rings are employed, top-compression, centre-scraper bottom-oil control. The two compression rings are marked 'TOP' and must be fitted the right way up. Stagger the ring gaps at three equidistant points of a circle to prevent gas blow by. (photos).

24 Piston, ring and cylinder bore wear - examination and renovation

1 Piston and cylinder bore wear are contributory factors to excessive oil consumption (over 1 pint to 300 miles) and general engine noise. They also affect engine power output due to loss of compression. If you have been able to check the individual cylinder pressures before dismantling so much the better. They will indicate whether one or more is losing compression which may be due to cylinders and pistons if the valves are satisfactory.
2 Determining the degree of wear on pistons and cylinders is complementary. In some circumstances the pistons alone may need renewal - the cylinders not needing reboring. If the cylinders need reboring then new pistons must be fitted. First check the cylinders. A preliminary check can be done simply by feeling the inside walls about ½ inch down from the top edge. If a ridge can be felt at any point then the bores should be measured with an inside micrometer or calipers to see how far they vary from standard. The measurement should be taken across the bore of the cylinder about 15 mm (0.6 inch) down from the top edge at right angles to the axis of the gudgeon pin. Then measure the piston, also at right angles to the gudgeon pin across the skirt at the bottom. The two measurements should not differ by more than 0.20 mm (0.008 inch).
3 Further measurement of the cylinder across the bore will indicate whether or not the wear is mostly on the piston. If the cylinder bore is uniform in size fitting new pistons in the original bore size is possible. However, it is a very short sighted policy. If new pistons are needed anyway the cost or reboring will add 20-25% to the cost of the pistons so it would be as well to get it done whilst the engine is out of the vehicle.
4 Another feature of the pistons to check is the piston ring side clearance in the grooves. This should not exceed 0.12 mm (0.0047 inch) for the top ring and 0.10 mm (0.004 inch) for the other two. Usually however, this wear is proportionate to the rest of the piston and will not occur in a piston which is otherwise apparently little worn. If you think that only a new set of rings is required it would be a good idea to take your pistons to the supplier of the new rings and check the new rings in the gaps. You may change your mind about how worn the pistons really are! Once a cylinder has been rebored twice (to 78 mm diameter) it must not be rebored again.
5 Remove the piston rings from each piston in turn and keep them identified for their respective bore. Similarly, if new rings are being fitted, keep them identified in respect of piston location and bore.
6 Press each ring squarely an inch or two (25 to 50 mm) down the cylinder bore and check the ring gap with feeler gauges. The gaps should be 0.010 to 0.018 inch (0.25 to 0.45 mm) for the oil control ring and 0.008 to 0.016 inch (0.20 to 0.40 mm) for the compression rings.

25 Flywheel - examination and renovation

1 The clutch friction disc mating surface of the flywheel should be examined for scoring. If this is apparent then it should either be exchanged for a new unit or if the scoring is very light it may be skimmed.
2 The starter ring gear should be examined and if the teeth are worn or chipped it must be renewed.

Fig. 1.24. Driving out the camshaft front bearing sealing cap (Sec. 21)

Fig. 1.25. Removing the camshaft bearings from the crankcase (Sec. 21)

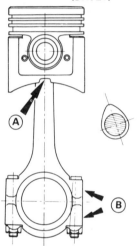

FIG. 1.26. CORRECT FITTING OF PISTON TO CONNECTING ROD (SEC. 23)

A Piston skirt cut-out

B Big end cap marks facing camshaft

Fig. 1.27. Pressing a gudgeon pin into position (Sec. 23)

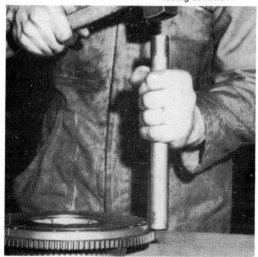

Fig. 1.28. Driving off the starter ring gear from the flywheel (Sec. 25)

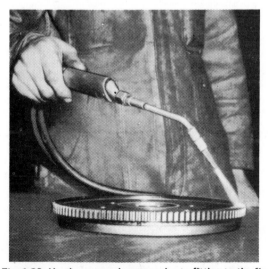

Fig. 1.29. Heating a new ring gear prior to fitting to the flywheel (Sec. 25)

3 To remove the ring, support the flywheel and drive off the ring gear using a bronze or steel bar.

4 Take care not to damage the flywheel locating dowels during this operation or they will have to be renewed.

5 Place the new ring gear in position on the flywheel ensuring that the teeth have their lead-ins (chamfer) facing the correct way as originally fitted.

6 Using a blow lamp or torch, heat the ring gear evenly all round until it just starts to drop into position.

7 Drive the ring gear squarely onto the flywheel shoulder using a drift.

8 If a new flywheel is fitted or it is skimmed, then the flywheel bolted to the crankshaft will have to be rebalanced as a unit by a SIMCA dealer.

26 Oil pump and drive shaft bushes - examination and renovation

1 The oil pump gears and drive shaft should be checked for wear and play compared with the tolerances given in Specifications. Renew components as required or exchange the complete unit.

2 Check the pressure relief valve components and renew as appropriate if the ball or body are scored or seats appear pitted.

3 Check the wear of the oil pump/distributor drive shaft bushes. Where these have to be renewed, either extract them using a threaded rod and nuts and distance pieces similar to the method used in Fig. 1.30 page 31.

4 Alternatively, tap a thread in each bush and use a bolt as an extractor.

5 Fit the shorter bush to the distributor side (M) pulling it in tight to the machined surface of the cylinder block. It is vital that the oil hole in the bush aligns with the crankshaft bearing oil passage.

6 Fit the bush to the oil pump side (N) again using the threaded rod and nut method and avoiding damage to the bush just fitted. There is no need to align the oil hole on this bush as it opens into a circular oil chamber in the cylinder block.

7 Test the drive shaft in the bushes for ease of rotation. A hard spot will indicate mis-alignment or distortion.

27 Cylinder head, rocker gear, valves - examination and renovation

1 As previously described, the alloy cylinder head must be handled very carefully to avoid scoring or damage. Do not stand it on a bench which is covered with filings or they may become embedded in the surface of the head.

2 Remove carbon using a blunt scraper taking great care not to damage the machined surfaces.

3 If there are any visible cracks the head should be scrapped. Cracks are most likely to occur round the valve seats or spark plug holes. Bearing in mind that head will cost (new) nearly 20% of the cost of a complete replacement engine economies should be considered as well as the likelihood of obtaining a used head from a breaker's yard. If the latter, make sure that the head you get is the same type as the old one - and in better condition!

4 The valve seats should be examined for signs of burning away or pitting and ridging. If there is slight pitting the refacing of the seats by grinding in the valve with carborundum paste will probably cure the problem. (photo) If the seat needs re-cutting, due to severe pitting, then the seat width should not exceed specification. Fitting new valve seat inserts is a specialist task as they are chilled and shrunk in order to fit them.

5 The rocker gear should be dismantled and thoroughly cleaned of the sludge deposits which normally tend to accumulate on it. The rocker arms should be a smooth fit on the shaft with no play. If there is any play it is up to the owner to decide whether it is worth the cost of renewal. The effects on engine performance and noise may not be serious although wear tends to accelerate once it is started. The valve clearance adjusting screws should also be examined. The domed ends that bear on the valve stems tend to get hammered out of shape. If bad, replacement is relatively cheap and easy.

6 The valves themselves must be thoroughly cleaned of carbon. The head should be completely free of cracks or pitting and must be perfectly circular. The edge which seats into the cylinder head should also be unpitted and unridged although very minor blemishes may be ground out when re-seating the valve face.

7 Replace the valve into its guide in the head and note if there is any sideways movement which denotes wear between the stem and guide. Here again the degree of wear can vary. If excessive, the performance of the engine can be noticeably affected and oil consumption increased. The maximum tolerable sideways rock, measured at the valve head with the end of the valve stem flush with the end of the guide, is 0.8 mm (0.031 inch). Wear is normally in the guide rather than on the valve stem but check a new valve in the guide if possible first. Valve guide renewal is a tricky operation and should be left to a SIMCA dealer.

8 Check that the end face of the valve stem is not 'hammered' or ridged by the action of the rocker arm. If it is, dress it square and smooth with an oilstone.

9 On later type engines, oil seals are fitted to the upper ends of the valve guides to reduce the escape of oil down the valve stems. Early model engines may be modified to accept these seals but this is an operation requiring the services of a SIMCA dealer.

28 Engine reassembly - general

1 Ensure absolute cleanliness during assembly operations and lubricate each component with clean engine oil before fitting.

2 Renew all lockwashers, gaskets and seals as a matter of course.

3 Take care to tighten nuts and bolts to the torque specified in Specifications and watch out for any differences in bolt lengths which might mean attempting to screw a long bolt into a short hole with subsequent fracturing of a casting.

4 Follow the sequence of reassembly given in the following Sections and do not skip any adjustment procedure essential at each fitting stage.

29 Crankshaft and main bearings - reassembly

1 Fit the new shell main bearings to the crankcase locations. (photo)

2 Fit the two semi-circular thrust washers.

3 The thrust washers should be retained in position with grease at each side of the main bearing centre web of the crankcase and must have their oil grooves facing outwards.

4 Oil the crankcase bearing shells liberally (photo).

5 Lower the crankshaft carefully into position in the crankcase (photo).

6 Fit the shell bearings to the main bearing caps (photo).

7 Place the main bearing caps in order, ready for fitting. The caps are numbered 1 to 5, number 1 being positioned nearest the flywheel. The shells in caps 2 and 4 have oil grooves, 1, 3 and 5 do not. Fit the main bearing caps in their correct order (photo).

8 Fit the main bearing cap bolts and tighten them to the correct torque of 47 lb/ft (photo).

9 The crankshaft end-float must now be checked. To do this, lever the crankshaft in one direction and then the other and using feeler gauges measure the gap between the thrust washers and the face of each side of the centre main bearing web. The total end-float should be between 0.0016 and 0.0031 in (0.040 and 0.078 mm), (photo). Where the clearance is outside the permitted tolerance then the thrust washers must be changed for ones of different thickness. These are available in a variety of different thicknesses.

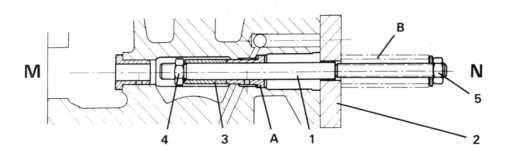

FIG. 1.30. METHOD OF EXTRACTING OIL PUMP/DISTRIBUTOR DRIVE SHAFT BUSHES (SEC. 26)

1 Rod	3 Sleeve	5 Nut	B Old gudgeon pin
2 Plate	4 Nut	A Shaft bush	M Side towards distributor
			N Side towards oil pump

23.6a Correct positioning of ring gaps

23.6b 'TOP' mark on compression rings

27.4 Grinding in a valve

29.1 Fitting main shells to crankcase

29.4 Oiling the crankcase shell bearings

29.5 Lowering the crankshaft into position

29.6 Fitting the main bearing cap shell bearing

29.7 Fitting a main bearing cap

29.8 Tightening a main bearing cap bolt

30 Flywheel, spigot bearing and oil seal - refiting

1 It is an advantage to fit the flywheel at this stage as it will provide a means of rotating the crankshaft when installing the connecting rod/piston assemblies.
2 Check the condition of the spigot bearing which is located in the centre of the flywheel mounting flange. If it is worn, extract it and drift in a new one.
3 Stick a new paper gasket in position on the cylinder block.
4 Fit a new oil seal to the inner rim of the crankshaft/flywheel flange oil seal cover.
5 Locate the oil seal cover so that the lip of the oil seal is not damaged and then fit and tighten the five securing bolts, each fitted with a lockwasher (photo).
6 If the paper gasket stands proud of the lower joint face, trim it.
7 Locate the flywheel on the crankshaft mounting flange (photo).
8 Locate the circular plate and insert the securing bolts and tighten them to 40 lb ft (photo).
9 The flywheel can only be fitted one way as the bolt holes are not equidistant and positioning dowels are designed to ensure correct location.

31 Connecting rod/piston asemblies - refiting to crankshaft

1 Fit the piston rings to the piston as described in Section 23. Oil them liberally and ensure that the gaps are staggered (photo).
2 Fit a piston ring clamp and then locate the shell bearings in the connecting rod big-end.
3 Oil the cylinder bores and insert the piston/connecting rod assembly into its cylinder. Take care not to damage the bore surfaces with the big-end bolts. (photo)
4 Correctly installed, the mark on the piston crown must be furthest from the flywheel and the connecting rod big-end reference number must face the camshaft. Do not knock the piston from the clamp into the cylinder bore but use hand pressure only.
5 Fit the shells to the big-end caps, ensuring that when the caps are correctly located, the notches of both halves of the shells will coincide.
6 Fit the big-end caps by hand pressure (photo), rotating the crankshaft by means of the flywheel to TDC or BDC to facilitate fitting.
7 Fit the big-end nuts and tighten them to a torque of 26 lb ft. (photo)
8 Fit the Woodruff key to the crankshaft. (photo).
9 Fit the crankshaft sprocket, using a tubular drift if necessary and ensuring that the countersunk side of the sprocket faces the engine. (photo)

32 Camshaft, timing gear, distributor/oil pump drive - reassembly

1 Oil the camshaft bearings liberally and insert the camshaft into the cylinder block taking care not to damage the bearings as the cam lobes pass through them (photo).
2 Fit the camshaft thrust plate so that it engages in the groove of the journal. (photo)
3 Fit and tighten the thrust plate retaining screws using new locking tabs. (photo)
4 At this stage check the camshaft endfloat, using either a dial gauge or feelers. The tolerance is between 0.005 and 0.008 inch (0.10 and 0.20 mm) and endfloat outside these recommendations should be rectified by the substitution of a new thrust plate or (if necessary due to wear) a new camshaft.
5 Bend over the thrust plate bolt locking tabs.
6 Where a split link type timing chain is fitted, proceed as follows. Fit the camshaft sprocket, the bolt holes not being equidistant, it can only be fitted correctly. (photo)

7 Tighten the securing bolts and bend over the locking tabs. (photo)
8 Rotate the crankshaft by means of the flywheel so that No 1 piston (flywheel end) is at TDC. Turn the camshaft until the alignment marks on both the camshaft and crankshaft sprockets are in alignment.
9 Fit the double roller timing chain round both sprockets and insert the link (open end of connecting plate spring away from direction of travel). (photo)
10 Check the alignment of the timing marks with a straight edge. (photo)
11 Where the timing chain is of endless type, then the crankshaft must be turned so that No 1 piston is at TDC and the chain engaged round the crankshaft sprocket. The camshaft sprocket must then be engaged within the loop of the chain so that when it is in perfect alignment for fitting to the camshaft flange. The timing marks on both sprockets are coincident. To achieve this it will be necessary to turn the camshaft and reposition the camshaft sprocket teeth in the chain on a trial and error basis.
12 Smear the oil pump drive shaft with engine oil and insert it in position. (photo)
13 Insert the shaft drive gear, engaging it with the camshaft worm. The gear must be fitted the correct way round so that the splined part of the bore is to the outside. (photo) Secure the gear with the circlip.
14 From the opposite side to the oil pump insert the distributor drive so that the large and small segments are in the position shown in the photo.
15 It is imperative that during the foregoing operations No 1 piston is held at TDC.
16 Locate the distributor base plate so that its boss is towards the timing cover and tighten the securing bolts. (photo)

33 Oil pump - refitting

1 Locate the oil pump body and a new gasket on the cylinder block. (photo)
2 Insert the oil pump gears. (photo)
3 Locate the oil pump cover and fit the securing bolts. (photo)
4 Tighten the bolts evenly to a torque of 8.5 lb ft. (photo)
5 If the relief valve has been dismantled, reassemble it and screw it securely into position.

34 Timing cover and seal and crankshaft pulley - refitting

1 Examine the timing cover oil seal for wear or damage and renew it, also if there has been previous evidence of oil leakage.
2 Extract the old oil seal and drive in the new one squarely using a suitable drift.
3 Before fitting the seal, check that the directional arrow on the seal follows the direction of rotation of the engine and that the seal spring faces inwards.
4 Using a new gasket, fit the timing cover to the cylinder block. (photo)
5 Tighten the retaining bolts noting that two different sizes of setscrews and one nut and bolt are used. (photo)
6 Fit the crankshaft pulley and retaining bolt. (photo).

35 Sump and oil strainer - refitting

1 Locate a new sump case gasket to the cylinder block, using grease to hold it in position. (photo)
2 Lower the sump case into position on the block. (photo)
3 Fit the oil pump strainer (3 bolts) into position. (photo)
4 The correct location of the strainer is as shown. (photo)
5 Locate the cork sump pan gasket in position. (photo)
6 Locate the sump pan (photo) and tighten the bolts evenly.

29.9 Checking crankshaft end-float

30.5 Fitting the crankshaft oil seal cover

30.7 Fitting the flywheel to the crank-shaft flange

30.8a Inserting the flywheel bolts

30.8b Tightening the flywheel securing bolts

31.1 Lubricating the piston rings prior to inserting piston in block

31.3 Fitting piston/con-rod assembly to block

31.6 Fitting a big-end cap

31.7 Tightening the big-end cap nuts

31.8 Fitting the key to the crankshaft

31.9 Fitting the sprocket to the crankshaft

32.1 Fitting the camshaft

32.2 Fitting the camshaft thrust plate

32.3 Fitting camshaft thrust plate screws
and locking tabs

32.6 Fitting the camshaft sprocket

32.7 Fitting camshaft sprocket bolts and
locking plate

Fig. 1.31. Fitting the crankshaft thrust washers to the crankcase
(Sec. 29)

Fig. 1.32. Drifting in a spigot bearing into the centre of the
crankshaft rear flange (Sec. 30)

Fig. 1.33. Drifting in a new timing cover oil seal (Sec. 34)

32.9 Fitting the timing chain link

32.10 Checking timing wheel alignment

32.12 Inserting the oil pump drive shaft

32.13 Inserting the oil pump drive shaft
gear

32.14 Correct location of distributor drive
(No. 1 piston at TDC)

32.16 Fitting the distributor base plate

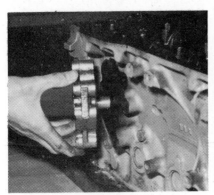

33.1 Fitting the oil pump body and
gasket

33.2 Inserting the oil pump gears

33.3 Fitting the oil pump cover and
gasket

33.4 Tightening the oil pump securing
bolts

34.4 Fitting the timing cover and gasket

34.5 Tightening the timing cover bolts

36 Water pump - refitting

1   Locate the water pump gasket to the sump case using grease to hold it in position.
2   Fit the water pump and tighten the securing bolts to the correct torque (photo) 8.5 lb ft.
3   Connect the water hose between the water pump and the crankcase outlet. (photo)
4   Re-fit the water pump drain plug and sealing washer.

37 Cylinder head, valves and rocker gear - reassembly and refitting

1   The components of the cylinder head should have been examined for wear, carbon removed and the valves ground in as described in Section 27.
2   Insert the first valve into its guide in the cylinder head, having kept them in strict order, the valve will be fitted to its original location. (photo)
3   Place the lower valve-spring seat in position. (photo)
4   Where fitted, place a new oil seal in position. (photo)
5   Place the valve spring and cotter collar in position on the valve stem (photo.) If the old valve springs have been in service for 15000 miles (24000 km) or more they should be renewed.
6   Using a suitable compressor, compress the valve spring and insert the split collets. (photo)
7   Release the valve spring compressor and check that the components of the valve are as shown in (photo). Place a small block of wood on the end face of the valve stem and give it a blow with a hammer in order to settle the collets and to ensure that later valve clearance adjustment is precise. Repeat the fitting operations on the other seven valves.
8   Insert the tappet blocks (cam followers) into their original sequence in the cylinder block. (photo)
9   Clean both mating surfaces of block and head, ensuring that no trace of carbon, scale or grit remains.
10 Locate a new cylinder head gasket in position on the block, ensuring that the word 'DESSUS' is visible on the upper surface. (photo)
11 Check that the two alignment dowels are correctly positioned through the gasket. The gasket should normally be fitted dry but if there has been evidence of oil or water leaks from the head gasket or if the surfaces of the block or head are scratched, then a thin film of non-setting compound such as Hermetite Red should be applied to both sides of the gasket. This compound also provides a protection against corrosion of the alloy head.
12 Lower the cylinder head gently into position on the cylinder block. (photo)
13 At this stage, check that the rocker pillar alignment dowels are securely in position on the top face of the cylinder head. (photo)
14 Fit the pushrods, carefully engaging their lower ends in the tappet blocks. (photo)
15 If the rocker shaft assembly has been dismantled for the renewal of worn components, it should now be reassembled with the parts fitted in the sequence shown in Fig. 1.34 page 37.
16 Fit new pins to **front** and **rear** rocker shaft pillars, ensuring that the plugged ends of the hollow pins face outwards.
17 Lower the assembled rocker shaft onto the locating dowels on the cylinder head. (photo)
18 Drop the cylinder head bolts into their holes, noting that the longer bolts locate in the thicker side of the rocker pillars. (photo)
19 Check that the push-rods locate correctly with each rocker arm. (photo) It will be essential to have slackened the rocker arm adjuster screws right off to ensure that there is no valve spring pressure applied when tightening down the cylinder head bolts.
20 Using a torque wrench, tighten the cylinder head bolts to 45 lb ft in the sequence shown in Fig. 1.13 page 21. (photo)
21 Adjustment of the valve clearances may be carried out now or at a later stage when the engine has been installed but if the operation is undertaken now, it will permit the rocker cover and other ancillaries to be installed and obviate their removal again later.
22 The clearance on inlet valves should be set to 0.012 inch (0.30 mm) COLD. 0.014 inch (0.35 mm) HOT. The clearance should be 0.014 inch (0.35 mm) COLD and 0.016 inch (0.40 mm) HOT for exhaust valves. Counting from the flywheel end, inlet valves are numbers 1, 3, 6, 8 exhaust valves are 2, 4, 5, 7.
23 Turn the engine by means of the flywheel and refer to the following table, adjusting each valve clearance in the sequence given.
Counting from flywheel end of block.

Valve clearances to adjust	Valves in balance
1 and 2	7 and 8
3 and 4	5 and 6
5 and 6	3 and 4
7 and 8	1 and 2

24 Insert the feeler blade between the heel of the rocker arm and the valve stem end face. Turn the adjuster screw until the feeler is a stiff sliding fit and then tighten the locknut. (photo)
24 Repeat the adjustment on the other valves, then recheck all clearances and fit the rocker cover. (photo)

38 Engine ancillaries - refitting

1   Fit the breather (using a new gasket) to the crankcase. (photo)
2   Place a new gasket either side of the insulating washer which locates between the fuel pump and the crankcase. (photo)
3   Fit the fuel pump to the crankcase ensuring that the pump actuating arm fits between the crankcase wall and the camshaft. (photo)
4   Fit the dipstick retainer to the crankcase, using a new gasket. (photo)
5   Provided the distributor drive gear has been correctly installed (Section 32), the distributor may now be pushed into position in the crankcase. Turn the distributor so that the vacuum capsule is towards the timing gear cover and engage the large and small segments of the driving shafts. (photo)
6   Fit the distributor retaining plate by sliding it behind the distributor mounting bolt head. (photo)
7   Provided the distributor has not been dismantled, the contact breaker points will not need adjusting otherwise refer to Chapter 4.
8   Fit the thermostat housing to the cylinder head (two bolts). (photo)
9   Fit the inlet manifold to the cylinder head using a new gasket. (photo) Before completing this operation, fit the pre-heat pipe from the thermostat elbow, pull the inlet manifold downwards and slide the pre-heat pipe under the manifold securing studs.
10 Connect the crankcase breather tube to the carburettor. (photo)
11 Fit the fuel pipe to the carburettor.
12 Fit the pre-heat pipe which runs between the water pump and the inlet manifold noting carefully its correct positioning against the crankcase. (photo)
13 Fit a new exhaust manifold gasket and bolt the manifold to the cylinder head, using only the specified brass nuts. (photo)
14 Fit the clutch assembly to the flywheel. Full details of the fitting procedure and centralising the driven plate are given in Chapter 5.
15 Position the thermostat in its housing, noting the tab for correct location. (photo)
16 Fit the thermostat housing cover, using a new gasket. (photo)
17 Fit the water pump pulley. (photo)
18 Fit the water pump pulley spacer and locking tab ring. Tighten the securing bolts and bend up the tabs. (photo)

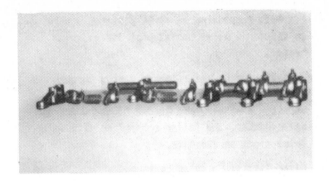

Fig. 1.34. Correctly assembled rocker shaft (Sec. 37)

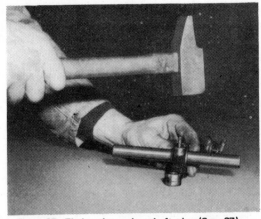

Fig. 1.35. Fitting the rocker shaft pins (Sec. 37)

34.6 Fitting the crankshaft pulley and bolt

35.1 Locating the sump case gasket

35.2 Fitting the sump case into position

35.3 Locating the oil pump strainer

35.4 Correct location of oil pump strainer

35.5 Fitting the sump pan gasket

35.6 Fitting the sump pan

36.2 Fitting the water pump

36.3 Connecting the pump to crankcase water hose

37.2 Inserting a valve into its guide

37.3 Fitting lower valve spring seat

37.4 Fitting valve stem oil seal

37.5 Fitting valve spring and cotter collar

37.6 Fitting the split cotters

37.7 Correct positioning of valve spring and components

37.8 Inserting a tappet block (cam follower)

37.10 Positioning the cylinder head gasket

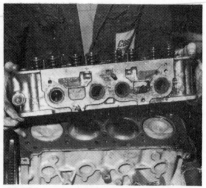

37.12 Lowering the cylinder head into position

37.13 Checking security of rocker pillar dowels

37.14 Inserting the push-rods

37.17 Lowering the rocker assembly into position

37.18 Fitting the cylinder head bolts

37.19 Engaging push-rods with rocker arms

37.20 Tightening the cylinder head bolts

37.24 Adjusting a valve clearance

37.25 Fitting the rocker cover

38.1 Fitting the crankcase breather and gasket

38.2 Location of fuel pump washers and spacer

38.3 Fitting fuel pump to crankcase

38.4 Fitting dipstick retainer to crankcase

38.5 Installing distributor

38.6 Fitting distributor retaining plate

38.8 Fitting thermostat housing to cylinder head

38.9 Fitting inlet manifold and gasket

38.10 Fitting crankcase breather tube to carburettor

38.12 Correct location of pre-heat pipe

38.13 Fitting exhaust manifold and gasket

38.15 Fitting thermostat

38.16 Fitting thermostat housing cover and gasket

38.17 Fitting the water pump pulley

38.18 Fitting the water pump pulley securing bolts and lock tabs

38.19 Fitting the heater box

39.2 Engine and gearbox ready for mating

39.3 Clutch assembly correctly aligned

39.5 Fitting cover plate (exhaust side)

39.6 Fitting flywheel dust shield plate

39.7 Fitting starter motor

40.1 Engine ready for installation

40.2 Location of engine/gearbox lifting slings

40.3 Hoisting the power/transmission unit into position

40.4 Installing left hand engine mounting bolts

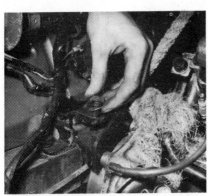
40.5 Entering right hand engine mounting bolts

40.6 Components of the engine rear mounting

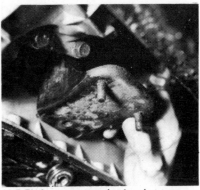
40.7 Fitting rear mounting bracket to cylinder block

40.8 Locating rear engine mounting clamp plate spring to cross member

40.9 Fitting rear mounting cover plate, bolts and locking tabs

40.12 Engaging a drive shaft with the differential unit

19 Lower the heater box (which provides warmed air to the carburettor) onto the rocker cover. Ensure that the nut underneath the heater box is tight before installing it. (photo)

39 Gearbox to engine - reconnection

1 If previously removed, reassemble the clutch operating mechanism, release bearing and fork as described in Chapter 5.
2 Position the engine and gearbox units as shown. (photo)
3 Having aligned the driven plate (Chapter 5) the gearbox should slide easily as the gearbox primary shaft passes through the splined hub of the driven plate and engages with the spigot bush which is located in the centre of the flywheel to crankshaft mounting flange. (photo)
4 Insert the gearbox to engine securing bolts and tighten to a torque of 32 lb ft.
5 Fit the cover plate on the exhaust side of the engine and secure with the three retaining bolts. (photo)
6 Fit the dust shield plate behind the flywheel. (photo)
7 Fit the starter motor in position and secure it with the three retaining bolts. (photo)

40 Combined engine/gearbox/differential unit - refitting to vehicle

1 Check that the vehicle is raised sufficiently high at the front to permit the engine/gearbox unit to pass beneath it. (photo)
2 Attach suitable lifting chains or slings. (photo)
3 Slide the power unit under the vehicle and then lift it upwards into the engine compartment using a suitable hoist. (photo)
4 Enter the two engine mounting bolts into the left hand mounting. (photo)
5 Enter the two engine mounting bolts on the right hand side. (photo)
6 Assemble the rear engine mounting. (photo)
7 Fit the rear mounting bracket to the cylinder block using two bolts each side only at this stage. (photo)
8 The engine may now have to be pulled forward slightly in order to fit the rubber mounting, followed by the clamp plate spring positioned on top of the crossmember. (photo)
9 Fit the mounting cover plate using the four bolts and lock tabs. (photo)
10 Screw in all the mounting bolts and bend up the locking tabs. Release the hoist and remove the lifting slings and ropes.
11 Lower the front of the vehicle until it can be supported on jacks or axle stands under the body frame.
12 Engage the drive shafts with the differential unit. (photo)
13 Connect the lower ball joint with the lower wishbone link. Reconnect the steering arm ball joints.
14 Fit the securing nut to the lower ball joint. (photo)
15 Connect the stub axle carrier to the upper suspension wishbone. This may necessitate the use of a lever to force the upper wishbone down. (photo)
16 Remove the temporary rods which were fitted to offset torsion bar reaction and refit the dampers.
17 Push the gear selector lever which connects with the gearbox sufficiently far up its shaft so that the spring may be compressed and the cotter inserted. (photo)
18 Fit the exhaust pipe clamp halves, bolts and brass nuts. (photo)
19 Connect the steering arm to the rack. (photo)
20 Fit the caliper unit to the stub axle carrier taking care not to strain the flexible hydraulic hose. (photo)
21 Bend over the caliper bolt lock tabs. (photo) Fit the brake disc pads and pins as fully described in Chapter 10.
22 Push the gear selector cable up through its hole so it can be engaged with the gear selector shaft. (photo)

23 The attachment of the selector cable at the base of the gearshift lever is shown. (photo)
24 Fit a new oil filter cartridge. (photo)
25 The road wheel may now be fitted and the jacks lowered so that the remaining assembly and refitting work can be carried out with the vehicle standing level on the ground.

41 Engine - final reassembly, connections and filling

1 Fit the alternator in position so that its top fits in between the 'U' clamp. The large bolt is inserted from beneath the front wing. (photo)
2 Fit the lower adjustment bracket to the alternator and to the lug provided on the sump case. (photo)
3 Fit the fan belt. This is accomplished by pushing in the alternator as far as possible towards the engine (mountings loosened). Slip the belt over all three pulleys. (photo) Pull the alternator away from the engine until the belt cannot be deflected at the centre of its top run. Tighten the alternator adjustment bracket and mounting bolts.
4 Refit the clutch operating cylinder, ensuring that the small spring clip on the pushrod clips up behind the clutch bearing lever. (photo)
5 Adjust the clutch free movement as described in Chapter 5.
6 Fit the rotor arm and the distributor cap, fit the spark plugs, the HT leads and reconnect the LT lead to the coil.
7 Fit the heater front pipe. (photo)
8 Reconnect the leads to the water temperature and oil pressure transmitter units. (photo)
9 Connect the accelerator linkage to the carburettor. (photo)
10 Connect the choke cable to the carburettor. (photo)
11 Connect the earthing strap to the cylinder head. (photo)
12 Unplug the fuel line from the tank and reconnect it to the fuel pump. (photo)
13 Fit the radiator. To do this, the expansion bottle will probably have to be removed. Note the radiator upper and lower mountings. (photo)
14 Fit the radiator top hose. (photo)
15 Fit the radiator bottom hose, noting its location on the sump case. (photo)
16 Secure the radiator overflow pipe to the right hand side of the radiator.
17 Lower the electric cooling fan down behind the radiator so that the captive nuts are to the top. These nuts tuck under the cross piece of the front trim. (photo)
18 Fit the pulley driving belt cover to the body under the front wing. (photo)
19 Fit the air cleaner, ensuring that its lower surface does not foul the choke or accelerator linkage. (photo)
20 Refit the bonnet. The help of an assistant will be required for this operation. (photo)
21 Fill the cooling system as described in the next Chapter, fill the engine with the correct grade and quantity of oil. Refill the gearbox and fill up the differential unit.
22 Reconnect the battery negative terminal. (photo)

42 Initial starting up

1 After a major overhaul, start the engine and allow it to run until it reaches normal working temperature. Check for oil and water leaks.
2 If necessary, adjust the carburettor as described in Chapter 3 and the ignition timing, Chapter 4.
3 After 500 miles (800 km) check the torque of the cylinder head bolts (cold) and subsequently check the valve clearances either hot or cold as previously described in Section 37.
4 Check the security of all nuts and bolts on the engine and gearbox, particularly those used on the inlet and exhaust manifolds.

40.14 Screwing nut onto lower ball joint

40.15 Levering upper suspension wishbone into connection with stub axle carrier

40.17 Inserting gear selector lever cotter

40.18 Fitting exhaust pipe clamp bolts

40.19 Connecting steering arm to rack

40.20 Fitting brake caliper to stub axle carrier

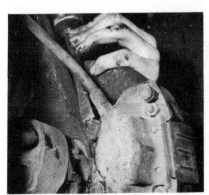
40.21 Bending over the caliper bolt locking tabs

40.22 Engaging gear selector cable with selector shaft

40.23 Attachment of gear selector cable to shaft

40.24 Fitting oil filter cartridge

41.1 Fitting alternator upper mounting bolt

41.2 Fitting alternator lower bracket

41.3 Fitting alternator/water pump driving belt

41.4 Fitting clutch operating cylinder

41.7 Fitting heater front pipe

41.8a Connecting water temperature transmitter lead

41.8b Connecting oil pressure switch lead

41.9 Connecting accelerator control

41.10 Connecting the choke operating cable

41.11 Connecting cylinder head earthing strap

41.12 Connecting fuel line to pump

41.13a Radiator upper mounting

41.13b Radiator lower mounting

41.14 Fitting radiator top hose

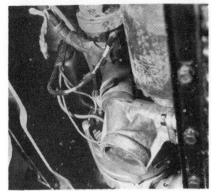
41.15 Fitting radiator bottom hose

41.17 Installing the radiator cooling fan assembly

41.18 Fitting the pulley driving belt cover

41.19 Fitting the air cleaner assembly

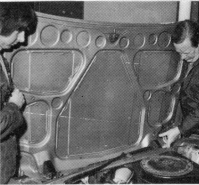
41.20 Re-fitting the bonnet (hood)

41.22 Re-connecting the battery negative terminal

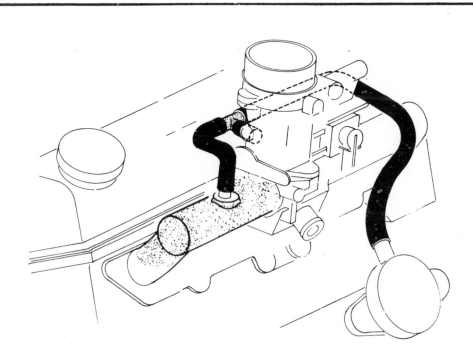
Fig. 1.36. Components of crankcase ventilation system fitted to vehicles supplied to German market (Sec. 45)

43 Engine removal where automatic gearbox fitted

1   Where an automatic gearbox is fitted, reference should be made to Chapter 6 (part 2) for a full description of the disconnection of controls and separation of the gearbox from the engine unit.

44 Modifications

The operations described in this Chapter apply to all engine types but it is essential when ordering spare parts that exact particulars of the vehicle (model, engine number etc.), are quoted. See 'Ordering spare Parts'.

45 Crankcase ventilation systems

1   All models are fitted with a crankcase fume extraction system.
2   Early 1118 cc models were fitted with a simple extractor tube.
3   Engines fitted to vehicles built for the German market are fitted with a system which utilises vacuum from the inlet manifold to assist fume extraction.
4   Later type vehicles fitted with series 353 engines are equipped with a system which draws crankcase fumes into the carburettor when the butterfly valve is open and draws them directly into the inlet manifold when the butterfly is closed. This by-pass system incorporates a filter and valve which must be

serviced every 15000 miles (25000 km) as described later in this Section.
5   The 1100 special models and vehicles fitted with series 366 engines have a system which draws fumes from the rocker cover and expels them into the air cleaner.
6   In order to maintain the efficiency of the crankcase ventilation system fitted to Series 353 and 366 engines, the following maintenance must be carried out.
a)   Check distributor, timing, spark plugs and contact breaker points every 3000 miles (4800 km) see Chapter 4.
b)   Check valve clearances (hot) every 6000 miles (9600 km) as described in Section 37 of this Chapter.
c)   Renew the air cleaner element every 6000 miles (10000 km).
d)   Check the idling speed adjustment and dashpot adjustment as described in Chapter 4.
e)   Check and clean the pressure adjusting valve aperture calibrated at 0.039 inch (1 mm) every 3000 miles (5000 km).
f)   Renew the pressure adjusting valve and clean the rubber connecting hoses every 15000 miles (25000 km).

46 North American models - special features

1   Vehicles exported to North America are fitted with a 1204 cc engine having a compression ratio of 8.7 : 1.
2   The engine conforms to strict anti-pollution requirements and in consequence modifications have been made to the pistons, cylinder head gasket, inlet manifold, distributor, flywheel, carburettor and controls. Each of the following Chapters includes a Section covering the deviation from standard models and any special adjustment or servicing requirements.

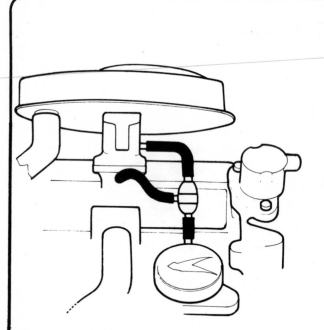

Fig. 1.37. Components of crankcase ventilation system fitted to Series 353 engines (Sec. 45)

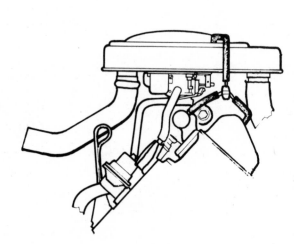

Fig. 1.38. Components of crankcase ventilation system fitted to Series 366 engines (Sec. 45)

47 Fault finding

Symptom	Reason/s	Remedy
Engine will not turn over when starter switch is operated	Flat battery Bad battery connections Bad connections at solenoid switch and/or starter motor Defective solenoid Starter motor defective	Check that battery is fully charged and that all connections are clean and tight. Remove starter and check solenoid. Remove starter and overhaul.
Engine turns over normally but fails to fire and run	No spark at plugs No fuel reaching engine Too much fuel reaching the engine (flooding)	Check ignition system according to procedures given in Chapter 4. Check fuel system according to procedures given in Chapter 3. Slowly depress accelerator pedal to floor and keep it there while operating starter motor until engine fires. Check fuel system if necessary as described in Chapter 3.
Engine starts but runs unevenly and misfires	Ignition and/or fuel system faults Incorrect valve clearances Burnt out valves	Check the ignition and fuel system as though the engine had failed to start. Check and reset clearances. Remove cylinder heads and examine and overhaul as necessary.
Lack of power	Ignition and/or fuel system faults Incorrect valve clearances Burnt out valves Worn out piston or cylinder bores	Check the ignition and fuel system for correct ignition timing and carburettor settings. Check and reset the clearances. Remove cylinder head and examine and overhaul as necessary. Remove cylinder head and examine pistons and cylinder bores. Overhaul as necessary.
Excessive oil consumption	Oil leaks from crankshaft oil seal, rocker cover gasket, oil pump, drain plug gasket, sump plug washer, oil cooler Worn piston rings or cylinder bores resulting in oil being burnt by engine Smoky exhaust is an indication Worn valve guides and/or defective valve stem seals	Identify source of leak and repair as appropriate. Fit new rings or rebore cylinders and fit new pistons, depending on degree of wear. Remove cylinder heads and recondition valve stem bores and valves and seals as necessary.
Excessive mechanical noise from engine	Wrong valve to rocker clearances Worn crankshaft bearings Worn cylinders (piston slap)	Adjust valve clearances. Inspect and overhaul where necessary.
Unusual vibration	Misfiring on one or more cylinders Loose mounting bolts	Check ignition system. Check tightness of bolts and condition of flexible mountings.

NOTE: When investigating starting and uneven running faults do not be tempted into snap diagnosis. Start from the beginning of the check procedure and follow it through. It will take less time in the long run. Poor performance from an engine in terms of power and economy is not normally diagnosed quickly. In any event the ignition and fuel systems must be checked first before assuming any further investigation needs to be made.

Chapter 2 Cooling system

Contents

Specifications

System type	Semi-sealed, thermo-syphon, water pump assisted with electric cooling fan.
Radiator material	Steel
Cooling area	194 in^2 (1250 cm^2)
Thermostat fully open	89ºC (192ºF) begins to open 78ºC (172ºF)
1100 Special (early models)	opens 72ºC (161ºF)
(later models)	opens 83ºC (181ºF)

Electric fan operation

Actuates at water temperature of	95ºC ($\pm$ 1.5ºC) 203ºF
Switches off at water temperature of	86ºC ($\pm$ 2ºC) 187ºF

Capacities

System including vehicle heater	1.3 gal (6 litres)
Difference between 'MAX' and 'MIN' marks on expansion bottle	4/5 pints (0.45 litres)

Tightening torque wrench settings

	lb ft
Thermoswitch to radiator	25
Radiator mounting bolts	12
Thermostat housing to cylinder head	8.5
Thermostat housing cover	8.5
Water temperature transmitter to cylinder head	10.5
Water pump to sump casing	8.5
Water pump inlet housing to sump casing	8.5
Water pump drain plug	11.5
Water pump pulley bolt	10.5
Water inlet housing to cylinder block	14.5
Water return manifold to cylinder block	12.0

1 General description

1 The cooling system is of conventional type and operates by means of thermo syphon action with the assistance of a belt driven water pump. A diagrammatic presentation of the circulation pattern and the location of the major components is shown in Fig. 2.1 page 49.

2 The water in the radiator flows from right to left instead of in the more common downward direction and the 'header' tanks are situated on either side of the radiator matrix.

3 Water heated in the cylinder jackets is cooled by the ram effect of air passing through the radiator matrix when the car is in motion and assisted by a thermostatically, electrically operated fan which operates within a pre-determined temperature range.

4 Water from the cooling system also circulates through the vehicle heater and is used to pre-heat the inlet manifold and carburettor body (not 1204 cc with special Weber carburettor).

5 The cooling system is semi-pressurized and incorporates an expansion bottle to accept coolant displaced when the engine is hot and to act as a coolant reservoir when the system cools down or in the event of minor leakage.

6 A thermostat is fitted in the system to restrict water circulation until normal engine operating temperature has been reached.

7 The original coolant is effective indefinitely but where loss of coolant has occurred or the strength of the coolant (anti-freeze mixture) is suspect, then the system should be drained, flushed and refilled as described in later Sections of this Chapter.

8 All flexible hose joints are secured by Corbin type clips and they should only be prised open sufficiently far to enable them to slide over the hose. Ordinary pliers may be used for their removal but special types are more satisfactory. However, the

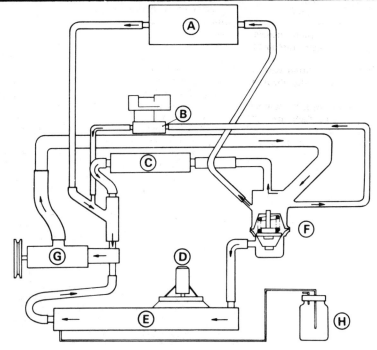

FIG. 2.1. DIAGRAMMATIC LAYOUT OF WATER COOLING AND VEHICLE INTERIOR HEATING SYSTEM

A Heater matrix
B Water heated base of carburettor

C Water heated inlet manifold
D Electric fan

E Radiator
F Thermostat

G Water pump
H Expansion bottle

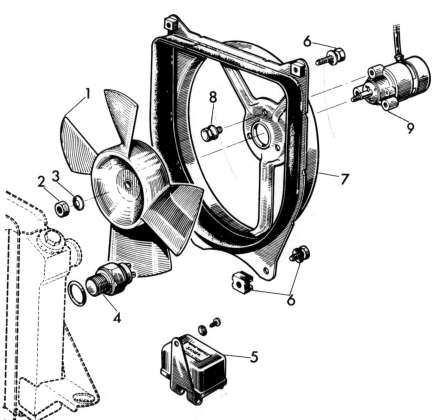

FIG. 2.2. RADIATOR COOLING FAN — EXPLODED VIEW

1 Fan
2 Securing nut

3 Lockwasher
4 Thermostatic contactor

5 Relay
6 Mounting bolt

7 Frame
8 Motor securing bolt
9 Electric motor

cost of these need not be incurred if the Corbin type are replaced by reliable worm drive clips.

2 Cooling system - draining

1 If it is wished to retain the coolant for further use, place a clean receptacle beneath the engine and then set the vehicle interior heater to the full on position.
2 Unscrew and remove the plug and sealing washer from the base of the water pump.
3 The coolant will drain into the receptacle, its displacement from the cooling system being replaced by air which enters through the valve in the lid of the expansion jar.
4 To expedite the draining operation, the radiator filler cap may be removed and the lid unscrewed from the expansion jar.
5 Do not allow the coolant to come into contact with the paintwork of the vehicle as its anti-freeze content will damage the surface of the finish.
6 The coolant should be retained in a covered vessel pending return to the system and any sediment which precipitates should be discarded.

3 Cooling system - flushing

1 Provided the cooling system is maintained in good order then periodic flushing should not be necessary. Where the coolant has discoloured or become contaminated with oil due to gasket failure, then the system should be thoroughly cleansed.
2 To do this, remove the radiator filler cap and insert a hose in the filler neck, then with the water pump drain plug removed and the heater control full on, allow the water to flow until it is quite clear when emerging from the water pump drain plug.
3 If the radiator appears blocked then it should be removed as described in Section 6 and reverse flushed. This is carried out by placing the hose in the right hand radiator outlet so that the water flow is in the opposite direction to normal.
4 The removal of scale from the system should not normally be a problem as with a semi-sealed circuit only initial scaling occurs unless due to leaks, continual topping-up is required.
5 The use of chemical de-scalers and cleansers is not recommended as unless specifically formulated, damage to the aluminium cylinder head and water pump and thermostat housings may occur.
6 Never flush a hot engine cooling system with cold water or cracks or distortion of the block or head may be caused.
7 In the event of blockages in the heater matrix then this should be removed as described in Chapter 11 and serviced as previously described for the radiator.

4 Cooling system - filling

1 Place the heater control to the full-on position.
2 Remove the expansion bottle cap.
3 Remove the radiator cap.
4 Fill the radiator slowly right to the top of the filler neck with coolant of the correct anti-freeze mixture strength (see next Section). If a new solution is being made up it is preferable to use soft or de-mineralised water. (photo)
5 Fill the expansion bottle to the 'maximum' mark.
6 Re-fit the radiator cap but do not overtighten it.
7 Re-fit the expansion bottle cap.
8 Start the engine and run it at an even speed until bubbles cease to be visible in the coolant contained in the expansion bottle.
9 Top up the level of coolant in the expansion bottle until it reaches the 'maximum' mark.
10 Do not allow coolant solution to contaminate the valve in the expansion bottle cap due to overfilling or gas pressure which could be caused by a blown gasket. The valve should be renewed in either event.

5 Anti-freeze mixture

1 The use of anti-freeze mixture in the cooling system fulfills two purposes. To protect the engine and heater components against fracture during periods of low ambient temperature and to utilise the effects of the rust and corrosion inhibitors incorporated in the anti-freeze product.
2 A 'long-life' type of anti-freeze mixture may be used but where a normal commercial type is used it is wise to renew it or at least check its strength with a hydrometer every year.
3 Ensure that the mixture is of a type compatible with aluminium components and refer to the following table for strength recommendations.

Quantity of anti-freeze	Gives protection to
1.7 pints (1 litre)	- 17.8° C (0° F)
2.0 pints (1.3 litres)	- 28.9° C (-20° F)
2.3 pints (1.43 litres)	-34.5° C (-30° F)
3.0 pints (1.7 litres)	-40° C (-40° F)

4 Due to the searching action of anti-freeze mixtures, always check the security of hose clips and gasket joints before filling.

6 Radiator - removal, inspection, cleaning and replacement

1 Drain the system as described in Section 2.
2 Remove the air cleaner from its location in the engine compartment.
3 Disconnect the battery earth lead.
4 Disconnect the electric leads to the radiator cooling fan.
5 Unscrew and remove the fan assembly securing bolts and withdraw the assembly from behind the radiator.
6 Disconnect the inlet hose from the radiator.
7 Disconnect the outlet hose from the radiator. (photo)
8 Disconnect the fan starting thermal-contractor earthing wire.
9 Remove the thermal contractor and relay, Fig. 2.2 page 49.
10 Disconnect the hose which connects the radiator to the expansion bottle. (photo)
11 Detach the radiator upper and lower mounting, Fig. 2.3. page 51.
12 Pull the radiator as far forward from the cross member as it will go, tilt it and then remove it by passing it under the cross member and out through the engine compartment. (photo)
13 The radiator matrix should be cleaned internally as described in Section 3. Any accumulation of flies on the radiator fins should be removed by lightly brushing and applying air from a tyre pump (from the rear).
14 If the radiator is leaking, do not attempt to repair it yourself as the heat used for soldering must be carefully localised if further leaks are not to be created. Take the unit to a specialist repairer or exchange the unit for a factory reconditioned one. The use of any type of leak sealant is at best, a temporary cure and its use may clog the fine tubes of the heater matrix and damage the water pump seals.
15 Refitting the radiator is a reversal of removal. Refill the system as described in Section 4.

7 Thermostat - removal, testing, and refitting

1 Drain the cooling system as previously described.
2 Unscrew and remove the two bolts which secure the thermostat housing cover in position.
3 Remove the cover and gasket and withdraw the thermostat. If it is stuck in its seat do not try to lever it out but cut round its seat joint with a pointed blade to break the seal.
4 To test whether the thermostat is serviceable, suspend it in a pan of water into which a thermometer has been placed. Heat

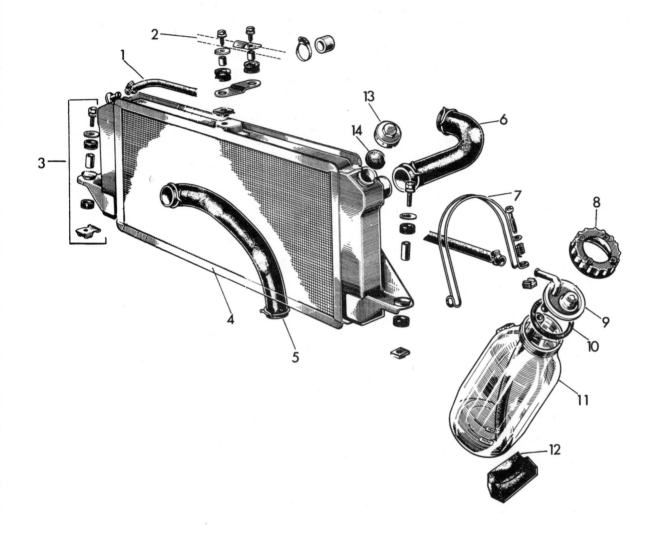

FIG. 2.3. RADIATOR – COMPONENTS AND EXPANSION BOTTLE

1 Tube to expansion bottle	4 Radiator	7 Expansion bottle strap
2 Upper mounting	5 Lower radiator hose	8 Expansion bottle cap
3 Lower mounting	6 Top radiator hose	9 Expansion bottle valve

10 Expansion bottle cap seal
11 Expansion bottle
12 Expansion bottle pad
13 Filler cap
14 Filler cap seal

6.7 Radiator bottom hose connection

6.10 Radiator to expansion bottle tube connection

6.12 Removing the radiator

the water and check that the thermostat begins to open when the water temperature reaches that at which the thermostat is rated (see Specifications).

5 Similarly, when the thermostat is fully open, place it into cooler water and observe its closure. Any failure in the opening or closing actions of the unit will necessitate renewal. Fit one with the specified temperature marked on it, nothing is to be gained by fitting one having a different operating temperature range and could cause cool running or overheating of the engine and heater inefficiency.

6 Refitting is a reversal of removal but ensure that the locating tab on the thermostat is correctly aligned and use a new cover gasket. Do not overtighten the cover securing bolts. (8.5 lb ft).

7 Refill the system as described in Section 4.

8 Water pump - removal and refitting

1 Disconnect the battery negative terminal.

2 Set heater control to full on, remove the expansion bottle cap and unscrew the drain plug at the base of the water pump. Retain the coolant if required.

3 Disconnect the leads from the radiator fan motor and remove the fan assembly as described in Section 6.

4 From under the wing remove the pulley driving belt cover as described in Chapter 1.

5 Slacken the adjuster bracket bolt on the alternator and having pushed the alternator in towards the engine, slip off the driving belt.

6 Disconnect the water pump to crankcase hose.

7 Unscrew and remove the four water pump cover retaining bolts and lift the pump from its crankcase location.

8 Peel off the old gasket and clean the mating faces of both the pump and crankcase.

9 Refitting is a reversal of removal but always use a new gasket.

10 Refill the cooling system and reconnect the battery.

9 Water pump - dismantling and reassembly

1 The water pump is designed for long trouble-free service and if it has been in operation for a considerable mileage then it will probably be realistic to exchange the complete unit for one which has been factory reconditioned rather than attempt to repair a pump without the necessary experience and tools.

2 Check the condition of the impeller for corrosion other than this, any fault will lie with a worn shaft seal, (12) Fig. 2.4 page 53.

3 Press off the hub (6) from the shaft (7). To achieve this, support the rear face of the hub and exert pressure on the end of the shaft. (If seal only to be renewed, do not remove hub).

4 Turn the pump over and again adequately supporting the rear face of the impeller (13) press the end of the shaft to expel it from the impeller bore.

5 Now immerse the pump body in boiling water for two or three minutes. Remove the pump quickly and drive out the shaft/bearing assembly by drifting it out from the seal end with a copper or plastic faced hammer.

6 Drive the seal from the water pump body by means of a drift inserted from the front end of the pump.

7 The shaft/bearing assembly cannot be separated and if necessary must be renewed as a single component.

8 Check the condition of the seal and shaft bearing mating surfaces of the pump body. Where necessary, these may be improved with grade '600' paper.

9 Press the water pump seal into its seating in the body, Fig. 2.5 page 53.

10 Again heat the pump body in boiling water and then press the shaft/bearing assembly into the body ensuring that the bearing seats securely against the bore inner shoulder. Note that the longer end of the shaft is at the seal end, Fig. 2.6 page 53.

11 Supporting the end face of the shaft at the seal end, press on the flanged hub so that its boss is towards the shaft bearing. The hub is correctly positioned on the shaft when there is a clearance of 0.050 in (1.270 mm) between the pump and hub faces measured with feeler gauges.

12 Support the front end face of the shaft and press on the impeller (vanes outwards) until there is again a clearance of 0.050 inch (1.270 mm) between the pump and impeller faces.

13 Check for free rotation by turning the vanes of the impeller.

10 Radiator cooling fan - description and servicing

1 The radiator cooling fan is shown in exploded form in Fig. 2.2 page 49.

2 The assembly comprises a four bladed fan attached to the driving spindle of an electric motor.

3 The electric motor is controlled by a relay which is located on the engine compartment cross member. The relay is actuated by a thermostatic contactor screwed into the left hand radiator header tank.

4 When the coolant temperature reaches 95⁰ C (203⁰ F) the contactor closes and through the relay, energises the fan. When the water temperature falls to between 86 and 88⁰ C (187 and 191⁰ F) the contactor opens and the fan is de-energised.

5 It must be realised that during adjustments within the engine compartment, with the engine at operating temperature, the fan blades may turn unexpectedly if the ignition is switched on as the contactor points may be closed if the water temperature is sufficiently high. From the point of view of safety, disconnect the battery negative terminal before carrying out adjustments in close proximity to the radiator.

6 In the event of incorrect functioning of the radiator cooling fan, check the security of connecting leads.

7 Using a test bulb, check the opening and closing of the thermal contactor points by warming up the engine and letting it cool down.

8 Check the relay by substitution.

9 Where the foregoing tests prove negative then the fault must lie with the motor.

10 Remove the fan motor and blade assembly after disconnecting the electrical leads and withdrawing the four securing bolts.

11 Unscrew and remove the nut and spring washer which secures the fan blades to the motor shaft. This has a left hand thread and the nut must therefore be unscrewed in a clockwise direction.

12 Unscrew and remove the three bolts which secure the motor to the fan assembly outer frame. Renew the motor on an exchange basis.

13 Reassembly and refitting of the fan cooling unit is a reversal of removal and dismantling.

11 Vee belt - adjustment, removal and refitting

1 The driving belt for the alternator and water pump obtains its power from the crankshaft pulley.

2 Removal of the belt is described in Chapter 1, Section 4.

3 Refitting and adjustment is described in Chapter 1, Section 41.

12 Water temperature gauge - fault finding

1 Correct operation of the water temperature gauge is important as the engine could attain a considerable degree of overheating, unnoticed, without it.

2 To check the correct operation of the installation, first disconnect the 'Lucar' connector from the sender unit plug screwed into the top of the inlet manifold. With the ignition 'on' the gauge should be at the cold mark. Then earth the lead to the engine block when the needle should indicate hot, at the opposite end of the scale. This test shows that the gauge on the dash is functioning properly. If it is not then it will need renewal. If there is still a fault in the system with this check completed satisfactorily, there will be a fault in the sender unit

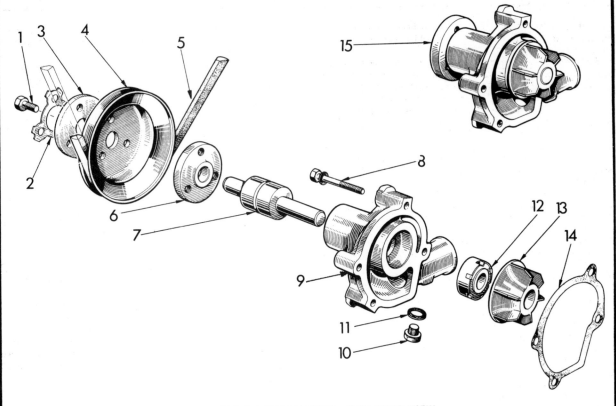

FIG. 2.4. WATER PUMP — EXPLODED VIEW

1 Pulley retaining bolt	5 Driving vee belt	9 Body	13 Impeller
2 Lockplate	6 Hub	10 Drain plug	14 Gasket
3 Plate	7 Shaft/bearing assembly	11 Drain plug seal	15 Assembled water
4 Pulley	8 Bolt	12 Seal	pump

Fig. 2.5. Fitting a new water pump shaft seal (Sec. 9)

Fig. 2.6. Fitting a water pump shaft/bearing assembly (Sec. 9)

or the wire leading from it to the gauge. Renew these as necessary.

13 Modifications

1 Reference should be made to Specifications for changes in thermostat temperature ratings.

2 Certain modifications have been carried out to the return flexible water hose which connects the inlet manifold (5) with the pump inlet collector housing (3) Fig. 2.7 page 55. .

3 The function of these hoses is essentially similar but they vary in detail according to the date of vehicle manufacture.

4 The layout of the return hose and manifold and carburettor hoses as fitted to the 1100 special is shown in the photograph.

Fault finding chart - cooling system

Symptom	Reason/s	Remedy
OVERHEATING Heat generated in cylinder not being successfully disposed of by radiator	Insufficient water in cooling system	Top up radiator.
	Cooling fan inoperative	Overhaul or renew fan.
	Radiator core blocked or radiator grille restricted	Reverse flush radiator, remove obstruction.
	Bottom water hose collapsed, impeding flow	Remove and fit new hose.
	Thermostat not opening properly	Remove and fit new thermostat.
	Ignition advance and retard incorrectly set (accompanied by loss of power, and perhaps, misfiring)	Check and reset ignition timing.
	Carburettor(s) incorrectly adjusted (mixture too weak)	Tune carburettor(s).
	Exhaust system partially blocked	Check exhaust pipe for constrictive dents and blockages.
	Oil level in sump too low	Top up sump to full mark on dipstick.
	Blown cylinder head gasket (water/steam being forced down the radiator overflow pipe under pressure)	Remove cylinder head, fit new gasket.
	Engine not yet run-in	Run-in slowly and carefully.
	Brakes binding	Check and adjust brakes if necessary.
UNDERHEATING Too much heat being dispersed by radiator	Thermostat jammed open	Remove and renew thermostat.
	Incorrect grade of thermostat fitted allowing premature opening of valve	Remove and replace with new thermostat which opens at a higher temperature.
	Thermostat missing	Check and fit correct thermostat.
LOSS OF COOLING WATER Leaks in system	Loose clips on water hoses	Check and tighten clips if necessary.
	Top, bottom, or by-pass water hoses perished and leaking	Check and replace any faulty hoses.
	Radiator core leaking	Remove radiator and repair.
	Thermostat gasket leaking	Inspect and renew gasket.
	Radiator cap seal ineffective	Renew radiator pressure cap seal.
	Blown cylinder head gasket (pressure in system forcing water/steam into expansion bottle.	Remove cylinder head and fit new gasket.
	Cylinder wall or head cracked	Dismantle engine, dispatch to engineering works for repair.

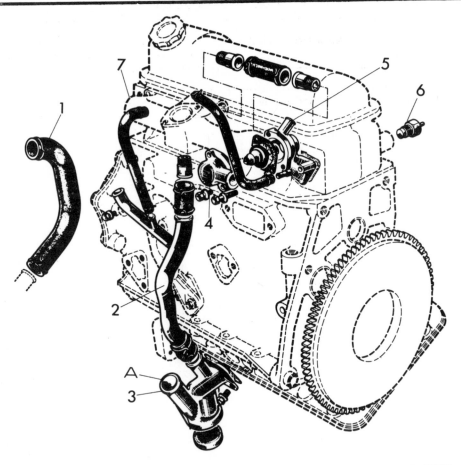

FIG. 2.7. LOCATION OF COMPONENTS OF THE COOLING SYSTEM

1 Pump outlet hose to cylinder block
2 Return hose from inlet manifold
3 Pump inlet collector housing
4 Thermostat housing cover and cylinder head outlet

5 Thermostat housing
6 Water temperature transmitter
7 Inlet manifold
A Radiator bottom hose connection

Layout of hose connections, 1100

Chapter 3 Fuel system and carburation

Contents

Specifications

Fuel pump

Type	Mechanical, camshaft operated
Make	S.E.V. AC or SOFABEX

Carburettors

Make	Solex
Types and applications	

Carburettor type	Key (see below)	Engine type	Engine number
32 BISA	1	350	to No 6030020
	2	350S	to No 6670020
32 BISA2	3	352	from No 5000021 to 5030020
32 BISA3	4	350	from No 6030021
	5	350S	from No 6670021
	6	352	from No 5030021
	7	353	to No 7310020
	8	353	from No 7310021
32 BISA4	9	353	(1972 H) anti-pollution equipment

DATA

Specification Key No.	1	2	3	4	5	6	7	8	9
Venturi dia.	24	24	24	25	25	27	25	24 27**	27
Main jet	125 120*	125 120*	120	130	130 125** 125***	120	125	120 122.5**	122.5
Main air correction jet	190	190	190	190	190	190	200	190 200**	200
Econostat jet	55	55	60	65	65	60 80****	65	80 90**	90
Idling jet	50	50	50	50	50	50	45	45	45
Idling air bleed	220	220	220	220	220	220	150	150	150
Emulsion tube	E2	E2	E			E2****	E2	E2 E7**	E7
Progression holes	2 x 100	2 x 100	2 x 100	2 x 100	2 x 100	2 x 100	100 x 100	100 x 100 100 x 130**	100 x 100 100 x 130**
Accelerator pump nozzle	45	45	45	45	45	45	45	45	45

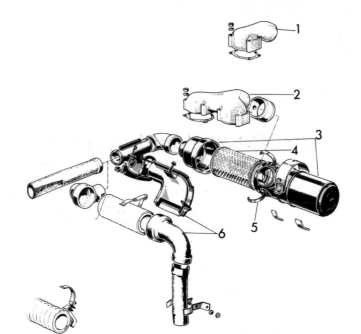

FIG. 3.1. EXPLODED VIEW OF CYLINDRICAL TYPE AIR CLEANER (SEC. 2)

1	Air intake (single carburettor)	2	Air intake (twin carburettor)	3	Body	5	Retaining clips
				4	Element	6	Air induction assembly

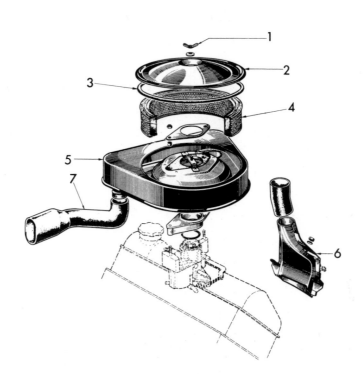

FIG. 3.2. EXPLODED VIEW OF PAN TYPE AIR CLEANER (SEC. 2)

1	Wing nut	3	Sealing ring	4	Element	5	Body
2	Cover					6	Heater box inlet

Accelerator pump stroke	3 mm	3 mm	3 mm	3 mm	3 mm	3 mm	3 mm	3 mm	3 mm
						4.5 - 5.0 mm****	4 mm**	4 mm**	4 mm**
Needle valve	1.5 mm	1.5 mm	1.5 mm	1.5 mm	1.5 mm	1.5 mm	1.5 mm	1.2 mm	1.2 mm
Fast idle setting	1 – 1.1 mm	1 – 1.1 mm	1 – 1.1 mm	1 – 1.1 mm	1 – 1.1 mm	1 – 1.1 mm		1 – 1.1 mm	
By-pass	2 x 100	2 x 100							

Rev/min

Idling speed, manual	650 – 700	650 – 700	650 – 700	650 – 700	650 – 700	650 – 700	800 – 900	800 – 900	800 – 900
Idling speed, automatic (D)	650	650		650	650		650	650	
Idling speed, automatic (N)	850	850		850	850		850	850	825 – 925

Dashpot stroke   2.3mm**

*	350S Engines before no. 6400021
**	Automatic transmission models only
***	1100LS from engine no. 6053038. 1100GLS from 6446518 except automatic transmission and certain non-pollution engines.
****	From engine no. 5050021 except for North American versions.

Weber

Types and applications:

Twin 36DCNF – 7 Left hand	353S engine
36DCNF – 8 Right hand	353S engine
Single 36DCNF 15	Series 366 engines

DATA

	TWIN	SINGLE
Main venturi dia. (mm)	30/30	28/28
Auxiliary venturi dia. (mm)	4.5/4.5	3.5/3.5
Main jet	110/110	155/155
Main air correction jet	220/220	165/165
Emulsion tube	F26/F26	F27/F27
Idling jet	45/45	50/50
Idling air bleed	120/120	160/160
Starting jet	F5 x 100/F5 x 100	80FI/80FI
Starting air jet	4.5/4.5	—
Accelerator pump nozzle	40	45
Needle valve	1.75	1.75
Accelerator pump cam	No 25 (14 from Sept. 1970)	42 (pos. 2)
Idling speeds (manual)	800/900	800/900
Idling speed (auto) N	—	850/950

TORQUE WRENCH SETTINGS

	lb ft
Inlet manifold	10.0
Exhaust manifold nuts	14.5
Carburettor mounting flange nuts	14.5
Air cleaner securing bolts	9.5
Fuel pump to crankcase	10.5

1 General description

1 The fuel system is conventional and incorporates a rear mounted fuel tank, a camshaft driven mechanical fuel pump mounted on the cylinder block and a downdraught type of carburettor with all the necessary fuel lines and controls.

2 The fuel pump encountered may be one of three types, AC, SEV or SOFABEX. In operating principle they are similar, detail differences will be observed from the relevant illustrations.

3 The carburettor fitted varies in type according to the vehicle model and date of manufacture. Cars and vans fitted with a 350 or 352 series engine have a SOLEX carburettor, those fitted with a 353S or 366T engine have a Weber carburettor. Full specifications and vehicle applications for all carburettors are given in the Specifications section of this Chapter.

4 Solex carburettors have a water heated jacket in the throttle block and the alloy inlet manifold incorporates a water-heated pre-heater.

5 Exhaust manifolds and exhaust pipe systems very according to vehicle model. They are described in a later Section of this Chapter.

6 Vehicles operating in certain territories are fitted with anti-pollution system. These are described in Section 26 of this Chapter.

2 Air cleaners - removal, servicing and refitting

1 All vehicles are fitted with a disposable paper element type air cleaner.

2 Model 1204 vehicles built in 1970 are fitted with an air cleaner of the type shown in Fig. 3.1 page 57.

3 Access to the filter element is obtained by releasing the two spring clips located on the body.

4 All other vehicles are fitted with a pan type air cleaner, Fig. 3.2 page 57.

5 Access to the element is obtained by removing the wing nut

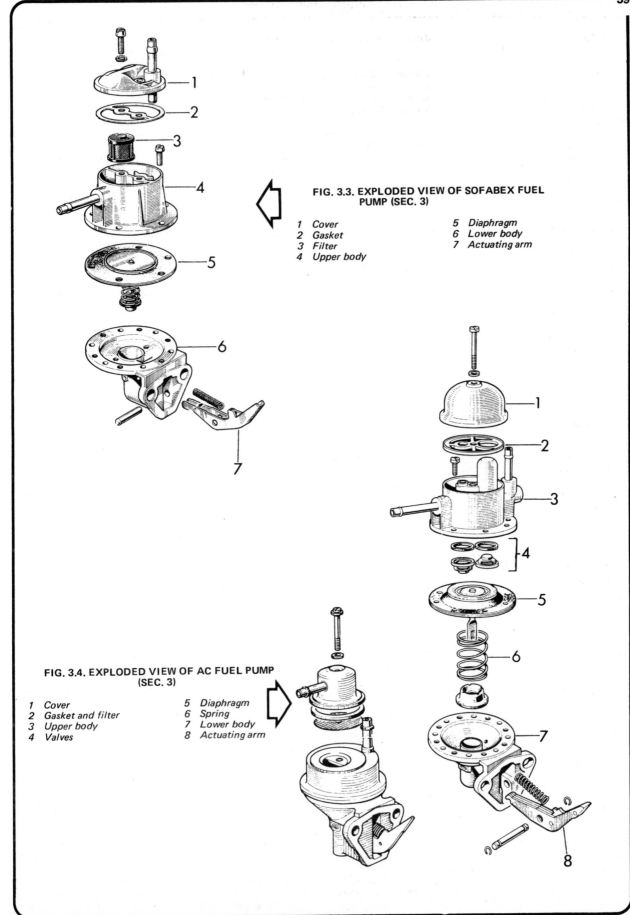

FIG. 3.3. EXPLODED VIEW OF SOFABEX FUEL PUMP (SEC. 3)

1 Cover
2 Gasket
3 Filter
4 Upper body
5 Diaphragm
6 Lower body
7 Actuating arm

FIG. 3.4. EXPLODED VIEW OF AC FUEL PUMP (SEC. 3)

1 Cover
2 Gasket and filter
3 Upper body
4 Valves
5 Diaphragm
6 Spring
7 Lower body
8 Actuating arm

and cover. The filter body may then be removed by unscrewing the two now exposed nuts. Retain the rubber cover ring and the flange washers or renew them should they have deteriorated. (photo)

6   All air cleaner types incorporate a device for warming the intake air and this is either a heater box attached to the rocker cover through which air warmed by the exhaust manifold is drawn (Solex carburettors) or in the case of the cylindrical type of cleaner fitted to the twin Weber 1204 cc engine, a heated intake system controlled by a flap valve.

7   Air cleaner element maintenance and renewal is described in 'Routine Maintenance' Section at the front of this manual.

3   Fuel pump - routine maintenance

1   Detach the fuel supply hose from the fuel pump and plug the hose to prevent loss of fuel.

2   Unscrew the cover retaining screw and remove the cover from the pump. The method of cover removal will differ in detail but will be made clear after reference to the appropriate illustration, Figs. 3.3, 3.4, 3.5 pages 59 and 61.

3   Withdraw the filter screen and wash it in petrol.

4   Remove all trace of dirt and sediment from the interior of the pump chamber.

5   Refit the filter screen, check that the cover gasket is in good condition. If it is not, renew it. Fit the cover but do not use excessive force on the retaining screw.

6   Reconnect the fuel line, start the engine and check for leaks.

4   Fuel pump - removal and refitting

1   Disconnect the fuel supply line from the pump and plug the line to prevent loss of fuel.

2   Disconnect the fuel line between the pump and carburettor. On engines fitted with twin Weber carburettors, the fuel line has a tee branch to feed both carburettors.

3   Unscrew and remove the two pump securing bolts and remove the pump, noting the insulating and sealing washers, fitted between the pump flange and the cylinder block.

4   Withdraw the pump in a downward direction so that the pump actuating arm can be extracted from between the crankcase wall and the camshaft.

5   Refitting is a reversal of removal but check the location and condition of the flange washers.

5   Fuel pump - servicing, repair and testing

1   Before deciding to overhaul a fuel pump, it will be wise to consider a factory exchange unit, particularly where the unit has been in service for a considerable mileage.

2   If you decide to overhaul the pump first obtain a repair kit which contains all necessary renewable items.

3   The method of overhaul applies to all makes of pump but components may vary in design detail.

4   Scribe a line on the two upper and lower body flange edges before dismantling so that they may be refitted in the same relative position. Withdraw the body flange securing screws.

5   Press down on the centre of the diaphragm and tilt it to disengage the lower end of the pull rod from the rocker arm. (AC pump eyelet and hook, SEV collar).

6   Remove the diaphragm assembly, spring, oil seal and washer. The diaphragm and pull rod cannot be separated and are renewed as an assembly. The rocker arm may be withdrawn after removal of its pivot circlips. If this component is sufficiently worn to warrant renewal then the pump should be renewed as a unit.

7   The valves in the AC pump are staked in position and should only be removed for renewal with new components. Locate new gaskets in the valve seats, press the new valves fully home and secure them in position by staking at several points. The valves in

the SEV pump are part of a plate assembly and the combined valve/plate unit is removed after withdrawal of the three securing screws. When refitting a new valve/plate assembly, use a new gasket.

8   When the fuel pump is dismantled, clean all parts in clean petrol and examine for wear and damage.

9   Reassembly is a reversal of dismantling. Use all the new components supplied in the repair kit. Tighten the body flange screws to finger tightness and then operate the rocker arm several times to centralise the diaphragm. Finally tighten the flange screws evenly and in diametrically opposite sequence.

10 When reassembly is complete, temporarily connect the fuel supply line from the tank. Operate the pump actuating rocker arm and after three or four movements of the arm, a well defined spurt of fuel should be ejected from the outlet nozzle of the pump.

11 Remove the fuel supply line and place a finger over the pump inlet nozzle. Operate the actuating arm when a distinct suction should be felt. Remove the finger when an inrush of air should be heard. These tests prove that the pump is in good operating condition and may be employed to test the pump at any time not only when the unit has been overhauled.

6   Fuel tank and transmitter unit - removal, servicing and refitting

1   The fuel tank is located to the rear and below the luggage boot floor (van loading floor) on the right hand side.

2   Components of the fuel tank are shown in Fig. 3.6 page 62.

3   The filler cap is of non-vented type, the tank having a separate vent tube to atmosphere. Tanks fitted to early model vehicles incorporated a small drain plug but this is deleted on later models.

4   Commence removal by lifting the luggage boot floor mat and withdrawing the tank protective cover.

5   Disconnect the leads from the transmitter unit and the plastic air vent tube from the filler neck.

6   From below the car, disconnect the tank to pump fuel line and plug the tank outlet.

7   Unscrew and remove the three tank securing bolts and cut round the sealing mastic bead at the edge of the fuel tank locating flange. Remove the tank upwards into the boot using a twisting motion in order to release the filler neck from its flexible grommet in the bodywork.

8   If the tank is dirty or contains sediment, use two or three lots of clean paraffin to wash it out and then let it drain thoroughly. Do not shake the tank too vigorously or use a stick to probe the interior or damage may be caused to the transmitter float and arm.

9   Do not try to solder a leak in a fuel tank. This is a specialists job. If the leak cannot be repaired with a cold setting compound then the tank should be replaced with a new one.

10 The fuel gauge (tank) transmitter unit may be tested as described in Section 23 of this Chapter and if renewal is called for it should be removed from the tank by unscrewing the flange retaining screws. The transmitter unit may be removed without removing the fuel tank from the vehicle but the unit will have to be released by using a key similar to the one shown in Fig. 3.7 page 62.

11 Refitting is a reversal of removal.

7   Carburettors - general description

1   A Solex carburettor is fitted to all SIMCA models except those fitted with series 353S and 366 engines to which Weber carburettors are fitted.

2   The Solex carburettor is of downdraught type with manually operated choke and may be type 32 B1SA, 32 B1SA2, 32 B1SA3 or 32 B1SA4 according to model of vehicle and the year of manufacture. These carburettors are essentially similar in

2.5 Removing the air cleaner body

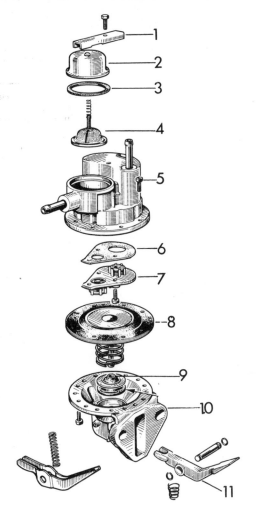

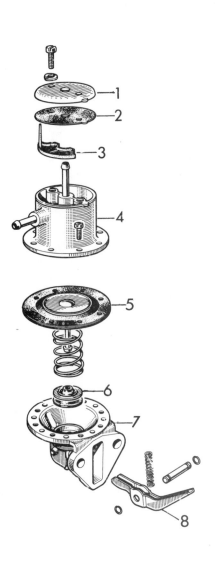

FIG. 3.5. S.E.V. FUEL PUMP — EXPLODED VIEWS (SEC. 3)

Left - 1968/9 - 1970 models
1 Cover retainer
2 Cover
3 Seal
4 Filter
5 Upper body
6 Gasket
7 Valve plate
8 Diaphragm
9 Seal
10 Lower body
11 Actuating arm

Right - all other models
1 Cover
2 Gasket
3 Filter
4 Upper body
5 Diaphragm
6 Seal
7 Lower body
8 Actuating arm

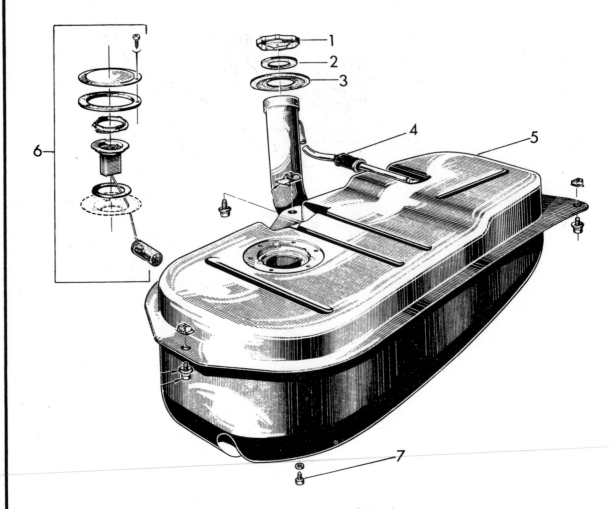

FIG. 3.6. FUEL TANK (SEC. 6)

1 Filler cap   3 Grommet   5 Tank   7 Drain plug and washer
2 Seal   4 Vent pipe   6 Fuel level transmitter

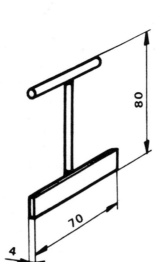

Fig. 3.7. Diagram of tool for unscrewing fuel tank transmitter
unit (dimensions in millimetres) (Sec. 6)

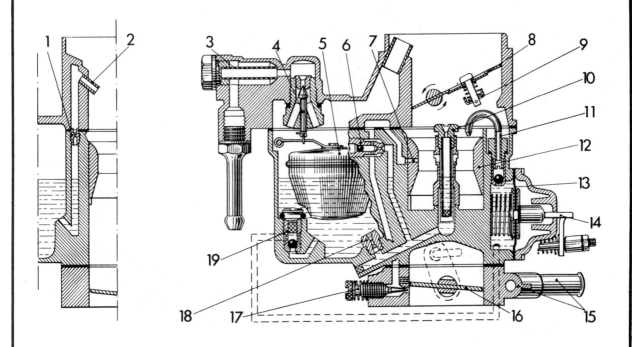

FIG. 3.8. SECTIONAL VIEW OF SOLEX 32 BISA CARBURETTOR (SEC. 7)

1 Econostat jet
2 Econostat discharge nozzle
3 Fuel filter
4 Fuel needle valve
5 Fuel float
6 Idling jet
7 Idling air bleed (calibrated drilling)
8 Choke plate
9 Choke plate by-pass valve
10 Emulsion tube and air correction jet
11 Accelerator pump discharge nozzle
12 Venturi (choke tube)
13 Accelerator pump diaphragm
14 Accelerator pump lever
15 Pre-heater water connections
16 Throttle plate
17 Idling mixture adjustment screw
18 Main jet
19 Accelerator pump non-return valve

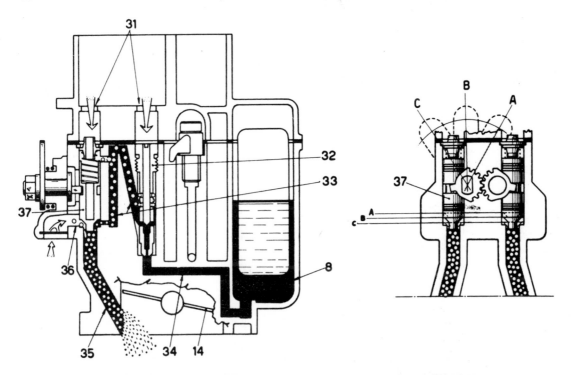

**FIG. 3.9 DIAGRAM OF WEBER CARBURETTOR WITH CHOKE IN OPERATION
FOR KEY TO LEFT HAND ILLUSTRATION, SEE TEXT SEC. 7.15**

Key to right hand illustration
A Choke control fully extended (engine cold)
B Choke control half way (engine warm)
C Choke fully in (engine at operational temperature)

operating principle but reference should be made to Specifications for exact details of jet and other differences.

3 The Solex 32 B1SA carburettor is shown in sectional form in Fig. 3.8 page 63.

4 It comprises three main units, the throttle block, the main body and the top cover. The throttle block embodies the throttle plate and control assembly and incorporates a water heated jacket connected to the engine cooling system to provide pre-heating of the carburettor.

5 The main body incorporates the choke tube, float chamber, accelerator pump and the jets, also the distributor vacuum and crankcase breather connections.

6 The top cover comprises the starting plate assembly, needle valve, inlet connection and filter and the econostat discharge nozzle.

7 The starting device comprises a choke plate fitted with a by-pass valve and a fast idle connecting link to the throttle control arm.

8 The accelerator pedal is connected to the throttle spindle which in turn actuates the accelerator pump to discharge neat fuel into the choke tube when accelerating hard.

9 The econostat device operates from the air intake flow and comes into action at high engine speeds only, to provide a rich mixture at full load conditions.

10 The twin type carburettors (Weber DCNF) fitted to the 353S engine are of twin choke downdraught design with manually operated choke. Each choke tube supplies one engine cylinder and the twin carburettors therefore provide the effect of four individual units.

11 The carburettors are identical in construction but the throttle control layout varies between left and right hand units. The left hand carburettor (master unit) is designated 36 DCNF-7 and the right hand one 36 DCNF-8.

12 The throttle and cold start controls are both connected to the master carburettor but the design of the control arms permits synchronising of the two carburettors and the individual cold-start devices are interconnected.

13 A single Weber type 36 DCNF carburettor is fitted to the series 366 engines and is similar in operating principle to the twin types fitted to the 353S engine.

14 The following diagrams show the various operating cycles of the Weber type carburettor.

15 **Choke in operation**, (Fig. 3.9 page 63), fuel from the bowl (8) passes through channels (34) and jets (32) and is emulsified by air from the holes (31). The fuel reaches the valve seat (37) through the channels (33) and again emulsified by air from the holes (36). It flows through channels (35) into the area below the butterfly valve (14).

16 **Idling and progression** (Fig. 3.10 page 65). The fuel flows to the idling jets (19) through the channels (18) and emulsified with air supplied through the jets (15). The volume of air admitted is regulated by adjustment of the idling screws (20). The fuel then passes through channels (17) and holes (16) to the tubes located below the butterfly valve (14). From idling, as the butterfly valves (14) are opened progressively the mixture reaches the tubes and flows through the progression holes (13) so enabling the engine speed to be increased progressively.

17 **Normal running at constant throttle opening** (Fig. 3.11 page 65). The fuel flows through the needle valve (12) towards the bowl (8) where the float (9) pivoted on the spindle (10) regulates the position of the inlet needle valve (11) and so maintains a pre-determined level of fuel in the bowl. The fuel then passes through jets (7) to the wells (6). It then mixes with air from the emulsion tubes (5) and correction jets (1) and as a vapour passes through holes (2) to reach the carburation area formed by the venturi components (3) and (4).

18 **Accelerator pump** (Fig. 3.12 page 66). The action of the pump is twofold. When the butterfly valve (14) is being closed, the lever (26) releases the diaphragm (28) which due to the effect of the spring (24) draws fuel by suction from the bowl (8) through the ball valve (30). As the butterfly valve is being opened by means of the cam (25) and lever (26) the diaphragm (28) ejects fuel into the carburettor tubes (23) through the valve

(22) and the jets (21). The spring (27) dampens the action of the butterfly valve and so extends the period of fuel injection. Excess fuel from the accelerator pump is returned to the carburettor bowl together with the fumes from the pump chamber through the calibrated hole (29).

8 Solex carburettors - idling adjustment

1 Before setting the idling adjustment, check the following for condition and adjustment. The contact breaker points, ignition timing, valve clearances, sparking plugs, air cleaner, fuel pump screen and the ease of operation of the accelerator control mechanism. (Fig. 3.13 page 66).

2 The most satisfactory method of adjusting the idling speed of the engine is by connecting a vacuum gauge to the inlet manifold. With the engine running at normal operating temperature, adjust the mixture and speed screws until the gauge needle indicates maximum depression.

3 Where a vacuum gauge is not available, run the engine until it reaches normal operating temperature. On automatic transmission vehicles, apply the handbrake fully and engage 'Drive'. The initial starting point for adjustment should be obtained by screwing the mixture control screw (W) fully home, without force and then unscrewing it between two and two and a half turns, Fig. 3.13.

4 Unscrew the idle speed adjustment screw (Z) until it just clears the throttle control arm stop, then screw it in about half a turn.

5 Run the engine and screw the mixture control screw in or out until the maximum engine speed is obtained. Adjust the speed screw and then repeat the operations until the desired tickover is reached (650-700 rev/min). With 353 series engines fitted to North American models the idling speed should be 800-900 rev/min (manual transmission). With all automatic transmission models, the idling speed with 'Drive' selected should be 650-700 rev/min.

6 On 1972 (H series) models fitted with anti-pollution (type 353) engines, the idling speed for manually operated transmission models is 800-900 rev/min and for automatic transmission models (selector in neutral) 825-925 rev/min. Adjust the idling on these models by turning the mixture control screw until maximum engine speed is obtained, then reduce the engine speed by unscrewing the idling speed screw. Now screw the mixture control screw in until a drop in engine speed of 50 rev/min is noticed. Readjust the idling speed if necessary by turning the speed adjustment screw until the recommended slow running rev/min is obtained.

9 Solex carburettors - removal and refitting

1 Remove the wing nut from the air cleaner cover, remove the cover and lift out the element. (photo)

2 Remove the two nuts which secure the air cleaner body to the top of the carburettor. Lift off the air cleaner assembly and disconnect the warm air intake hose at the rear of the cleaner body. Retain the rubber jointing ring.

3 Disconnect the choke and accelerator cables.

4 Disconnect the two water hoses from their throttle block connections and plug both hoses to prevent loss of coolant.

5 Unscrew and remove the two carburettor securing nuts and lockwashers, lift off the carburettor and peel off the gasket.

6 Refitting is a reversal of removal but use a new flange gasket and check the satisfactory operation of the choke and accelerator cables.

7 Top up the cooling system expansion bottle if required.

10 Solex carburettors - setting and adjustment of components

1 **Float level**. Incorrect setting will be indicated by flooding or fuel leakage at the carburettor or evidence of fuel starvation

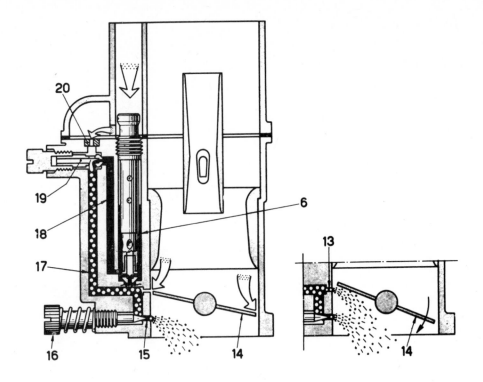

Fig. 3.10 Diagram of idling and progression cycle, Weber carburettor. For key see text, section 7.16

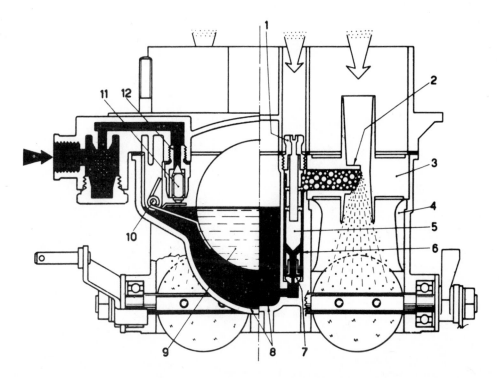

Fig. 3.11 Diagram of Weber carburettor, normal running at constant throttle opening. For key see text, section 7.17

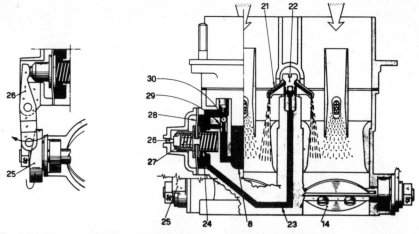

Fig. 3.12 Diagrammatic view of accelerator pump action (Weber). For key see text, section 7.18

FIG. 3.13. ADJUSTMENT SCREWS LOCATED ON SOLEX
CARBURETTOR (SEC. 8)

W   Mixture control   Z   Idling speed

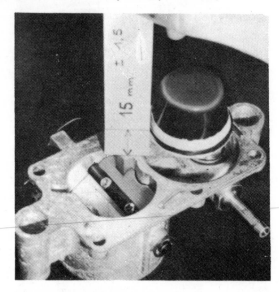

Fig. 3.14. Measuring the float position (Solex) (Sec. 10.6)

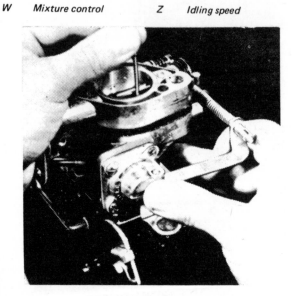

Fig. 3.15. Checking the adjustment of the accelerator pump
(Solex) (Sec. 10.10)

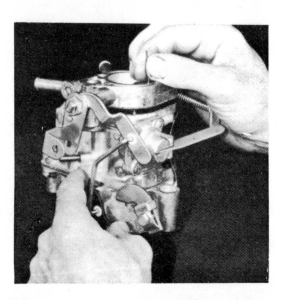

Fig. 3.16. Checking the fast idle setting (Solex) (Sec. 10.13)

9.1 Air cleaner element removal

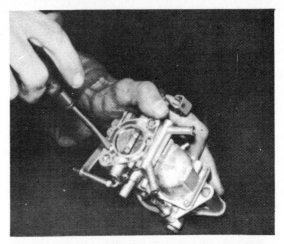

Fig. 3.17. Location of throttle block to carburettor (Solex) securing screws (Sec. 11.7)

Fig.3.18 Removing the fast idle link (Solex)

Fig.3.19 Removing the accelerator pump operating rod (Solex)

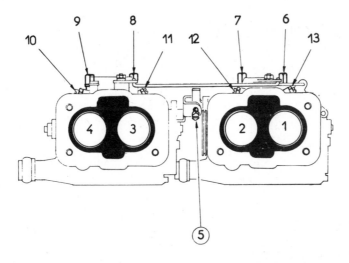

Fig.3.20 Adjustment screws (twin Weber installation)

1 to 4 Carburettor throats
6 to 9 Idling mixture adjustment
screws

10 to 13 Fuel flow rate control
screws (not to be al-
tered

causing stalling or loss of power of the engine.

2   Remove the air cleaner and disconnect the fuel pipe and choke cable from the carburettor.

3   Disconnect the fast idle link from the throttle control arm.

4   Remove the retaining screws and lift off the carburettor top cover.

5   Invert the top cover so that the float arm rests against the fuel inlet needle valve.

6   Use a small rule and measure the distance between the cover mating face of the carburettor and the upper edge of the float collar, Fig. 3.14 page 66.

7   The correct distance is 0.5315 to 0.6496 inch (13.5 to 16.5 mm) and should be adjusted if necessary by gently bending the float operating arm.

8   Flooding of fuel from the float chamber may sometimes be caused by the needle valve housing not being fully tightened in its seat or a damaged sealing washer. Fuel would, in these circumstances, enter the float chamber without passing through the needle valve orifice.

9   **Accelerator pump stroke**, this adjustment will necessitate removal of the carburettor from the manifold. Invert the carburettor and close the throttle butterfly valve. To ensure complete closure, the idling speed adjustment screw will have to be unscrewed.

10 Pull the accelerator pump operating lever fully back gently and using twist drills, test the distance between the edge of the butterfly valve plate and the choke tube wall. A 2.5 mm diameter drill should pass but a 4 mm one should not, Fig. 3.15 page 66.

11 If the clearance is found to be incorrect, renew the accelerator pump control rod with a new type having an adjuster nut and a locknut.

12 **Throttle butterfly valve plate, fast idle setting.** This adjustment will again require removal of the carburettor. Invert the carburettor and close the butterfly valve plate.

13 Pull the choke plate to the fully closed position and check the clearance between the edge of the plate and the choke tube wall, Fig. 3.16 page 66.

14 Again using twist drills as gauges, a 1 mm diameter drill should pass through but a 1.1 mm drill should not.

15 Where the clearance is incorrect, bend the fast idle connecting link gently in the centre of its length.

---

11 Solex carburettors - dismantling, servicing and reassembly

1   Disconnect the fast idle link (9) Fig. 3.21 page 69.

2   Remove the top cover securing screws and remove the cover and gasket.

3   Remove the fuel filter retaining plug (15) and extract the filter (14).

4   Unscrew and remove the fuel inlet valve (5) and retain the sealing washer.

5   If absolutely necessary, the choke plate (3) and spindle (4) may be removed after removal of the two retaining screws and the spindle circlip.

6   Disconnect the accelerator pump operating rod (13).

7   Remove the two screws which secure the throttle block (11) to the carburettor body, Fig. 3.17 page 67.

8   Withdraw the throttle block and gasket, (and spacer if fitted).

9   If absolutely necessary, the throttle spindle (17) and throttle valve plate (10) may be removed after unscrewing the spindle nut and the two plate retaining screws.

10 Remove the float (6) and unscrew the various jets.

11 Remove the four securing screws from the accelerator pump cover assembly (12) and withdraw the diaphragm and return spring.

12 With the carburettor now dismantled, clean the components in clean fuel. Blow out the jets using air from a tyre pump; never probe with wire.

13 Examine the spindles and their housing bores for wear and slackness in operation. If this is evident then it will be realistic to exchange the complete unit for a reconditioned one on an exchange basis.

14 Check the jet sizes and other calibrated components against the specification listed at the front of this Chapter and renew any that have previously been incorrectly substituted.

15 Obtain a repair kit which will contain a complete set of new gaskets and washers and other essential items.

16 Reassembly is a reversal of dismantling but remember to check the various settings and adjustments as described in the preceding Section. Use all the items found in the repair kit and replace the original sealing washer beneath the inlet valve housing. Any alteration in the washer will affect the fuel level in the carburettor bowl.

---

12 Solex 32 B1SA to 32 B1SA2 - conversion

1   It is possible to convert a 32 B1SA type carburettor to a model 32 B1SA by removing the unit from the manifold.

2   Remove the fast idle link. Fig. 3.18 page 67.

3   Remove the throttle block. Fig. 3.17 page 67.

4   Remove the accelerator pump operating rod, Fig. 3.19 page 67.

5   Obtain a special spacer and two gaskets from the SIMCA dealer and fit them between the throttle block and the carburettor body. Two longer setscrews will be required, also a new accelerator pump rod and fast idle link.

6   Check the clearance of the choke plate as described in the preceding Section.

---

13 Weber (twin) carburettors - idling, adjustment and synchronising

1   Before adjusting the carburettors, run through the check list given in Section 8.

2   The flow rates through the balancing channels are set in production and the screws 10, 11, 12 and 13 should not be altered, Fig. 3.20 page 67.

3   With the engine at normal operating temperature, set the idling speed adjustment screw (12) Fig. 3.22 page 70, so that the engine speed is 850 rev/min.

4   Screw the first mixture control screw (6) Fig. 3.20 page 67, in or out until the engine speed is the highest obtainable. Adjust the idling speed screw so that the engine again runs at approximately 850 rev/min.

5   Repeat the sequence of operations with each of the other mixture control screws (7, 8 and 9) in turn.

6   Test check the four screws again to obtain the best balance at the required engine speed and note that screw number (9) will require unscrewing two turns more than the others to achieve the best idling adjustment as there is an additional air flow connection to its internal passage.

7   With the mixture control screws now correctly set, the units must be synchronised. To do this it is preferable to obtain one of the several proprietary balancing devices which indicate (visually) correct synchronisation of twin carburettor installations. This is achieved simply by balancing the intake suction of each carburettor by locating the device in the intake of each carburettor in rotation and turning the screw (5) (Fig. 3.20 page 67) until the correct readings are obtained. An alternative method of synchronising is to place a length of hose in each of the carburettor intakes in turn and attempt to match the 'hiss' from each carburettor. At best this is a temporary expedient until more precise turning can be carried out.

---

14 Weber (single) carburettor - idling adjustment

1   Adjust the idling mixture control screws (two only) in a similar manner to that already described for the twin carburettor installation.

2   No synchronisation will of course, be required.

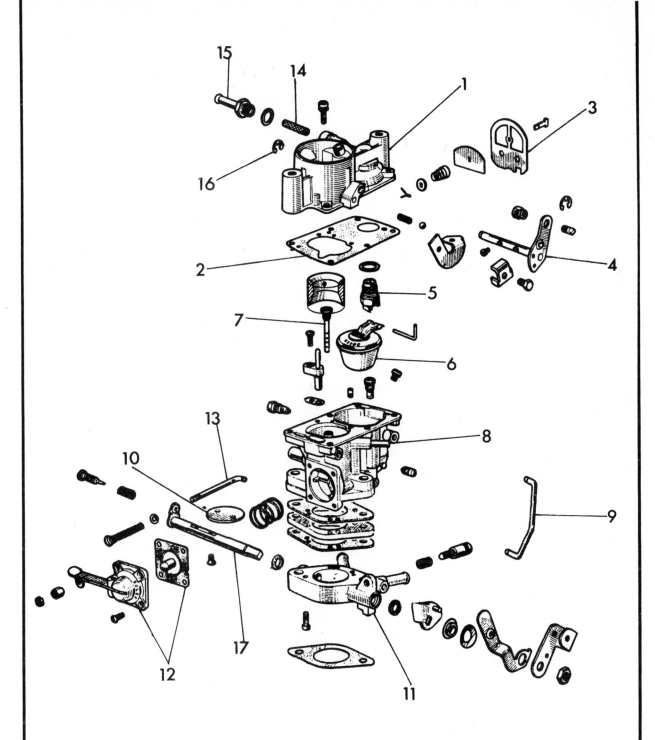

FIG. 3.21. EXPLODED VIEW OF THE SOLEX 32 BISA CARBURETTOR (SEC. 11)

1 Top cover	6 Float	11 Water heated throttle	14 Filter
2 Cover gasket	7 Air correction jet	block	15 Inlet tube and filter
3 Choke plate	8 Body	12 Accelerator pump assembly	retaining plug
4 Choke spindle	9 Fast idle link	13 Accelerator pump	16 Choke spindle circlip
5 Inlet valve	10 Throttle plate	operating rod	17 Throttle spindle

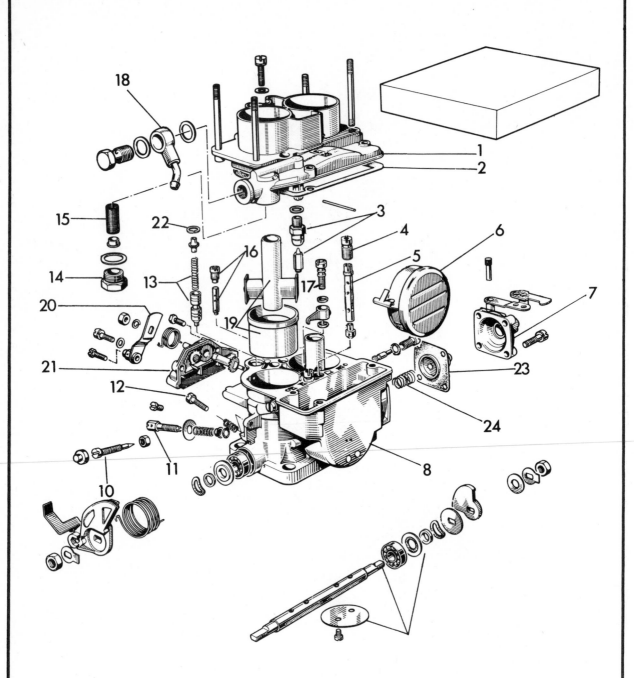

FIG. 3.22. EXPLODED VIEW OF 1972 WEBER CARBURETTOR (1970/71 MODELS VARY SLIGHTLY IN DETAIL) (SEC. 15)

Key to major components
1 Cover
2 Gasket
3 Inlet needle valve
4 Main air correction jet
5 Emulsion tube
6 Float
7 Accelerator pump

8 Body
9 Throttle spindle and butterfly
10 Flow rate screw
11 Idling mixture screw
12 Idling speed screw
13 Starting device piston
14 Filter plug

15 Filter
16 Starting fuel jet
17 Pump discharge valve
18 Fuel inlet coupling
19 Venturi
20 Choke control arm
21 Starting device cover

22 Circlip (starting device piston)
23 Accelerator pump diaphragm
24 Accelerator pump return spring

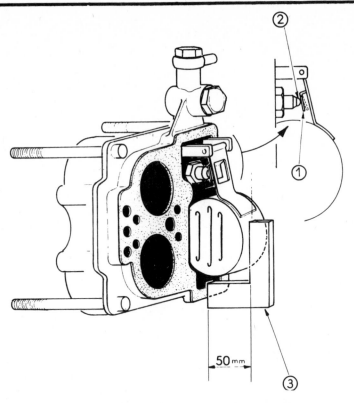

**FIG. 3.23. CHECKING FLOAT LEVEL POSITION ON
A WEBER CARBURETTOR (SEC. 16.2)**

1   *Float arm tab*   3   *Measuring tool*
2   *Needle valve*

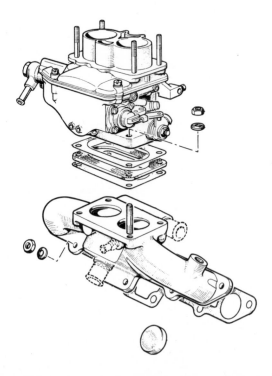

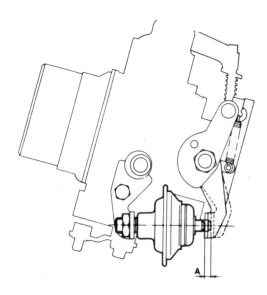

**Fig. 3.25 Inlet manifold with single Weber carburettor
(Sec. 18)**

Fig. 3.24. Diagram showing dashpot clearance (A) (Sec. 16.5)

15 Weber carburettors - removal and refitting

1   Remove the air cleaner.
2   Disconnect the fuel inlet pipe (18) Fig. 3.22 page 70.
3   Plug the fuel line to prevent loss of fuel (it will probably be easier to detach the line from the tank at its connection with the fuel pump and to plug it as it has no banjo fitting to contend with.
4   Disconnect the choke and accelerator controls.
5   Unscrew and remove the four nuts and lockwashers which secure each carburettor to the inlet manifold.
6   Lift away the carburettor and flange gasket.
7   Refitting is a reversal of removal but use new flange gaskets and check that the choke and accelerator controls operate correctly.

16 Weber carburettors - setting and adjustment of components

1   **Float level adjustment,** this may be required where there is evidence of flooding or fuel starvation.
2   Remove the carburettor and detach the cover. With the carburettor body in the altitude shown in Fig. 3.23 page 71 and the tab (1) in contact with the fuel inlet valve ball, the distance between the exposed surface of the gasket and the outside face of the float should be 1.9685 inch (50 mm).
3   Where this dimension varies from that specified, bend the tab to rectify.
4   **Dashpot adjustment;** this device is only fitted to models having full anti-pollution fume control systems and automatic transmission. Its purpose is to slow down the closing action of the throttle.
5   Correct setting can be checked by either measuring the distance travelled by the end of the dashpot as the throttle returns to the idle position after revving the engine or by using a rev counter and checking the speed at which the end face of the dashpot contacts the throttle control lever. The correct clearance should be 2 to 3 mm or contact made at an engine speed of 1200 rev/min, Fig. 3.24 page 71.
6   Variations in these specifications should be noted: 1204 cc models for Sweden (1971 onwards) clearance 4.5 to 5.0 mm engine speed 825 to 925 rev/min. On 366 type engines (anti-pollution) clearance 4.5 to 5.0 mm engine speed 850 to 950 rev/min with gear selector in neutral.
7   Adjustment of the dashpot stroke should be carried out by releasing the locknut and rotating the dashpot up or down in relation to its bracket.

17 Weber carburettors - dismantling, servicing and reassembling

1   Refer to Fig. 3.22 page 70.
2   Unscrew and remove the cover securing screws and withdraw the lid and gasket.
3   Remove the float arm pivot pin and withdraw the float (6).
4   Unscrew and remove the inlet needle valve and its housing retaining the sealing washer located beneath it.
5   Remove the filter plug (14) and withdraw the filter (15).
6   Remove the venturis (19) from the carburettor body.
7   Unscrew the jets and adjusting screws (not flow rate screws see Fig. 3.20 page 67).
8   Disconnect the link from the choke control arm (20) and the starting device operating lever. Remove the retaining screw and detach the choke control arm.
9   Remove the retaining screws and the starting device cover (21).
10 The starting device piston assembly (13) may be dismantled after removal of the retaining circlip (22).
11 Remove the four retaining screws from the accelerator pump assembly cover (7).
12 Withdraw the diaphragm (23) and return spring (24).
13 Dismantle the throttle plate and spindle only if essential. The throttle plate may be slid from its locating slot after the two retaining screws have been removed.
14 Having dismantled the carburettor into its components, carefully inspect them for wear, damage or distortion and renew as appropriate. If there are any cracks in the carburettor body exchange the complete unit for a reconditioned one.
15 Blow all jets clear with air from a tyre pump, never probe with wire.
16 Obtain a repair kit, specifying carefully the exact carburettor type number.
17 Reassembly is a reversal of dismantling, use the new components and gaskets supplied in the repair kit and carry out the settings and adjustments described in the preceding Section.
18 When the carburettor is refitted to the engine, carry out the idling (and synchronising if applicable) adjustments as described in Sections 13 and 14.
19 Do not screw the mixture control screws fully home or damage to their seating may result. Do not alter the thickness of the inlet needle valve seating washer and check that the chamfer on the throttle plate is fitted so that it seals against the choke tube when closed.

18 Inlet manifolds and exhaust systems

1   The inlet manifolds fitted in conjunction with Solex and Weber carburettors are shown in Figs. 3.25 page 71, and Fig. 3.26 page 73.
2   The exhaust manifold and silencer system fitted to single carburettor models are shown in Figs. 3.28 page 74 and 3.29 page 74.
3   The silencer supports used on early models were of flexible strap type not the suspension rings shown.
4   The exhaust manifold and downpipes used in twin carburettor models are shown in Fig. 3.30 page 74, otherwise the silencer assembly is similar to that used on single carburettor vehicles.
5   The exhaust system may be renewed in sections as necessary.
6   Removal of the flexible sections will be difficult unless the manifold securing nuts are first removed and the exhaust pipe connection to the silencer disconnected. The complete front assembly including the manifold may then be removed for dismantling on the bench.

19 Fuel system - fault finding

There are three main types of fault to which the fuel system is prone. They may be summarised as follows:-
a) Lack of fuel at engine
b) Weak mixture
c) Rich mixture

20 Lack of fuel at engine

1   If it is not possible to start the engine, first check that there is fuel in the fuel tank, and then check the ignition system as detailed in Chapter 4. If the fault is not in the ignition system then disconnect the fuel inlet pipe from the carburettor and turn the engine over by the starter relay switch.
2   If petrol squirts from the end of the inlet pipe, reconnect the pipe and check that the fuel is getting to the float chamber. This is done by unscrewing the bolts from the top of the float chamber, and lifting the cover just enough to see inside.
3   If fuel is there then it is likely that there is a blockage in the starting jet, which should be removed and cleaned.
4   No fuel in the float chamber, is caused either by a blockage in the pipe between the pump and float chamber or a sticking float chamber valve. Alternatively on the Weber carburettor the gauze filter at the top of the float chamber may be blocked. Remove the securing nut and check that the filter is clean. Washing in petrol will clean it.

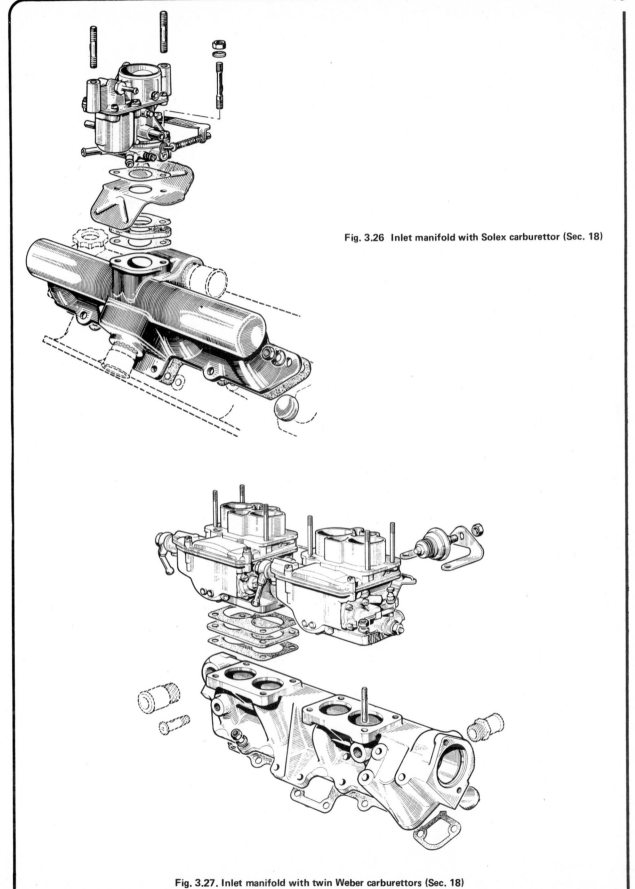

Fig. 3.26 Inlet manifold with Solex carburettor (Sec. 18)

Fig. 3.27. Inlet manifold with twin Weber carburettors (Sec. 18)

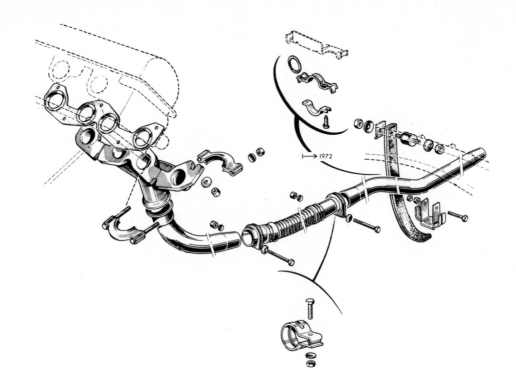

Fig. 3.28. Exhaust manifold and downpipe (single carburettor) (Sec. 18)

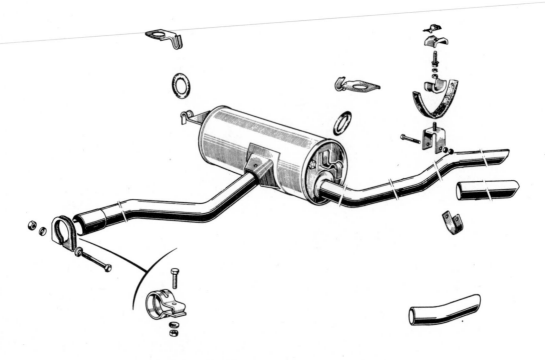

Fig. 3.29. Silencer and tailpipe (all models) (Sec. 18)

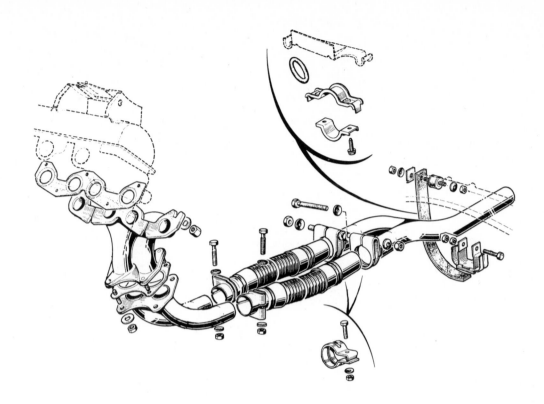

Fig. 3.30. Exhaust manifold and downpipes (twin Weber models) (Sec. 18)

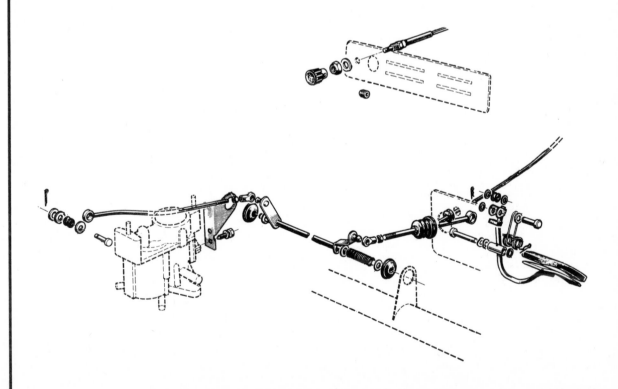

Fig. 3.31. Layout of accelerator and choke controls (Solex) (Sec. 24)

5 If it is decided that it is the float chamber valve that is sticking, remove the fuel inlet pipe, and lift the cover, complete with valve and floats, away.

6 Remove the valve needle and valve and thoroughly wash them in petrol. Petrol gum may be present on the valve or valve needle and this is usually the cause of a sticking valve. Replace the valve in the needle valve assembly, ensure that it is moving freely, and then reassemble the float chamber. It is important that the same washer be placed under the needle valve assembly as this determines the height of the floats and therefore the level of petrol in the chamber.

7 Reconnect the fuel pipe and refit the air cleaner.

8 If petrol does not squirt from the end of the pipe leading to the carburettor then disconnect the pipe leading to the inlet side of the fuel pump. If fuel runs out of the pipe then there is a fault in the fuel pump, and the pump should be checked as has already been detailed.

9 No fuel flowing from the tank when it is known that there is fuel in the tank indicates a blocked pipe line. The line to the tank should be blown out. It is unlikely that the fuel tank vent would become blocked, but this could be a reason for the reluctance of the fuel to flow. To test for this, blow into the tank down the fill orifice. There should be no build up of pressure in the fuel tank, as the excess pressure should be carried away down the vent pipe.

21 Weak mixture

1 If the fuel/air mixture is weak there are six main clues to this condition:-
a) The engine will be difficult to start and will need much use of the choke, stalling easily if the choke is pushed in.
b) The engine will overheat easily.
c) If the spark plugs are examined (as detailed in the Section on engine tuning), they will have a light grey/white deposit on the insulator nose.
d) The fuel consumption may be light.
e) There will be a noticeable lack of power.
f) During acceleration and on the overrun there will be a certain amount of spitting back through the carburettor.

2 As the carburettors are of the fixed jet type, these faults are invariably due to circumstances outside the carburettor. The only usual fault likely in the carburettor is that one or more of the jets may be partially blocked. If the car will not start easily but runs well at speed, then it is likely that the starting jet is blocked, whereas if the engine starts easily but will not rev. then it is likely that the main jets are blocked.

3 If the level of petrol in the float chamber is low this is usually due to a sticking valve or incorrectly set floats.

4 Air leaks either in the fuel lines, or in the induction system, should also be checked for. Also check the distributor vacuum pipe connection as a leak in this is directly felt in the inlet manifold.

5 The fuel pump may be at fault as has already been detailed.

22 Rich mixture

1 If the fuel/air mixture is rich there are also six main clues to this condition:-
a) If the spark plugs are examined they will be found to have a black sooty deposit on the insulator nose.
b) The fuel consumption will be heavy.
c) The exhaust will give off a heavy black smoke, especially when accelerating.
d) The interior deposits on the exhaust pipe will be dry, black and sooty (if they are wet, black and sooty this indicates worn bores, and much oil being burnt).
e) There will be a noticeable lack of power.
f) There will be a certain amount of back-firing through the exhaust system.

2 The faults in this case are usually in the carburettor and most usual is that the level of petrol in the float chamber is too high. This is due either to dirt behind the needle valve, or a leaking float which will not close the valve properly, or a sticking needle.

3 With a very high mileage (or because someone has tried to clean the jets out with wire), it may be that the jets have become enlarged.

4 If the air correction jets are restricted in any way the mixture will tend to become very rich.

5 Occasionally it is found that the choke control is sticking or has been maladjusted.

6 Again, occasionally the fuel pump pressure may be excessive so forcing the needle valve open slightly until a higher level of petrol is reached in the float chamber.

23 Fuel gauge transmitter unit - fault finding

1 If the fuel gauge does not register, check that the fuel tank is not empty. Examine the cable between the unit and the gauge to ensure that the connections are secure and that due to perished insulation, the cable is not earthing.

2 Check that the fuel gauge case is not earthed.

3 Where the fuel gauge registers full at the time, then almost certainly the cable between the transmitter unit and the gauge has become disconnected.

24 Accelerator and choke controls

1 The layout of the carburettor controls is shown according to type in Figs. 3.31, 3.32 and 3.33 pages 75 and 77.

2 Ensure that the accelerator cable has enough slack in the idling position for correct closure of the butterfly valve to occur when the accelerator pedal is released.

3 Check that the accelerator cable cannot contact the radiator fan blades and if necessary secure it to the heater hose to avoid this possibility.

4 Should vibration of the accelerator outer cable occur then a rubber washer (A) may be fitted between the outer cable and its stop, Fig. 3.34 page 78.

5 Keep the moving parts and swivels of the controls lubricated (regularly) with engine oil.

25 Modifications

1 Few modifications have been carried out to the fuel system and carburettors.

2 The accelerator pump contours have been changed.

3 The float design of the Weber carburettors has been altered.

4 Weber carburettor adjustment screws have been changed to self-locking types.

5 On 1100 special H series vehicles, ensure that a minimum clearance of 0.6 mm is maintained between the idling speed stop and the accelerator outer cable support plate, Fig. 3.35 page 78.

6 If necessary, file the support plate to achieve this clearance.

26 Maintenance of minimal fume emission (U.S.A. and other territories)

1 The design and operating principles of simple crankcase fume recycling devices are described in Chapter 1.

2 The adjustment of the dashpot fitted to vehicles having fume control systems and automatic transmission is described in Section 16.

3 On vehicles fitted with comprehensive anti-pollution fume emission control equipment then three major adjustments must be regularly carried out.

4 Check the vacuum unit pull-rod stop setting, Fig. 3.36 page 78. With the engine at idling speed, press on the end of the pull rod so that the stop (6) contacts the vacuum unit body (8). The

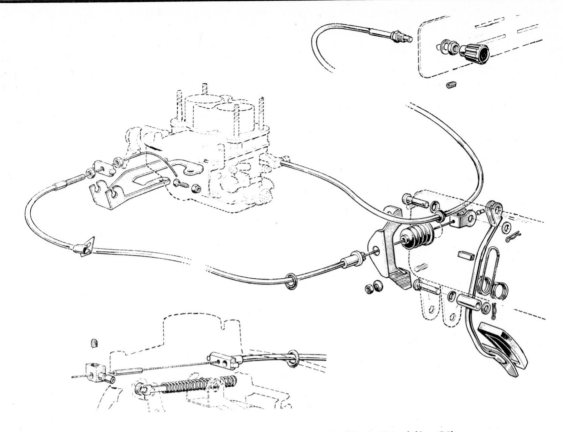

Fig. 3.32. Layout of accelerator and choke controls (Single Weber) (Sec. 24)

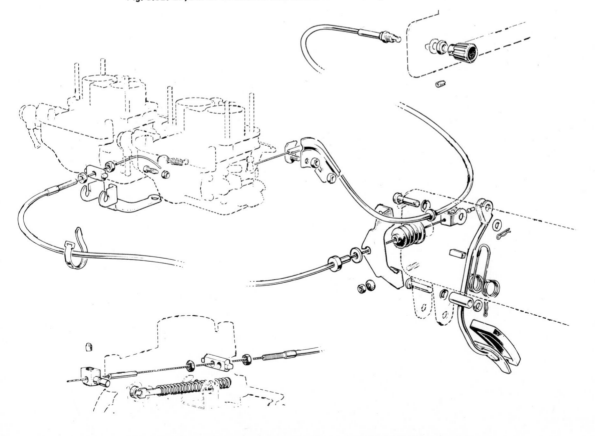

Fig. 3.33. Layout of accelerator and choke controls (Twin Weber) (Sec. 24)

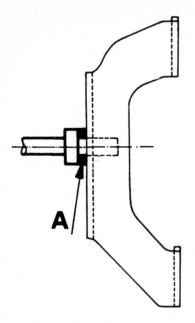

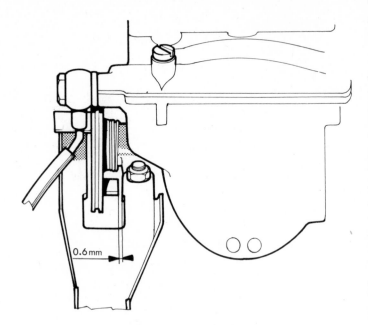

FIG. 3.34. DIAGRAM SHOWING METHOD OF RECTIFICATION OF ACCELERATOR CABLE VIBRATION (SEC. 24)

A   Rubber washer

Fig. 3.35. Diagram showing possible modification required to 1100 special H series vehicles (Sec. 25.5)

0.6 mm

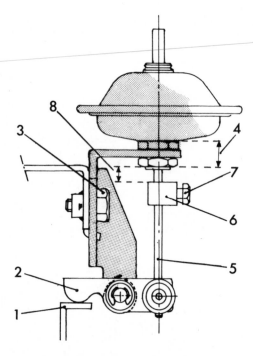

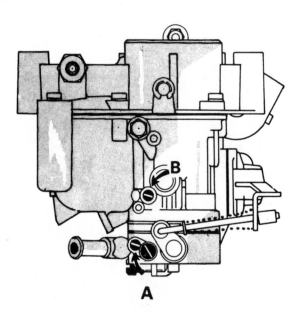

FIG. 3.36. VACUUM UNIT STOP ROD ADJUSTMENT DIAGRAM (U.S.A. VEHICLES) (SEC. 26.4)

1 Lever on throttle control arm
2 Intermediate lever
3 Bracket fixing bolt
4 Bracket adjustment
5 Diaphragm pull-rod
6 Adjustable stop
7 Lock screw
8 Stop in position against vacuum unit

Fig. 3.37. Additional adjustment screws A and B fitted to Solex carburettors installed in North American vehicles (Sec. 25)

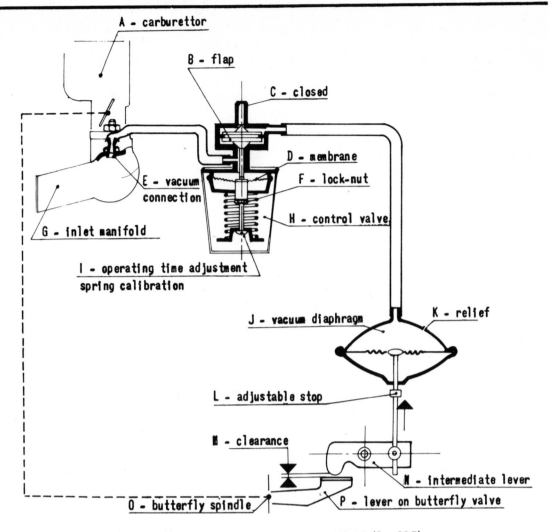

Fig. 3.38. Layout of the fume emission control circuit (Sec. 26.5)

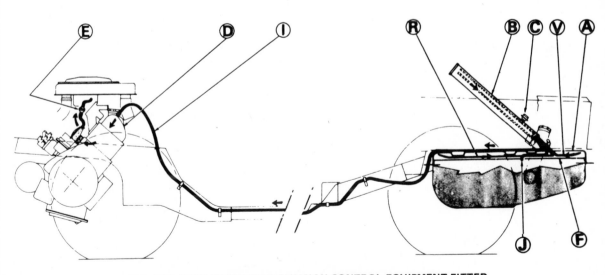

FIG. 3.39. FUEL TANK FUME EMISSION CONTROL EQUIPMENT FITTED
TO NORTH AMERICAN VEHICLES (SEC. 27.3)

E   Flame trap
D   Rocker arm cover
I   Fume recovery tube
R   Vent tube
B   Fume recuperator
C   Bivalve flap
V   Vent tube
A   Strainer
J   Filler vent tube
F   Intermediate partition

speed of the engine will now have increased to between 1800 and 1900 rev/min. If the engine speed is not at this level, slacken the stop lock screw (7) and push the rod in until it is obtained and then, holding the rod still, bring the stop into contact with the vacuum unit and tighten the lockscrew. Release the rod, permit the engine to resume its idling speed before rechecking the pull rod stop setting.

5   Check the vacuum unit and control valve operation, Fig. 3.38 page 79.

6   Correct operation is indicated when the intermediate lever takes 3 to 4 seconds to return to its initial idling position after releasing the accelerator pedal when the engine is running at 4000 rev/min. Where this is not the case, adjust the tension of the spring in the vacuum control unit. To do this, remove the plastic cover from the valve. Using two thin spanners (8 mm) inserted through the coils of the spring, hold the diaphragm nut and release the locknut. Adjust the valve screw (screwing in reduces closure time, unscrewing increases it) until the correct setting is obtained and then retighten the locknut.

7   Where adjustment of the valve screw has no effect upon the time taken for the intermediate lever to return then this is due to an air leak in the circuit, a defective vacuum control valve, an unserviceable vacuum unit or the intermediate lever binding. Renew as appropriate.

8   Check the clearance of the intermediate lever (2) Fig. 3.36 page 78. This should be between 0.032 and 0.047 inch (0.8 and 1.2 mm). Adjust if necessary, by moving the position of the vacuum unit bracket.

9   In addition to the foregoing operations, the following items must be checked and any necessary adjustments carried out at intervals not greater than every 6000 miles (10000 km).
(i)   Ignition timing.
(ii)   Engine idling adjustment.
(iii)   Sparking plug gaps.
(iv)   Contact breaker points gap.
(v)   Smooth operation of the accelerator controls.
(vi)   Leak free condition of the tube which connects the manifold to the control valve.

27 North American models - differences

1   Where a Solex carburettor is fitted then it will have two additional adjustment screws (A.B) Fig. 3.37 page 78.

2   These screws are set during production and must not be altered.

3   The fuel tank has a device for controlling the discharge of fumes, Fig. 3.39 page 79.

4   When dismantling the recuperator or fuel tank assembly note the colour identification on the connecting tubes for exact refitting.

Fault finding chart

Symptom	Reason/s	Remedy
FUEL CONSUMPTION EXCESSIVE		
Carburation and ignition faults	Air cleaner choked and dirty giving rich mixture	Remove, clean and replace air cleaner.
	Fuel leaking from carburettor(s), fuel pumps or fuel lines	Check for and eliminate all fuel leaks. Tighten fuel line union nuts.
	Float chamber flooding	Check and adjust float level.
	Generally worn carburettor(s)	Remove, overhaul and replace.
	Distributor condenser faulty	Remove, and fit new unit.
	Balance weights or vacuum advance mechanism in distributor faulty	Remove, and overhaul distributor.
Incorrect adjustment	Carburettor(s) incorrectly adjusted mixture too rich	Tune and adjust carburettor(s).
	Idling speed too high	Adjust idling speed.
	Contact breaker gap incorrect	Check and reset gap.
	Valve clearances incorrect	Check rocker arm to valve stem clearances and adjust as necessary.
	Incorrectly set sparking plugs	Remove, clean, and regap.
	Tyres under-inflated	Check tyre pressures and inflate if necessary.
	Wrong sparking plugs fitted	Remove and replace with correct units.
	Brakes dragging	Check and adjust brakes
INSUFFICIENT FUEL DELIVERY OR WEAK MIXTURE DUE TO AIR LEAKS		
Dirt in system	Petrol tank air vent restricted	Remove petrol cap and clean out air vent.
	Partially clogged filters in pump and carburettor(s)	Remove and clean filters.
	Dirt lodged in float chamber needle housing	Remove and clean out float chamber and needle valve assembly.
	Incorrectly seating valves in fuel pump	Remove, dismantle, and clean out fuel pump.
Fuel pump faults	Fuel pump diaphragm leaking or damaged	Remove, and overhaul fuel pump.
	Gasket in fuel pump damaged	Remove, and overhaul fuel pump.
	Fuel pump valves sticking due to petrol gumming	Remove, and thoroughly clean fuel pump.
Air leaks	Too little fuel in fuel tank (prevalent when climbing steep hills)	Refill fuel tank.
	Union joints on pipe connections loose	Tighten joints and check for air leaks.
	Split in fuel pipe on suction side of fuel pump	Examine, locate, and repair.
	Inlet manifold to block or inlet manifold to carburettor(s) gasket leaking.	Test by pouring oil along joints - bubbles indicate leak. Renew gasket as appropriate.

Chapter 4 Ignition system

Contents

Specifications

System type	12v battery, coil and distributor
Firing order	1 3 4 2 (No 1 next to flywheel)

Distributor

Make	Ducellier or SEV
Type	Centrifugal and vacuum advance
Direction or rotation (viewed from top)	Clockwise
Contact breaker points gap	0.018 in (0.45 mm) *
Condenser capacity	0.2 to 0.3 micro farad
Dwell angle	$56^o \pm 1^o$

This may vary on some models; refer to the manufacturer's handbook supplied with the car.

Distributor type, application and static advance

Type	Engine application	Static advance BTDC
4258A	352 to number 5000021	6°
4301A	352 from number 5030021	6°
4354A	352 from number 5050021	6°
4199A	350 to number 6002416	9°
4214A/4222A/4222A	350 from number 6002417	12°
4286A	350 from number 6030021	12°
4286B	350 from number 6780431	12°
4199A	350S to number 6566462	9°
4248A/4249A	350S from number 6566463	10°
4287A	350S from number 6670021	10°
4287B	350S from number 6780431	10^D
4304B (manual)	353S from number 7310021	0°
4305A (automatic)	353S from number 7310021	4°
4343A	H series engines (1972)	12°
4342	353S from number 7700021	12°
4332A	H series engines (1972) type 366	12°
4389A ,..	366T engine (1972 H series)	12°
4389A	366T engine (1972 H series)	12°
—	353 to number 7310020, anti-pollution USA version	4° ATDC

Coil

Type	Ducellier or SEV oil filled
Primary resistance	3.0 to 3.5 ohms
Secondary resistance	5000 to 5500 ohms

Sparking plugs

Type (all models except*)	Champion N6Y
* Anti-pollution engines	Champion N7Y
* Type 366 and 353 engines (1972 H series)	Champion N7Y
* Type 366TT engines (1972 H series)	Champion N7Y
Gap	0.024 in (0.6096 mm)

TORQUE WRENCH SETTINGS

	lb ft
Sparking plugs	20.0
Distributor bracket bolt	14.5
Distributor to bracket	6.5

1 General description

In order that the engine can run correctly it is necessary for an electrical spark to ignite the fuel/air mixture in the combustion chamber and at exactly the right moment in relation to engine speed and load. The ignition system is based on feeding low tension voltage from the battery to the coil where it is converted to high tension voltage. The high tension voltage is powerful enough to jump the spark plug gap in the cylinders many times a second under high compression pressures providing that the system is in good condition and that all adjustments are correct.

The ignition system is divided into two circuits. The low tension circuit and the high tension circuit (Fig. 4.1 page 85).

The low tension (sometimes known as the primary) circuit consists of the battery; lead to the control box; lead to the ignition switch; lead from the ignition switch to the low tension or primary coil windings (coil terminal CB) to the contact breaker points and condenser in the distributor.

The high tension circuit consists of the high tension or secondary coil windings; the heavy ignition lead from the centre of the coil to the centre of the distributor cap; the rotor arm; and the spark plug leads and spark plugs.

The system functions in the following manner: Low tension voltage is changed in the coil into high tension voltage by the opening and closing of the contact breaker points in the low tension circuit. High tension voltage is then fed via the carbon brush in the centre of the distributor cap to the rotor arm of the distributor cap, and each time it comes in line with one of the four metal segments in the cap, which are connected to the spark plug leads the opening and closing of the contact breaker points causes the high tension voltage to build up, jump the gap from the rotor arm to the appropriate metal segment and so via the spark plug lead to the spark plug, where it finally jumps the spark plug gap before going to earth.

The ignition is advanced and retarded automatically, to ensure the spark occurs at just the right instant for the particular load at the prevailing engine speed.

The ignition advance is controlled both mechanically and by a vacuum operated system. The mechanical governor mechanism comprises two weights, which move out from the distributor shaft as the engine speed rises due to centrifugal force. As they move outwards they rotate the cam relative to the distributor shaft, and so advance the spark. The weights are held in position by two light springs and it is the tension of the springs which is largely responsible for correct spark advancement.

The vacuum control consists of a diaphragm, one side of which is connected via a small bore tube to the carburettor, and the other side to the contact breaker plate. Depression in the inlet manifold and carburettor, which varies with engine speed and throttle opening, causes the diaphragm to move, so moving the contact breaker plate, and advancing or retarding the spark. A fine degree of control is achieved by a spring in the vacuum assembly.

The distributor is mounted on the forward facing side of the engine crankcase and is driven by a shaft in mesh with the camshaft.

The type of distributor fitted is critical to the particular engine model and reference should be made to Specifications before purchasing a new one.

2 Contact breaker - adjustment

1 Every 6000 miles (10000 km) the distributor contact breaker points should be examined and adjusted if required.
2 Pull off the two spring clips which secure the distributor cap in position and lift off the cap. (photo)
3 Clean the inside and outside of the distributor cap with a dry cloth and examine the cap contact segments for excessive burning. If evident, then the cap must be renewed.
4 Pull off the rotor arm (photo)

5 Gently prise the contact breaker points apart and examine the condition of their faces. If they are rough, pitted or dirty they must be removed for dressing or renewal as described in the following Section.
6 If the condition of the points is satisfactory, turn the engine over (it will be easier to do this if the sparking plugs have first been removed) until the heel of the breaker arm is on a high point of the cam.
7 Measure the gap between the points with a feeler gauge. (photo).
8 The gap should be as given in the Specifications. Where adjustment is required, slacken the contact breaker base plate securing screw and move the fixed arm by inserting a screwdriver in the notches provided. (photo)
9 When the gap is correct, the feeler blade should just fall under its own weight. Tighten the breaker arm securing screw.
10 Refit the rotor, distributor cap and retaining clips.

3 Contact breaker points - removing and refitting

1 If the contact breaker points are worn or pitted then they must be removed and either dressed on an oilstone or renewed. Any 'pips' or craters must be removed by rubbing each contact face perfectly squarely on a fine oil or carborundum stone. Excessive pitting of the faces may be caused by a poor earth either at the battery lead or at the cylinder head earthing strap.
2 Remove the distributor cap and rotor. Detach the long spring clip which secures the moveable breaker arm to its pivot post. Lift the breaker arm from its post and then loosen the spade terminal at the end of the supply lead by unscrewing the nut within the boss on the exterior of the distributor body. The breaker arm may now be removed complete with captive lead.
3 Unscrew and remove the fixed contact breaker arm from the base plate.
4 Refitting is a reversal of removal but remember to adjust the points gap as described in the preceding Section and apply a smear of petroleum jelly to the distributor cam faces.

4 Condenser - removal, testing and refitting

1 The purpose of the condenser, (sometimes known as a capacitor) is to ensure that when the contact breaker points open there is no sparking across them which would cause wear.
2 The condenser is fitted in parallel with the contact breaker points. If it develops a short circuit, it will cause ignition failure as the points will be prevented from interrupting the low tension circuit.
3 If the engine becomes very difficult to start or begins to miss after several miles running and the breaker points show signs of excessive burning, then the condition of the condenser must be suspect. A further test can be made by separating the points by hand with the ignition switched on. If this is accompanied by a flash it is indicative that the condenser has failed.
4 Without special test equipment the only sure way to diagnose condenser trouble is to replace a suspected unit with a new one and note if there is any improvement.
5 The condenser is externally mounted on the distributor body and may be withdrawn by removing its retaining screw and disconnecting its lead from the LT terminal.
6 Refitting is a reversal of removal.

5 Coil - description and maintenance

1 The ignition coil is oil filled and is mounted on the right hand side of the engine compartment.
2 The HT connection is a push-in type. (photo)
3 The LT connections are 'Lucar' type. (photo)
4 Always ensure that the LT connections are correctly made to the coil. From the distributor, the LT lead should be fitted to

Measuring plug gap. A feeler gauge of the correct size (see ignition system specifications) should have a slight 'drag' when slid between the electrodes. Adjust gap if necessary

Adjusting plug gap. The plug gap is adjusted by bending the earth electrode inwards, or outwards, as necessary until the correct clearance is obtained. Note the use of the correct tool

Normal. Grey-brown deposits lightly coated core nose. Gap increasing by around 0.001 in (0.025 mm) per 1000 miles (1600 km). Plugs ideally suited to engine and engine in good condition

Carbon fouling. Dry, black, sooty deposits. Will cause weak spark and eventually misfire. Fault: over-rich fuel mixture. Check: carburettor mixture settings, float level and jet sizes; choke operation and cleanliness of air filter. Plugs can be re-used after cleaning

Oil fouling. Wet, oily deposits. Will cause weak spark and eventually misfire. Fault: worn bores/piston rings or valve guides; sometimes occurs (temporarily) during running-in period. Plugs can be re-used after thorough cleaning

Overheating. Electrodes have glazed appearance, core nose very white - few deposits. Fault: plug overheating. Check: plug value, ignition timing, fuel octane rating (too low) and fuel mixture (too weak). Discard plugs and cure fault immediately

Electrode damage. Electrodes burned away; core nose has burned, glazed appearance. Fault: initial pre-ignition. Check: as for 'Overheating' but may be more severe. Discard plugs and remedy fault before piston or valve damage occurs

Split core nose (may appear initially as a crack). Damage is self-evident, but cracks will only show after cleaning. Fault: pre-ignition or wrong gap-setting technique. Check: ignition timing, cooling system, fuel octane rating (too low) and fuel mixture (too weak). Discard plugs, rectify fault immediately

2.2 Removing the distributor cap

2.4 Removing the rotor arm

2.7 Checking the contact breaker gap

2.8 Adjusting the gap with a screwdriver

5.2 HT lead connection to coil

5.3 LT lead connection to coil

the coil negative (–) terminal. Keep the exterior of the coil free from oil and grease.

6 Distributor - removal and refitting

1 The distributor is secured to its crankcase mounting bracket (see Chapter 1) by one bolt.
2 Detach the HT leads from the plugs and coil and the LT lead from the coil.
3 Unscrew and remove the single securing bolt and withdraw the distributor unit.

4 To refit the distributor, turn the engine so that number one piston (flywheel end of engine block) is at TDC. This will be indicated when with the rocker cover removed, both No 1 cylinder valves are closed and No 4 cylinder valves are in balance. It will be easier to rotate the engine if the sparking plugs are first removed from the cylinder head.
5 Hold the distributor so that the vacuum capsule is towards the timing gear cover.
6 Turn the rotor arm so that it points towards No 1 HT contact in the distributor cap. Fig. 4.3 page 86.
7 Engage the large and small segments of the distributor drive shaft with the driving sleeve segments.

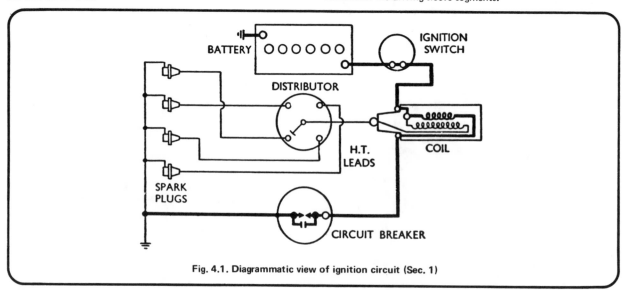
Fig. 4.1. Diagrammatic view of ignition circuit (Sec. 1)

8 Insert the securing bolt which retains the distributor to its bracket.

9 Reconnect the HT and LT leads and then carry out the ignition timing adjustment as described in Section 10.

7 Distributor - dismantling

1 When major overhaul of the distributor becomes necessary it is usually more economical to exchange the unit on a factory reconditioned basis.

2 However, the following procedure should be followed if servicing and repair of the original unit is preferred. Whether the unit is a SEV or Ducellier type the operations are similar, the two units differing only in detail. The Ducellier unit is the subject of this Section.

3 Remove the distributor cap (1) Fig. 4.2 page 86.

4 Withdraw the rotor (2).

5 Disconnect the condenser lead from the LT terminal and remove the condenser securing screw and lift the condenser (12) from its location.

6 Remove the spring clip which secures the vacuum unit operating rod to the link pivot pin, (photo).

7 Remove the two vacuum capsule securing screws and detach the capsule.

8 Disconnect the spring contact breaker (3) lead from the LT terminal. Remove the screws which secure the distributor cap retaining spring clips (14) and the baseplate (6). Lift out the baseplate assembly complete with fixed contact breaker (5) moveable contact breaker arm (3) and vacuum advance link (4).

9 The contact breaker arms may be removed if required as described in Section 3.

10 Pick out the felt lubricating pad (20) from the top of the distributor shaft. Unscrew the retaining screw and lift the cam assembly from the shaft.

11 Where essential, the control springs (8) can be unhooked from the centrifugal weights and the plate and weights lifted from their pivots.

12 The distributor shaft and plate assembly can be removed after the pin (19) has been drifted out of its location in the driving dog (18). Note carefully the sequence of fitting of spacers, washers and seals which are fitted between the distributor body and the driving dog.

8 Distributor - inspection and repair

1 Check the points as described in Section 3. Check the distributor cap for signs of tracking, indicated by a thin black line between the segments. Replace the cap if any signs of tracking are found.

2 If the metal portion of the rotor arm is badly burned or loose, renew the arm. If only slightly burned clean the end with a fine file. Check that the contact spring has adequate pressure and the bearing surface is clean and in good condition.

3 Check that the carbon brush in the distributor cap is unbroken and stands proud of its holder.

4 Examine the fly weights and pivots for wear and the advance springs for slackness. They can best be checked by comparing with new parts. If they are slack they must be renewed.

5 Check the points assembly for fit on the breaker plate, and the cam follower for wear.

6 Examine the fit of the lower shaft in the distributor body. If this is excessively worn it will be necessary to fit a new assembly.

9 Distributor - reassembly

1 Reassembly is a reversal of dismantling but the following points should be observed.

2 Lubricate all components except the rotor and contact breaker with clean engine oil before reassembling.

3 Ensure that the spacers and washers are properly fitted at the

7.6 Circlip retaining vacuum advance link to pivot

lower end of the distributor shaft.

4 Use a new pin to secure the driving dog to the distributor shaft, peening both ends of the pin well over.

5 Clean the contact breaker points with clean petrol or methylated spirit and adjust the gap as described in Section 2.

10 Ignition - timing

1 Two ignition timing scales are provided, one on the timing cover and crankshaft pulley wheel and the other on the flywheel and clutch housing, Fig 4.4 page 86.

2 The latter scale is the more accurate and is visible after removal of the plate (A).

3 In order to rotate the engine for timing adjustment or setting, remove the sparking plugs and either engage first gear and push the car, jack up the front left hand road wheel and turn it with gear engaged or with neutral selected, turn the crankshaft pulley by using a spanner on the pulley retaining bolt. The last method is the only way to rotate the engine on automatic transmission vehicles.

4 Rotate the engine until number 1 piston is at TDC. This is indicated by removing the rocker cover and observing the moment when the inlet and exhaust valves of number 4 cylinder are in balance (exhaust just closing, inlet just opening). An alternative method is to place a finger over number 1 plug and feel the compression created as the piston ascends on compression stroke. Use the timing cover/crankshaft pulley alignment marks as basic TDC.

5 Refer to Specifications and ascertain the number of degrees of static ignition setting applicable to your particular engine type.

6 Rotate the engine a fraction of a turn at a time until the mark on the flywheel is aligned with the correct BTDC mark on the clutch housing scale. Each division of the scale represents 2°.

7 Slacken the bolt which secures the distributor to its support bracket and with the ignition switched on and a test bulb connected between the LT terminal of the distributor and earth, turn the distributor unit until the test bulb just lights. Tighten the securing bolt.

8 Excessive movement of the distributor should not be needed to achieve the correct position of the distributor and such movement will indicate re-checking of the distributor and drive gear alignment being required as described in Section 6 of this Chapter and in Chapter 1 of this manual.

9 The use of a stroboscope will entail the acquisition of an electric rev. counter. This must be used to establish the number of degrees of advance which are to be added to the static ignition

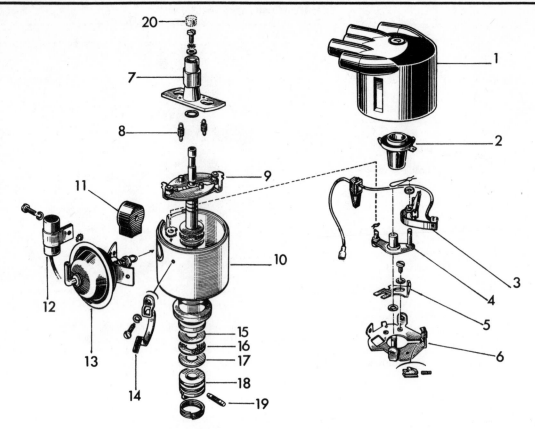

FIG. 4.2. EXPLODED VIEW OF DUCELLIER TYPE DISTRIBUTOR (SEC. 7)

1 Cap	6 Contact breaker baseplate	10 Body	15 Thrust washer
2 Rotor	7 Cam assembly	11 LT insulator	16 Sealing ring
3 Moveable breaker arm	8 Centrifugal advance weight	12 Condenser	17 Spacer washer
4 Vacuum advance link	control springs	13 Vacuum capsule	18 Driving dog
5 Fixed contact breaker	9 Drive shaft and plate	14 Cap retaining spring	19 Retaining pin
			20 Felt pad

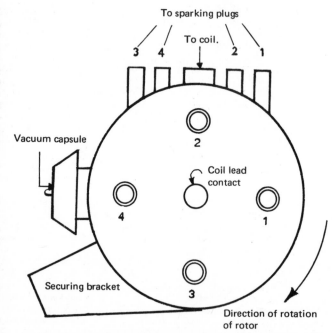

Fig. 4.3. Diagram showing location of segments in distributor cap and sequence of HT lead connections to sparking plugs (Sec. 6 and 11)

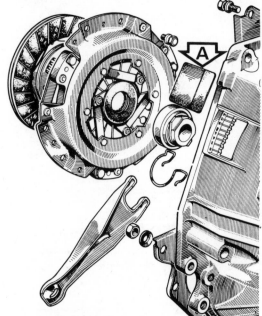

FIG. 4.4. CLUTCH OR CONVERTOR HOUSING IGNITION TIMING SCALE (SEC. 10)

"A" —   Snap-in type cover plate

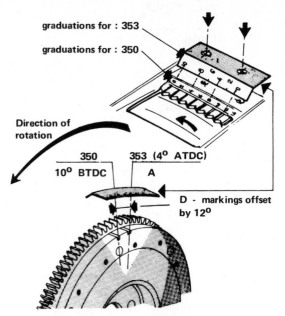

graduations for : 353

graduations for : 350

Direction of rotation

350   353 (4° ATDC)

10° BTDC   A

D - markings offset by 12°

Fig. 4.5. Timing marks and index scale used on Type 353 engines having fume control equipment and operating in U.S.A. (Sec. 10)

setting due to the movement of the centrifugal advance weights in the distributor when the engine is running. This additional number of degrees of advance varies according to index number of the distributor and to the indicated number of revs. at tick-over.

10 A stroboscope is also used to check the operation of the vacuum and centrifugal advance but if the distributor cap is removed and the vaccum tube detached from the carburettor, the movement of the vacuum capsule operating arm may be observed if the tube is sucked hard.

11 Should no movement occur during this test, then faults will be indicated in the advance mechanism and the distributor must be dismantled only sufficiently to check for weak or damaged weight control springs or an unserviceable vacuum capsule or leaking vacuum pipe.

12 On type 353 engines fitted to USA anti-fume pollution engines, the flywheel carries two timing marks and the clutch or convertor housing scale is the additional, offset one, located to the rear of the standard one, Fig. 4.5.

13 With this type of engine, the second mark on the flywheel (A) should be emphasised with white chalk and a stroboscope used to align it with the 4° ATDC mark on the 353 engine scale.

14 A stroboscope should be used to time the ignition setting on all engines fitted with fume control equipment and with all types of engines check the condition and gap of the contact breaker points before carrying out the operation.

11 Spark plugs and leads

1 The correct functioning of the spark plugs is vital for the correct running and efficiency of the engine.

2 At intervals of 6,000 miles (9500 km) the plugs should be removed, examined, cleaned, and if worn excessively, replaced. The condition of the spark plugs will also tell much about the overall condition of the engine.

3 If the insulator nose of the spark plug is clean and white, with no deposits, this is indicative of a weak mixture, or too hot a plug. (A hot plug transfers heat away from the electrode slowly - a cold plug transfers it away quickly).

4 The plugs fitted as standard are Champion as listed in Specifications at the beginning of this Chapter. If the tip and insulator nose is covered with hard black looking deposits, then this is

indicative that the mixture is too rich. Should the plug be black and oily, then it is likely that the engine is fairly worn, as well as the mixture being too rich.

5 If the insulator nose is covered with light tan to greyish brown deposits, then the mixture is correct and it is likely that the engine is in good condition.

6 If there are any traces of long brown tapering stains on the outside of the white portion of the plug, then the plug will have to be renewed, as this shows that there is a faulty joint between the plug body and the insulator, and compression is being allowed to leak away.

7 Plugs should be cleaned by a sand blasting machine, which will free them from carbon more thoroughly than cleaning by hand. The machine will also test the condition of the plugs under compression. Any plug that fails to spark at the recommended pressure should be renewed.

8 The spark plug gap is of considerable importance, as, if it is too large or too small, the size of the spark and its efficiency will be seriously impaired. The spark plug gap should be set to the figure given in Sepcifications at the beginning of this Chapter.

9 To set it, measure the gap with a feeler gauge, and then bend open, or close, the outer plug electrode until the correct gap is achieved. The centre electrode should never be bent as this may crack the insulation and cause plug failure if nothing worse.

10 When replacing the plugs, remember to use new plug washers, and replace the leads from the distributor in the correct firing order, which is 1 - 3 - 4 - 2, No 1 cylinder being the one nearest the flywheel. No 1 lead from the distributor runs from the 4 o'clock position when looking down on the distributor cap, Fig. 4.3 page 87.

11 The plug leads require no routine attention other than being wiped over regularly and kept clean. At intervals of 6,000 miles (9500 km) however, pull the leads off the plugs and distributor one at a time and make sure no water has found its way onto the connections. Remove any corrosion from the brass ends, wipe the collars on top of the distributor, and refit the leads.

12 Ignition system - fault finding

By far the majority of breakdown and running troubles are caused by faults in the ignition system either in the low tension or high tension circuits.

13 Ignition system - fault symptoms

There are two main symptoms indicating ignition faults. Either the engine will not start or fire, or the engine is difficult to start and misfires. If it is a regular misfire, i.e. the engine is only running on two or three cylinders the fault is almost sure to be in the high tension circuit. If the misfiring is intermittent, the fault could be in either the high or low tension circuits. If the car stops suddenly, or will not start at all, it is likely that the fault is in the low tension circuit. Loss of power and overheating, apart from faulty carburation settings, are normally due to faults in the distributor or incorrect ignition timing.

14 Fault diagnosis - engine fails to start

1 If the engine fails to start and the car was running normally when it was last used, first check there is fuel in the petrol tank. If the engine turns over normally on the starter motor and the battery is evidently well charged, then the fault may be in either the high or low tension circuits. First check the HT circuit. NOTE: If the battery is known to be fully charged; the ignition light comes on, and the starter motor fails to turn the engine CHECK THE TIGHTNESS OF THE LEADS ON THE BATTERY TERMINALS and also the security of the earth lead to its CONNECTION TO THE BODY. It is quite common for the leads to have worked loose, even if they look and feel secure. If one of the battery terminal posts gets very hot when trying to

work the starter motor this is a sure indication of a faulty connection to that terminal.

2   One of the commonest reasons for bad starting is wet or damp spark plug leads and distributor. Remove the distributor cap. If condensation is visible internally dry the cap with a rag and also wipe over the leads. Replace the cap.

3   If the engine still fails to start, check that current is reaching the plugs, by disconnecting each plug lead in turn at the spark plug end, and hold the end of the cable about 3/16th inch (4.762 mm) away from the cylinder block. Spin the engine on the starter motor.

4   Sparking between the end of the cable and the block should be fairly strong with a regular blue spark. (Hold the lead with rubber to avoid electric shocks). If current is reaching the plugs, then remove them and clean and regap them to 0.025 inch (0.64 mm). The engine should now start.

5   If there is no spark at the plug leads take off the HT lead, from the centre of the distributor cap and hold it to the block as before. Spin the engine on the starter once more. A rapid succession of blue sparks between the end of the lead and the block indicate that the coil is in order and that the distributor cap is cracked, the rotor arm faulty or the carbon brush in the top of the distributor cap is not making good contact with the spring on the rotor arm. Possibly the points are in bad condition. Clean and reset them as described in Sections 2 and 3.

6   If there are no sparks from the end of the lead from the coil, check the connections at the coil end of the lead. If they are in order start checking the low tension circuit.

7   Use a 12v voltmeter on a 12v bulb and two lengths of wire. With the ignition switch on and the points open test between the low tension wire to the coil (it is marked SW or +) and earth. No reading indicates a break in the supply from the ignition switch. Check the connections at the switch to see if any are loose. Refit them and the engine should run. A reading shows a faulty coil or condenser or broken lead between the coil and the distributor.

8   Take the condenser wire off the points assembly and with the points held open, test between the moveable point and earth. If there is now a reading then the fault is in the condenser which must be renewed.

9   If there is no reading from the moveable point to earth, take a reading between earth and the CB or − terminal of the coil. A reading here shows a broken wire which will need to be replaced between the coil and distributor. No reading confirms that the coil has failed and must be replaced, after which the engine will run once more. Remember to refit the condenser wire to the points assembly. For these tests it is sufficient to separate the points with a piece of dry paper while testing with the points open.

15 Fault diagnosis - engine misfires

1   If the engine misfires regularly run it at a fast idling speed. Pull off each of the plug caps in turn and listen to the note of the engine. Hold the plug cap in a dry cloth or with a rubber glove as additional protection against a shock from the HT supply.

2   No difference in engine running will be noticed when the lead from the defective circuit is removed. Removing the lead from one of the good cylinders will accentuate the misfire.

3   Remove the plug lead from the end of the defective plug and hold it about 3/16th inch (4.762 mm) away from the block. Restart the engine. If the sparking is fairly strong and regular the fault must lie in the spark plug.

4   The plug may be loose, the insulation may be cracked, or the points may have burnt away giving too wide a gap for the spark to jump. Worse still, one of the points may have broken off. Either renew the plug, or clean it, reset the gap, and then test it.

5   If there is no spark at the end of the plug lead, or, if it is weak and intermittent, check the ignition lead from the distributor to the plug. If the insulation is cracked or perished, renew the lead. Check the connections at the distributor cap.

6   If there is still no spark, examine the distributor cap carefully for tracking. This can be recognised by a very thin black line running between two or more electrodes, or between an electrode and some other part of the distributor. These lines are paths which now conduct electricity across the cap thus letting it run to earth. The only answer is a new distributor cap.

7   Apart from the ignition timing being incorrect, other causes of misfiring have already been dealt with under the section dealing with the failure of the engine to start. To recap - these are that:-

a) The coil may be faulty giving an intermittent misfire.

b) There may be a damaged wire or loose connection in the low tension circuit.

c) The condenser may be short circuiting.

d) There may be a mechanical fault in the distributor (broken driving spindle or contact breaker spring).

8   If the ignition timing is too far retarded, it should be noted that the engine will tend to overheat, and there will be a quite noticeable drop in power. If the engine is overheating and the power is down, and the ignition timing is correct then the carburettor should be checked, as it is likely that this is where the fault lies.

16 Modifications

1   Vehicles manufactured after November 1971 incorporate a shield to protect the distributor from water spray.

2   Protective rubber caps are fitted to the spark plugs (to prevent dirt entering the cylinders when the plugs are removed) installed in late type 352, 350 and 350S engines. These caps are not designed to fit the engines built prior to the following numbers. 352 engine - 5005106, 350 engine 6012919, 350S 6565275.

17 North American models - differences

1   A modified flywheel timing mark and clutch or convertor housing scale are fitted to these vehicles. Reference should be made to Section 10, paragraph 13 for a detailed description.

Chapter 5 Clutch

Contents

Specifications

Type	Ferodo 180D, single dry plate
Pressure plate	Diaphragm spring
Outer diameter	9.17 in (233 mm)
Total depth of assembly	1.77 in (45 mm)
Driven plate (friction disc)	
Friction lining outer diameter	7.15 in (181.5 mm)
Friction lining inner diameter	4.88 in (124 mm)
Thickness (under load)	0.31 to 0.33 in (7.8 to 8.4 mm)

Hydraulic system

Make	Lockheed
Clutch free movement	
at release bearing	0.030 to 0.045 in (0.75 to 1.15 mm)
at release fork arm end	0.040 to 0.060 in (1.0 to 1.5 mm)

TORQUE WRENCH SETTING

	lb ft
Clutch assembly to flywheel	10.5
Slave cylinder to clutch housing	16.0
Release fork pivot pin to gearbox face	32.0
Release bearing support tube to gearbox	10.5

1 General description

The clutch assembly comprises a single (dry) driven plate, a pressure plate, release bearing and mechanism. The driven plate (friction disc) is free to slide along the gearbox primary shaft and is held in position between the flywheel and pressure plate faces by the pressure exerted by the diaphragm spring of the pressure plate. The friction linings are riveted to the driven plate which incorporates a spring cushioned hub to absorb transmission shocks and to assist smooth take up of the drive.

The diaphragm spring is mounted on shouldered pins and is held in place in the cover by fulcrum rings. The clutch is actuated by a pendant type foot pedal which operates a hydraulic master and slave cylinder, Fig. 5.1 page 91. Depressing the clutch pedal pushes the release bearing, mounted on its hub, forward to bear against the spring fingers of the diaphragm. This action causes the diaphragm spring outer edge to deflect and move the pressure plate rearwards to disengage the pressure plate face from the driven plate linings. When the clutch pedal is released, the diaphragm spring forces the pressure plate into contact with the friction linings and sandwiches the driven plate between it and the flywheel so taking up the drive.

As the friction linings wear, the pressure plate automatically moves closer to the driven plate to compensate.

The release bearing is a ball bearing, grease packed and sealed for life. Correct clutch free movement must be maintained and provision is made for adjustment. Components of the clutch are shown in Fig. 5.7 page 95. A cross sectional view of pressure plate, driven plate and release bearing is given in Fig. 5.3 page 93.

2 Clutch free movement - adjustment

1 In order to prevent abnormal wear of the thrust bearing and pressure plate thrust surfaces and to ensure full engagement and withdrawal of the clutch, the correct free movement (A) must be maintained, Fig. 5.4 page 93.
2 The correct clearance (A) is 0.030 to 0.045 inch (0.75 to 1.15 mm). As this obviously cannot be measured, adjustment should be carried out in the following manner.
3 Slacken the locknut (1). (photo)
4 Detach the spring clip (2) which secures the push rod to the release fork.
5 Screw the adjuster nut (3) down the push rod until there is no free play between the nut and the fork.
6 Now screw the adjuster nut back 1 to 1½ turns. Fit the spring clip and tighten the locknut. The free movement will now be correct.

3 Clutch hydraulic system - bleeding

1 Gather together a clean jam jar, a length of rubber tubing which fits tightly over the bleed nipple in the slave cylinder, a tin of hydraulic brake fluid, and a friend to help.
2 Check that the master cylinder is full and if not fill it, and cover the bottom inch of the jar with hydraulic fluid.
3 Remove the rubber dust cap from the bleed nipple on the slave cylinder and with a suitable spanner, open the bleed nipple one turn.
4 Place one end of the tube securely over the nipple and insert the other end in the jam jar so that the tube orifice is below the level of the fluid.
5 The assistant should now pump the clutch pedal up and down slowly until air bubbles cease to emerge from the end of the tubing. He should also check the reservoir frequently to ensure that the hydraulic fluid does not disappear so letting air into the system.
6 When no more air bubbles appear, tighten the bleed nipple on the downstroke.
7 Replace the rubber dust cap over the bleed nipple. Allow the hydraulic fluid in the jar to stand for at least 24 hours before using it, to allow all the minute air bubbles to escape.

4 Clutch pedal - removal and refitting

1 Disconnect the clutch master cylinder push rod from the clutch pedal by removing the split pin and cotter.
2 Remove the split pin from the pedal cross shaft (1), Fig. 5.2 page 93.
3 Detach the pedal return spring (4).
4 Withdraw the cross shaft sufficiently far to enable the clutch pedal to be removed downwards. Take care to note the sequence of fitting of the various cross shaft washers, spacers and springs.
5 Refitting is a reversal of removal but grease the cross shaft and use new split pins.

5 Clutch - removal and refitting

1 Access to the clutch may be gained in one of two ways. Either the complete engine/transmission unit should be removed as described in Chapter 1 and the gearbox/transmission separated from the engine or the engine left in the car and the gearbox/transmission unit removed independently. The latter procedure is fully described in the next Chapter.
2 Note the alignment of the paint spots on both the flywheel and the pressure plate assembly for exact replacement.
3 Unscrew the six pressure plate retaining bolts from the flywheel, working in a diametrically opposite removal sequence and slackening the bolts only a few turns at a time.
4 Withdraw the pressure plate assembly and driven plate. (photo)
5 It is important that no oil or grease gets on the clutch disc friction linings, or the pressure plate and flywheel faces. It is advisable to replace the clutch with clean hands and to wipe down the pressure plate and flywheel faces with a clean dry rag before assembly begins.
6 Place the clutch disc against the flywheel with the shorter end of the hub, which is the end with the chamfered splines, facing the flywheel. On no account should the clutch disc be replaced with the longer end of the centre hub facing the flywheel as on reassembly it will be found quite impossible to operate the clutch in this position.
7 Replace the clutch cover assembly loosely on the two dowels. Replace the six bolts and spring washers and tighten them finger-tight so that the clutch disc is gripped but can still be moved.
8 The clutch disc must now be centralised so that when the engine and gearbox are mated the gearbox input shaft splines

will pass through the splines in the centre of the driven plate hub.
9 Centralisation can be carried out quite easily by inserting a round bar or long screwdriver through the hole in the centre of the clutch, so that the end of the bar rests in the small hole in the end of the crankshaft containing the input shaft bearing bush.
10 Using the input shaft bearing bush as a fulcrum, moving the bar sideways or up and down will move the clutch disc in whichever direction is necessary to achieve centralisation.
11 Centralisation is easily judged by removing the bar and viewing the driven plate hub in relation to the hole in the release bearing. When the hub appears exactly in the centre of the release bearing hole all is correct.
12 Tighten the clutch bolts in a diagonal sequence to ensure that the cover plate is pulled down evenly and without distortion of the flange.
13 Grease the splines of the gearbox primary shaft sparingly with molybdenum type grease.
14 Refit the gearbox as described in the next Chapter.
15 Adjust the clutch free movement as described in Section 2.

6 Clutch - inspection

1 Examine the clutch disc friction linings for wear and loose rivets and the disc for rim distortion, cracks, broken hub springs, and worn splines. The surface of the friction linings may be highly glazed, but as long as the clutch material can be clearly seen this is satisfactory. Compare the amount of lining wear with a new clutch disc at the stores in your local garage, and if the linings are more than three quarters worn replace the disc.
2 It is always best to renew the clutch driven plate as an assembly to preclude further trouble, but, if it is wished to merely renew the linings, the rivets should be drilled out and not knocked out with a punch. The manufacturers do not advise that only the linings are renewed and personal experience dictates that it is far more satisfactory to renew the driven plate complete than to try and economize by only fitting new friction linings.
3 Check the machined faces of the flywheel and the pressure plate. If either is grooved it should be machined until smooth or renewed.
4 If the pressure plate is cracked or split, or if the pressure of the diaphragm spring is suspect, it is essential that an exchange unit is fitted.
5 Check the release bearing for smoothness of operation. There should be no harshness and no slackness in it. It should spin reasonably freely bearing in mind it has been prepacked with grease. (photo)

7 Clutch release bearing - removal and refitting

1 With the gearbox and engine separated to provide access to the clutch, attention can be given to the release bearing located in the bellhousing, over the input shaft.
2 The release bearing is a relatively inexpensive but important component and unless it is nearly new it is a mistake not to replace it during an overhaul of the clutch.
3 To remove the release bearing, first pull off the release arm rubber gaiter.
4 The release arm and bearing assembly can then be withdrawn from the clutch housing.
5 To free the bearing from the release arm simply unhook it, and then with the aid of two blocks of wood and a vice press off the release bearing from its hub.
6 Refitting is a reversal of removal but note the fitting of the retaining spring clip to the bearing hub. (photo)
7 Observe the method of engagement of the spring clip to the release arm. (photo)

2.3 Slackening the clutch push-rod lock-nut

5.4 Removing the pressure plate and driven plate

6.5 The sealed ball type release bearing

7.6 Fitting the spring to the release bearing hub

7.7 Connecting the spring to the release arm

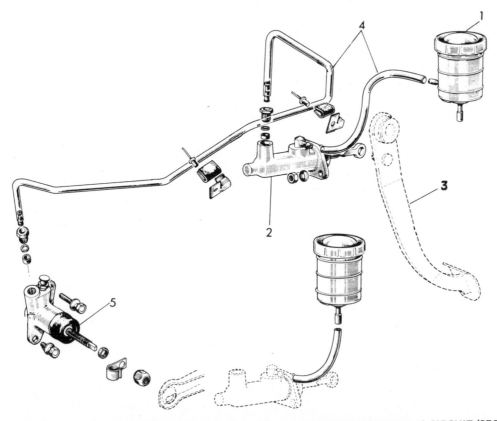

FIG. 5.1. LAYOUT AND COMPONENTS OF THE CLUTCH OPERATING HYDRAULIC CIRCUIT (SEC. 1)

| 1 | Fluid reservoir | 3 | Foot pedal | 4 | Fluid lines | 5 | Slave cylinder |
| 2 | Master cylinder | | | | | | |

8 Clutch master cylinder - removal, servicing, and refitting

1   Disconnect the operating push rod from the clutch pedal.
2   Disconnect the fluid line from the base of the reservoir and allow the reservoir fluid to drain into a clean vessel.
3   Hydraulic brake fluid will damage the vehicle paintwork and must not be allowed to come into contact with it.
4   Disconnect the fluid line which supplies the slave cylinder by detaching it at the master cylinder union. Plug the line to prevent entry of dirt.
5   Unscrew and remove the master cylinder retaining nuts and lift the unit from the bulkhead.
6   Expel the fluid from the master cylinder by depressing the push rod two or three times.
7   Obtain a master cylinder repair kit which will contain the essential seals and components most likely to require renewing.
8   Pull off the rubber dust excluder (1) Fig. 5.5.
9   Withdraw the push rod.
10 Extract the circlip (2) and ring (3).
11 The piston assembly (5) to which is fitted the seals (4) and (6) may now be expelled from the master cylinder body. Tapping the end of the master cylinder on a block of wood may effect removal or alternatively apply air pressure from a tyre pump to the master cylinder fluid line union.
12 Remove the piston return spring (7).
13 With the master cylinder now completely dismantled, wash all components and the interior of the cylinder body with methylated spirit or clean hydraulic fluid.
14 Discard the old seals, first noting (and sketching if necessary) the way they are fitted to the piston in respect of chamfers and lips.
15 Examine the master cylinder bore and the piston surfaces for scoring or 'bright' spots. If these are evident, then the complete unit should be reassembled and exchanged for a factory reconditioned one.
16 Commence reassembly by dipping the new seals, supplied in the repair kit, in clean brake fluid and fitting them to the piston assembly, using the fingers only to manipulate them into position. Take particular care that their lips and chamfered edges have not been deformed or cut during storage in the repair kit packet.
17 Locate the return spring in the cylinder bore and then lubricate the bore liberally with clean hydraulic fluid. Insert the piston assembly using a twisting motion and ensuring that the lips of the seals are not trapped or pinched during the operation.
18 Refitting of the remaining components is a reversal of dismantling.
19 Refit the master cylinder to its bulkhead location and reconnect the pedal push rod. Connect the hydraulic fluid line to the slave cylinder and fill the reservoir with clean fluid which has been standing in an air-tight container and has not been shaken for at least 24 hours. These conditions should always be complied with, as hydraulic fluid absorbs moisture rapidly from the atmosphere and if used from an uncapped container will cause corrosion to the internal parts of the hydraulic system. Fluid which has been shaken will take at least 24 hours for the air bubbles to emerge and the use of aerated fluid will cause sponginess of operation when the pedal is depressed, due to the compression of the air trapped within the system. Bleed the system as described in Section 3.

9 Clutch slave cylinder - removal, servicing and refitting

1   Slacken the locknut (3) Fig. 5.6 page 94.
2   Unscrew and remove the adjustment nut (1) and detach the clip (2) which retains the operating rod to the clutch release arm.
3   Uncouple the fluid pipe at its connection with the body of the cylinder and plug the pipe to prevent loss of fluid. Remove the master cylinder reservoir cap and place a thin sheet of polythene over the top of the reservoir body and then screw the cap on again. This operation will effectively seal the air vent hole

in the cap and enable the vacuum created to prevent the fluid running out of the open end of the hydraulic line at the slave cylinder.
4   Unbolt the slave cylinder from the clutch bellhousing.
5   Obtain a clutch slave cylinder repair kit which will contain all necessary seals and renewable components.
6   Unscrew and remove the locknut from the push rod and pull off the rubber dust excluding boot (4).
7   Using a screwdriver as a lever, prise out the metal cap (5) from the body (11) catching the return spring (6) as it is ejected.
8   Withdraw the push rod (7) and its retainer (8).
9   Remove the piston (9) and seal (10) by tapping the end of the body on a block of wood or applying air pressure from a tyre pump at the hydraulic fluid union.
10 Remove the spacer (11) (if necessary).
11 Inspection and reassembly procedure is as described for the master cylinder in the preceding Section with the following exceptions. A new metal cap (5) must be fitted. Maintain pressure on the return spring and crimp the tabs of the cap into the groove in the body using a small chisel.
12 Refit the pushrod and locknut and rubber boot.
13 Refit the slave cylinder to the clutch bellhousing, reconnect the fluid line, the release arm, push rod clip and adjuster nut.
14 Bleed the system (Section 3) and remove the plastic sheet (if fitted) between the reservoir cap and body.
15 Adjust the clutch free movement (Section 2).

10 Clutch - faults

There are four main faults to which the clutch and release mechanism are prone. They may occur by themselves or in conjunction with any of the other faults. They are; clutch squeal, slip, spin, and judder.

11 Clutch squeal - diagnosis and cure

1   If on taking up the drive or when changing gear, the clutch squeals, this is a sure indication of a badly worn clutch release bearing.
2   As well as regular wear due to normal use, wear of the clutch release bearing is much accentuated if the clutch is ridden, or held down for long periods in gear, with the engine running. To minimize wear of this component the car should always be taken out of gear at traffic lights and for similar holds up.
3   The clutch release bearing is not an expensive item but difficult to get at.

12 Clutch slip - diagnosis and cure

1   Clutch slip is a self-evident condition which occurs when the clutch friction plate is badly worn; the release arm free travel is insufficient; the flywheel or pressure plate face are contaminated with oil or grease; or the pressure plate itself is faulty.
2   The reason for clutch slip is that, due to one of the faults listed above, there is either insufficient pressure from the pressure plate, or insufficient friction from the friction plate, to ensure solid drive.
3   If small amounts of oil get onto the clutch, they will be burnt off under the heat of clutch engagement, and in the process, gradually darken the linings. Excessive oil on the clutch will burn off leaving a carbon deposit which can cause quite bad slip, or fierceness, spin and judder.
4   If clutch slip is suspected, and confirmation of this condition is required, there are several tests which can be made:
5   With the engine in second or third gear and pulling lightly up a moderate incline, sudden depression of the accelerator pedal may cause the engine to increase its speed without any increase in road speed. Easing off on the accelerator will then give a definite drop in engine speed without the car slowing.
6   In extreme cases of clutch slip the engine will race under

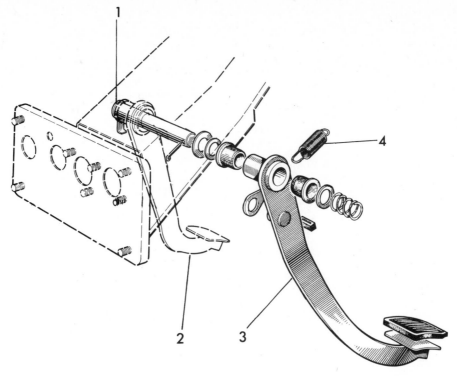

FIG. 5.2. CLUTCH PEDAL — COMPONENTS (SEC. 4)

1 Cross shaft   2 Brake pedal   3 Clutch pedal   4 Pedal return spring

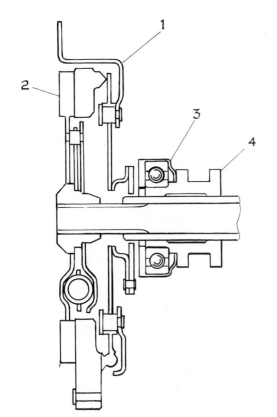

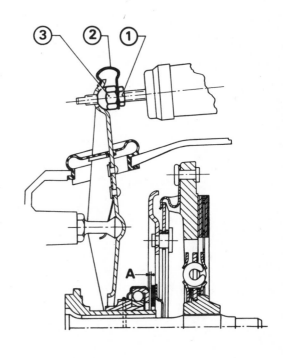

FIG. 5.3. CLUTCH MECHANISM — CROSS SECTION (SEC. 5)

1 Pressure plate cover   3 Release bearing
2 Driven plate   4 Release bearing hub

FIG. 5.4. CLUTCH FREE MOVEMENT (SEC. 2)

1 Push rod locknut   3 Adjuster nut
2 Spring clip   A Free movement

normal acceleration conditions.

7 If slip is due to oil or grease on the linings a temporary cure can sometimes be effected by squirting carbon tetrachloride into the clutch lining. The permanent cure is, of course, to renew the clutch driven plate and trace and rectify the oil leak.

13 Clutch spin - diagnosis and cure

1 Clutch spin is a condition which occurs when there is a leak in the clutch hydraulic actuating mechanism; the release arm free travel is excessive; there is an obstruction in the clutch either on the primary gear splines, or in the operating lever itself; or the oil may have partially burnt off the clutch linings and have left a resinous deposit which is causing the clutch disc to stick to the pressure plate or flywheel.

2 The reason for clutch spin is that due to any, or a combination of, the faults just listed, the clutch pressure plate is not being completely freed from the centre plate even with the clutch pedal fully depressed.

3 If clutch spin is suspected, the condition is confirmed by extreme difficulty in changing gear, and very sudden take-up of the clutch drive at the fully depressed end of the clutch pedal

travel as the clutch is released.

4 Check the clutch master and slave cylinders and the connecting hydraulic pipe for leaks. Fluid in one of the rubber boots fitted over the end of either the master or slave cylinders is a sure sign of a leaking piston seal.

5 If these points are checked and found to be in order then the fault lies internally in the clutch, and it will be necessary to remove the clutch for examination.

14 Clutch judder - diagnosis and cure

1 Clutch judder is a self-evident condition which occurs when the gearbox or engine mountings are loose or too flexible; when there is oil on the faces of the clutch friction plate; or when the clutch pressure plate has been incorrectly adjusted.

2 The reason for clutch judder is that due to one of the faults just listed, the clutch pressure plate is not freeing smoothly from the friction disc, and is snatching.

3 Clutch judder normally occurs when the clutch pedal is released in first or reverse gears, and the whole car shudders as it moves backwards or forwards.

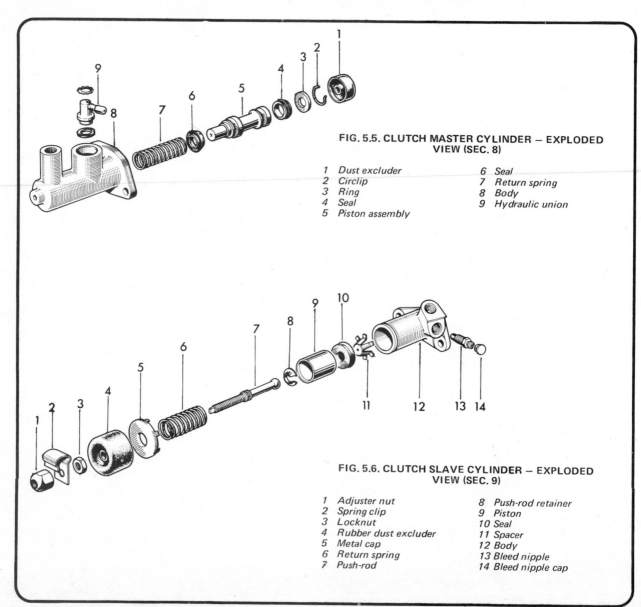

FIG. 5.5. CLUTCH MASTER CYLINDER — EXPLODED
VIEW (SEC. 8)

1 Dust excluder   6 Seal
2 Circlip   7 Return spring
3 Ring   8 Body
4 Seal   9 Hydraulic union
5 Piston assembly

FIG. 5.6. CLUTCH SLAVE CYLINDER — EXPLODED
VIEW (SEC. 9)

1 Adjuster nut   8 Push-rod retainer
2 Spring clip   9 Piston
3 Locknut   10 Seal
4 Rubber dust excluder 11 Spacer
5 Metal cap   12 Body
6 Return spring   13 Bleed nipple
7 Push-rod   14 Bleed nipple cap

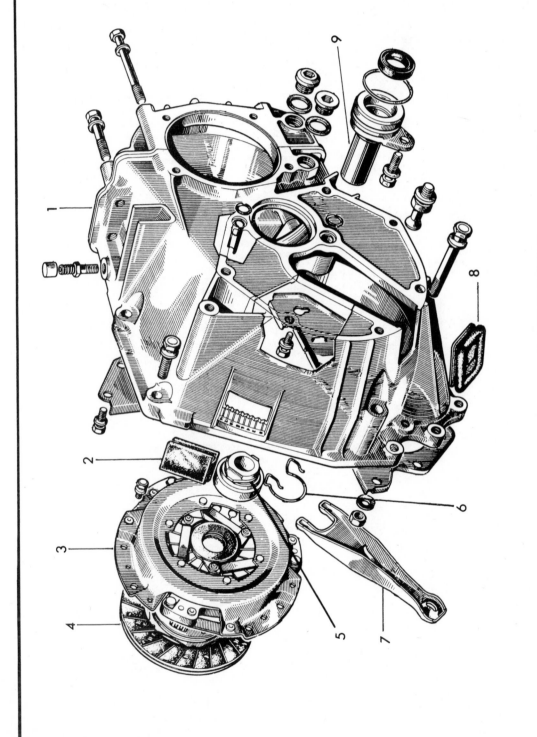

FIG. 5.7. CLUTCH – EXPLODED VIEW (SEC. 5)

1 Clutch bellhousing
2 Ignition timing scale

3 cover plate
3 Pressure plate assembly

4 Driven plate
5 Release bearing and hub

6 Release hub to arm retaining spring

7 Release arm
8 Release arm grommet

9 Release bearing hub support tube

Chapter 6 Gearbox

Contents

PART 1. Manual Gearbox

Specifications

Type	four forward speeds (all with synchromesh) and reverse.

Gear ratios

1st	3.9:1
2nd	2.31:1
3rd	1.52:1
4th	1.08:1
Reverse	3.77:1

Final drive

Type	Helical gears
Ratio 1100cc engine	3.937:1
1204cc and 1296cc engines	3.706:1
Capacities	
Gearbox	1.2 pts
Final drive	1.0 pts

TORQUE WRENCH SETTINGS

	lb ft
Clutch bellhousing to cylinder block bolts	32.0
Gearbox to clutch bellhousing bolts	16.0
Gearbox selector fork cover to gearbox bolts	8.5
Gearbox and final drive drain and filler plugs	25.0
Clutch release fork pivot pin to gearbox	10.5
Clutch thrust bearing support tube to gearbox bolts ...	10.5
Output shaft locknut (LH thread)	120.0
Differential half housing bolts	16.0
Large bearing thrust plate bolts	22.0

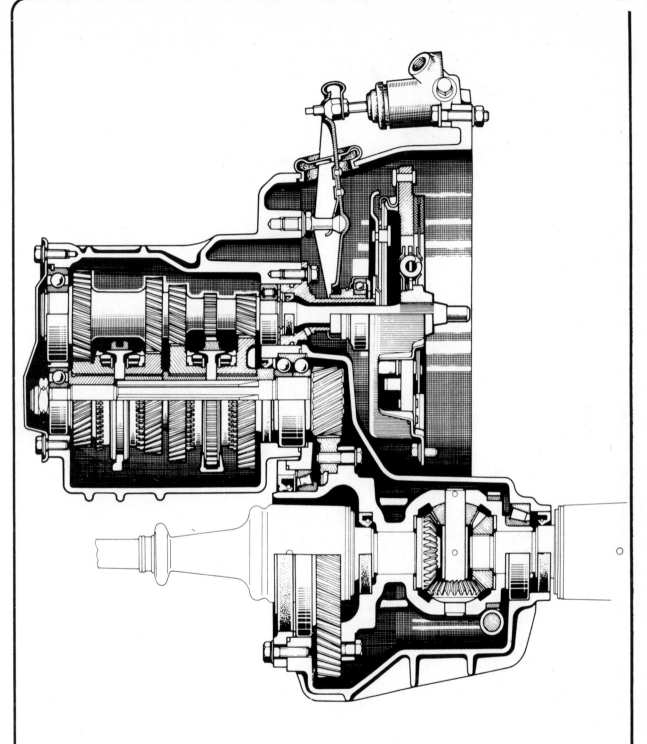

Fig. 6.1. GEARBOX AND FINAL DRIVE (SEC. 1)

1 General description

1   The integrated manual gearbox and final drive unit is located on the right hand end of the engine when viewed from the front of the car.

2   The front road wheels are driven through drive shafts of unequal lengths.

3   The clutch bellhousing incorporates the final drive unit and the gearbox is mounted on the outer face of the clutch housing, Fig. 6.1 Page 97.

4   The differential assembly is of conventional design having the inner ends of the drive shafts splined to the differential gears.

5   Semi-automatic transmission is fitted as an option. This is described in Part 2 of this Chapter.

2 Gearbox - removal and refitting

1   The removal of the gearbox with the engine is described in Chapter 1. The gearbox may be removed without removing the engine using the following method.

2   Disconnect the leads from the battery terminals.

3   Raise the front of the vehicle and support it on stands.

4   Disconnect the gearshift rod or cable assembly from the gearbox, see Section 10.

5   Unbolt the clutch slave cylinder from the clutch bellhousing and unclip the push rod from the clutch release arm. The slave cylinder may now be tied up out of the way either disconnecting the hydraulic fluid line.

6   Make up an engine support which will take the weight of the unit when the gearbox mounting is removed. An example of this type of support is shown (photo).

7   Remove the left hand front road wheels.

8   Remove the left hand damper and then drain the oil from the gearbox.

9   Disconnect the left hand front engine mounting as described in Chapter 1.

10 Obtain two guide studs each 2.17 inch (55 mm) in length and threaded (8 x 125) over 0.6 inch (15 mm) of their length. Insert them in the holes (A) (photo).

11 Take out the bolts which secure the gearbox to the clutch bellhousing.

12 Withdraw the gearbox, carefully retaining the shims fitted at (A) (photo)

13 Before refitting the gearbox, secure the clutch release arm in the position shown (photo) using a strong rubber band.

14 Select a gear and then replace the shims removed at (A) photo 2.12, using grease to retain the shims in position.

15 Check that the two small sealing 'O' rings are correctly located round the gearbox to differential connecting oil passages.

16 Where major overhaul or renewal of internal components has been carried out, then the correct sealing of the gearbox to the clutch bellhousing/final drive unit must be checked. To do this, first drive the pinion fully home using a soft faced mallet, (photo).

17 Fit the original shims into the recess in the clutch/final drive housing (photo).

18 Place four lengths of 1 mm diameter soft soldering wire at equidistant points on the bearing mating surface of the clutch/final drive recess.

19 Remove the 'O' ring seal from the gearbox pinion bearing recess (photo).

20 Carefully locate the gearbox onto the clutch/final drive housing. (photo) To facilitate this, remove clutch assembly.

21 Tighten the securing bolts to 16 lb ft.

22 Remove the bolts and gearbox and measure the thickness of the crushed wire and then add shims to the equivalent thickness.

23 Refit the 'O' ring seal into the groove surrounding the output shaft pinion.

24 Pass the clutch release bearing through the aperture in the clutch bellhousing and insert the gearbox input shaft into the splined hub of the driven plate. The driving gear may require moving slightly to facilitate meshing of the splines and to engage the gearbox housing on the two guide studs.

25 Screw in and tighten the gearbox retaining bolts evenly to a torque of 16 lb ft.

26 Remove the guide bolts and fit the engine mounting assembly and spacer.

27 Remove the temporary engine support bar.

28 Refit the clutch slave cylinder and check the clutch free movement as described in the preceding Chapter.

29 Reconnect the gearshift control mechanism (cable or rod) and adjust if necessary, see Section 10.

30 Refit the damper and road wheel.

31 Fill the gearbox and check the oil level in the final drive unit.

32 Reconnect the battery leads and remove the jacks from the front of the vehicle.

3 Gearbox - dismantling

1   Clean the external surfaces of the gearbox and dry thoroughly. Place the unit in a servicing frame or secure it to a bench. Remove the mounting assemblies from the outside of the gearbox housing.

2   Remove the gearshift selector cover, using a swivelling action to clear the forks. (photo)

3   Remove the rear cover (5) Fig. 6.2 page 100 and the clutch release bearing guide tube.

4   Slide two gears into engagement to lock the gearbox.

5   Remove the nut (20) which locks the rear bearing (19) to the output shaft, Fig. 6.4 page 101.
Note that it has a left hand thread.

6   Make up a plate to the dimensions shown in Fig. 6.5. page 101.

7   Fit this between the face of the first gear wheel and the inside face of the gearbox housing. Using a strengthening plate on the outside of the gearbox and a bridge piece and bolt, press the output shaft out of its bearing (photo).

8   Withdraw the 3rd and 4th gears together with synchroniser unit (photo).

9   Withdraw the 1st and 2nd gears together with synchroniser units.

10 Remove the circlip which retains the reverse gear idler shaft, (photo).

11 Remove the pin (2) which locates the reverse gear shaft in position, Fig. 6.3 page 100.

12 Using a suitable extractor, remove the reverse gear (1) and shaft (3).

13 Unscrew and remove the two securing bolts from the clutch release bearing guide tube and withdraw the guide tube, retaining the spacer (4) located on the face of the primary shaft.

14 Remove the circlip (5) which retains the bearing to the primary shaft.

15 Using a length of tubing as a drift, drive out the primary shaft complete with two bearings (photo). The tubular drift must bear on the outer track of the front bearing.

16 Do not attempt to remove the primary shaft bearings or the output shaft bearings unless you have a press and extractors suitable for the job. It is better to take them to a SIMCA agent.

17 If necessary, the gearshift control and selector fork assembly may be dismantled. Commence by setting the selector shafts and forks in neutral, and removing the fork shaft end cover.

18 Unscrew and remove the 3rd/4th selector fork securing screw, withdraw the selector shaft slowly and retain the detent ball as it is removed (photo).

19 Remove the 3rd/4th selector fork.

20 Remove the 1st/2nd selector fork screw, withdraw the shaft just sufficiently far to permit removal of the 1st/2nd selector fork.

21 Rotate the 1st/2nd selector shaft through 90° to facilitate removal of the detent ball, (photo).

22 Withdraw the 1st/2nd selector shaft completely but retaining the detent balls and springs during the operation.

2.6 Engine support bar in position

2.10 Location of gearbox guide studs

2.12 Location of gearbox primary shaft bearing shims

2.13 Securing the clutch release arm with an elastic band

2.16 Seating the drive shaft pinion and bearing

2.17 Fitting the shims to the primary shaft bearing recess in the clutch bellhousing

2.19 Removing the output shaft pinion bearing 'O' ring seal

2.20 Locating the gearbox on the clutch/final drive housing

3.2 Removing the gearshift selector cover

3.7 Pressing the output shaft from its bearing

3.8 Removing the 3rd/4th gear and synchro assembly from the gearbox

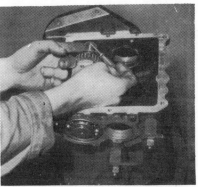
3.10 Removing the reverse gear idler shaft circlip

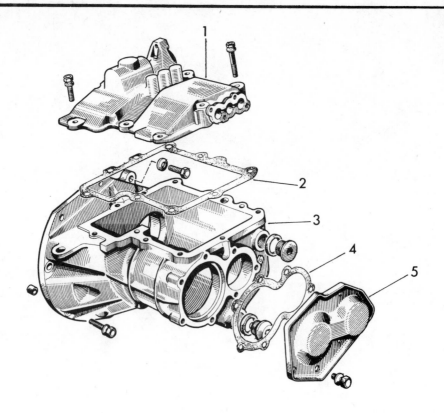

FIG. 6.2. GEARBOX – STATIC COMPONENTS (SEC. 3)

1 Gearshift selector cover	3 Housing	4 Gasket (rear cover)	5 Rear cover
2 Gasket			

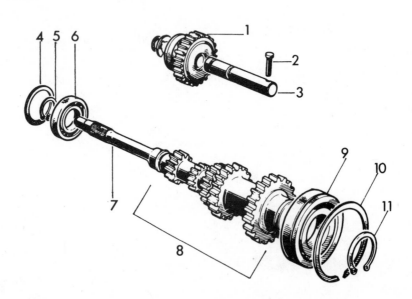

FIG. 6.3. REVERSE GEAR AND PRIMARY SHAFT – COMPONENTS (SEC. 3.11)

1 Reverse gear	4 Spacer	7 Primary shaft	10 Bearing snap ring
2 Pin	5 Circlip	8 Gear assembly	11 Circlip
3 Reverse idler shaft	6 Bearing	9 Bearing	

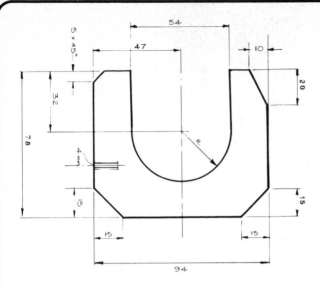

Fig. 6.5. Support plate diagram for output shaft removal
(Sec. 3.6) (dimensions in mm)

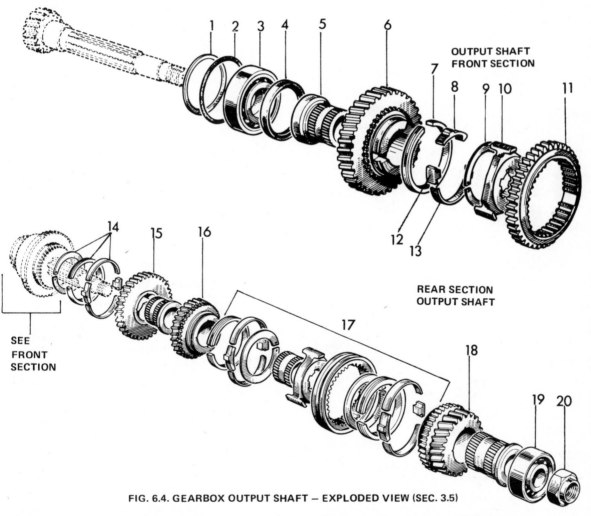

OUTPUT SHAFT
FRONT SECTION

REAR SECTION
OUTPUT SHAFT

SEE
FRONT
SECTION

FIG. 6.4. GEARBOX OUTPUT SHAFT – EXPLODED VIEW (SEC. 3.5)

1	Spacer	6	1st gear	11	Reverse gear & 1st/2nd synchro sleeve (reverse on periphery)	15	2nd gear
2	'O' ring seal	7	Synchroniser ring			16	3rd gear
3	Double ball race	8	Synchro locking piece	12	Retainer stop	17	3rd/4th synchro assembly
4	Oil seal	9	Synchro circlip	13	Spring	18	4th gear
5	Bush	10	Synchro hub	14	1st/2nd gear synchro assembly (part)	19	Bearing
						20	Locking nut

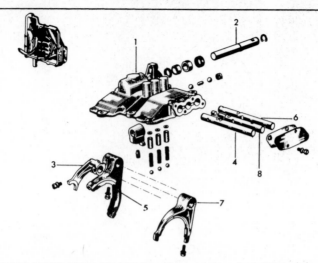

FIG. 6.6 GEAR SHIFT FORK SELECTOR MECHANISM – EXPLODED VIEW (SEC. 3)

1 Cover	3 Reverse selector fork	5 1st/2nd selector fork	7 3rd/4th selector fork
2 Fork control lever	4 Reverse selector shaft	6 1st/2nd selector shaft	8 3rd/4th selector shaft

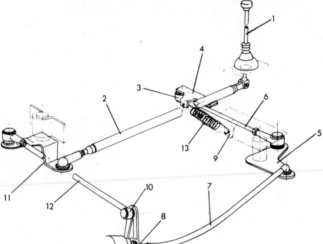

FIG, 6.7. GEAR SHIFT MECHANISM – ALL ROD TYPE FITTED 1970 ONWARDS (SEC. 10.1)

1 Gearshift lever	4 Plate	7 Selector rod	10 Engagement lever
2 Control tube	5 Bell crank lever	8 Fork control shaft	11 Bell crank lever
3 Ball joint	6 Adjustable link	9 Plate	12 Link rod
			13 Return spring

23 Remove the reverse selector fork securing screw, drift out the reverse shaft sufficiently far to enable the fork to be removed. Withdraw the reverse shaft completely and retain the detent and interlocking balls and springs.

24 Remove the securing screw from the fork control lever, (photo).

25 Withdraw the spindle and fork control lever and the three springs which impinge upon the detent balls.

26 The gearbox is now completely dismantled and both the inside of the gearbox case and all components should be thoroughly washed in paraffin so that examination may be carried out as described in the following Section.

4 Gearbox - examination

1 Examine each component for wear, distortion, chipping or scoring and renew if apparent.

2 Examine the gear wheels, particularly for wear and chipping of teeth and renew as necessary.

3 Check all ball and roller bearings for play. If even the slightest wear is evident then they must be withdrawn from their shafts and renewed.

4 The serviceability of the synchromesh units will be known from previous gearchange experience and they should be renewed as complete assemblies.

5 Examine the ends of the selector forks at their points of contact. Comparison of their profiles with new components will give a guide to renewal requirements.

6 Check the gearbox casing for cracks, particularly around the shaft bearing and bolt holes.

5 Gearbox - reassembly

1 Assemble the primary and output shafts temporarily to check for correct positioning of the various gears and components. (photo)

2 Fit the retaining circlips to the primary shaft bearings. (photo)

3 Tap the primary shaft assembly into its location using a soft faced hammer until the bearing snap ring is seated against the housing (photos).

3.15 Drifting out the primary shaft

3.18 Removing the 3rd/4th selector shaft and fork

3.21 Rotating the 1st/2nd selector shaft to remove the detent ball

3.24 Removing the fork control lever securing screw

5.1 Correctly assembled primary and output shafts

5.2a Fitting circlip to the primary shaft large bearing

5.2b Fitting the circlip to the other bearing of the primary shaft

5.3a Locating the primary shaft and bearings

5.3b Driving the shaft home

5.4 Inserting the reverse idler shaft

5.5 Reverse shaft 'O' ring

5.6 Reverse shaft stop bolt

4 Locate the reverse sliding gear in position (fork groove on differential side) and insert the reverse shaft (photo).
5 Fit a new 'O' ring seal to the reverse shaft before fitting. (photo)
6 Engage the reverse shaft stop bolt (photo)
7 Fit the reverse shaft circlip. (photo)
8 Drive the output shaft rear bearing into position in the gearcase so that its face is flush with the external gearcase surface. (photo)
9 Check the condition of the output shaft (drive pinion end) oil seal and renew if necessary. (photo)
10 Insert the original spacer into the output shaft bearing seat. (photo) Insert the output shaft into the gear case. (photo) Should the output shaft, its bearings or the gear case have been renewed, then the thickness of the spacer must be determined as described in Section 2, paragraphs 16 to 22 inclusive.
11 As the shaft passes through the gear and synchroniser assemblies, they should be positioned ready to receive the shaft as shown. (photo)
12 Ensure that the gear hubs are correctly positioned. (photo)
13 If the 3rd/4th synchro unit has been dismantled then it should be reassembled as shown. (photos)
14 If the 1st/2nd synchro unit has been dismantled, then it should be reassembled as shown: also shown are the synchro assembly components as they should have been fitted. (photos)
15 Check that the gears mesh correctly and then drive the bearing into the gearcase to locate correctly the output shaft assembly.
16 Engage two gears to lock the gearbox and fit and tighten the locknut (LH thread) to 120 lb ft. (photo)
17 Lock the nut by indenting its collar into the groove provided in the shaft. (photo)
18 Disengage the locked gears.
19 If new bearings have been fitted or the drive shaft or thrust bearing bracket have been renewed, then the thickness of the primary shaft bearing spacers must be established in the following manner.
20 Fit the original spacers onto the primary shaft front bearing. (photo) Remove the peripheral 'O' ring seal from the clutch release bearing guide tube. (photo)
21 Measure the gap between the face of the guide tube flange and the face of the gearbox. This should be between 0.13 and 0.15 inch (0.33 and 0.38 mm). Add or remove shims (available in 0.1, 0.2, 0.5 and 1 mm thicknesses), until the clearance is correct while pressing down on the guide tube.
22 Renew the clutch release bearing guide tube internal oil seal. (photo)
23 Insert the guide tube complete with peripheral 'O' ring into position over the primary shaft. (photo)
24 Bolt the guide tube into position.
25 Prise out the oil seal for the fork control lever spindle. Ensure that the seal housing is clean then fit a new seal with the lip towards the inside of the cover.
26 Smear the seal lip with gearbox oil, then push the spindle carefully through the oil seal to engage with the fork control lever so that the control lever finger is towards the oil seal. Tighten the finger retaining screw.
27 Fit the three neutral locking ball springs.
28 Fit the 3rd/4th (control) locking ball in position then insert the 3rd/4th shaft, passing it through the gear fork. Ensure that the securing side of the fork is facing outwards, and rotate the shaft so that the notch is uppermost for easier engagement (photo).
29 Compress the ball and spring using a screwdriver, and push the shaft in so that the ball is held by the shaft (photo).
30 Install the shaft pin, then push the shaft further on and rotate it through 180°. Ensure that the shaft and fork are in the neutral position, then tighten the fork retaining screw (photo).
31 Fit the reverse and the 3rd/4th shaft interlocking ball, then install the neutral locking ball (this ball also locks reverse gear when engaged).
32 Insert the reverse shaft with the two locking notches aligned,

and with the fork fastening hole initially horizontal.
33 Compress the ball and spring using a screwdriver, and push the shaft into position.
34 Locate the reverse fork on the shaft (photo).
35 Engage the reverse shaft in its neutral position in the 2nd locking notch, then tighten the fork retaining screw.
36 Fit the 1st/2nd and 3rd/4th shaft interlocking ball in position, then the 1st/2nd shaft neutral locking ball.
37 Insert the 1st/2nd shaft with the fork fastening hole horizontal to ensure easier engagement of the neutral locking ball in its housing.
38 Compress the ball and spring using a screwdriver, then push in the 1st/2nd gear shaft until the ball is held beneath the shaft.
39 Rotate the 1st/2nd shaft through 90° and install the 1st/2nd fork (photo).
40 Position the 1st/2nd shaft in neutral and secure the fork by tightening the retaining screw.
41 Refit the fork shaft and cover using a new gasket.
42 Fit a new gasket to the gearshift fork cover. (photo)
43 Engage the selector forks and locate and bolt the cover into position. (photo)
44 Fit a new rear cover gasket.
45 Fit the cover and gasket to the gearbox.
46 If the clutch release arm pivot has been removed then it should be refitted. (photo)
47 Refit the mounting plates. (photo).

---

6 Final drive (differential unit) - removal and refitting

1 Remove the gearbox as described in Section 2 of this Chapter.
2 Drain the oil from the differential unit by removing the drain plug.
3 Unbolt the speedometer cable from the lower differential unit.
4 Remove the left hand drive shaft/stub axle assembly as described for engine removal (Chapter 1) or in Chapter 7.
5 Unscrew and remove the gearbox guide bolts which were fitted to facilitate removal of the gearbox.
6 Remove the starter motor.
7 Remove both flywheel shields, one from the starter motor and one from the differential unit.
8 Remove the bolts which secure the clutch bellhousing to the engine block.
9 Pull the combined clutch bellhousing, final drive unit outwards sufficiently far to disengage the right hand drive shaft. Do not allow the driveshaft to drop but have an assistant support it and lower it gently.
10 To refit the clutch bellhousing/final drive unit, first screw in a guide stud as shown at (A) (photo).
11 Offer up the transmission unit and engage it on the guide stud, (photo).
12 Engage the right hand drive shaft in the differential.
13 Slowly push the clutch bellhousing/final drive unit into its correct position, turning the driveshaft at the same time.
14 Fit the securing bolts and tighten them to a torque of 32 lb ft. Remove the guide stud.
15 Refit the left hand drive shaft, stub axle and brake disc as described in Chapter 1.
16 Reconnect the speedometer drive cable to the final drive unit.
17 The gearbox may now be refitted as described in Section 2 of this Chapter.

---

7 Final drive (Differential) unit - dismantling

1 Place the clutch bellhousing face downwards on the bench and remove the securing bolts from the bearing thrust plate, (photo).
2 Remove the thrust plate, retain the shims fitted below it and

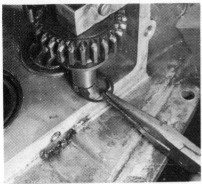
5.7 Fitting reverse idler shaft circlip

5.8 Fitting output shaft rear bearing

5.9 Output shaft oil seal

5.10a Locating output shaft bearing spacers

5.10b Inserting output shaft into gear-case

5.11 Locating gear assemblies ready for insertion of output shaft

5.12 Inserting a gear hub

5.13a 3rd/4th gear synchro ready for assembly

5.13b 3rd/4th gear synchro

5.14a 1st/2nd gear synchro ready for assembly

5.14b 1st gear synchro assembly

5.14c Synchro assembly - typical for 2nd, 3rd and 4th gears

5.16 Tightening the output shaft locknut

5.17 Locking the shaft nut in position

5.20a Fitting the primary shaft front bearing spacers

5.20b Removing the 'O' ring seal from the clutch release bearing guide tube

5.22 Renewing clutch release bearing guide tube oil seal

5.23 Locating the clutch release bearing guide tube

5.28 Insert the 3rd/4th shaft and rotate so notch is uppermost

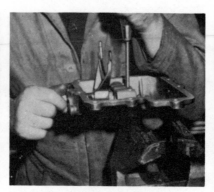
5.29 Compress ball and spring with screwdriver

5.30 Ensure shaft and fork are in neutral **position**

5.34 Locate reverse fork on shaft

5.39 Installing 1st/2nd fork

5.42 Fitting gearshift selector fork cover gasket

5.43 Fitting the selector fork cover

5.46 Tightening the clutch release arm pivot

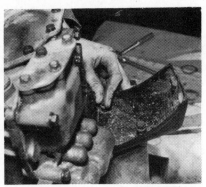
5.47 Fitting a gearbox mounting plate bolt

6.10 Guide studs (A) for refitting clutch/final drive housing

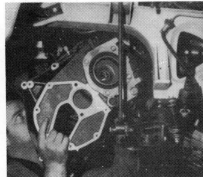
6.11 Engaging the clutch/final drive housing on the guide studs

7.1 Removing the bearing thrust plate from the final drive unit

8.3 Removing the crownwheel securing bolts

8.4 Pulling off a differential bearing

8.6 Speedometer gear in lower differential housing

8.9 Drifting in a new inner differential oil seal

8.10 Fitting a new oil seal to differential small bearing recess

8.11 Fitting new oil seal to differential large bearing flange

remove the 'O' ring seal.

3   Remove the securing bolts from the differential half housing and then remove the half housing complete with the seal located on smaller bearing side.

4   Lift the differential assembly from the casing. (photo)

5   Wash all components and the interior of the differential housing in paraffin.

8   Final drive (differential) unit - inpsection and servicing

1   Inspect each component for wear, scoring or damage. Examine the teeth of the crownwheel for chipping, also the gear wheels in the differential cage.

2   Examine the roller bearings for wear and cracks in the inner and outer tracks.

3   To remove the crownwheel, (if this component is renewed, the gearbox output shaft with matched pinion will also have to be renewed) support the unit in a vice and unscrew the securing bolts (photo).

4   The differential bearings may be renewed if a suitable extractor is available (photo).

5   The speedometer drive gear is a press fit on the outside of the differential cage. An extractor will be needed to remove it.

6   Refitting of bearings and speedometer drive gear will require the use of a press and it will be better to let a service station carry out this work if the correct tools are not available. Where the speedometer drive gear is to be renewed, then the meshing gear in the lower differential half housing must also be renewed as a matched pair (photo).

7   Dismantling of the sun and planet bevel gears is not recommended. It is better to obtain a reconditioned factory exchange differential cage complete.

8   The differential oil seals should be renewed as a matter of course. These may be renewed without removing the unit from the vehicle but the oil must first be drained and the gearbox pulled forward.

9   Extract the inner oil seal and carefully drift in a new one ensuring that its lip is towards the differential cage. (photo)

10 Drift out the oil seal from the small bearing end of the housing and fit a new one squarely with its lip towards the roller bearing. (photo)

11 Tap out the oil seal from the large bearing flange and fit a new one using a soft faced hammer ensuring that the lip will be towards the large bearing when it is bolted up, (photo)

12 The differential and final drive assembly is now ready for refitting to its housing but certain adjustments are necessary. They are described in the following Section.

9   Final drive (differential) unit - reassembly and adjustment

1   Lower the assembled final drive unit into the housing and at the same time locate the large roller bearing track ring. (photo)

2   Fit the lower half housing into position but do not tighten the bolts more than finger tight. (photo)

3   A thrust plate dummy tool should now be borrowed or hired from your Simca dealer (PN 20886K) or a substitute made up. Its purpose is to align the surface of the upper and lower differential housings and to locate the differential bearings correctly in their seats.

4   Bolt the tool first to the main housing face and then to the lower housing, (photo).

5   Tighten the central threaded plate of the tool until the roller bearings are seated, rotating the differential housing at the same time. Repeat this operation several times and then release the plate of the tool and tighten the half housing bolts to 16 lb ft (photo).

6   Remove the dummy thrust plate tool and check that the

differential housing will turn easily without binding or tight spots.

7   Fit the original bearing shims. (photo)

8   Place four lengths of 1 mm diameter soft soldering wire (or Plastigage) at equal points on top of the original shims, bolt the thrust plate (without 'O' ring seal) into position, tightening the bolts to 22 lb ft.

9   Remove the thrust plate, measure the thickness of the crushed wire with a micrometer and this thickness plus 0.10 inch (0.2540 mm) will be the required **additional** shim pack thickness to provide the necessary bearing pre-load. Shims are available in a range of thicknesses to suit most requirements. The next higher thickness should be used however where an exact tolerance cannot be matched precisely by a combination of shim thicknesses.

10 Locate the shim pack in position.

11 Fit a new 'O' ring to the thrust plate. (photo)

12 Bolt the thrust plate to the housing, tightening the bolts to a torque of 22 lb ft. (photo)

13 The final drive (differential) unit is now ready for fitting to the vehicle as described in Section 6, followed by the gearbox, Section 2.

10 Gearshift lever and mechanism - adjustment

1   The gearshift control mechanism may be part cable and rod or completely rod operated according to the date of vehicle manufacture, Figs. 6.9 page 111 and 6.7 page 102.

2   Adjustment of cable type gearshift may be carried out by altering the position of the nuts (6). The gearshift lever, inside the car, should be vertical when in the neutral position. Adjust the nut and locknut until this is achieved.

3   Correct gear engagement may be achieved by loosening the locknuts on the rods (1) and (2) and screwing the rods either in or out. Retighten the locknuts when gear selection in all positions proves positive and smooth.

4   Adjustment of the later rod-operated type of gearshift control is achieved by altering the lengths of the selector rods, link rods or gearchange control tube. Where adjustment of the linkage is badly out, it will be a more precise operation to remove all the rods and links pre-set them to the dimensions indicated in Fig. 6.8 page 110.

11 Gearshift control cable - renewal

1   Detach the balljoint assembly from the gearshift lever, (photo)

2   Unhook the return spring and then unscrew the outer cable locknuts at the balljoint support bracket.

3   Detach the inner and outer cables, (photo).

4   Loosen the locknut which secures the inner cable to the fork of the gearbox control shaft, (photo)

5   Loosen the outer cable locknut which secures it to the support bracket (gearbox side).

6   Unscrew and remove the combined inner and outer cable asembly, (photo).

7   Refitting a new cable is a reversal of removal but check the adjustment as described in the preceding Section.

12 Modifications

1   The only modification so far is the provision of an additional mounting bolt (gearbox to clutch bellhousing) on vehicles manufactured after May, 1970, (photo).

9.1 Fitting final drive assembly into housing

9.2 Locating differential lower half housing

9.4 Location of thrust plate dummy tool to determine differential bearing pre-load

9.5 Tightening the differential lower half housing bolts

9.7 Fitting shims to differential large bearing recess

9.11 Fitting differential bearing thrust plate 'O' ring

9.12 Tightening thrust plate securing bolts

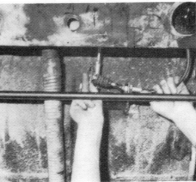

11.1 Detaching the balljoint assembly from the gearshift lever (cable type mechanism)

11.3 Detaching the inner and outer gearshift cables

11.4 Location of inner cable locknut at gearbox end

11.6 Removing the inner and outer gearshift cable assembly

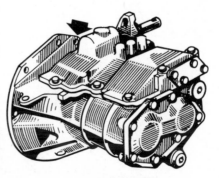

12.1 Additional gearbox to clutch bellhousing securing bolt hole (after May 1970)

13 Fault diagnosis - Gearbox (Manual)

Symptom	Reason/s	Remedy
General wear	Synchronising cones worn, split or damaged Baulk ring synchromesh dogs worn, or damaged	Dismantle and overhaul gearbox. Fit new gear wheels and synchronising cones. Dismantle and overhaul gearbox. Fit new baulk ring synchromesh.
General wear or damage	Broken selector rod spring Gearbox coupling dogs badly worn Selector fork rod groove badly worn	Remove plug and replace spring. Dismantle gearbox. Fit new coupling dogs Fit new selector fork.
Lack of maintenance	Incorrect grade of oil in gearbox or oil level too low	Drain, refill or top up gearbox with correct grade of oil.
General wear	Bush or roller bearings worn or damaged Gearteeth excessively worn or damaged	Dismantle and overhaul gearbox.Renew bearings. Dismantle, overhaul gearbox. Renew gearwheels. Dismantle and overhaul gearbox.
Clutch not fully disengaging	Clutch pedal adjustment incorrect	Adjust clutch pedal correctly.

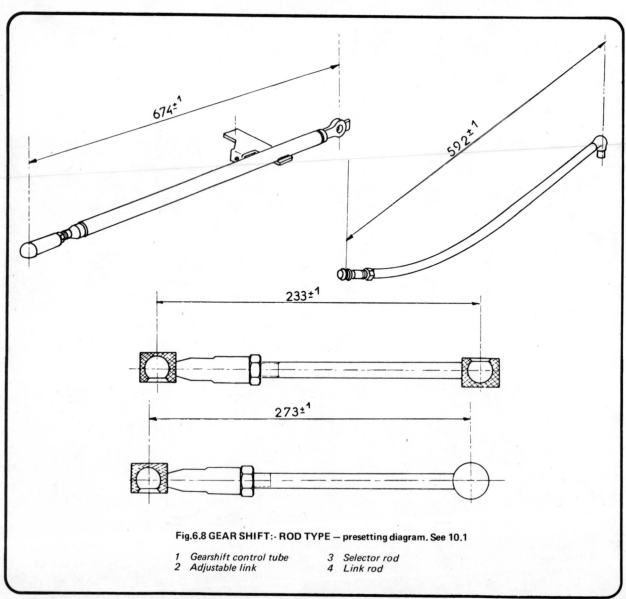

Fig.6.8 GEAR SHIFT:- ROD TYPE — presetting diagram. See 10.1

1   Gearshift control tube   3   Selector rod
2   Adjustable link   4   Link rod

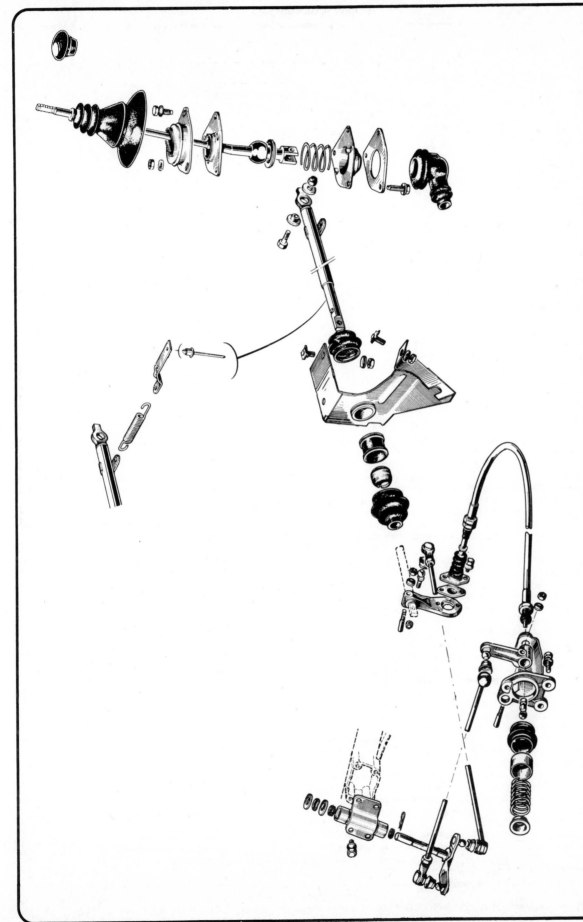

Fig. 6.9. GEAR SHIFT MECHANISM – Cable and rod type fitted prior to 1970 (Sec. 10.4)

PART 2. Automatic Transmission

Specifications

Type ...   .   Ferodo semi-automatic with torque converter and single plate clutch (sealed unit). 3 speed

Ratios: 1st   ...   .   2.47 : 1
           2nd   ...   .   1.65 : 1
           3rd   ...   .   1.08 : 1
           reverse ...   .   3.77 : 1

All forward gears have synchromesh

Final drive   ...   .   Identical to unit fitted to manually operated gearbox. Refer to manually operated gearbox and final drive specifications.

Capacity
Torque converter (including cooler and reservoir tank) ...   ...   7.5 pints

Torque wrench settings (for final drive see manually operated gearbox specifications)

	lb/ft
Drive plate to crankshaft flange bolts	40.0
Drive plate to torque converter bolts	26.0
Converter housing to engine bolts	32.0
Gearbox to converter housing bolts	16.0
Gearbox selector fork cover to gearbox bolts	8.5
Gearbox output shaft locknut (L.H)	120.0
Gearbox large bearing thrust plate bolts	22.0
Solenoid valve cover bolts	9.0

14 General description

1   Ferodo semi-automatic type transmission is available as an optional extra on vehicles marketed in certain territories.
2   A torque converter is used instead of a conventional clutch pedal and actuating mechanism. There is a three speed gearbox.
3   Operation of the oil filled clutch is automatically controlled by solenoid operated valves which are energised when the gearshift lever is moved.
4   A sectional view of the automatic transmission is shown in Fig. 6.10 page 114.
5   The torque converter impeller (A) is connected to the engine crankshaft. As the engine rotates the impeller blades cause the oil contained within the converter housing to move and turn the blades of the rotor (B). The rotor is connected through the medium of a single plate clutch to the input (primary) shaft of the gearbox.
6   Oil pressure controls the engagement or withdrawal of the clutch plates. This pressure is controlled by a solenoid operated valve which operates upon movement of the gearshift lever. Certain overriding safety features are built into the system to prevent starting the engine in gear with clutch engaged and to ensure that the clutch is disengaged fractionally in advance of a gearchange to avoid 'dragging' of gears during a change. These arrangements are effected by the ignition switch and gearshift lever switch circuit layouts, Fig. 6.11 page 115.
7   A delay feature is built into the system to shorten the period of clutch engagement during acceleration and to lengthen the period during deceleration or overrun. The method employed is to use a rocking flap which by covering or uncovering the bypass controls the oil pressure to the clutch plates to regulate their unequal velocities, (photo).
8   The automatic transmission fluid is kept to the correct level by provision of a reservoir, (photo), which should be maintained as described in 'Routine Maintenance' Section.
9   The fluid temperature rises rapidly during operation. An oil cooler is provided to control the temperature level, Fig. 6.14 page 120.
10 A valve is incorporated in the oil cooler fluid line to maintain specified pressure within the torque converter.
11 The final drive unit is identical to that fitted to manually operated gearbox vehicles.
12 The gearbox is similar to that used in manually controlled gearbox vehicles but has only three forward speeds (synchromesh) and reverse.

15 Automatic transmission - removal and refitting

1   The gearbox may be removed as a separate component while the power/transmission unit is still in position in the vehicle.
2   The torque converter assembly cannot be removed unless the engine is also withdrawn from the vehicle.
3   Reference should be made to Chapter 1 and Part 1 of this Chapter for the operations necessary for either complete power/transmission unit or 'gearbox only' removal but the following additional procedure must also be carried out, whichever method is used.
4   Remove the neutral contactor plug from the gearbox, (photo).
5   Disconnect the converter fluid supply hose at the Tee connection and swivel the hose upwards to retain the fluid, (photo).
6   Remove the gearbox stone guards.
7   Remove the oil cooler fluid hose from the Tee piece and from the pressure control valve and tie them up out of the way. Plug the hoses to prevent the ingress of dirt.
8   Refitting of either the complete engine/transmission unit or the gearbox alone is a reversal of the procedure described in either Chapter 1 or Part 1 of this Chapter and must include refitting of the additional components detailed in this Section.

16 Torque converter - removal and refitting

1   Having removed the engine/transmission from the car as a combined unit, the torque converter may now be removed.
2   Six bolts (1) are used to secure the starter ring to the converter housing, (photo).
3   Three of these bolts act as securing bolts to attach the converter housing to the triangular attachment plate which itself

14.7a Clutch rocker valve, (b) rocker valve (c) splined shaft

14.7b Clutch rocker valve, (a) bypass orifice (b) rocker valve (c) splined shaft

14.8 Location of fluid reservoir (late models) (1) support bracket (2) reservoir (3) supply hose (4) lower attachment hole

15.4 Neutral contactor plug and lead

15.5 Removing the reservoir to tee piece supply hose

16.10a Aligning the crankshaft pulley

16.2 Torque converter attachment plate and temporary clamp (1) attachment plate bolt (2) clamp fabrication diagram

16.10b Aligning the convertor ignition timing

17.7 Sectional view of convertor splined shaft (A) splined shaft (B) securing circlip

17.8 Lowering torque convertor into its housing with driving lugs correctly aligned (arrowed)

18.2 Reservoir filling diagram (1) initial fill (2) level after fitting cap

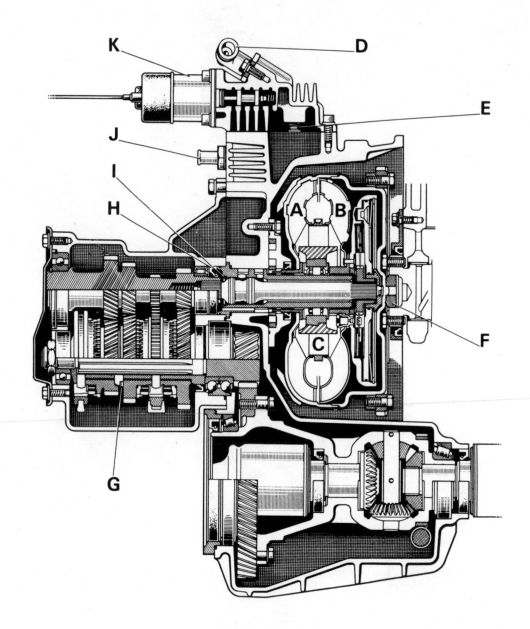

FIG. 6.10. AUTOMATIC TRANSMISSION/FINAL DRIVE — CROSS SECTION (SEC. 14)

A Impeller	D Tee piece corrector	G Clutch brake	J Oil cooler valve
B Rotor	E Relief valve	H Seal	K Solenoid
C Stator	F Convertor support bearing	I Circlip	

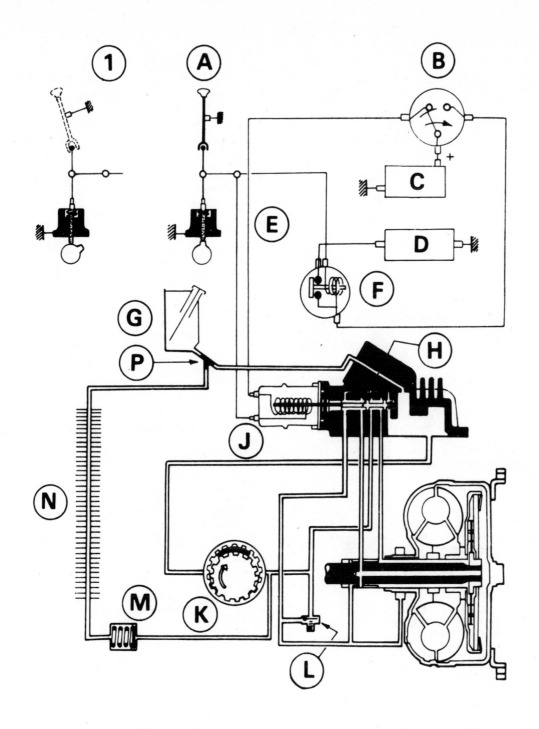

FIG. 6.11. AUTOMATIC TRANSMISSION — ELECTRIC AND HYDRAULIC CIRCUITS (SEC. 14.6)

I	Gear shift lever and neutral switch in neutral mode	G	Fluid reservoir
A	Gear shift lever in gear selected mode	H	Solenoid valve
B	Ignition/starter switch	J	Solenoid
C	Battery	K	Fluid pump
D	Starter motor	L	Relief valve
E	Neutral switch	M	Oil cooler valve
F	Relay	N	Oil cooler
		P	Tee piece

is secured to the crankshaft flange by six bolts.

4 Remove the three attachment plate bolts. This is achieved by working through the hole which is left when the starter motor is removed. Unscrew and remove one bolt and then rotate the engine by means of the crankshaft pulley bolt until each of the remaining two bolts comes into position within the starter motor aperture.

5 Fit a retaining clamp (2) to retain the torque converter within its housing once the attachment plate bolts have been withdrawn. This may be made up to the dimensions shown and it should be secured through one of the starter motor bolt holes as shown (photo 16.2).

6 Remove the gearbox, unless this was previously done while the power/transmission unit was still in position in the vehicle.

7 Unscrew and remove the bolts which secure the converter housing to the engine block, noting the position of individual bolts as their lengths vary. Withdraw the housing.

8 When installing a new or reconditioned engine in vehicles equipped with automatic transmission, it is imperative that the crankshaft flange is checked and if a clutch spigot bearing is fitted to the centre of the flange it must be removed before mating of the torque converter housing to the engine block takes place.

9 Refitting is largely a reversal of removal but the following additional procedure must be carried out.

10 Before bolting the converter housing to the engine block, the crankshaft pulley and converter ignition timing marks must be synchronised. Set both alignment marks to zero on their respective scales, (photo).

11 Before fitting the gearbox to the converter housing, renew the 'O' ring seal on the converter sleeve and the two small ones at the oil passages either side of the output shaft aperture.

12 Position the output shaft pinion bearing spacers on the converter housing using thick grease to retain them.

13 When refitting the gearbox to the converter housing observe the pressure of the converter splined shaft spring and ensure that the 'O' ring seals and the bearing spacers are not displaced as you counter its action to engage the gearbox and converter housing mating faces.

17 Torque converter assembly - dismantling and reassembly

1 Drain the final drive (differential) unit.

2 Clean the exterior of the converter housing with paraffin.

3 Remove the temporary retaining clamp used to retain the converter in its housing.

4 Place the housing open end, face down on the bench and lift it upwards leaving the converter on the bench.

5 Drain the fluid from the converter.

6 The converter is a sealed assembly and on no account should any attempt be made to separate its components. Any damage or malfunction to the impeller, stator, rotor or clutch mechanism will necessitate renewal of the complete unit.

7 To reassemble the converter to its housing, remove the splined shaft (A) which is retained by a circlip (B) (photo).

8 Position the converter housing on a bench so that its bell mouth is uppermost. Observe the position of the grooves in the pump gear and align the driving lugs with these lugs as the converter is lowered gradually into its housing, (photo).

9 Engagement must be smooth, if necessary lift it slightly and rotate it a fraction to ensure ease of fitting.

10 Fit the converter retaining clamp pending refitting of the unit to the engine.

11 Refit the splined shaft and its circlip and re-fill the converter after the power/transmission unit has been refitted to the vehicle. The refilling procedure is described in the next Section. Fill the final drive unit. It cannot be too strongly emphasised that a high standard of cleanliness must be observed at all times when filling or servicing the automatic transmission assembly. The ingress of dirt or grit can cause serious damage to the unit.

18 Torque converter - filling with fluid

1 Either of two methods may be used to fill the converter with hydraulic fluid.

2 With the engine switched off, fill the reservoir with the correct grade of automatic transmission fluid to the top of the filler tube, (photo).

3 Fit the filler cap and let the fluid level settle. Repeat as necessary until the dipstick shows a fluid level between the 'minimum' and 'maximum' marks.

4 Check the dipstick level again after a few miles of running on the road.

5 The alternative method of filling the converter is to run the engine at tick-over speed for ten minutes and to fill the reservoir until the level no longer drops. Move the gearshift lever in and out of engagement until it is established that no further topping up is required to maintain the correct fluid level.

19 Gearbox - servicing

1 Servicing the gearbox is similar to that described for the manually operated type in Part 1 of this Chapter. The differences between the two units must, however be borne in mind. The 1st and 2nd gear ratios are different in the automatic box.

2 A friction type clutch brake is fitted at the forward end of the output shaft to compensate for clutch drag (due to oil immersion) by holding gears at rest when neutral is selected and to therefore ensure smooth gearshifts.

3 The gearshift selector cover has been modified to incorporate the neutral switch.

20 Electrical circuit - checking and testing

1 The following operations should be carried out periodically as a preventative maintenance measure, as some of the electrical equipment and control gear is vulnerable to weather and road dirt.

2 Detach the lead from the neutral contact switch which is screwed into the gearbox cover, (photo).

3 Connect a 12v bulb between the switch terminal and the battery + terminal. With the ignition switched 'ON' the lamp should light when the gearshift lever is in neutral and should be extinguished when the lever is in any other position. Any deviation from the function described will mean renewal of the switch.

4 Following upon the check just described, the starter relay should be tested if faulty operation occurs. The relay is mounted on the engine bulkhead, (photo).

5 When the combined ignition/starter switch is turned to the starting position, a distinct click should be heard within the relay box and the starter motor should turn. Failure of the starter motor to operate may be due to a faulty starter motor or ignition switch or their connecting leads. These should be checked before renewing the relay.

6 Check the gearshift lever contact switch. Photo and Fig. 6.13 page 118.

7 This component is liable to the effects of corrosion and the terminals and lead ends should be examined for security of contact before carrying out a test with a lamp. Connect a 12v lamp between the battery + terminal and the lever earth wire. The lamp should light when the lever is actuated and go out when it is released. Failure to operate correctly may be due to faulty insulation of a lead allowing contact between the wire and the body underframe, or an accumulation of dirt inside the lever socket, or the soldered wire within the insulating stud having become detached. Rectify as necessary.

8 The final remaining check to be carried out is on the clutch actuating solenoid. The solenoid actuates the oil pump valve gear which controls the flow of fluid within the torque converter and clutch assemblies.

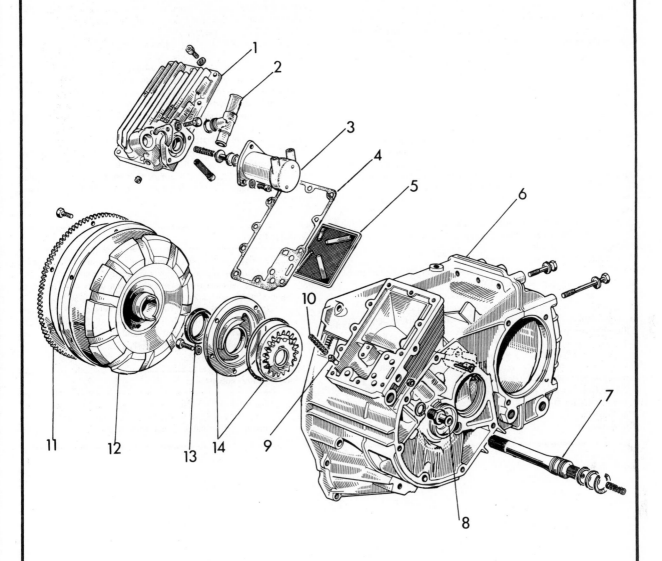

FIG. 6.12. TORQUE CONVERTOR — EXPLODED VIEW (SEC. 22.3)

1	Valve cover	5	Main filter	9	Relief valve	13	Oil seal
2	Tee piece	6	Convertor housing	10	Spring	14	Fluid pump
3	Solenoid	7	Splined shaft	11	Starter ring		
4	Gasket	8	Oil cooler connector valve	12	Convertor		

9 Clean all external dirt away and remove the solenoid from the valve cover which is located on the torque converter housing, (photo). A hexagonal (allan) key will be needed to remove the socket headed securing bolts.

10 Take a lead directly from the battery + terminal to the terminal on the solenoid and check that the plunger stroke is 7 mm in all rotary positions.

11 Fit a new sealing 'O' ring before refitting and check the fluid level in the reservoir once refitting has been completed.

21 Solenoid operated valve - dismantling and reassembly

1 Lower the level of the fluid in the valve chamber by disconnecting the by-pass hose at its upper end and draining the fluid into a container held below the outlet union. Plug or cap the upper end of the by-pass hose and also the open end of the main supply hose.

2 Discard the fluid which has been drained.

3 Unscrew the cover socket screws and remove the cover and its paper gasket, (photo).

4 Extract the main filter, (photo).

5 Withdraw the relief valve complete with coil spring, (photo).

6 Withdraw the tubular filter, (photo).

7 Remove the sliding valve from its housing, (photo).

8 Examine components for wear and renew as necessary.

9 Reassembly is a reversal of dismantling but observe the following points.

10 Always use a new cover gasket and tighten the securing bolts to a torque of 9 lb ft in the sequence shown in (photo).

11 Reconnect the hoses and top-up the oil reservoir to the correct level as previously described.

12 The fluid supply hose tee connecter need not normally be removed unless there is evidence of oil leakage, in which case, the securing clamp should be released and a new sealing 'O' ring fitted, (photo).

22 Fluid pump and seals - servicing

1 The fluid pump which is located at the rear of the converter should not be removed or refitted without the use of special centralising and locating tools. It is therefore recommended that when the fluid pump is suspect its removal and refitting should be left to a SIMCA dealer.

2 Incorrectly fitted fluid pumps may cause noise during operation.

3 The fluid pump oil seal (13) which is located in a recess in the torque converter housing, may be renewed without disturbing the fluid pump or its securing bolts, Fig. 6.12 page 117.

4 Remove the converter from its housing as described in Section 15 and carefully prise out the seal after removal of the circlip and splined shaft, (photo).

5 Lubricate the new seal with automatic transmission fluid and fill the cavity between the seal lips with Molykote BR2 grease. Drive it into position using a tubular drift so that its lip is towards the fluid pump. Do not drift it in any further once its face is flush with the housing outer surface. Refit the splined shaft and circlip.

23 Modifications

1 Vehicles having a 1294 cc capacity engine are fitted with a strengthened torque converter. As the re-inforcement is to the impeller blades which cannot be seen, these units are identified by means of a dab of purple paint.

2 After manufacture of the first few gearboxes, the thickness of the clutch brake (Section 18) was increased. Fitting the new thicker component will necessitate removing one of the two spring support washers fitted to the early type gearboxes.

24 Fuel system - adjustments

1 Certain adjustments to the idling speed of carburettors fitted to automatic transmission models and to the dashpot capsule will be required periodically. Refer to Chapter 3 for full details.

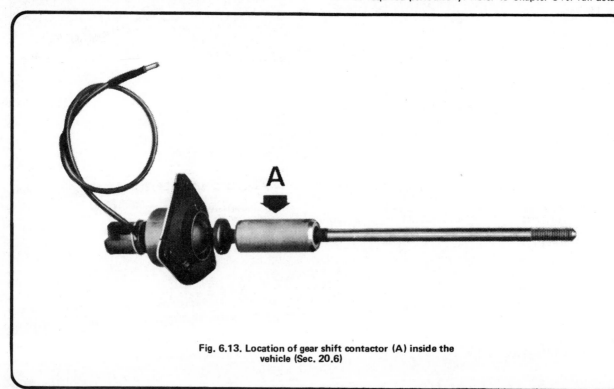

Fig. 6.13. Location of gear shift contactor (A) inside the vehicle (Sec. 20.6)

20.2 Location of neutral contactor switch lead and fluid reservoir

20.4 Location of relay on engine bulk-head

20.6 Location of gearshift lever contact switch (below floor)

20.9 Removing the solenoid from the valve cover

21.3 Removing the valve cover

21.4 Extracting the main filter

21.5 Withdraw the relief valve complete with spring

21.6 Withdrawing the tubular filter from the valve chamber

21.7 Removing the sliding valve from its housing

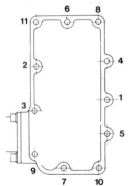
21.10 Bolt tightening sequence from the valve cover

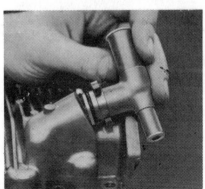
21.12 Valve cover tee piece fluid hose connectors showing 'O' ring seal and forked securing clamp

22.4 Removing the circlip from the splined shaft

25 Fault diagnosis — Automatic Transmission

Symptom	Reason/s	Remedy
Poor performance	Blocked filters in solenoid operated valve	Clean filters.
Difficult or noisy gearshifts	Relief valve jammed or spring broken Damaged or worn convertor	Renew as necessary. Renew convertor.
Starter motor does not operate	Faulty relay Defective starter motor Neutral contact switch faulty	Renew. Repair or renew. Service or renew.
No drive when gear selected	Solenoid valve slide (core) locked in position Earthed cable	Check or renew solenoid valve. Test cable insulation and replace cable if necessary.
Transmission locked in engagement	Earthed cable Solenoid slide valve stuck	Check circuit. Service or renew solenoid valve.
Reverse gear squeaks when selected but vehicle remains stationary	Gearbox clutch brake worn	Renew.
Excessive oil consumption	Leaks at hoses or joints or oil seals	Dismantle and rectify.
Transmission excessively hot during operation	Blocked cooling circuit Tee piece valve stuck Fault in torque convertor	Check and clear. Renew valve. Renew as unit.

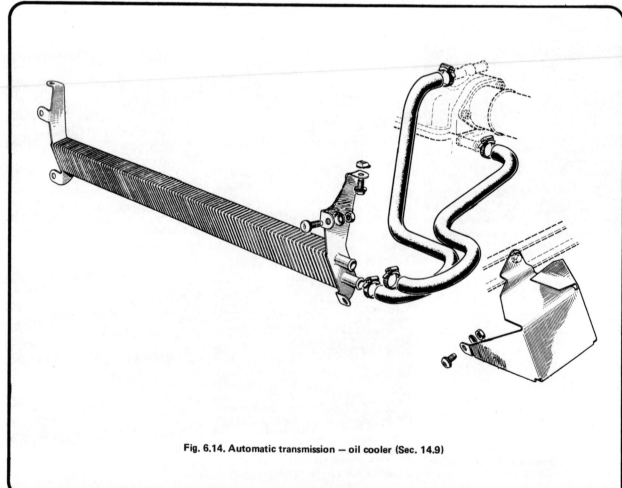

Fig. 6.14. Automatic transmission — oil cooler (Sec. 14.9)

Chapter 7 Front suspension; drive shafts and hubs

Contents

Specifications

Suspension type ...   .   Torsion bar, anti-roll bar and telescopic hydraulic dampers.

Driveshafts
Type   ...   .   Three piece solid shaft comprising inner, intermediate and stub axle sections.

Driveshaft joints
Inner to intermediate shaft   ...   .   Tripod needle bearing, sliding homokinetic
Intermediate to stub axle shaft
Early vehicles   ...   .   Double universal type
Later vehicles (from vehicle no. F2 1301 423)   ...   Single GLAENZER type

TORQUE WRENCH SETTING

	lb ft
Hub nut	145
Lower suspension arm pivot pin nut	54
Upper suspension arm pivot pin nuts	40
Stub axle carrier lower ball joint nut castellated ring ...	250
Upper suspension arm ball joint nut	25
Lower crossmember to body bolts	34
Damper upper mounting	9.5
Damper lower mountint	16
Anti-roll bar securing bolts	16
Torsion bar link pin bolt	54
Upper suspension arm securing bolts	34
Wheel bearing screwed sleeve to stub axle carrier ...	210
Roadwheel nuts	45

1 General description

1   The front suspension is of independent type and incorporates torsion bars and telescopic, hydraulic shock absorbers.
2   Components of the left hand suspension components are shown in Fig. 7.1 page 122.
3   The torsion bars terminate at each end in hexagon heads. At the road wheel end, the torsion bar locates in a hexagon socket (2) built into the swivel end of the lower suspension arm, Fig. 7.2 page 122.
4   The rear end of the torsion bar locates in a splined cup (4) which is retained in the cross member (1) by a circlip (8), Fig. 7.3 page 123.
5   Adjustment of the suspension is by means of tensioning the

torsion bars by rotating the adjuster nut (5).
6   Details of the upper suspension components and the stub axle carrier are shown in Fig. 7.5 page 124. Early models have a slightly modified cross member.
7   An anti-roll stabilizer bar is fitted and one end of its attachment to the lower suspension arm is shown in Fig. 7.4 page 123.
8   The drive shafts comprise inner, intermediate and stub axle sections. The intermediate shaft incorporates a sliding homokinetic type joint at its inner end. On vehicles built after mid 1970 (from vehicle F2-1301423) the attachment of the stub axle shaft to the intermediate shaft is by means of a single GLAENZER type joint, Fig. 7.6 page 125.
9   On earlier vehicles the stub axle shaft is connected to the intermediate shaft by means of a double universal joint, Fig. 7.7 page 125.

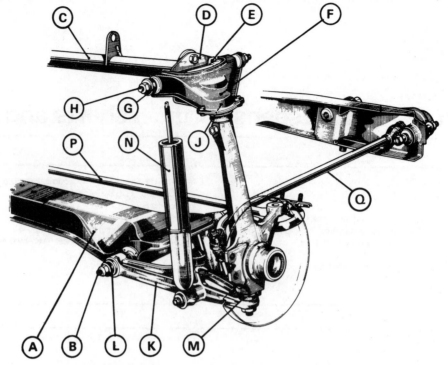

FIG. 7.1. FRONT SUSPENSION – GENERAL ARRANGEMENT (SEC. 1.2)

A Lower crossmember
B Lower suspension arm
   pivot pin
C Upper crossmember (early
   type pre 1970)

D Upper suspension arm bracket
E Spacers for camber adjustment
F Upper suspension arm
G Swivel bush

H Swivel pin
J Ball joint assembly
K Lower suspension arm
L Swivel bush

M Stub axle carrier lower
   balljoint
N Damper
P Anti-roll bar
Q Torsion bar

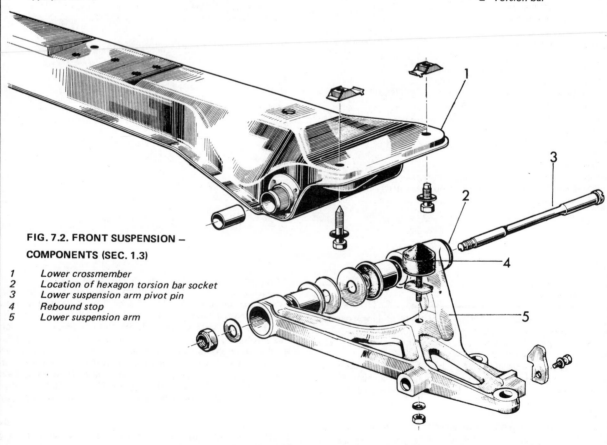

FIG. 7.2. FRONT SUSPENSION –

COMPONENTS (SEC. 1.3)

1   Lower crossmember
2   Location of hexagon torsion bar socket
3   Lower suspension arm pivot pin
4   Rebound stop
5   Lower suspension arm

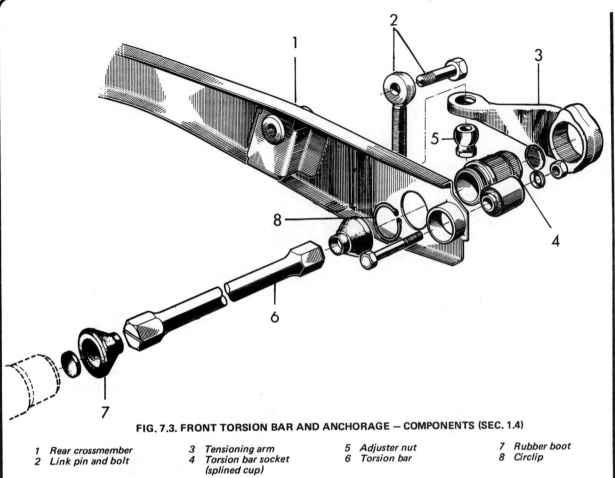

FIG. 7.3. FRONT TORSION BAR AND ANCHORAGE — COMPONENTS (SEC. 1.4)

1 Rear crossmember	3 Tensioning arm	5 Adjuster nut	7 Rubber boot
2 Link pin and bolt	4 Torsion bar socket (splined cup)	6 Torsion bar	8 Circlip

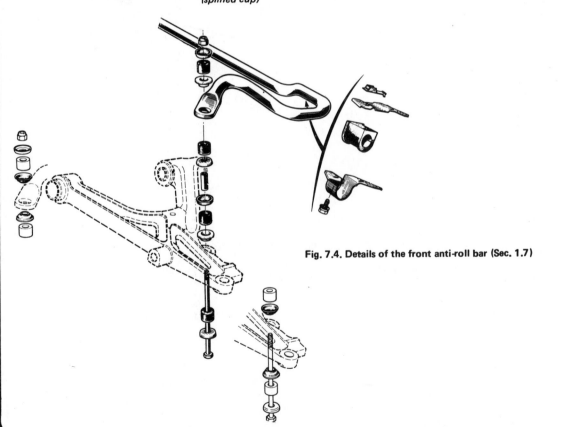

Fig. 7.4. Details of the front anti-roll bar (Sec. 1.7)

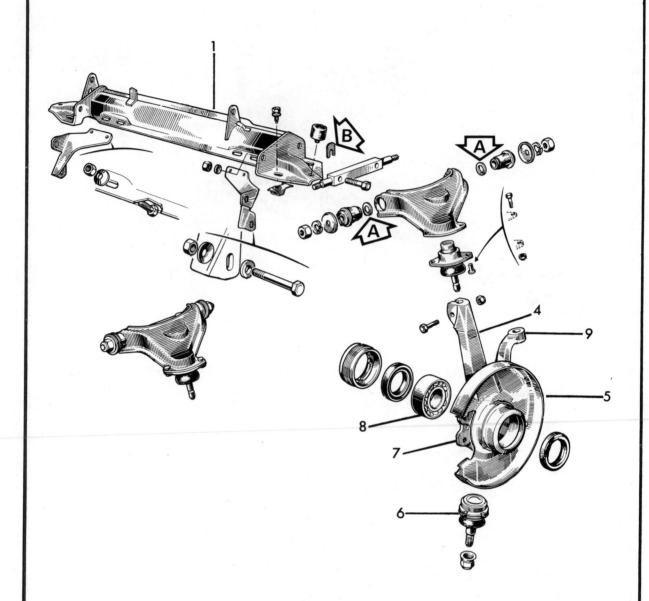

FIG. 7.5. EXPLODED VIEW OF ONE SIDE OF THE FRONT SUSPENSION

A	Washers (fitted to early models only)		6	Lower balljoint
1	Late type (1970 on) crossmember		7	Brake caliper unit anchorage
2	Upper suspension arm		8	Hub bearing
3	Upper balljoint		9	Steering arm
4	Stub axle carrier		B	Camber shim
5	Splash guard			

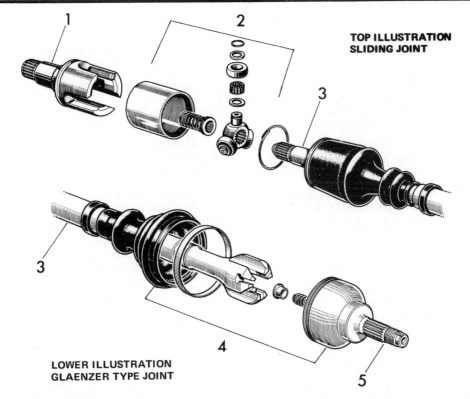

**TOP ILLUSTRATION
SLIDING JOINT**

**LOWER ILLUSTRATION
GLAENZER TYPE JOINT**

FIG. 7.6. DRIVE SHAFT JOINTS (INNER AND OUTER) 1970 ONWARDS (SEC. 1.8)

1	Inner shaft (to differential) and tulip yoke	4	Glaenzer type joint
2	Components of sliding joint and tripod bearings	5	Stub axle shaft
3	Intermediate shaft		

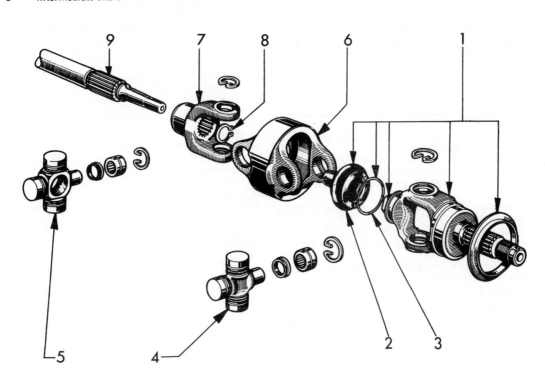

FIG. 7.7. DRIVE SHAFT JOINT (OUTER) PRE 1970 (SEC. 1.9)

1	Yoke assembly	4	Tee piece	6	Double yoke	9	Intermediate shaft
2	Rubber boot	5	Tee piece (hollow centre)	7	Splined yoke		
3	Snap ring			8	Circlip		

2 Driveshaft - removal and refitting

1 Remove the hydraulic damper and fit a substitute restraining rod to offset the torque of the torsion bars. Diagram and details of the method of constructing the rod are given in Chapter 1. The rod fitted in position is shown in Fig. 7.8 page 127.
2 Jack up the front of the vehicle and place supports securely under the body frame.
3 Remove the road wheel.
4 Unscrew and remove the hub nut and thrust washer. It will probably be necessary to apply the foot brake in order to prevent the hub rotating during this operation.
5 Remove the two bolts which retain the brake caliper unit to the anchorage (7) on the splash guard, Fig. 7.5 page 124.
6 Tie the caliper unit up out of the way using a length of wire to prevent strain on the brake hose. The fluid line need not be disconnected and therefore the hydraulic system will not require bleeding on reassembly.
7 Disconnect the lower swivel joint at the base of the stub axle carrier by using a suitable extractor.
8 Disconnect the track rod to steering arm ball joint.
9 Withdraw the driveshaft carefully from the final drive (differential) unit, using a tilting motion, as the upper stub axle ball joint is still connected to the upper suspension arm, Fig. 7.9 page 127.
10 Support the drive shaft during the operation to prevent damage to the driveshaft oil seals or rubber bellows.
11 Expel the driveshaft from the stub axle carrier and disc/hub assembly by carefully and squarely striking the end of the shaft with a soft-faced mallet, Fig. 7.10 page 127. It is a wise precaution to screw the axle nut on a few turns before using the mallet as a protection against thread damage.
12 If desired, the stub axle may be withdrawn by disconnecting the upper swivel balljoint, again using a suitable extractor.
13 Refitting is a reversal of removal but take great care not to dismantle the shaft sliding joints by pulling them apart or they will have to be reassembled as described in the next Section. Do not damage the oil seals or joint bellows and also use a new hub nut finally tightening to 145 lb ft and peening well over to lock it.
14 Full details of refitting the caliper unit and disc pads are given in Chapter 10.

3 Driveshaft joints - servicing

(a) Inner homokinetic sliding joint

1 Secure the driveshaft in a vice and remove the snap ring which retains the wider mouth of the bellows, Fig. 7.11 page 127.
2 Draw the tulip shaped yoke upwards and remove it, Fig. 7.12 page 127.
3 Remove the spring and cap and then wipe out as much grease as possible from the joint assembly.
4 Fit masking or insulating tape round the ends of the three joint trunnions to prevent the bearings becoming dislodged, Fig. 7.13 page 127.
5 Using a press, press the splined driveshaft from the joint spider, Fig. 7.14 page 127. It must be noted that with later type vehicles, the spider on the inner driveshaft joint is offset by 57° $\pm3°$) compared with the spider on the outer joint. The position of the spider in relation to the shaft should therefore be marked before removal as shown in Fig. 7.15 page 127.
6 Obtain a repair kit which will contain all renewable components except the tulip shaped yoke and intermediate shaft. Check all renewable parts for wear, damage, or corrosion, and replace if necessary.
7 Hold the intermediate shaft vertically in a vice. During the assembly it is necessary to make sure that every part is clinically clean.
8 Fit the new rubber retaining ring and sealing bellows to the shaft.
9 Fill the bellows and the tulip shaped yoke, complete with its metal cover, with grease.
10 Secure the new needle roller bearings on the new joint tripod and retain them with tape as previously described.
11 Fit the joint spider complete with bearings to the intermediate splined shaft, using a tubular drift, Fig. 7.16 page 128.
12 Peen the end of the intermediate shaft at three equidistant points to secure the joint tripod in position.
13 Remove the temporary retaining tape from the needle bearings.
14 Fit the cap and spring onto the curved end of the intermediate shaft.
15 Insert the tulip shaped yoke and metal cover into position in the bellows, Fig. 7.17 page 128.
16 Fit the smaller mouth of the bellows into the groove in the intermediate shaft and secure with the rubber retaining ring, Fig. 7.18 page 128.
17 Check the movement of the assembled joint for tight spots.
18 Where the rubber bellows only are to be renewed then they and the rubber retaining ring should be cut off. Without any further dismantling, the new bellows and ring may be slid into position using a tripod type expanding former similar to the one shown in Fig. 7.19 page 128.
19 This will permit the bellows and rubber ring to ride over the tripod joint and needle bearing assembly.

(b) Outer (road wheel end) joint

20 Early model vehicles were fitted with double universal joints linking the intermediate and stub axle shafts, Fig. 7.7 page 125.
21 These joints can be reconditioned in the conventional manner by removing the circlips and by striking the shaft adjacent to the joint cause the bearing cup to emerge from the yoke. The cups may then be twisted from their locations by gripping them in the jaws of a vice.
22 Due to the unreliable performance of these joints however, it is recommended that they are renewed with the later GLAENZER type joint, Fig. 7.6 page 125. (lower illustration).
23 Fitting the GLAENZER type joint will however necessitate removing the old intermediate shaft as the new joint comprises intermediate shaft and stub axle shaft as inseparable components of the joint assembly.

4 Hubs and outer bearings - dismantling and reassembly

1 Carry out the operations described in paragraphs 1-6 inclusive in Section 2 of this Chapter.
2 Unscrew and remove the four bolts which secure the brake disc to the wheel hub, Fig. 7.20 page 128.
3 Rotate the brake disc just enough so that two suitable bolts may be screwed into the hub (road wheel fixing) bolt holes and by bearing against the brake disc with equal pressure extract the hub, Fig. 7.21 page 128.
4 Withdraw the hub together with the oil seal and bearing, Fig. 7.22 page 128.
5 Remove the brake disc and then pick out the bearing balls from their plastic cage and then remove the cage, Fig. 7.23 page 129.
6 Pull the bearing ring from the hub with the aid of a suitable extractor, Fig. 7.24 page 129.
7 Disconnect the lower stub axle carrier balljoint and the track rod to steering arm balljoint.
8 Pull the drive shaft from the stub axle carrier but do not disengage it from the final drive unit, Fig. 7.25 page 129.
9 Fit the new bearing balls and their plastic cage to the bearing ring. Pack with wheel bearing grease and then fit the assembly to the stub axle carrier, Fig. 7.26 page 129.
10 Fit a new oil seal (lip inwards) into the stub axle carrier, using a suitable tubular drift, Fig. 7.27 page 129.
11 Refit the brake disc to the hub, tightening the securing bolts to a torque of 35 lb ft.
12 Using a suitable bolt and plates, draw the disc/hub assembly into position on the stub axle carrier, Fig. 7.28 page 131.
13 Fit the drive shaft into the stub axle carrier and reconnect

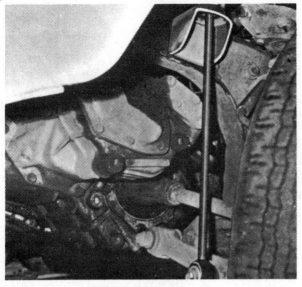

Fig. 7.8. Hydraulic damper substitute rod in position (Sec. 2.1)

Fig. 7.9. Withdrawing a driveshaft from its connection with the differential unit (Sec. 2.9)

Fig. 7.10. Drifting the stub axle shaft from the carrier (Sec. 2.11)

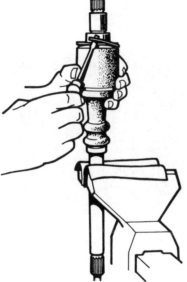

Fig. 7.11. Removing the snap ring from the driveshaft bellows (Sec. 3.1)

Fig. 7.12. Drawing the tulip shaped yoke from the driveshaft bellows (Sec. 3.2)

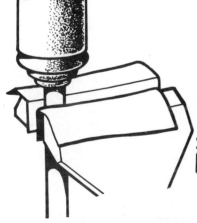

Fig. 7.13. Driveshaft joint bearings taped to prevent dislodging (Sec. 3.4)

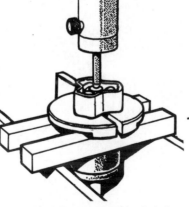

Fig. 7.14. Pressing the driveshaft from the joint spider (Sec. 3.5)

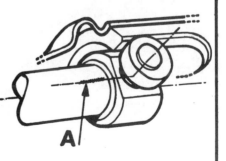

Fig. 7.15. Driveshaft joint spider alignment mark (A) (Sec. 3.5)

128

Fig. 7.18. Fitting the rubber retaining ring to the driveshaft bellows (Sec. 3.16)

Fig. 7.16. Drifting a new spider into position on the driveshaft (Sec. 3.11)

Fig. 7.17. Fitting the driveshaft joint yoke and cover into the bellows (Sec. 3.15)

Fig. 7.19. Using a former/guide to fit the driveshaft bellows (Sec. 3.18)

Fig. 7.20. Removing wheel disc to hub securing bolts (Sec. 4.2)

Fig. 7.21. Extracting a front wheel hub (Sec. 4.3)

Fig. 7.22. Removing a front wheel hub, oil seal and bearing (Sec. 4.4)

Fig. 7.23. Removing a front hub bearing cage (Sec. 4.5)

Fig. 7.24. Extracting a hub bearing ring (Sec. 4.6)

Fig. 7.25. Disconnecting a driveshaft stub axle and stub axle carrier (Sec. 4.8)

Fig. 7.26. Fitting a hub bearing to a stub axle carrier (Sec. 4.9)

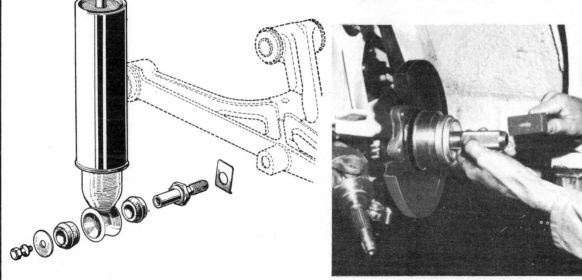

Fig. 7.34. Hydraulic telescopic damper and mounting details (Sec. 8.2)

Fig. 7.27. Fitting a new oil seal to a stub axle carrier (Sec. 4.10)

the lower ball joint and the track rod to steering arm balljoint.

14 Refit the brake caliper ensuring that a new locking plate is used.

15 Fit a new hub nut, tightening it onto the thrust washer to a torque of 145 lb ft. Peen the nut.

16 Refit the telescopic damper, refit the road wheel and lower the jack.

5 Inner hub bearings - dismantling and reassembly

1 These bearings are retained within the stub axle carrier by a screwed sleeve and it is recommended that the stub axle carrier be removed from the vehicle if the inner bearings are to be renewed. Location of the inner and outer hub bearings are shown in Fig. 7.29 page 131.

2 Carry out the operations described in paragraphs 1 to 8 of the preceding Section.

3 Disconnect the stub axle carrier upper ball joint and remove the stub axle carrier, leaving the driveshaft in engagement with the final drive unit.

4 Relieve the peening on the threaded sleeve at the rear of the stub axle carrier and unscrew the sleeve nut which will require the use of removal tool 20908H or one made up to perform the operation, Fig. 7.30 page 131.

5 Using a tubular drift, drive the inner bearing from the stub axle carrier, Fig. 7.31 page 131.

6 Before fitting the new bearing, pack it with wheel bearing grease. Pull it into position in the stub axle carrier by using a bolt and two plates as shown in Fig. 7.32 page 131.

7 Use a new threaded sleeve as the required peening on installation makes the original unsuitable for re-use.

8 Fit a new oil seal into the threaded sleeve and screw it and its nut into position using the fitting tool. The lip of the oil seal will face inwards when correctly positioned, and the sleeve nut must be tightened to a torque of 210 lb ft.

9 Lock the sleeve in position by peening it at two points.

10 Carry out the operations described in paragraphs 9 to 14 in Section 4.

11 Reconnect the stub axle carrier upper balljoint.

6 Stub axle carrier lower balljoint - renewal

1 Remove the stub axle carrier as described in Section 5.

2 Place the carrier in a vice with the balljoint uppermost.

3 Relieve the peening at the balljoint slotted ring.

4 A removal tool must now be employed (20909A) and it should be positioned and secured by the balljoint nut, Fig. 7.33 page 131.

5 Unscrew and remove the balljoint.

6 Fitting the new balljoint is a reversal of removal but take care not to pinch or tear the rubber cover. Tighten the slotted securing ring to a torque of 250 lb ft.

7 Remove the tool and peen the ring at one notch to lock it.

8 Refit the stub axle carrier as described in Section 5.

7 Upper suspension arm balljoint - renewal

1 Refer to Fig. 7.5 page 124. Remove the damper and fit the restraining rod to offset the torque of the torsion bar.

2 Jack up the front of the vehicle and support it on stands. Remove the road wheel.

3 Disconnect the stub axle carrier from the upper suspension arm by removing the securing nut and bolt.

4 Drill out the two rivets which secure the balljoint assembly to the upper suspension arm.

5 The new balljoint will be supplied as a kit complete with nuts and bolts as replacement for the rivets.

6 Fitting is a reversal of dismantling but ensure that the balljoint securing nuts are located on the top surface of the upper suspension arm and correctly locked.

8 Shock absorber - removal, testing and refitting

1 The telescopic type hydraulic shock absorber cannot be repaired and in the event of evidence occurring of bad cornering, steering wander or an unusually soft ride then the units should be removed from the vehicle and tested.

2 Disconnect the upper and lower mountings, details of which are shown in Fig. 7.34 page 129.

3 Secure the lower damper mounting in a vice and in the vertical position. Operate the damper for the full length of its travel ten times. There should be good resistance in both directions of travel. If the action is jerky, or there is no resistance at all, renew the unit.

4 Refitting is a reversal of removal but note carefully the fitting sequence of the mountings.

9 Anti-roll bar - removal, inspection and refitting

1 The anti-roll bar is connected at each end to the lower suspension arm by a long bolt, nut and bush assembly as shown in Fig. 7.4 page 123.

2 It is also supported by rubber bushes retained by semi circular clamps.

3 Removal of the bar is carried out by withdrawing the anchor bolts and the rubber bush clamps.

4 Inspect the bar closely for cracks and also the rubber mounting components for deterioration. Renew as appropriate.

5 Refitting is a reversal of removal but do not exceed a tightening torque for the anchor or clamp nuts of 16 lb ft.

10 Torsion bars - removal and refitting

1 Jack up the front of the vehicle and support securely on stands or blocks.

2 Remove the front road wheels and unbolt both the brake caliper units and tie them to the body frame out of the way.

3 The tension on each torsion bar must now be relieved to enable the tensioning arm adjuster nut (5) Fig. 7.3 page 123 to be released. To do this, either use the recommended SIMCA servicing tool (20916Q) or make up a suitable lever welded to the splined portion of an old tensioning arm.

4 With the tool offsetting the torque of the torsion bar, unscrew the bolt (A) two or three turns, Fig. 7.35 page 132.

5 Remove the adjuster nut and prise the tensioning arm with the tool so that it clears the link pin. Swivel the link pin up out of the way and release the tension of the torsion bar slowly. Remove the tool and the tensioning arm, Fig. 7.36 page 132.

6 On the other side of the crossmember, peel back the rubber cover and remove the circlip which retains the splined hub, Fig. 7.37 page 132.

7 Withdraw the splined hub from the torsion bar, Fig. 7.38 page 132.

8 Withdraw the torsion bar from the lower suspension arm by moving it to the rear and then remove it from the vehicle by pulling it forward out of the crossmember.

9 Refitting is a reversal of removal but grease the splines of the torsion bar and the hubs into which it locates with wheel bearing type grease. The left hand torsion bar is identified by a blue paint spot, the right hand by a red paint spot. The torsion bars are not interchangeable. Never mark a torsion bar by scratching or filing as this may cause premature failure.

10 With the torsion bars correctly installed in the vehicle, the tensioning arms should be fitted to the torsion bars at the angle shown in the diagram, Fig. 7.39 page 132.

11 A template should be used to obtain this initial setting and then the procedure described in the following Section must be carried out.

Fig. 7.28. Drawing a disc/hub assembly into position (Sec. 4.12)

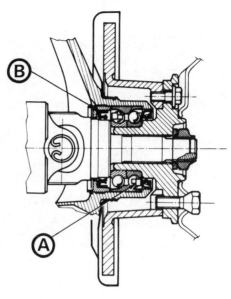

Fig. 7.29. Cross sectional view of a front hub assembly
A Outer ball bearing assembly   B Inner bearing

Fig. 7.30. Unscrewing a sleeve nut from a stub axle carrier
(Sec. 5.4)

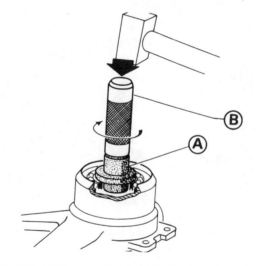

Fig. 7.31. Drifting out a hub inner bearing from the stub axle
carrier (Sec. 5.5)

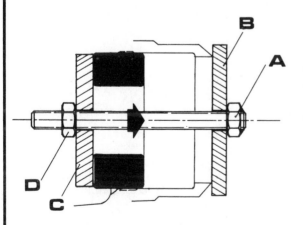

Fig. 7.32. Pulling a new hub inner bearing into position, using
plates (B and C) a threaded bolt and nuts (A and D) (Sec. 5.6)

Fig. 7.33. Removing a stub axle carrier lower balljoint (Sec. 6.4)

Fig. 7.35. Undoing adjuster screw and link bolt (A). Balance torsion bar torque with tool as shown (Sec. 10.4)

Fig. 7.36. Removing the torsion bar tensioning arm (Sec. 10.5)

Fig. 7.37. Removing the torsion bar splined hub circlip (Sec. 10.6)

Fig. 7.38. Withdrawing the splined hub from the torsion bar (Sec. 10.7)

60°

FIG. 7.39. TEMPLATE FOR TORSION BAR INITIAL SETTING (SEC. 10.10)

A   *Crossmember (rear)*
B   *Link pin bolt hole*
C   *Tensioner arm*

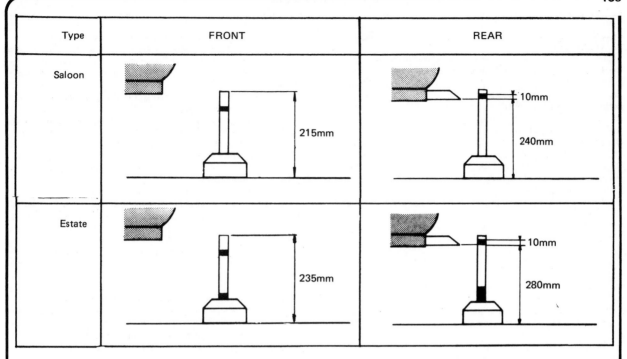

Type	FRONT	REAR
Saloon	215mm	10mm / 240mm
Estate	235mm	10mm / 280mm

Fig. 7.40. Torsion bar setting diagrams showing jacking point pointer and measuring stands (Sec. 11.4)

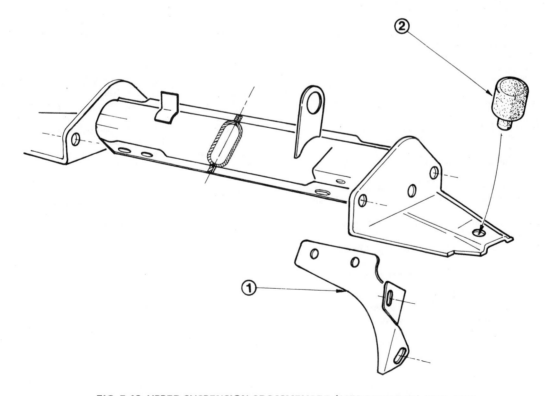

FIG. 7.43. UPPER SUSPENSION CROSSMEMBER (1970 ONWARDS) (SEC. 15.1)

1   Mounting bracket   2   Upper suspension arm rebound stop

11 Torsion bars - setting

1 The torsion bars must be set to ensure correct ride and cornering characteristics. If the front or rear torsion bars have been removed, either singly, in pairs or all four at once, the following operations must be carried out.

2 Place the vehicle on a level surface with the tyres correctly inflated and the fuel tank filled.

3 Set the steering in the straight ahead position and disconnect the telescopic damper lower mountings.

4 Fit a pointer to each of the four jacking points so that the point may be read off against simple measuring stands as shown in Fig. 7.40 page 133.

5 When the tip of the pointer is in alignment with the highest point of the measuring band this is the standard setting. The lowest point of the band indicates the 'soft' setting and the higher one goes, the harder the ride.

6 Adjust the nuts on the tensioning arms until each of the four pointers is indicating exactly similar points on the four measuring stands.

7 Rotate each nut a little at a time and 'bounce' the car between adjustments to settle the suspension. Note that in the case of the rear torsion bars, the right hand adjuster screw acts on the left hand wheel and the left hand screw acts on the right hand wheel.

8 Reconnect the dampers when adjustment is complete and check the setting of the brake equalizer as described in Chapter 10.

9 Lowering or raising of the suspension beyond the limits specified is permissible where road conditions require it but it is recommended that a distance of not more than ½ inch (12.7 mm) in either direction on the measuring stand should be traversed by the pointer (beyond the standard band) otherwise an exceptionally hard or soft ride will result.

12 Lower suspension arm - servicing

1 If wear is evident in the lower suspension arm bushes or swivel pin, then the assembly must be removed and the worn components renewed. Jack up the car and remove the wheel.

2 Refer to Fig. 7.2 page 122 and note the sequence of fitting of the various swivel components before dismantling.

3 Remove the torsion bar as described in Section 10.

4 Disconnect the anti-roll bar at its attachment to the lower suspension arm.

5 Disconnect the stub axle carrier lower balljoint as described in Section 6.

6 Unscrew and remove the nut from the swivel pin, withdraw the pin, remove the bush components and lift away the suspension arm.

7 Refitting is a reversal of removal but tighten the swivel pin nut to a torque of 54 lb ft.

8 Fit and set the torsion bar as described earlier in this Chapter.

13 Upper suspension arm - servicing

1 It will be necessary to remove the upper suspension arm when there is evidence of wear in the swivel bushes or pin. Its removal will also make easier the renewal of the balljoint assembly described in Section 7.

2 Remove the shock absorber and fit the restraining rod previously described.

3 Jack up the front of the vehicle and support it on stands.

4 Place a restraining strap round the stub axle carrier and secure it to the damper substitute rod, Fig. 7.41 page 135.

5 Disconnect the upper suspension arm to stub axle carrier balljoint.

6 Remove the two bolts which secure the upper suspension arm to the upper crossmember, Fig. 7.42 page 135.

7 As the upper suspension arm is withdrawn, note carefully the location of the spacers and retain them for future replacement. These spacers are used to adjust the front wheel camber as described in Chapter 8.

8 Unscrew and remove the swivel pin nut and remove the various components.

9 Renew bushes and other parts as necessary.

10 Refitting is a reversal of removal. Tighten the swivel pin nut to a torque of 40 lb ft, and ensure that the spacers are returned to their original positions before tightening the upper suspension arm securing bolts to 34 lb ft.

11 Whenever the suspension has been removed and refitted, the steering geometry should be checked as described in Chapter 8.

14 Upper suspension crossmember - removal and refitting

1 Substitute restraining rods for both front dampers.

2 Jack up the front of the vehicle and support on stands.

3 Disconnect the accelerator control rod balljoints.

4 Remove the accelerator control link rod.

5 Bend back the tab and pull the wiring harness from the crossmember.

6 Disconnect the leads from the brake light switch on the master cylinder.

7 Bend back the tab which retains the air conditioner hose to the crossmember.

8 Unscrew and remove the upper suspension arm securing bolts, retaining the camber adjustment spacers.

9 Withdraw the upper suspension arms partly through the side bulkhead apertures and restrain their sideways movement by strapping the stub axle carriers to the damper substitute rods, Fig. 7.41 page 135.

10 Unscrew and remove the crossmember securing bolts from the angle reinforcement and support plate brackets.

11 Remove the crossmember through one of the side panel appertures.

12 Refitting is a reversal of removal but should the thread strip in the tapped holes in the crossmember side plates, the upper suspension arms may be secured by drilling out the tapped holes to 0.413 inch (10.5 mm) (drill size Z), and fitting bolts and nuts instead.

15 Modifications

1 The tubular upper crossmember used on early models has been replaced by a welded plate type with integral upper suspension arm mounting brackets, Fig. 7.43 page 133.

2 The modification applies as follows: L.H.D. saloon from body FO-9080678. L.H.D. estate from body FO-9080728 R.H.D. vehicles from body F1-1120655.

3 From body No F2-2251500 the washers (A) fitted on each side between the swivel pin and the upper suspension arm pressings are omitted, Fig. 7.5 page 124. The pin has been modified to compensate and may be used as a renewal component on old units provided the washers originally fitted are removed.

Fault diagnosis

Symptom	Reason/s	Remedy
General wear	Tyre pressures uneven	Check and adjust if necessary.
	Shock absorbers inoperative	Test and renew.
	Suspension balljoints worn	Disconnect and renew.
	Wheels out of balance	Balance wheels correctly.
	Hub bearings worn	Renew.
Poor road holding	Torsion bars incorrectly set	Reset correctly.
	Incorrect steering geometry	See Chapter 8
	Brakes binding on one side of vehicle	Dismantle and service (Chapter 10).

Fig. 7.41. Stub axle carrier secured to the damper substitute rod pending removal of the upper balljoint (Sec. 13.4)

Fig. 7.42. Removing a bolt which secures the upper suspension arm to the upper crossmember (Sec. 13.6)

Chapter 8 Steering

Contents

Specifications

Type	... Rack and pinion
Pinion shaft end play	... 0.004 inch (0.1 mm)

Distance between (track rod) inner face of locknut and end face
of steering housing ... ... 2.93 inch ($\pm$ 0.035 inch)
(75 mm) $\pm$ 0.90 mm)

Toe-in/toe-out ... ... 0.019 inch (0.5 mm) toe-in to 0.059 inch (1.5 mm) toe-out

Camber:—
To vehicle No.E21110563 (car)	... 0° 15' ($\pm$ 30') positive
From vehicle No.E21110564 (car)	... 0° 15 ($\pm$ 30') negative
To vehicle No.E21110563 (estate)	... 0° 30' ($\pm$ 30') negative
From vehicle No.E21110564 (estate)	... 1° 0' (− 30') negative

Torque wrench settings

	lb/ft	mkg
Track rod yoke to eyebolt bolts 29	29	4.0
Track rod locknuts 50	50	6.9
Track rod end taper nut 21	21	2.9
Steering gear to mounting bracket bolts 16	16	2.2
Gearshift coupling bracket to steering gear bolts 54	54	7.5
Steering gear support bracket to bodyframe side member bolts ... 16	16	2.2
Pinion shaft nut 18	18	2.4
Rack damper adjuster locknut 43	43	5.9
Steering wheel nut 38	38	5.3
Steering column upper attachment bolt 16	16	2.2
Early type universal joint to shaft 7.2	7.2	1.0
Late type universal joint to shaft 14.5	14.5	2.0

1 General description

1 The design of the steering gear is of rack and pinion type, Fig.8.1.
2 Models built up to 1971 are fitted with a two spoke steering wheel which transmits motion through a universally jointed (collapsible) shaft to the steering gear pinion, Fig.8.2.
3 Models built after 1971 are fitted with a three spoke steering wheel and the shaft universal joint is clamped to the pinion shaft extension, Fig.8.3.
4 The steering rack terminates in two eyebolts to which are connected the two half track rod assemblies and track rod end ball joints. The track rods incorporate a hexagonal connecting piece to permit shortening or lengthening of each half track rod and so vary the setting of the front roadwheel tracking.

5 The track rods are connected to the steering arms which are integral with the stub axle carriers.
6 Shims are used between the rack and pinion steering gear mounting points and brackets and these have a direct bearing upon the track setting during movements of the front suspension.

2 Maintenance

1 No routine maintenance is required but check that the rubber bellows on the steering gear assembly and the balljoints have not deteriorated or split. Should this be evident, then renew these components.
2 Should the steering gear become stiff after a high mileage then 25cc of recommended grease should be introduced to the

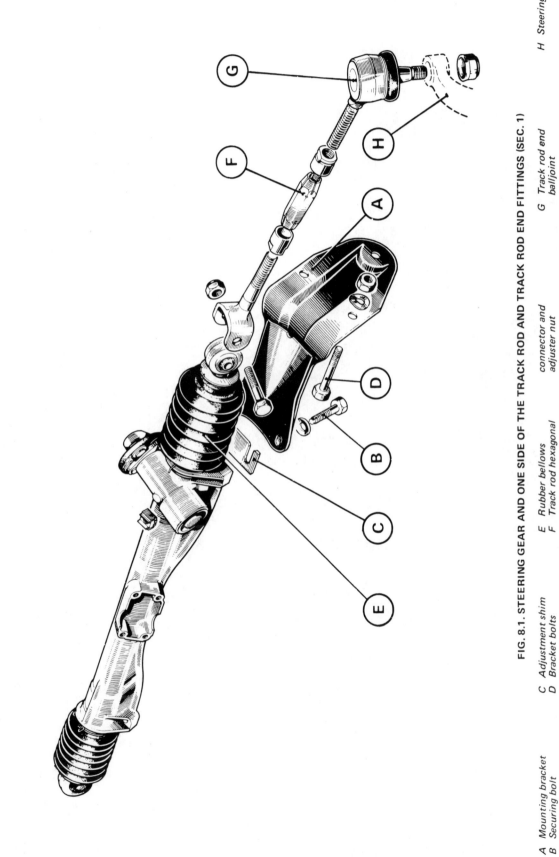

FIG. 8.1. STEERING GEAR AND ONE SIDE OF THE TRACK ROD AND TRACK ROD END FITTINGS (SEC. 1)

A Mounting bracket
B Securing bolt

C Adjustment shim
D Bracket bolts

E Rubber bellows
F Track rod hexagonal

   connector and
   adjuster nut

G Track rod end
   balljoint

H Steering arm

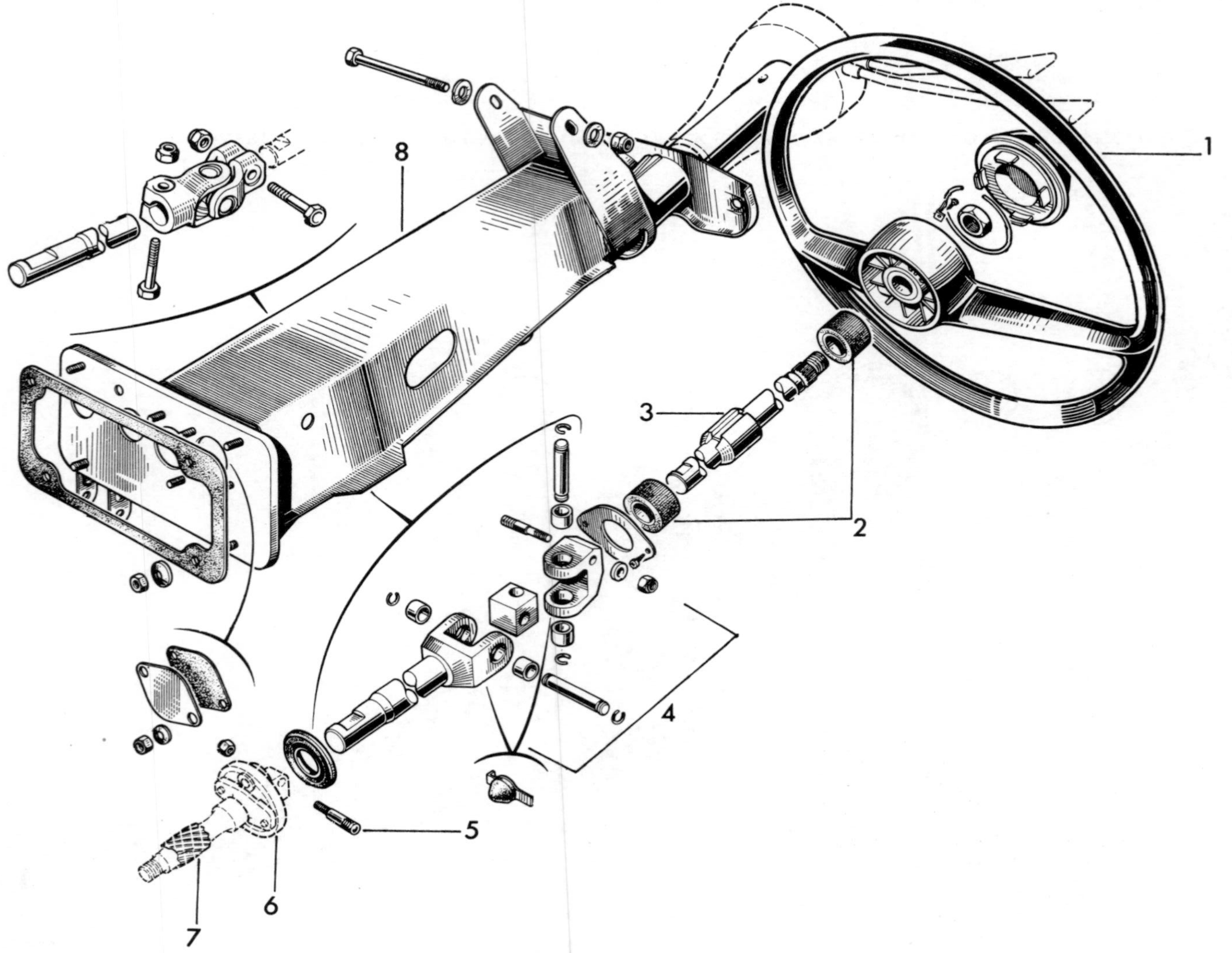

FIG. 8.2. EXPLODED VIEW OF THE STEERING COLUMN ASSEMBLY FITTED TO VEHICLES BUILT
BEFORE 1972 (SEC. 1.2)

1 Steering wheel
2 Bushes

3 Steering lock groove
4 Column universal joint

5 Flexible joint to
   assembly

6 Flexible joint
   shaft cotter pin

7 Pinion

8 Steering column
   shroud

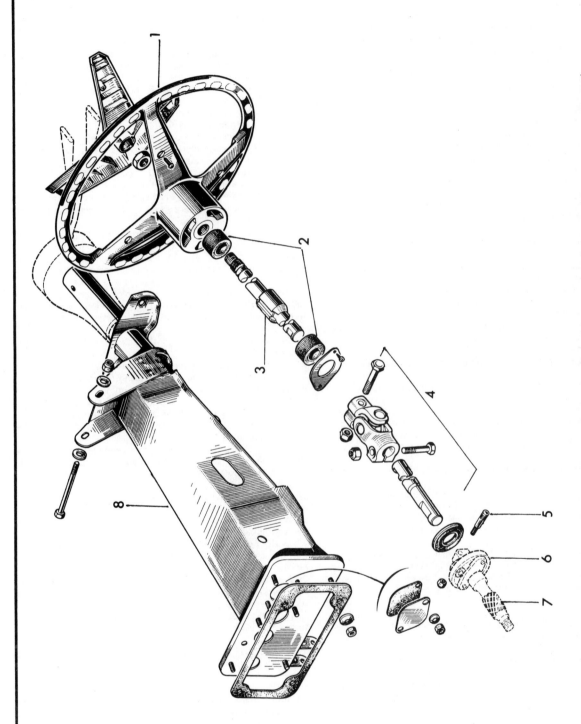

Fig. 8.3. Exploded view of the steering column assembly fitted to vehicles built after 1972 (Sec. 1.3) (For part nos. see Fig. 8.2)

steering unit through the rack damper aperture, see Section 5.

3 Keep all connecting bolts tightened to the torque wrench settings specified in Specifications.

3 Steering gear - adjustment of rack plunger play

1 Evidence that adjustment is required will be provided by a slapping sound coming from the steering gear.

2 Disconnect both track rods from the rack eyebolts.

3 Release the plunger cap lock nut (20) Fig.8.4.

4 Remove the nut and the locking tab washer (21).

5 Now tighten the plunger cap (19D) until it bears against the plunger (19A) but do not force.

6 Mark the location of the notch in the plunger cap in relation to the steering gear housing. Loosen the plunger cap fractionally by an amount equal to half the width of the notch.

7 Jack up the front of the vehicle and turn the steering wheel slowly from lock to lock and check for tight spots. Should one be found then carry out the plunger adjustment procedure with the steering remaining in the 'tight spot' position. Again check from lock to lock.

8 Fit a new locking tab washer, fit the locknut and tighten it to 43 lb/ft (5.9 mkg). Bend over the locking tab.

9 Reconnect the track rods and lower the jacks.

4 Steering gear - removal and refitting

1 Jack up the front of the vehicle and support securely on stands or blocks.

2 Remove the cotter pin (5) from the column to flexible joint connection, Figs.8.2 or 8.3.

3 Disconnect the track rods from the rack eyebolts.

4 Remove the gearshift linkage from the steering gear mounting.

5 Disconnect the anti-roll bar at both ends and lower it as far as possible.

6 Unscrew and remove the four bolts which secure the steering gear housing to its brackets. Remove any adjustment shims which may be fitted and note carefully their original location so that they may be refitted if the original steering gear is to be refitted.

7 Withdraw the steering gear downwards from under the vehicle.

8 Refitting is a reversal of removal where the original steering gear is being replaced in the vehicle. Refit the original shims in their correct location. After major steering dismantling, always check the tracking of the front wheels as described in Section 10 of this Chapter.

9 Where a new or factory reconditioned steering gear unit is fitted, the calculation of fitting shim thickness must be left to your Simca dealer due to the specialised nature of the equipment required and its effect upon the front wheel alignment.

5 Steering gear - dismantling, servicing and reassembly

1 Having removed the steering gear as described in the preceding Section consider whether in view of the mileage covered it would be more economical to obtain a factory exchange unit rather than recondition the existing unit. Where only minor components require renewal or the internal parts require cleaning and packing with fresh grease, then proceed as follows.

2 Remove the gearshift linkage bracket from the steering gear housing.

3 Secure the unit in a vice fitted with jaw protectors and do not overtighten.

4 Refer to Fig.8.4 and remove the circlips (23) and (24) from both ends of the housing and remove the two bellows.

5 Loosen the locknuts (8) and unscrew and remove the eyebolts (7).

6 Unscrew and remove the rack plunger assembly (19), retain-

ing any spacers (19c) which may be fitted.

7 Remove the bearing cover plate (15) the nut (14) and shim (13).

8 Drive the pinion from its location by using a brass or copper drift.

9 Withdraw the rack (6) from the pinion end of the housing.

10 The pinion bearing (10) may be renewed by removing the circlips (12) and shims (11).

11 The bearing (16) is renewable after extracting its securing circlip (17) and then driving out the ring using a stepped drift up to the dimensions given in the diagram, Fig.8.5.

12 Extract the circlip (5) shim (4) and the rubber guide ring (2). Remove the sleeve (3).

13 Thoroughly wash all components in paraffin and dry them with a piece of non-fluffy cloth.

14 Examine all components for wear and renew as appropriate.

15 Commence reassembly by inserting the sleeve (3) so that its slot is opposite the lubrication groove.

16 Fit the rubber guide ring (2) grease it with recommended grade grease and then locate the shim (4) and circlip (5).

17 Using the tool previously described, fit the anti-friction ring so that it is flush with the surface of the steering gear housing. Grease the anti-friction ring.

18 Fit the pinion bearing assembly by including an excessive number of shims so that the circlip (12) will not fit into its groove. Remove one shim at a time until the circlip will just locate correctly. This will provide an end-float of 0.1 mm (0.004 in).

19 Install the rack from the pinion end of the housing, fit a new rubber 'O' ring seal to the pinio , fit the pinion, its washer and securing nut, tightening the latter to a torque of 18 lb/ft (2.5 mkg).

20 Fit the pinion bearing cap, the bellows and their retaining circlips.

21 Measure out 80 cc of the recommended grade of grease and insert it into the steering gear by using the rack plunger as an injector, Fig.8.6. During this operation, move the rack from lock to lock over the full length of its travel. Do not exceed the stipulated quantity of grease or the bellows may burst in service.

22 Fit the rack damper plunger assembly and adjust it as described in Section 3 of this Chapter.

23 Screw in the two eyebolts complete with circular type locknuts until the between eyebolt centres measurement and the distance between the centre of each eyebolt and the inner face of each locknut is as shown in Fig.8.6a.

24 The dimension required ·between the inner face of the rack housing must be as indicated in Fig.8.7.

25 It will be realised that a certain amount of trial and error will be required until all the measurements specified are attained. When the operation is complete, place the rack on a perfectly flat surface and set the eyebolts in their correct operational plane as shown in Fig.8.8.

26 A simple gauge may be made for this operation or an adjustable woodworker's angle used. When the eyebolts are correctly set, tighten locknuts to a torque of 43 lb/ft (5.9 mkg).

27 Refit the rubber bellows and securing circlips taking care not to tear the rubber during the operation.

6 Steering column - removal and refitting

1 Disconnect the brake and clutch pedal push rods and also the acclerator pedal linkage. The master cylinders can be unbolted and supported without disconnecting the fluid lines.

2 Remove the nuts from the steering column universal joint clevis bolts and withdraw the bolts by screwing the nuts onto their reverse ends (early models). On later models, the nut should be removed from the clamp bolt and the nut then used to extract the lower clevis bolt, Figs.8.2 and 8.3.

3 Disconnect the electrical leads from the fascia switches making quite sure to mark the leads before removing them.

4 Working from within the engine compartment, unscrew the nuts which secure the bottom of the steering column to the

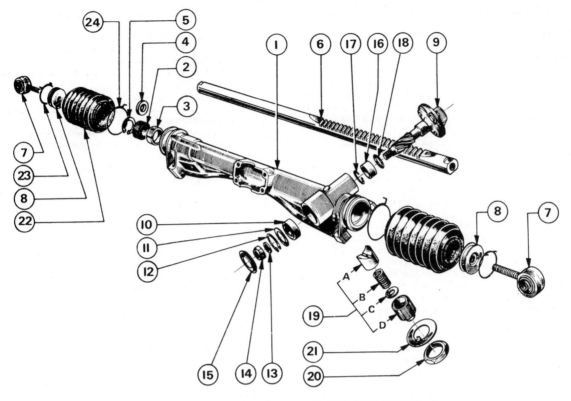

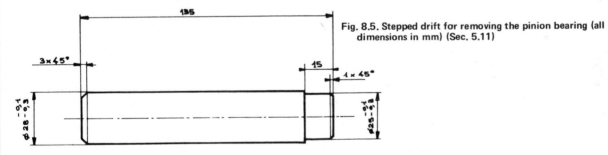

FIG. 8.4. STEERING GEAR – EXPLODED VIEW (SEC. 5)

1	Casing	8	Locknut	15	Cover plate	19D	Cap
2	Guide ring	9	Pinion and joint	16	Bearing	20	Locknut
3	Sleeve	10	Pinion bearing	17	Circlip	21	Tab washer
4	Shim	11	Shims	18	'O' ring	22	Bellows
5	Circlip	12	Circlip	19a	Plunger	23	Circlip
6	Rack	13	Shim	19b	Spring	24	Circlip
7	Eyebolt	14	Nut	19c	Shim (to Feb. 71 only)		

Fig. 8.5. Stepped drift for removing the pinion bearing (all dimensions in mm) (Sec. 5.11)

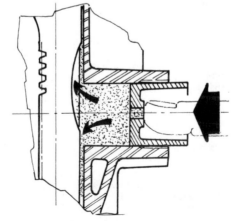

Fig. 8.6. Method of injecting grease into the steering gear using the rack damper plunger (Sec. 5.21)

bulkhead. Remove the bolt and nut from the upper support bracket and withdraw the complete steering column assembly with steering wheel attached into the interior of the car.

5 Refitting is a reversal of removal but set the wheel spokes in the horizontal position and ensure that the road wheels are in the 'straight ahead' position before coupling the column universal joint to the steering gear pinion. Insert the clevis pin in the flexible coupling and tighten its nut to 7 lb/ft (0.97 mkg).

7 Steering column flexible coupling - renewal

1 Remove either the steering column assembly or the steering gear as already described in this Chapter.
2 Remove the pinion assembly complete with flexible coupling as described in Section 5.
3 Obtain a repair kit which will contain a new flexible coupling piece and the necessary rivets (Part nos. 35748A and 23730Y).
4 Cut off the heads of the original rivets and drift them from their locations. As the upper flange is released, note the earthing spring which fits in the recess of the flexible coupling. Breakage of this spring in service can account for failure of horn and control switches and can easily be overlooked.
5 Use a bolt and nut to temporarily secure the flexible coupling components together while the new rivets are inserted.

8 Steering column - dismantling and reassembly

1 Prise out the central boss from the steering wheel, also the horn button and circlip, Fig. 8.2 and 8.3.
2 Unscrew and remove the steering wheel securing nut.
3 Withdraw the horn control bracket and spring and pull the steering wheel from the column splines. Should the steering wheel be difficult to remove, either use an extractor or invert the column and temporarily screw on the securing nut a turn or two. Place a small block under the nut and press down on the underside of the steering wheel hub.
4 Remove the steering column combined ignition switch and lock which is secured by two screws. Disconnect the two electrical lead connectors and then slide the switch over the top of the steering column.
5 Unscrew the retaining plate and remove the flexible bushing. The steering column shroud complete with switch and electrical leads can now be withdrawn.
6 Remove the upper and lower retaining plates and bushes from the shroud and withdraw the steering shaft upper section downwards.
7 Examine all components, particularly the bushes, for wear and renew as appropriate.
8 Reassembly is a reversal of dismantling.

9 Track rod ends - renewal

1 Refer to Fig.8.1.
2 Unscrew and remove the nut from the ball joint to steering arm tapered pin.
3 Using an extractor or wedges, disconnect the ball joints from the steering arms.
4 Holding the hexagonal adjuster nut (F) with one spanner unscrew the outer locknut ¼ turn. Unscrew the track rod end from the hexagonal nut without moving the position of the outer locknut.
5 With the track rod end removed, measure the length of the exposed threaded portion between the face of the locknut and the end of the threaded rod.
6 Position the locknut on the new track rod at the same position as originally fitted. Lightly grease the threads of the track rod end and screw it into the hexagonal adjuster nut until the adjuster nut abuts the locknut. Unscrew the track rod end ¼ turn and tighten the locknut, finger tight only.
7 Repeat the procedure for renewal of the opposite track rod

end. Fit the track rod ends to the steering arms.
8 The method described will provide an approximate setting of the original front wheel tracking but before the track rod lock nuts are fully tightened, the track must be checked as described in the following Section 11.

10 Steering geometry

1 Accurate front wheel alignment is essential for good steering and minimum tyre wear.
2 Wheel alignment embraces four factors: Camber, which is the angle at which the front wheels are set from the vertical, when viewed from the front of the vehicle. Positive camber is the amount (in degrees) that the wheels are inclined outwards from the vertical at their tops.
  Castor is the angle between the steering axis and a vertical line when viewed from each side of the vehicle. Positive castor is when the steering axis is included rearwards at the top.
  Steering axis inclination is the angle, when viewed from the front of the vehicle, between the vertical and an imaginary line drawn between the upper and lower stub axle carrier swivel ball joints.
  Toe-in is the amount by which the distance between the front inside edges of the road wheels (measured at hub height) is less than the diametrically opposite distance measured between the rear inside edges of the road wheels. Toe-out is specified for some vehicles and this is a greater measurement at the front inside edges of the wheel.
3 Checking and adjustment of toe-in (tracking) is described in the next Section.
4 The steering angles just described are either set during manufacture or in the case of the Camber angle, this can be altered by varying the shims (B) Fig. 7.5 shown in the preceding Chapter. Any variation of the Camber angle should be left to your Simca dealer who will have the necessary equipment for measuring these critical angles.
5 Two steering angles are shown in diagrammatic form in Fig.8.9 and reference should be made to the Specifications Section of this Chapter for the precise angles (in degrees).

11 Front wheel track - checking and adjustment

1 Although it is preferable to leave these operations to your Simca dealer, an approximate setting may be made which will be useful after renewal of any of the steering or suspension components and will at least permit the vehicle to be driven to the dealers for a more accurate check to be made, if necessary.
2 Place the vehicle on level ground with the tyres correctly inflated. Position the wheels in the 'straight ahead' position.
3 Obtain or make an alignment gauge. One may be easily made up from a piece of tubing or bar, suitably cranked to clear the engine/transmission unit with a bolt at one end to permit adjustment of its overall length.
4 With the gauge, measure the distance between the two inner wheel rims (at hub height) at the fronts of the road wheels.
5 Mark the tyre and then roll the vehicle either forward or backwards so that the mark on the tyre rotates 180°.
6 Measure the distance between the inner edges of the wheel rims at hub height at the rear of the road wheels. This second measurement should vary from that taken previously by being either between 0.019 in (0.5 mm) greater to give a toe-in characteristic or 0.059 in (1.5 mm) shorter to give a toe-out characteristic.
7 If the specified wheel alignment is not evident, loosen both locknuts on each of the two track rods and rotate the hexagon adjuster nuts (by an equal amount) ¼ turn at a time until on rechecking, the front wheel alignment falls within the tolerances specified.
8 Fully lighten the track rod locknuts, keeping the adjuster nuts still during the process and ensuring that the track rod end ball joints are in their correct attitudes to permit a full arc of

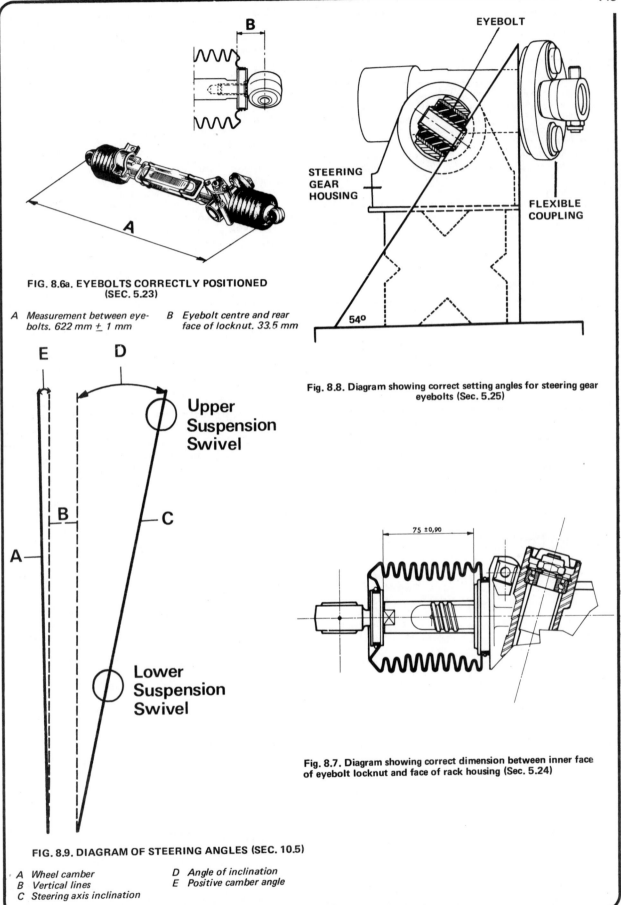

FIG. 8.6a. EYEBOLTS CORRECTLY POSITIONED (SEC. 5.23)

A Measurement between eyebolts. 622 mm ± 1 mm

B Eyebolt centre and rear
face of locknut. 33.5 mm

Fig. 8.8. Diagram showing correct setting angles for steering gear eyebolts (Sec. 5.25)

Fig. 8.7. Diagram showing correct dimension between inner face of eyebolt locknut and face of rack housing (Sec. 5.24)

FIG. 8.9. DIAGRAM OF STEERING ANGLES (SEC. 10.5)

A Wheel camber
B Vertical lines
C Steering axis inclination

D Angle of inclination
E Positive camber angle

travel during road use.

12 Wheels and tyres

1 The road wheels fitted to the Simca 1100 range are of pressed steel type, four bolt fixing, Fig.8.10.
2 To minimise tyre wear and to prevent steering wobble or vibration it is imperative to have the wheels balanced when the tyres are first fitted.
3 From time to time, check the security of the securing bolts and check that the bolt head recess in the wheel has not become enlarged or elongated. Where this is the case, the road wheel must be renewed.
4 Any deviation from even tread wear will indicate the need for rebalancing of the wheels or checking and adjusting of the steering angles.

13 Modifications

1 Track rod yokes have been redesigned for later vehicle and may be used for renewal of original components provided both left and righthand ones are changed and also the eyebolts renewed.
2 As from April 1970, the specified amount of lubricant in steering gear housing increased to 80 cc.
3 As from December 1970, steering gear bellows have been redesigned for installation without retaining rings.
4 As from February 1971, rack damper plunger shim omitted and a new longer spring fitted. When renewing plunger components, renew as complete assembly.
5 Certain changes to the steering column and universal joint design have been carried out. The shafts are interchangeable with earlier models but the ignition/steering lock switches may need renewal at the same time dependent upon make.

Fault finding chart/Steering

Before diagnosing faults from the following chart, check that any irregularities are not caused by:—

1 Binding brakes
2 Incorrect 'mix' of radial or crossply tyres
3 Incorrect tyre pressures
4 Misalignment of bodyframe.

Symptom	Reason/s	Remedy
Steering wheel can be moved before any sign of road wheel movement is apparent	Wear in linkage, gear or column couplings or track rod ends	Check for movement in all joints and gear and renew as required
Vehicle wanders and difficult to hold to a straight line	As above or wheel alignment incorrect or hub bearings loose or worn. Upper or lower suspension ball joints worn	Adjust or renew as necessary.
Steering stiff and heavy	Incorrect wheel alignment
Seizure of suspension or steering ball joints	Adjust or renew.
Wheel wobble and vibration	Roadwheels out of balance
Roadwheels buckled	Balance wheels
Renew wheels.
	Incorrect wheel alignment
Wear in steering joints
Wheel nuts loose	Check and adjust.
Renew.
Tighten.

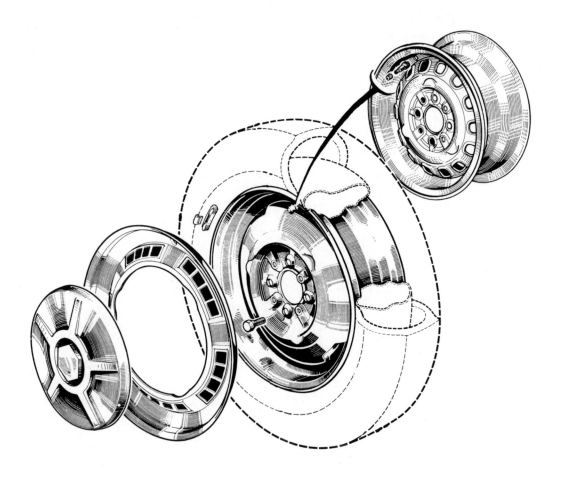

Fig. 8.10. Components of a roadwheel (Sec. 12.1)

Chapter 9 Rear suspension and hubs

Contents

Specifications

Type	Independent, trailing arms with torsion bars with anti-roll bar and telescopic type hydraulic dampers.

Torsion bars

Car	0.823 inch diameter
Identification	R.H. green paint spot
	L.H. yellow paint spot
Estate and van	0.874 inch diameter
Identification	R.H. red paint spot
	L.H. blue paint spot

Torque wrench settings

	lb/ft	mkg
Anchor bracket to crossmember bolts	50	6.9
Eyebolt to anchor bracket	54	7.5
Brake backplate to trailing arm bolts	16	2.2
Brake equaliser lever to anti-roll bar	15	2.1
Outer pivot housing to crossmember bolts	45	6.2
Anti-roll bar bracket to anchor bracket	12	1.7
Anti-roll bar link to trailing arm	16	2.2
Damper upper mounting nuts	9.5	1.3
Damper lower mounting bolts	16	2.2
Assembly attachment to bodyframe bolts	54	7.5

1 General description

1 The independent type rear suspension, Fig.9.1 comprises trailing arms and transverse torsion bars assisted by telescopic type hydraulic dampers.

2 The rear suspension assembly is an independent unit attached to the bodyframe by means of four rubber mountings, Fig.9.2.

3 The rear suspension crossmember supports the brake equaliser bracket and the trailing arms have stub axles located at their rear ends upon which the hub assemblies run on two roller bearings, Fig.9.3.

4 An anti-roll bar is fitted and located upon it is the brake equaliser actuating lever.

2 Rear hubs - removal, dismantling, reassembly, refitting

1 Jack up the rear of the vehicle and support adequately on stands or blocks.

2 Remove the road wheel and the brake drum (two screws).

3 Using a screwdriver, prise the grease cap from the hub.

4 Unscrew and remove the hub nut after relieving the peening and withdraw the thrust washer.

5 Withdraw the hub complete with the two roller bearings from the stub axle.

6 If the bearings are to be renewed due to wear, then their tracks must be removed by drifting them from the hub. Drift in new tracks using a tubular drift.

7 Every 12,000 miles (19000 km) the hub should be withdrawn as described and the bearings thoroughly washed in paraffin (not removed) and repacked with recommended wheel bearing grease.

8 Remove the oil seal from the recess in the brake back plate and drift a new one into position.

9 Check that the space between the bearings within the hub is half filled over its entire length with the correct grade of grease and fit the hub assembly to the stub axle.

10 Fit the thrust washer, engaging its tongue correctly, screw on the hub nut and tighten it to a torque of 10 lb/ft (1.4 mkg) at the same time rotating the hub. Back off the nut until the hub turns freely without my end-float. Peen the nut collar into the stub axle groove to retain it in the predetermined position.

11 Refit the brake drum and securing screws, fill the grease cap half full with grease and tap it into position in the hub.

12 Fit the road wheel and lower the jack.

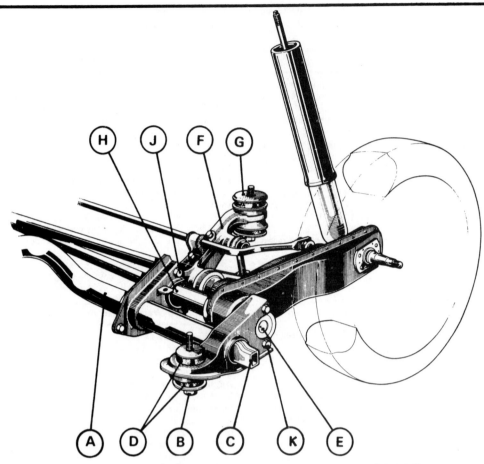

FIG. 9.1. REAR SUSPENSION — GENERAL ARRANGEMENT (SEC. 1.1)

A Tubular crossmember	C Jacking point	F Anchor bracket	J Anchor bracket bolt
B Bodyframe mounting bracket	D Mounting bushes	G Bodyframe rubber mounting	K Outer pivot housing bolt
	E Outer pivot	H Trailing arm pivot shaft	

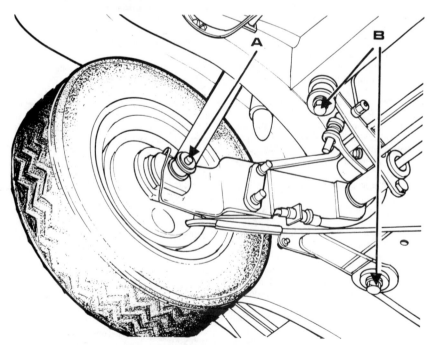

FIG. 9.2. REAR SUSPENSION ASSEMBLY ATTACHMENT POINTS (SEC. 3.12)

A   Rear damper lower mounting   B   To bodyframe

3 Suspension assembly - removal

1 Where major servicing of the rear suspension is intended, it is recommended that the assembly is first removed from the vehicle.
2 Jack up the rear of the vehicle and support securely on blocks or stands. Remove the rear roadwheels.
3 If the rear suspension assembly is to be dismantled extensively for a major overhaul then the torsion bars should be released at this stage.
4 Using a tool similar to the one described in Chapter 7 for the front torsion bars, counter the tension of one bar sufficiently to unscrew the adjuster nut (F) from the anchor lever (B) Fig.9.4.
5 Unscrew and remove the eyebolt (E) eyebolt retaining bolt (G).
6 Withdraw the anchor lever until it reaches the smooth recess of the splined hub (H).
7 Remove the tool slowly against the reaction of the torsion bar torque then repeat the foregoing operations for the other torsion bar.
8 Disconnect the hydraulic hose from the brake equaliser inlet union (See Chapter 10) and plug the hose and union to prevent loss of fluid and any dirt entering.
9 Disconnect and remove the exhaust silencer as described in Chapter 3.
10 Disconnect the handbrake cable from the equaliser on the handbrake operating rod.
11 Disconnect the damper lower mountings.
12 Place a trolly jack or other suitable support under the suspension assembly and then unscrew and remove the two bolts (B) and the rear damper lower mounting bolt (A) see Fig.9.2.
13 Lower the suspension assembly and remove it from beneath the vehicle.

4 Suspension assembly - dismantling and reassembly

1 Having removed the assembly from the vehicle and released the torsion bar tension, further dismantling may be undertaken to permit renewal of any worn or damaged components.
2 Disconnect the flexible brake hoses from the brake back plates and plug the hoses and the orifices in the back plates.
3 Disconnect the handbrake cables from the drums. This is achieved by first compressing the springs and extracting the grooved bushes which retain the outer cables to the backplate. Remove the brake drums and hub assemblies as described in Section 2 of this Chapter.
4 Remove the brake equaliser spring and the anti-roll bar from its end connections and brackets, Fig.9.5.
5 Unscrew and remove the securing bolts which retain the suspension control arm outer brackets and the torsion bar anchor brackets to the crossmember. Remove both suspension arms, torsion bars and anchor brackets from the crossmember as one assembly.
6 Remove the suspension arm and anchor bracket assemblies from the ends of the torsion bars.
7 Unscrew and remove the splined hub from each of the anchor brackets.
8 Due to the need for special extraction and fitting tools, the suspension arm, anchor bracket and outer pivot must not be further dismantled. Should wear be observed in the rubber bushes or other mounting components then the complete assembly should be either exchanged for a reconditioned unit or serviced by your Simca dealer who will have the necessary refitting jigs.
9 Reassembly should commence by screwing the splined hubs (H). Fig.9.4 into the anchor brackets until they seat and then unscrewing one half turn.
10 Clean the ends of the torsion bars and lightly grease with

wheel bearing grease.
11 Renew the rubber dust covers if they show signs of deterioration.
12 The torsion bars are indentified for left and righthand fitting as follows: car R.H. green L.H. yellow, estate and van R.H. red L.H. blue. Never attempt to mark a torsion bar by filing or scratching as this may lead to premature failure.
13 Pull the suspension arms towards each other and at the same time insert the torsion bars into their splined hubs at each side of the suspension assembly.
14 Fit the assembled components (torsion bars and suspension arms) to the crossmember and locate the retaining bolts, retaining the nuts with new tab washers.
15 Refit the anti-roll bar.
16 Reconnect the brake backplate, hubs and drums and the brake hoses and cables. Refit the brake equaliser spring.
17 Locate the anchor levers to the smooth recesses of the splined hubs.
18 The suspension assembly is now ready for fitting to the vehicle as described in the next Section.

5 Suspension assembly - refitting and torsion bar setting

1 Refitting is essentially a reversal of removal but great care must be taken to ensure that the sequence of mounting components at the points of attachment is as shown in Fig.9.2.
2 Reconnect the hydraulic brake hose to the brake equaliser and bleed the brakes as described in the next Chapter.
3 If the torsion bars were disconnected during the dismantling operations then refit each of the anchor levers to the torsion bar splines so that the ends of the levers almost impinge on the boss of the eyebolt securing bolt hole, Fig.9.6.
4 Apply the necessary leverage, using the tool referred to in removal procedure, so that the eyebolt can be fitted to the anchor and then bolted to the anchor bracket.
5 Remove the tool and then check and adjust the torsion bar setting in conjunction with the front torsion bars to provide the specified ground clearance as described in Chapter 7.
6 Check and adjust if necessary, the setting of the brake equaliser as described in the next Chapter.

6 Rear wheel alignment

1 The suspension angles at the rear are all set during manufacture and no adjustment is possible.
2 Should the track or other angles be suspect and be reflected in abnormal wear to the rear tyres (and there is no distortion of the suspension components due to collision damage), the hub bearings and the trailing arm bonded rubber bushes should be checked for wear and renewed if necessary.

7 Dampers - removal, testing - refitting

1 The procedure for these operations is similar to that described for the front dampers in Chapter 7.
2 Take particular care to ensure that the upper and lower mounting components are fitted in the correct sequence, Fig.9.7.

8 Anti-roll bar - removal and refitting

1 The rear anti-roll bar is attached at each of its ends to the trailing suspension arm and to the anchor bracket. Rubber mountings are fitted and these should be checked regularly for deterioration and renewed if necessary.
2 Components of the anti-roll bar mountings are shown in Fig.9.5.

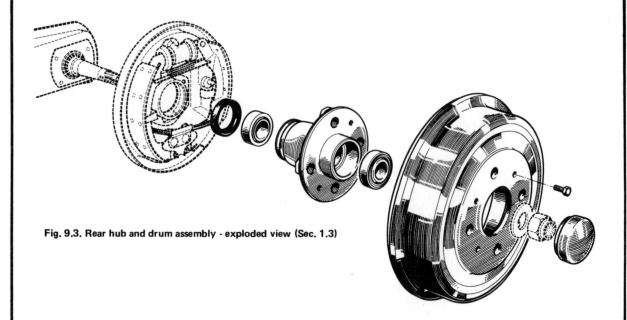

Fig. 9.3. Rear hub and drum assembly - exploded view (Sec. 1.3)

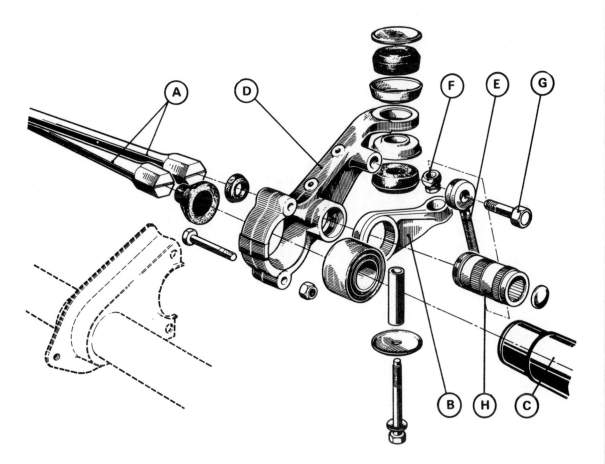

FIG. 9.4. REAR SUSPENSION TORSION BAR AND ANCHOR BRACKET — EXPLODED VIEW (SEC. 3.4)

A Torsion bars C Trailing arm pivot shaft E Eyebolt G Eyebolt retaining bolt
B Anchor lever D Anchor bracket F Adjuster nut H Splined hub

Fault finding chart/Rear suspension and hubs

Symptom	Reason/s	Remedy
Excessive tyre wear	Wear in hub bearings	Renew bearings.
	Dampers inoperative	Renew.
	Wear in trailing arm bushes	Arrange renewal with Simca dealer.
	Tyre pressures too low	Inflate to specified pressures (cold).
Wheel wobble and vibration	Road wheels out of balance	Re balance on or off car
	Road wheels buckled	Renew.

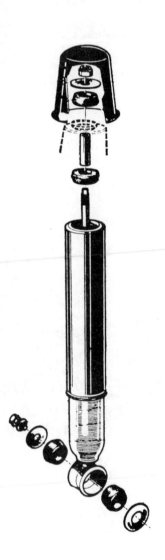

Fig. 9.7. Rear damper upper and lower mounting components
(Sec. 7)

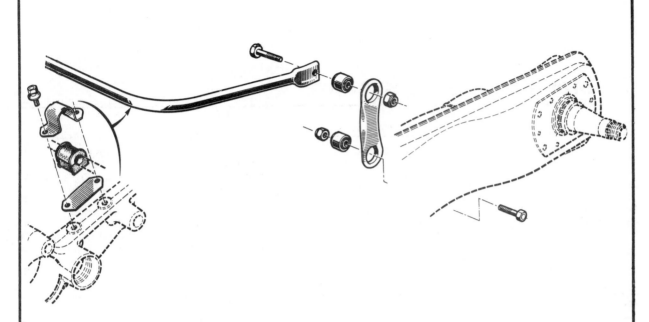

Fig. 9.5. Components of the anti-roll bar mounting (one side) (Sec. 9.5)

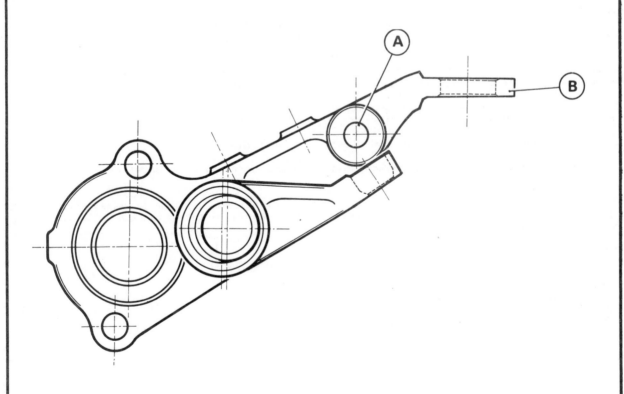

FIG. 9.6. DIAGRAM FOR INITIAL SETTING OF REAR SUSPENSION
ANCHOR LEVER TO TORSION BAR SPLINED HUB (SEC. 5.3)

A   Eyebolt securing bolt hole boss in anchor bracket   B   Anchor bracket

Chapter 10 Braking system

Contents

Specifications

System type ... ... Front disc and rear drum, hydraulically operated with servo assistance on specified models or as option. Single or dual hydraulic circuit according to operating territory regulations. Handbrake - mechanical, rear wheels only.

Application

Dual circuit, Lockheed 17.5 mm diameter master cylinder, remote fluid reservoir (combined for clutch and brake), residual check valve and leak indicator switch

E series 1969 on U.S.A.
F series 1970 on Sweden

Dual circuit, Teves 17.5 mm diameter master cylinder, twin interconnected fluid reservoirs, leak indicator switch

U.S.A. and Sweden from vehicle No F2/4091192
Norway from G series (Dec. 70) on

Dual circuit, Lockheed 19 mm diameter, twin interconnected fluid reservoirs. Leak indicator and direct (master-vac) servo*

G. series (1971 on) U.S.A.
H series (1972 on) Sweden, Norway, Switzerland

Single circuit, Teves 17.5 mm master cylinder, servo option*

F series (1970 on)

Single circuit, Lockheed 17.5 mm master cylinder, servo option*

As an alternative to the Teves (single) master cylinder

*For LHD vehicles, the direct action Master-vac type servo is fitted and for RHD vehicles, the Hydro-vac remote type unit is installed due to the lack of space ahead of the bulkhead mounted master cylinder. (LHD - 19.0 mm diameter Lockheed or Teves master cylinder - RHD 25.4 mm diameter Lockheed master cylinder).

Front brakes

Type	Teves disc and caliper
Minimum friction pad thickness (before renewal) (not including backing plate)	3/32 in
Disc diameter	9.173 in
Disc thickness	0.433 in
Maximum permissible disc run-out	0.008 in
Minimum thickness after regrinding	0.39 in

Rear brakes

Type	Bendix drum with single operating cylinder and leading and trailing shoes
Drum inside diameter	8.275 in
outside diameter	9.764 in
Friction linings (leading)	8.189 in x 1.378 in
(trailing)	6.141 in x 1.378 in
Wheel operating cylinder (diameter)	
up to 1970	11/16 in
from 1970	¾ in
Brake hydraulic fluid	Lockheed 55

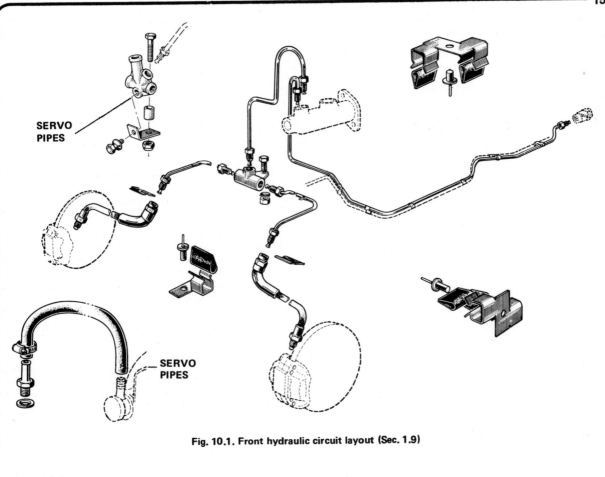

SERVO
PIPES

SERVO
PIPES

Fig. 10.1. Front hydraulic circuit layout (Sec. 1.9)

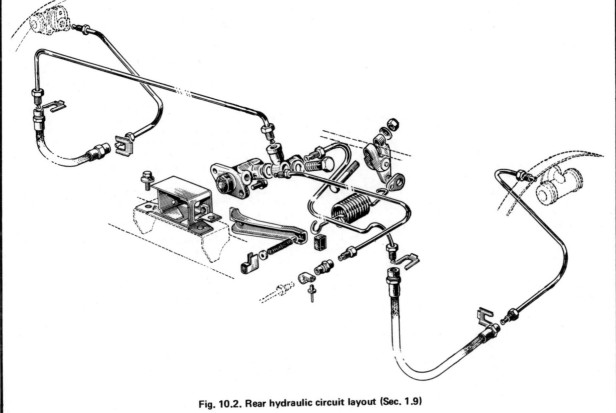

Fig. 10.2. Rear hydraulic circuit layout (Sec. 1.9)

Torque wrench settings

	lb ft
Brake drum to rear hub	11.5
Equalizer lever to anti-roll bar	15
Stop lamp switch to master cylinder	45
Rear brake backplate to suspension arm	16
Caliper to stub axle carrier	35
Reservoir to master cylinder securing nut	51
Master cylinder screwed end plug	72
Residual valve (Lockheed master cylinder)	36
Master cylinder stop screw	7.2

1   General description

1   The braking system is of hydraulic type with discs on the front wheels and drums on the rear.
2   The handbrake operates mechanically on the two rear wheels only.
3   The brakes are actuated by a foot operated pedal and the hydraulic circuit is supplied by fluid contained in a reservoir.
4   Single line hydraulic circuits are fitted as standard but dual circuits are specified in many territories.
5   The assistance of servo is available as an option on all models.
6   A brake equaliser valve is mounted on the rear suspension crossmember and is actuated by the position of the anti-roll bar under varying loads. The valve automatically varies the braking effort to the rear wheels according to the vehicle load. Adjustment of the valve is critical to ensure the correct braking forces are applied under all loading and road surface conditions.
7   The front disc brakes are self adjusting but the rear drums require adjustment as described in Section 3 of this Chapter.
8   Master cylinders used in single circuit systems may be of Lockheed or Teves manufacture and the units are not interchangeable.
9   The layout of the front and rear hydraulic circuits is shown in Figs. 10.1 and 10.2.
10   According to year of manufacture, the design of components will vary slightly and with a dual circuit, the supply pipes for front and rear circuits will come independently from each cylinder of the dual (tandem) master cylinder unit.

2   Disc brake pads - inspection, removal and refitting

1   Although the disc brakes are self adjusting, pad wear should be checked every 3000 miles.
2   Jack up the vehicle and remove the roadwheels.
3   Inspect the caliper unit for signs of oil or grease. Where these are evident, then the source must be found and the leak cured. Almost certainly it will be due to a defective hub oil seal or leaking caliper unit piston seals.
4   Prise out the cover plate (1) Fig.10.3.
5   Withdraw the retaining pins (2 and 3) and the spring (4).
6   Extract the brake pads (5 and 6) using pliers if necessary to pull them out.
7   Clean the inside of the caliper unit using a rag moistened with clean fuel.
8   Check the thickness of the friction pad (not including its metal backing plate). If the thickness is 3/32 in or less, renew the pads. Pads must be renewed as complete front wheel sets of four to maintain even braking.
9   If new pads are to be fitted, the caliper unit pistons must be pushed back into their cylinders to accommodate the thicker pads. Use a flat lever to do this but ensure that each piston is pressed squarely in and only sufficiently to enable the pad to enter the caliper unit opening. During this operation, the fluid reservoir level will rise and it may be necessary to syphon some off.
10   Fit the pads into the caliper unit recess (photo).
11   Fit the spring which retains the pads (photo).

12   Fit the pins, using a screwdriver if necessary to ensure their alignment with the pad and caliper unit holes (photo).
13   Fit the cover plate (photo).
14   Depress the brake foot pedal several times and then check the reservoir level, topping up if necessary.

3   Drum brakes - adjustment

1   Every 3000 miles, or should excessive travel of the foot pedal indicate it necessary, adjust the rear brakes.
2   Jack up each rear road wheel in turn and check that the handbrake is fully released.
3   Looking directly at the heads of the two cam adjusters located on the upper half of the brake backplate, turn the left hand adjuster anti-clockwise until the wheel locks, release the cam adjuster just enough to permit the wheel to turn without any drag.
4   Turn the right hand adjuster clockwise until the wheel locks and then again release it until the wheel is just free to turn without any drag.
5   Repeat the procedure on the opposite rear wheel.
6   It is probable that in the absence of a proper brake adjusting spanner, an ordinary open-ended type will have to be ground down due to the restricted access to the cam adjuster heads.
7   Lower the jacks.

4   Drum brakes - shoe inspection, removal and refitting

1   Every 6000 miles, the rear brake shoe friction linings should be examined for wear.
2   Jack up the rear of the vehicle, ensure that the handbrake is fully released and remove the roadwheels.
3   Unscrew and remove the two drum retaining screws (photo).
4   Remove the drum (photo). If the drum is slightly grooved due to wear, it may be necessary to slacken the cam adjusters before the drum can be withdrawn.
5   Inspect the linings for wear. If they are worn down to the rivet heads or nearly so, the shoes must be renewed. If they are stained or saturated with oil or grease they must be renewed and the source of leakage found. This will almost certainly be a leaking wheel cylinder or a defective hub oil seal.
6   The two linings in each drum may be found to have worn at different rates, in which case, renew the identical shoe in each drum simultaneously.
7   Always renew linings on an exchange shoe basis as hand riveted linings are never satisfactory and take a long time to bed down as they are not ground to contour, after fitting, as exchange shoes are.
8   Remove the brake shoes by first referring to Fig.10.4.
9   Unhook the longer shoe retracting spring, noting carefully the shoe web hole into which it locates.
11   At this stage note the position of the shoes in respect of leading and trailing edges (where the friction lining abuts the end of the shoe or leaves a portion of the shoe surface exposed). Where necessary, make a sketch to ensure exact replacement of the shoe assembly.
12   Prise the shoe steady clips (13) from their location by

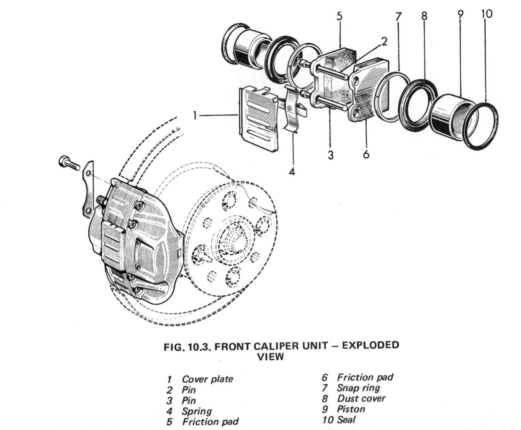

FIG. 10.3. FRONT CALIPER UNIT — EXPLODED VIEW

1 Cover plate	6 Friction pad
2 Pin	7 Snap ring
3 Pin	8 Dust cover
4 Spring	9 Piston
5 Friction pad	10 Seal

2.10 Fitting a disc pad

2.11 Fitting disc pad retaining spring

2.12 Inserting the disc pad retaining pins

2.13 Fitting the caliper cover plate

4.3 Removing a drum securing screw

4.4 Removing a rear brake drum

inserting a screwdriver behind them. Remove clips (4) and washer (5) and withdraw the handbrake operating lever (9).

13 Pull the upper ends of the shoes apart and remove the link (2).

14 Press both shoes in the downward direction until their lower ends are disengaged from their pivot guides.

15 Remove the shoes complete with small spring (12).

16 Place a stout elastic band round the wheel cylinder to retain the pistons in their cylinder and on no account depress the brake foot pedal while the shoes or drum are removed or the pistons will be ejected from the wheel cylinder and the hydraulic system will have to be bled.

17 Clean the inside surfaces of the brake drum by brushing or wiping with a fuel soaked rag if necessary. Examine the friction surfaces of the drum for scoring and if this is severe then the drum must either be exchanged for a reconditioned one or machined by a workshop equipped for the task (section 20).

18 Commence refitting by placing the shoes, correctly positioned (with respect to leading and trailing ends) flat down on a bench. Engage the lower, smaller, retracting spring. Set the cam adjusters to the fully released position.

19 Maintain outward pressure and locate the lower ends of the shoes in the backplate pivot guides. Prise the upper ends of the shoes apart behind the hub flange so that the link can be inserted between the two shoe webs.

20 Connect the ends of the upper, longer retracting spring in the web holes by using a pair of pliers.

21 Locate the end of one shoe in the wheel cylinder piston and then prise the opposite shoe into position against the force of the retracting spring. An adjustable spanner makes a useful levering tool for this (photo).

22 Fit the shoe steady springs into position (photo).

23 Fit the handbrake operating lever (9) the clip (4) and washer (5) and reconnect the handbrake cable to the operating lever.

24 Grease the handbrake cable guide on the backplate and the cam adjusters, very sparingly with high melting point grease.

25 Refit the brake drum and the two securing screws.

26 Adjust the brakes as described in the preceding Section, refit the roadwheel and lower the jacks.

5 Handbrake - adjustment

1 The handbrake is normally automatically adjusted when the rear drum brakes are adjusted. However, after extended service, the cable may stretch and the following procedure should be carried out. This method should also be used when a new cable or handbrake assembly has been installed.

2 Fully release the handbrake and then pull the handbrake up three notches (clicks).

3 Release the locknut (A) on the cable equalising yoke and adjust nut (B) Fig.10.5

4 Adjustment is correct when the cables are just taut and the rear wheels are fully locked when the lever is pulled up four notches (clicks).

5 When adjustment is complete, hold nut (B) quite still and tighten the locknut (A).

6 Handbrake assembly - renewal

1 The handbrake assembly comprises three sub assemblies, the lever, the operating rod and yoke and the cable.

2 A broken or overstretched cable can only be renewed as a unit as fittings and ends are not detachable.

3 Wear or damage to the rod and yoke can be repaired by renewal of the components affected.

4 It is possible to renew the lever ratchet as a separate component after dismantling by removal of the circlips and crosspins. Occasional application of grease to the ratchet and quadrant notches will help to reduce wear. Application of the handbrake with the ratchet button depressed will also increase the life of the lever components.

5 Details of the handbrake assembly are shown in Fig.10.6.

7 Hydraulic brake pipes - inspection, removal and refitting

1 Periodically inspect the rigid pipes for corrosion. It is advantageous to spray the pipe runs occasionally with zinc based paint to arrest and prevent rust. An alternative method is to wipe them over from time to time with a grease soaked rag. Road de-icing chemicals currently in use will quickly attack exposed hydraulic pipes even if they are specified as 'stainless' double walled type.

2 Periodically inspect the front and rear flexible brake hoses. Check them for chafing and rubbing and pinch them in a tight radius so that any perishing or cracking will be immediately obvious. Renew the flexible hoses should they show any sign of deterioration.

3 The front flexible hoses should be removed by first unscrewing the rigid to flexible pipe unions. Hold the flexible hoses perfectly still during this operation. With the union uncoupled, unscrew the flexible hose from the caliper unit, rotating the hose at the same time so that it does not twist or kink.

4 Refitting the front flexible hoses is a reversal of removal, screwing the hoses first into the caliper units and then holding them quite still with a spanner while the rigid pipe is connected and the union tightened.

5 Removal and refitting the rear flexible hoses is similar to that for the front hoses except that both ends are retained by securing clips and the hose should be held quite still while the union at each end is screwed into it, Fig.10.2.

6 Always wipe any oil or grease from a flexible hose as quickly as possible, using a fuel soaked rag.

8 Disc brake calipers - removal, servicing, refitting

1 Jack up the front of the vehicle and support securely.

2 Remove the road wheel.

3 Withdraw the disc pads as described in Section 2.

4 Unscrew and remove the two bolts which secure the caliper to the mounting lugs on the backplate.

5 Slide the caliper sideways from the backplate.

6 If the caliper is to be removed entirely, then the flexible hose must be disconnected from it and both the hose and the caliper orifice plugged to prevent loss of hydraulic fluid and ingress of dirt. Where the caliper is not to be removed from the vehicle, it may be tied up with wire to avoid strain on the hose.

7 Withdraw the spring rings (7) which secure the rubber dust excluder (8) Fig.10.3.

8 Remove the dust excluders and then unscrew and remove the bleed nipple (11) from the caliper body.

9 Seal the fluid inlet port with a finger and retain the piston on the side nearer this port.

10 Apply a tyre pump to the bleed nipple hole and expel the piston furthest from the hole.

11 Insert a fine drift or rod through the fluid inlet port and eject the other piston from its cylinder bore. Take care during these operations that the pistons do not drop to the floor and do not score the cylinder walls with the drift. Identify the pistons with a piece of masking tape so that they will be refitted to their original bores.

12 Pick out the two seals (10) from the grooves in the cylinder bores. Use a sharp probe for this and do not let it slip or it may score the cylinder walls.

13 This should be the limit of dismantling, do not separate the two halves of the caliper body but if leaks or corrosion are evident, change the unit for a factory exchange assembly.

14 Examine the surfaces of the piston and the internal surfaces of the cylinders. If any scratches, scoring or 'bright' areas are evident, renew the complete caliper.

15 Obtain a repair kit which will contain all the necessary seals. Observe absolute cleanliness during the following operations.

16 Smear the inside of the cylinders with clean hydraulic fluid and locate the new seals into their grooves, using the fingers only to manipulate them.

17 Dip the ends of the pistons in clean hydraulic fluid and insert

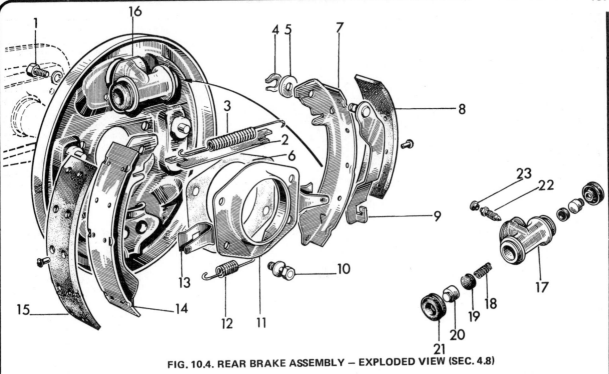

FIG. 10.4. REAR BRAKE ASSEMBLY — EXPLODED VIEW (SEC. 4.8)

1 Bolt	7 Brake shoe (trailing)	13 Clip	18 Spring
2 Connecting link	8 Friction lining	14 Brake shoe (leading)	19 Seal
3 Spring	9 Handbrake operating lever	15 Friction lining	20 Piston
4 Clip	10 Bolt	16 Wheel cylinder	21 Dust excluder
5 Washer	11 Oil seal carrier	17 Wheel operating	22 Bleed nipple
6 Gasket	12 Spring	cylinder (exploded view	23 Dust cap

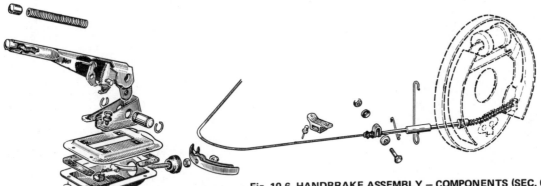

Fig. 10.6. HANDBRAKE ASSEMBLY — COMPONENTS (SEC. 6.5)

4.21 Prising a brake shoe in or out of its location

4.22 Fitting a shoe steady spring

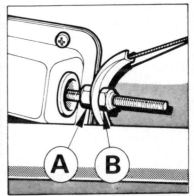

Fig. 10.5. Handbrake cable adjusting nut (B) and locknut (A) (Sec. 5.3)

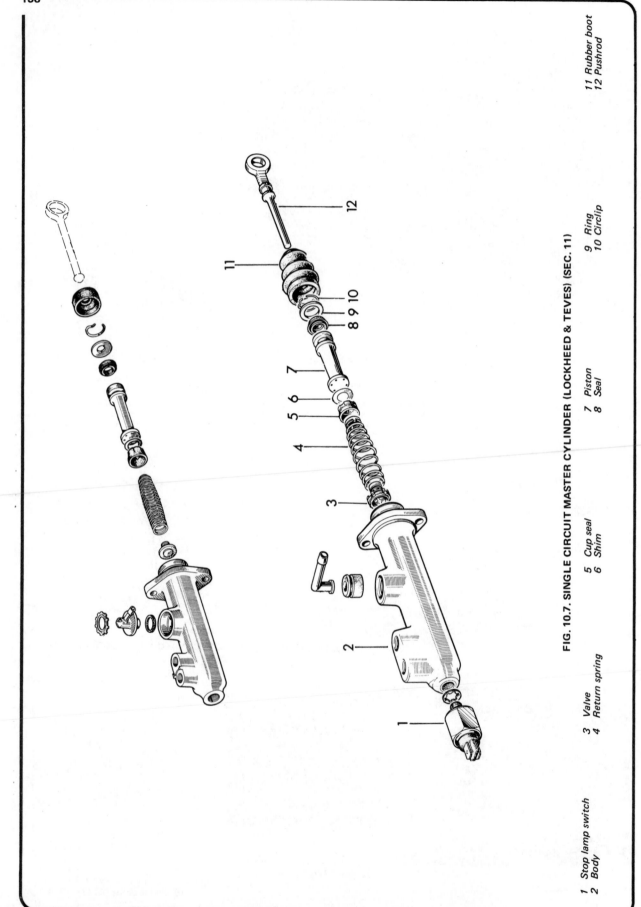

FIG. 10.7. SINGLE CIRCUIT MASTER CYLINDER (LOCKHEED & TEVES) (SEC. 11)

1 Stop lamp switch
2 Body
3 Valve
4 Return spring
5 Cup seal
6 Shim
7 Piston
8 Seal
9 Ring
10 Circlip
11 Rubber boot
12 Pushrod

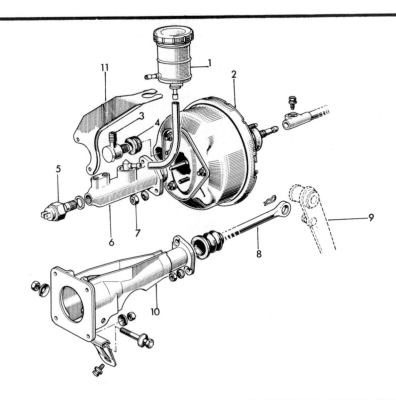

FIG. 10.8. MASTER CYLINDER, SINGLE CIRCUIT, TEVES FITTED WITH SERVO (SEC. 11.b)

1	Fluid reservoir	4	Seal
2	Servo unit	5	Stop lamp switch
3	Connection to manifold	6	Master cylinder

7	Master cylinder securing nut	9	Brake pedal arm
8	Operating rod	10	Servo unit support
		11	Reservoir support

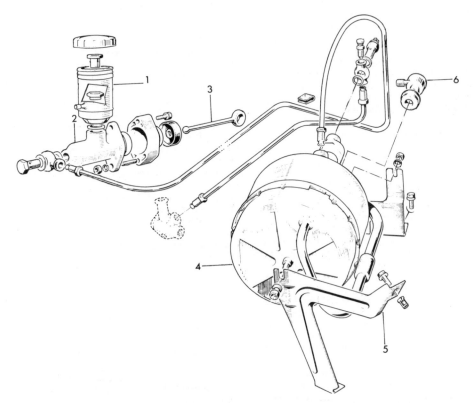

FIG. 10.9. SERVO UNIT (HYDRO VAC) AND MASTER CYLINDER — REMOTE (SEC. 11.C.1)

1	Fluid reservoir	4	Servo unit
2	Master cylinder	5	Servo support bracket
3	Pushrod	6	Non-return valve and manifold connection

them (solid end first) into the cylinder bores. Use a twisting motion and keep them quite square as they are pushed in to their fullest extent. The rims at the open ends of the pistons are very slightly stepped for the purpose of reducing brake squeal. The angle of the step must lie at 45° to the horizontal when viewed through the friction pad opening with the cut back portion of the rim at the top and the apex of the angle furthest from your view. This setting must be borne in mind when pressing the pistons into their bores and twisting the pistons before they are fully inserted.

18 Fit the rubber dust excluders and their spring rings.

19 Secure the caliper unit to the backplate lug, reconnect the fluid hose and refit the friction pads and spring and pins as described in Section 2.

20 Bleed the brakes as described in Sections 18 or 19 according to circuit type.

21 Refit the roadwheel, lower the jack.

9 Drum brake wheel operating cylinder - removal, servicing, refitting

1 Jack up the rear of the vehicle, remove the roadwheel.

2 Remove the drum and brake shoes as described in Section 4.

3 Disconnect the hydraulic fluid hose from the wheel cylinder and plug the hose.

4 Remove the two securing bolts which retain the wheel cylinder to the backplate, Fig.10.4.

5 Remove the wheel cylinder.

6 Peel off the rubber dust excluders (21) from each end of the unit and the eject the internal components - pistons, spring and seals. This may be done by tapping the cylinder carefully on a piece of wood until the pistons emerge or by removing the bleed nipple and applying a tyre pump to the nipple orifice.

7 Wash all components in hydraulic fluid and examine the piston and cylinder internal surfaces for scratches, scoring or bright areas. Where these are evident, renew the complete wheel cylinder assembly on an exchange basis.

8 Obtain a repair kit which will contain all the necessary seals. Observe absolute cleanliness during the following operations.

9 Lubricate the bore of the cylinder with clean hydraulic fluid and insert one seal, one piston and one dust excluder at one end of the unit. Insert the spring from the opposite end, followed by the seal, piston and dust cover. Note that the lips of both seals face inwards.

10 Refit the cylinder to the backplate, refit the shoes and drum. Reconnect the fluid hose.

11 Bleed the brakes as described in either Section 18 or Section 19 according to circuit type.

12 Adjust the rear brakes (Section 3) refit the road wheel, lower the jack.

10 Master cylinders - servicing - general

1 A number of different types of master cylinder have been fitted according to vehicle model. The master cylinder may be of Lockheed or Teves manufacture for single or tandem operation according to the circuit employed. Where servo assisted brakes are installed then the master cylinder may be designed as an integral part of the servo assembly operated directly by the foot pedal operating rod (LHD vehicles). The servo is installed remotely from the master cylinder on RHD vehicles due to the lack of space ahead of the master cylinder/brake pedal assembly.

2 Modifications have been carried out to the internal components of some master cylinders and in view of this and the differing types of cylinder which may be encountered it is imperative to specify the vehicle manufacturing details as extensively and completely as possible when ordering spares or repair kits. If in doubt, exchange the complete master cylinder for the correct replacement unit.

3 In the following Sections one of each type of master cylinder is covered but apart from component detail differences, the operations for all types are similar.

11 Master cylinder (single circuit) - removal and refitting

a) Without servo assistance, Fig.10.7.

1 Disconnect the master cylinder push-rod (12) from the brake pedal by removing the split pin from the cross shaft.

2 Disconnect the leads from the brake stop lamp switch (1).

3 Remove the filler cap from the remote reservoir and plug the feed tube to the master cylinder from within the reservoir.

4 Disconnect the single inlet and two outlet fluid pipes from the master cylinder.

5 Plug the three holes in the master cylinder to prevent the entry of dirt.

6 Remove the two retaining nuts and washers which secure the master cylinder to the engine bulk head and lift off the unit.

7 Expel the fluid from the master cylinder by depressing the operating rod several times. **Do not allow hydraulic brake fluid to come into contact with the bodywork or it will act as a paint stripper.**

8 Refitting is a reversal of removal, finally bleed the brakes as described in Section 18.

b) With servo assistance (LHD)

1 On left hand drive models, the servo forms part of the master cylinder assembly, Fig.10.8.

2 Disconnect the leads from the stop lamp switch.

3 Remove the fluid reservoir filler cap and plug the hole through which fluid is supplied to the master cylinder.

4 Disconnect the fluid pipes from the master cylinder by unscrewing the unions. Plug the holes to prevent entry of dirt.

5 Unscrew and remove the two retaining nuts (7) and withdraw the master cylinder from its locating studs.

6 Expel fluid from the master cylinder by depressing the piston several times, using a thin rod.

7 Refitting is a reversal of removal, finally bleed the brakes as described later in this Chapter.

c) With servo assistance (RHD)

1 On right hand drive models, due to lack of space within the engine compartment ahead of the brake pedal, the servo unit is sited remotely from the brake master cylinder, Fig.10.9.

2 Syphon out the hydraulic fluid from the reservoir.

3 Unscrew and remove the securing nut from within the reservoir, retaining the rubber seal, Fig.10.10.

4 Swing the reservoir to one side but do not disconnect the clutch fluid supply pipe which uses the same reservoir.

5 Uncouple the banjo union at the end of the master cylinder, Fig.10.11.

6 Unscrew and remove the two securing nuts and lift the master cylinder from its studs, Fig.10.12.

7 Expel hydraulic fluid from the master cylinder by depressing the piston several times.

8 Refitting is a reversal of removal but ensure that the two copper sealing washers (A) are correctly fitted, one each side of the banjo union, Fig.10.13.

9 Bleed the system as described later in this Chapter.

12 Master cylinder (dual circuit) - removal and refitting

a) Lockheed without servo assistance.

1 Disconnect the brake pedal operating rod.

2 Plug the internal outlet holes of the fluid reservoir.

3 Disconnect both inlet pipes from the master cylinder.

4 Disconnect both outlet pipes from the master cylinder (front circuit from union nearest engine bulkhead).

5 Plug the holes in the master cylinder to prevent the entry of dirt.

6 After removal of the nuts remove the master cylinder from the bulkhead securing studs.

7 Expel the fluid from the master cylinder by operating the pushrod.

8 Refitting is a reversal of removal, finally bleed the system as

Fig. 10.10. Unscrewing the securing nut from within the reservoir, - single type master cylinder (Sec. 11.C.2)

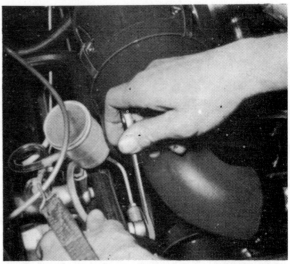

Fig. 10.11. Disconnecting the master cylinder outlet pipe, single type master cylinder fitted with servo (Sec. 11.C.5)

Fig. 10.12. Removing the master cylinder (single) leaving the clutch master cylinder in position (Sec. 11.C.6)

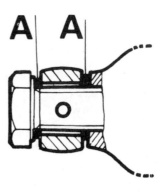

Fig. 10.13. Master cylinder fitted with servo - sealing washers on banjo union (Sec. 11.C.8)

Fig. 10.14. TEVES master cylinder (17.5 mm) - disconnecting the front circuit supply pipe (Sec. 12.B.2)

Fig. 10.15. Teves master cylinder (17.5 mm) - disconnecting the rear circuit supply pipe (Sec. 12.B.3)

described later in this Chapter.

b) Teves without servo assistance.

1 Disconnect the leads from the two stop lamp switches and the leak indicator switch.

2 Disconnect the front circuit outlet pipe from the top of the master cylinder, Fig.10.14.

3 Disconnect the rear circuit outlet pipe from the master cylinder, Fig.10.15.

4 Plug the holes in the master cylinder to prevent the entry of dirt.

5 Remove the nuts and withdraw the master cylinder from its bulkhead securing studs. Empty the fluid reservoir.

6 Expel the hydraulic fluid by depressing the piston.

7 Refitting is a reversal of removal, finally bleed the system as described later in this Chapter.

c) All models with servo assistance

1 The removal and refitting procedure is similar to that described for single circuit master cylinders in Section 11 except that the positions of the two circuit feed pipes at the master cylinder unions should be noted for exact replacement. Early model master cylinders had integral fluid reservoirs while later models have remote ones.

13 Master cylinder (single circuit) - servicing

1 Refer to Fig.10.7.

2 Unscrew and remove the stop lamp switch (1).

3 Remove the rubber boot (11) and pushrod (12).

4 Extract the circlip (10) and withdraw the ring (9), piston (7), seals (8) and (5), return spring (4) and valve (3). These internal components may be extracted by tapping the master cylinder body on a block of wood or applying pressure from a tyre pump at one hole and blanking the others with the fingers.

5 Examine the internal cylinder bore and the piston surface for scratches or 'bright' areas. If these are evident, renew the complete master cylinder.

6 Wash all components in clean hydraulic fluid or methylated spirit. Obtain a repair kit which will contain all necessary seals. Any internal components which have been modified since originally designed will be supplied in the spares kit but where such additional items are included, they must all be used and the original components discarded.

7 Observe strict cleanliness during reassembly and dip each component in clean hydraulic fluid before fitting. Use the fingers only to manipulate the seals into their locations and check carefully that their lips face the correct way as originally fitted and in accordance with the illustrations.

8 Reassembly is otherwise a reversal of dismantling. It is not recommended that the plastic connection on the master cylinder through which the fluid from the reservoir enters the unit should be removed as it requires the renewal of all components and special tools for fitting.

14 Master cylinder (dual circuit) - servicing

1 Dual or tandem master cylinders of either Teves or Lockheed type may be encountered, Figs. 10.16 and 10.17.

2 There are detail differences between the types and also dates of manufacture and although both are of 'in-line' type, the Teves has a side cylinder for leak switch actuation. The Teves dual master cylinder (1970-71) is covered in this Section but the essential principles apply equally to other models.

3 Pull the double (equalising) reservoir from the master cylinder body, Fig.10.18.

4 Unscrew and remove the two stop lamp warning switches (3) and the leakage indicator switch (4), Fig.10.16.

5 Remove the inlet connectors (1).

6 Remove the rubber boot (5) and pushrod (6).

7 Push the piston assemblies sufficiently down their bore to

enable the stop screw (7) to be removed.

8 Carefully secure the master cylinder in a vice fitted with jaw protectors, ensuring that the unit is secured squarely by its bosses and do not overtighten. With an Allen Key, unscrew the end plugs. With early Lockheed master cylinders, a blade will have to be used to remove the end plug, Fig. 10.19.

9 Detach the circlip (8) from the opposite end of the cylinder and extract the thrust washer (9).

10 Remove the primary piston assembly (10) and then the secondary piston assembly (11) pushing them out from the rear of the cylinder by inserting a wooden dowel through the front plug hole.

11 Extract the double piston assemblies (13) from the leakage warning switch cylinder.

12 Examine all components for corrosion and the surfaces of the pistons and internal cylinder bores for scoring or bright spots. Where these are evident, exchange the complete master cylinder for a factory reconditioned unit.

13 Wash all components in clean hydraulic fluid or methylated spirit. Obtain a repair kit which will contain all the necessary components for reconditioning. Quote the make and type of cylinder and the vehicle fabrication number and date of manufacture to ensure the correct replacement parts are obtained.

14 With Lockheed dual master cylinders, the residual valve may be removed if required, Fig.10.20 but it is not recommended that the two inlet unions are dismantled as refitting of the new union clamping rings will require the use of a special tool.

15 Commence reassembly by fitting the new seals with the fingers only and setting out the internal components in the correct sequence. Lubricate the parts with clean hydraulic fluid. Insert the primary piston assembly from the screwed plug end of the master cylinder taking care not to damage the lips of the seal as they pass up the bore. The use of a 3 mm diameter rounded end pin is recommended to assist the seals to pass the inlet ports without damage. Insert the pin in the inlet port sufficiently far to depress the seal lip and enable it to avoid contact with the sharp edge of the port on the internal surface of the cylinder bore.

16 Insert the secondary piston assembly, again from the screwed plug end of the master cylinder.

17 Fit a new copper washer and screw the end plug into position, tightening to 72 lb/ft torque.

18 Using a wooden dowel, depress both piston assemblies to permit the stop screw to be refitted. Use a new stop screw 'O' ring. Tighten the screw to 7.2 lb/ft torque.

19 If the residual valve was removed (Lockheed) refit it using a new copper washer and tighten to 36 lb/ft.

20 Using the wooden dowel, depress the primary piston so that the thrust washer and a new circlip may be fitted. Fit the rubber boot and pushrod.

21 With the Teves type master cylinder, refit the stop lamp switches and the leakage indicator switch and piston assemblies if these were removed during dismantling.

15 Vacuum servo assistance - general description

1 As previously described, vacuum servo assisted braking may be optionally specified. On left hand drive vehicles, the servo unit is part of the master cylinder assembly and is mounted directly ahead of the brake pedal on the engine rear bulk head. On right hand drive vehicles, the servo unit is mounted remotely from the foot pedal operated master cylinder due to the lack of space.

2 The principle of operation is that a flexible diaphragm, sealed at its outer edges between two hermetically sealed halves of a vacuum chamber, acts as a piston. The chamber on one side of the diaphragm is connected, through a tube and non-return valve to the engine inlet manifold and is always at partial vacuum, dependent upon the engine running and consequent manifold depression. The opposite side of the diaphragm is open to atmosphere. Both types of servo unit are shown in sectional form in Figs. 10.21 and 10.22.

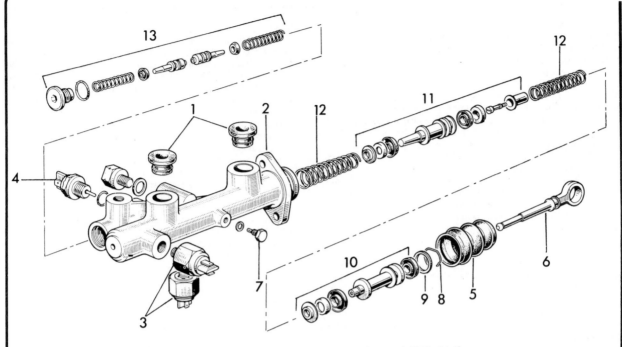

FIG. 10.16. MASTER CYLINDER (DUAL) (TEVES) (SEC. 14.1)

1	Inlet connector	5 Rubber boot	9 Thrust washer	13 Leak indicator
2	Body	6 Pushrod	10 Primary piston	piston
3	Stop lamp switches	7 Stop screw	11 Secondary piston	
4	Leak indicator switch	8 Circlip	12 Springs	

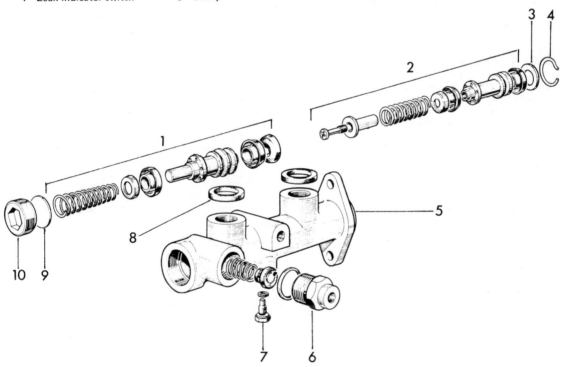

FIG. 10.17. MASTER CYLINDER (DUAL) (LOCKHEED) (SEC. 14.1)

1 Secondary piston	3 Thrust washer	5 Body	8 Seal
2 Primary piston	4 Circlip	6 Pressure valve	9 Sealing disc
		7 Stop screw	10 Plug

3 With the brake pedal fully released, the diaphragm is fully recuperated and held against the rear shell by the return spring.

The valve rod assembly is also fully recuperated by the brake pedal return spring. With the valve rod in this position, the vacuum port is fully open and there is a vacuum each side of the diaphragm.

4 With the brake pedal applied, the valve rod assembly moves forward until the control valve closes the vacuum port. Atmospheric pressure then enters behind the diaphragm and is assisted by the valve rod to push the diaphragm plate forward to enable the pushrod to actuate the master cylinder plunger.

5 With the pressure on the brake pedal released, the vacuum port is opened and the atmospheric pressure in the rear chamber is extracted to the front chamber and thence to the inlet manifold through the non-return valve. The atmospheric pressure port remains closed whilst the valve rod assembly returns to its original position, assisted by the diaphragm return spring. The diaphragm then remains suspended in vacuum until the next occasion on which the brake pedal is depressed when the cycle of operations is repeated.

6 It is emphasised that the servo unit provides asistance only to the braking effort of the hydraulic master cylinder and in the event of failure of the servo system normal braking by foot pressure only will remain unimpaired.

7 It is not recommended that the servo unit is dismantled or repaired but in the event of failure it should be exchanged for a guaranteed reconditioned unit.

16 Brake equaliser valve - checking and adjusting

1 The brake equaliser valve assembly exerts a compensating and regulating effect upon the front and rear braking effort according to the vehicle load. The equaliser valve is mounted on the rear suspension crossmember and is actuated by the pull of a spring fitted between the valve operating lever and an arm on the rear anti-roll bar. It is essential to safe and effective braking that the following operations are correctly carried out.

2 A sectional view of the equaliser valve is given in Fig.10.23.

3 Set the vehicle on level ground with tyres correctly inflated and the torsion bar settings as specified according to vehicle model and type (Chapter 7). Detach the exhaust silencer bracket to allow access to the equaliser valve assembly.

4 Using a vernier caliper gauge, measure the length of the equaliser spring as shown in Fig.10.24.

5 With vehicles built before 1970 the dimension should be 7.683 in. $\pm$ 0.039 in.) and for vehicles built after 1970, 7.917 in. $\pm$ 0.039 in. If adjustment is required, loosen the clamp on the anti-roll bar and move the operating lever, retighten the clamp. Refit the silencer bracket.

6 The principle of adjustment is that increasing the length of the spring increases the braking effort to the rear wheels.

7 The spring specification varies between car and estate models and according to year of manufacture. When renewing a spring check that it is of correct type and application.

17 Bleeding the system - single hydraulic circuit

1 Check that the level in the master cylinder reservoir is correct. Fully actuate the equaliser valve operating lever by inserting a block between it and the vehicle underframe.

2 Where a servo unit is fitted, depress the brake pedal several times to exhaust the vacuum.

3 Remove the rubber dust caps from all bleed nipples.

4 Assemble a bleed tube and a glass jar containing an inch or two of brake fluid. Have ready a new supply of the correct grade of hydraulic fluid which has been stored in an airtight container and has not been shaken for 24 hours (hydraulic fluid absorbs air and moisture and if used in a braking system will cause corrosion to the internal components).

5 Fit one end of the bleed tube to the nipple on one of the front caliper units and then immerse the other end in the fluid in the jar.

6 Open the bleed nipple half a turn and have an assistant depress the foot brake pedal fully and then let it return unassisted. Depress the pedal alternately sharply and then slowly until air bubbles cease to emerge from the end of the tube below the fluid in the jar. With the foot pedal held in the fully depressed position, tighten the bleed nipple (do not overtighten) and remove the bleed tube. Refit the nipple dust cap.

7 Replenish the fluid in the master cylinder reservoir using only hydraulic fluid which is new, of the correct specification and has not been shaken for the previous 24 hours and has been stored in an airtight container. During bleeding operations, should the fluid level in the reservoir fall to expose the outlet port then the complete bleeding operation will have to be repeated on **all** wheels due to the fact that air will have been drawn into the system.

8 Repeat the bleeding operations on the opposite front caliper followed by the rear brakes.

9 Finally repeat the bleeding operation on the original front wheel caliper, top up the reservoir to the correct level.

10 An additional bleed nipple is fitted to the hydraulic cylinder of the servo units fitted to G series (1971) models and this should be bled at the commencement of bleeding operations, Fig.10.25.

18 Bleeding the system - dual (tandem) hydraulic circuit.

1 Carry out operations 1 to 5 described in the preceding Section but noting that both reservoirs (or compartments) must be maintained with fluid to the correct level.

2 Bleed in the manner described in the preceding Section in the sequence LH front, RH front, RH rear LH rear. Unscrew each nipple only enough (½ turn max.) to permit the fluid to be pumped out. Depress the brake pedal lightly until resistance is felt and allow it to return slowly under control of the foot. **Do not test the braking efficiency by depressing the pedal hard until the complete bleeding sequence is completed.**

3 Where a leak indicator switch is fitted and the failure indicator lamp lights up during these operations, close the nipple which is open and open one in the opposite circuit. Apply a steady pressure at the foot pedal until the lamp goes out, release the pedal and close the nipple, the leak switch pistons will have resumed their balance.

4 Continue the bleeding operations and repeat the procedure described in paragraph 7 of the preceding Section.

5 Should any difficulty be experienced in obtaining satisfactory bleeding on a dual circuit system, the system will have to be pressurised (28 lb/in^2) and each circuit bled for 1½ to 2 minutes. This is obviously a job for the service station having the necessary equipment.

19 Brake operating pedal - removal and refitting

1 The brake pedal   operates on a common cross shaft with the clutch pedal   Fig.10.26.

2 The method of removal and refitting is as described for the clutch pedal in Chapter 5, Section 4.

20 Discs and drums - reconditioning

1 After extended mileage it is possible that the brake discs and drums will become scored. Any skimming must be carried out professionally and within the tolerances specified in Specifications.

2 Ovality in brake drums may be corrected by skimming, but excessive run-out in discs is best obviated by renewing the disc.

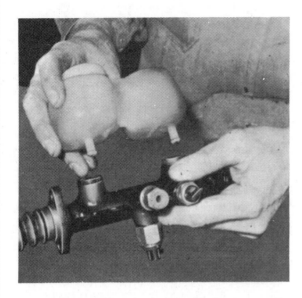

Fig. 10.18. Removing the twin (equalizing) fluid reservoir from a Teves (dual) 17.5 mm diameter master cylinder (Sec. 14.3)

Fig. 10.19. Using a blade made up to unscrew the end plug on a Lockheed master cylinder (Sec. 14.8)

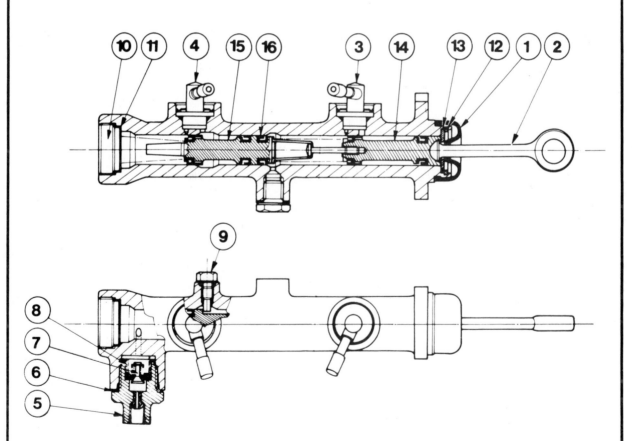

FIG. 10.20. MASTER CYLINDER (DUAL) (LOCKHEED 17.5 MM DIA) (SEC. 14.14)

1 Rubber boot	5 Outlet connection	9 Stop screw	13 Thrust washer
2 Pushrod	6 Sealing washer	10 Plug	14 Primary piston
3 Fluid inlet	7 Residual pressure valve	11 Seal	15 Secondary piston
4 Fluid inlet	8 Spring	12 Circlip	16 Cup seal

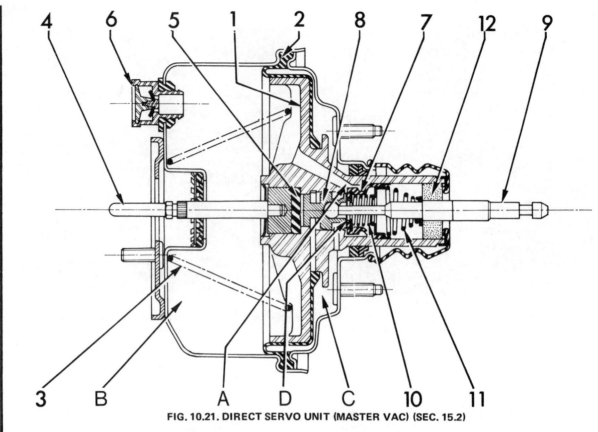

FIG. 10.21. DIRECT SERVO UNIT (MASTER VAC) (SEC. 15.2)

1 Diaphragm plate	5 Reaction disc	9 Operating rod	A Air inlet channel
2 Diaphragm	6 Non-return valve	10 Spring	B Vacuum chamber
3 Return spring	7 Seal	11 Spring	C Atmospheric pressure
4 Pushrod	8 Piston	12 Air filter	D Washer

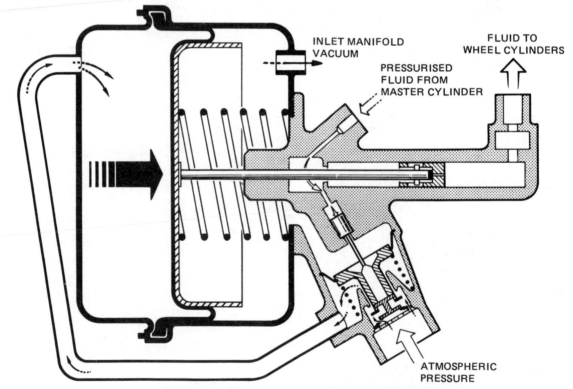

INLET MANIFOLD VACUUM

FLUID TO WHEEL CYLINDERS

PRESSURISED FLUID FROM MASTER CYLINDER

ATMOSPHERIC PRESSURE

Fig. 10.22. Remote (Hydro-vac) servo unit (Section) (Sec. 15.2)

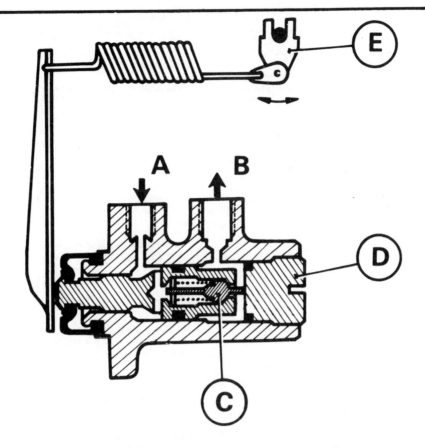

FIG. 10.23. BRAKE EQUALIZER VALVE (SEC. 16.2)

A Inlet port
B Outlet port
C Valve

D Plug
E Anti-roll bar clamp and arm

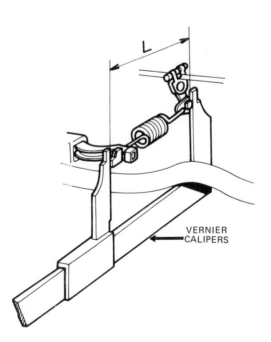

Fig. 10.24. Brake equalizer spring setting. Method of checking using vernier calipers (Sec. 16.4)

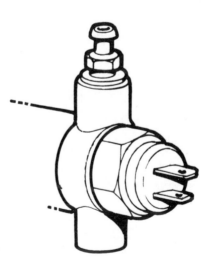

Fig. 10.25. Bleed nipple fitted to later type Hydro-vac servo units (Sec. 17.10)

21 Modifications

1 In order to avoid the trapping of air, certain changes of location of the master cylinder reservoir have been carried out.
   Single circuit systems for 1970 F series vehicles (LHD) without servo, Fig.10.27 with servo, Fig.10.28.
2 With RHD vehicles, the hydraulic supply line only has been repositioned, Fig.10.29.
3 Friction pad and lining grades have been changed and when renewing these components, they must be changed in full sets on each axle.
4 Rear wheel cylinder diameter changes means that any renewal of one cylinder must be matched by the replacement of the one at the opposite wheel.

Brake Fault Diagnosis

Brake grab
   Brake shoe linings or pads not bedded-in
   Contaminated with oil or grease
   Scored drums or discs
   Servo unit faulty

Brake drag
   Master cylinder faulty
   Brake foot pedal return impeded
   Blocked filler cap vent
   Master cylinder reservoir or compartments overfilled
   Seized wheel caliper or cylinder
   Incorrect adjustment of handbrake
   Weak or broken shoe return springs
   sCrushed or blocked pipelines

Brake pedal feels hard
   Friction surfaces contaminated with oil or grease
   Glazed friction material surfaces
   Rusty disc surfaces
   Seized caliper or wheel cylinder
   Faulty servo unit

Excessive pedal travel
   Low fluid level in reservoir
   Rear shoe adjusters faulty
   Excessive disc runout
   Worn front wheel bearings

System requires bleeding
Worn pads or linings

Pedal creep during sustained application
   Fluid leak
   Faulty master cylinder
   Faulty servo

Pedal spongy or springy
   System requires bleeding
   Perished flexible hose
   Loose master cylinder
   Cracked brake drum
   Linings not bedded-in
   Faulty master cylinder

Fall in master cylinder fluid level
   Normal disc pad wear
   Leak
   Internal fluid leak from servo

Servo Unit Fault Diagnosis

Hard pedal, lack of assistance with engine running
   Lack of vacuum due to:
   Loose connections
   Restricted hose
   Major fault in unit

Slow action of servo
   Faulty vacuum hose

Lack of assistance during heavy braking
   Air leaks in:
   Non-return valve O ring
   Non-return valve
   Dust cover
   Hoses and connections

Loss of fluid
   Major failure in unit

Brake pedal pushes back against foot pressure
   Hydraulic inlet and outlet pipes incorrectly connected
   Major fault in unit

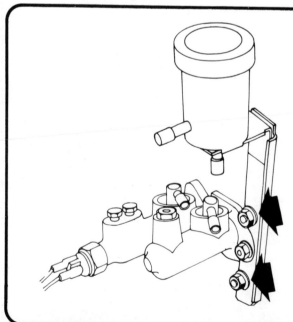

Fig. 10.27. Modified location of fluid reservoir on master cylinders without servo assistance to prevent air being trapped in system (Sec. 21.2)

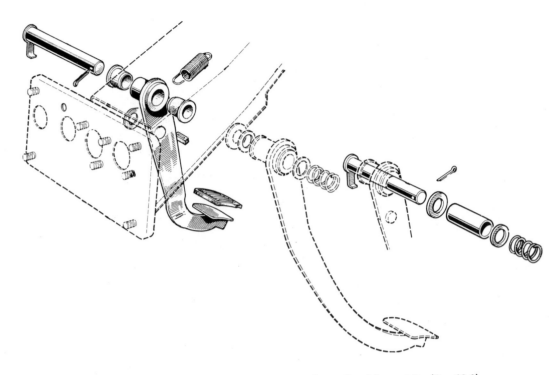

Fig. 10.26. Components of the brake and clutch (dotted) pedal assemblies (Sec. 19.1)

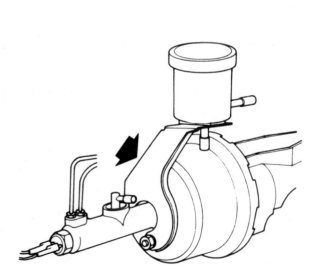

Fig. 10.28. Modified location of fluid reservoir on master cylinders with servo assistance to prevent air being trapped in system. (Support bracket arrowed)

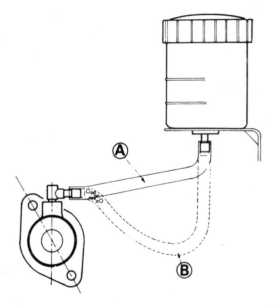

Fig. 10.29. Correct fitting of reservoir to master cylinder supply hose (A) to prevent trapping of air within system. (B) shows incorrect layout

Chapter 11 Electrical system

Contents

Specifications

System type	12 volt negative earth
Battery	lead acid
Capacity	40 amp/hour
Alternator (not 1100 special)	
Make ,..	Ducellier or Paris-Rhone
Rated voltage	14 volts
Maximum output	23 amps (330 watts)
Alternator (1100 special)	
Maximum output	30 amps (430 watts)
Other details as previously listed	
Alternator rear bearing (Ducellier)	
Diameter up to 1969	40 mm
Diameter after 1969	32 mm
Alternator control unit	
Make	Ducellier or Paris-Rhone
Regulating voltage	14.6 to 15.3 volts
Condenser capacity	470 mfd
Starter motor	
Make	Ducellier or Paris-Rhone
Type	pre-engaged
No of teeth (drive pinion)	10
No of teeth (ring gear)	112
Pinion end float	0.020 to 0.090 in
Windscreen wiper motor	
Make	Bosch, Marchal or Siem
Speeds	Two
Bulb ratings	Wattage
Front parking lights	5

	Wattage
Front flashers	21
Headlamp - main filament	40
Headlamp - dipped filament	45
Interior lights (festoon)	4
Instrument panel	5
Brake stop light	21
Rear lamps	5
Rear flashers	21
Rear lamps/flashers (estate car)	21/5

Torque wrench settings	lb/ft
Alternator to mounting bracket	35
Alternator to adjustment bracket	15
Starter motor to clutch or converter housing	16

1 General description

1 The electrical system is of 12 volt negative earth type and is shown in diagrammatic form in Fig.11.1.

2 A belt driven alternator charges the battery which in turn provides power for the starter motor, ignition system, lights and ancillary equipment.

3 A regulator is mounted within the engine compartment on the wheel arch for the purpose of controlling the voltage and charging rate.

4 The starter motor is of pre-engaged drive type and a full electrical specification is provided to include a thermostatically controlled radiator fan, heater blower, cigar lighter and electric clock. Electric windscreen wipers are fitted and a booster blower for the interior heater.

5 Electric windscreen washers are fitted to all models except the 1100 LS which has a 'one wash and wipe' type foot operated control.

6 The lighting system is conventional.

7 When fitting electrical accessories to cars with a negative earth system it is important, if they contain Silicone Diode or Transistors, that they are connected correctly, otherwise serious damage may result to the components concerned. Items such as radios, tape recorders, electronic ignition systems, electronic tachometer, automatic dipping etc., should all be checked for correct polarity.

8 It is important that the battery positive lead is always disconnected if the battery is to be boost charged when an alternator is fitted. Also if body repairs are to be carried out using electronic arc welding equipment the alternator must be disconnected otherwise serious damage can be caused to the more delicate instruments. When the battery has to be disconnected it must always be reconnected with the negative terminal earthed.

2 Battery - removal and refitting

1 The battery is located to the rear of the engine compartment just below the air intake grille, Fig.11.2.

2 The battery should be removed periodically for cleaning of its mounting tray. Any signs of corrosion should be cleared away with a wire brush as fully described in the next Section.

3 Lift the battery carefully from the engine compartment, keep it quite level and ensure that electrolyte does not spill on the vehicle paintwork or immediate damage will result.

4 Refitting is a reversal of removal but note that the negative lead should be refitted before the positive ones (the positive terminal has two cables attached to it).

3 Battery - maintenance and inspection

1 Normal weekly battery maintenance consists of checking the

a) Loss of electrolyte from the battery at sometime caused by spillage or a leak, resulting in a drop in the specific gravity of the electrolyte when the deficiency was replaced with distilled water instead of fresh electrolyte.

b) An internal short circuit caused by buckling of the plates or similar malady pointing to the likelihood of total battery failure in the near future.

7 The specific gravity of the electrolyte for fully charged conditions at the electrolyte temperature indicated, is listed in Table A. The specific gravity of a fully discharged battery at different temperatures of the electrolyte is given in Table B.

electrolyte level of each cell to ensure that the separators are covered by ¼ inch of electrolyte. If the level has fallen, top up the battery using distilled water only. Do not overfill. If a battery is overfilled or any electrolyte attacks and corrodes any metal it comes into contact with very rapidly. If the electrolyte level in any of the cells is below the bottom of the filling tube top up as follows:

a) Lift off the vent chamber cover or unscrew the plugs.

b) With the battery level, pour distilled water into the trough until all the filling tubes and trough are full.

c) Immediately replace the cover to allow the water in the trough and tubes to flow into the cells. Each cell will automatically receive the correct amount of water, to ensure the electrolyte level is just above the plates.

2 As well as keeping the terminals clean and covered with petroleum jelly, the top of the battery, and especially the top of the cells, should be kept clean and dry. This helps prevent corrosion and ensures that the battery does not become partially discharged by leakage through dampness and dirt.

3 Once every three months remove the battery and inspect the battery securing bolts, the battery clamp plate, tray and battery leads for corrosion (white fluffy deposits on the metal) which are brittle to touch). If any corrosion is found, clean off the deposit with ammonia and paint over the clean metal with an anti-rust/anti-acid paint.

4 At the same time inspect the battery case for cracks. If a crack is found, clean and plug it with one of the proprietary compounds marketed by such firms as Holts for this purpose. If leakage through the crack has been excessive then it will be necessary to refill the appropriate cell with fresh electrolyte as detailed later. Cracks are frequently caused to the top of the battery cases by pouring in distilled water in the middle of winter AFTER instead of BEFORE a run. This gives the water no chance to mix with the electrolyte and so the former freezes and splits the battery case.

5 If topping up the battery becomes excessive and the case has been inspected for cracks that could cause leakage, but none are found, the battery is being overcharged and the voltage regulator will have to be checked for serviceability (Section 36).

6 With the battery on the bench at the three montly interval check, measure the specific gravity with a hydrometer to determine the state of charge and condition of the electrolyte. There. should be very little variation between the different cells and, if a variation in excess of 0.025 is present it will be due to either:

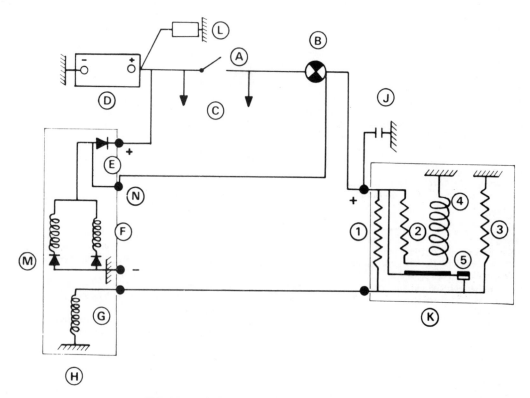

FIG. 11.1. CHARGING CIRCUIT DIAGRAM (SEC. 1.1)

A	Ignition switch	F	Alternator stator	K	Control unit
B	Charge indicator lamp	G	Alternator rotor	L	Starter motor
C	Electrical ancillaries	H	Alternator	M	Rectifying diode
D	Battery	J	Indicator lamp	N	Alternator terminal (awx.)
E	Isolating diode		protection condenser	I	Regulator resistor

2	Compensating resistor
3	Absorption resistor
4	Relay winding
5	Relay contact

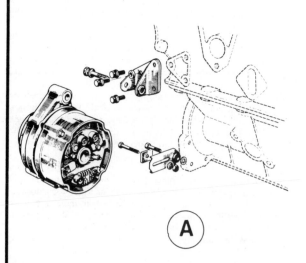

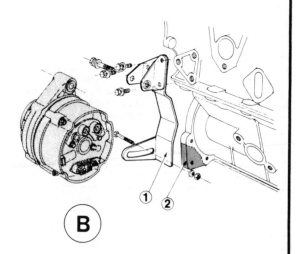

FIG. 11.3. ALTERNATOR MOUNTING BRACKETS (SEC. 8)

A   Early models   B   Later models

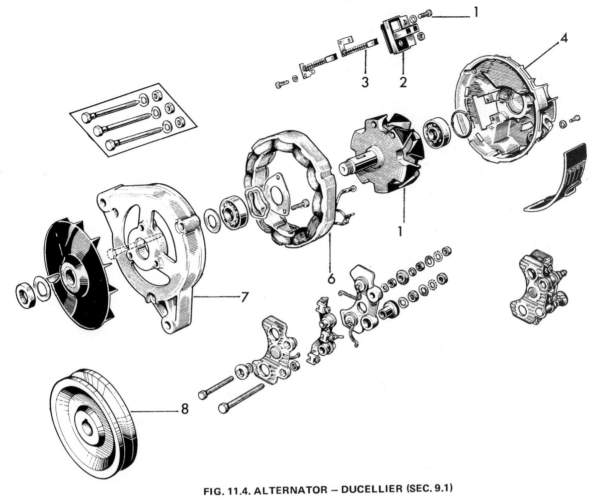

FIG. 11.4. ALTERNATOR — DUCELLIER (SEC. 9.1)

| 1 Brush holder screw | 3 Brush | 5 Rotor | 7 Front housing |
| 2 Brush holder | 4 Rear housing | 6 Stator | 8 Drive pulley |

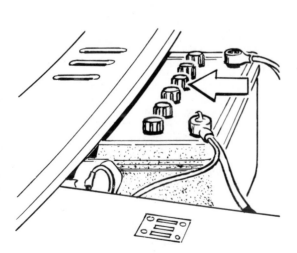

Fig. 11.2. Battery location (Sec. 2.1)

8.5 Alternator terminal connections and leads

TABLE A

Specific Gravity - Battery Fully Charged

1.268 at 100°F or 38°C electrolyte temperature
1.272 at 90°F or 32°C electrolyte temperature
1.276 at 80°F or 27°C electrolyte temperature
1.280 at 70°F or 21°C electrolyte temperature
1.284 at 60°F or 16°C electrolyte temperature
1.288 at 50°F or 10°C electrolyte temperature
1.292 at 40°F or   4°C electrolyte temperature
1.296 at 30°F or -1.5°C electrolyte temperature

TABLE B

Specific Gravity - Battery Fully Discharged

1.098 at 100°F or 38°C electrolyte temperature
1.102 at 90°F or 32°C electrolyte temperature
1.106 at 80°F or 27°C electrolyte temperature
1.110 at 70°F or 21°C electrolyte temperature
1.114 at 60°F or 16°C electrolyte temperature
1.118 at 50°F or 10°C electrolyte temperature
1.122 at 40°F or   4°C electrolyte temperature
1.126 at 30°F or -1.5°C electrolyte temperature

4 Electrolyte - replenishment

1 If the battery is in a fully charged state and one of the cells maintains a specific gravity reading which is .025 or more lower than the others, and a check of each cell has been made with a voltage meter to check for short circuits (a four to seven second test should give a steady reading of between 1.2 to 1.8 volts), then it is likely that the electrolyte has been lost from the cell with the low reading at some time.
2 Top up the cell with a solution of 1 part sulphuric acid to 2.5 parts of water. If the cell is already fully topped up draw some electrolyte out of it with a pipette. The total capacity of each cell is ¾ pint.
3 When mixing the sulphuric acid and water NEVER ADD WATER TO SULPHURIC ACID - always pour the acid slowly onto the water in a glass container. IF WATER IS ADDED TO SULPHURIC ACID IT WILL EXPLODE.
4 Continue to top up the cell with the freshly made electrolyte and then recharge the battery and check the hydrometer readings.

5 Battery - charging

1 DISCONNECT THE BATTERY (+) TERMINAL BEFORE ATTEMPTING TO CHARGE FROM A MAINS CHARGER OR DAMAGE TO THE ALTERNATOR WILL OCCUR.
2 In winter time when heavy demand is placed upon the battery, such as when starting from cold, and much electrical equipment is continually in use, it is a good idea to occasionally have the battery fully charged from an external source at the rate of 3.5 or 4 amps.
3 Continue to charge the battery at this rate until no further rise in specific gravity is noted over a four hour period.
4 Alternatively, a trickle charger charging at the rate of 1.5 amps can be safely used overnight.
5 Specially rapid 'boost' charges which are claimed to restore the power of the battery in 1 to 2 hours are most dangerous as they can cause serious damage to the battery plates.

6 Alternator driving belt - checking and adjustment

1 The correct belt tension must be maintained at all times, to ensure the correct charging rate and to avoid strain on the alternator bearings.

2 Remove the drive belt protective shield and slacken the alternator mounting bolts and the bolts which secure the adjustment strap.
3 Prise the alternator away from the engine block and tighten the adjustment strap bolts when there is a total free movement of ½ in at the centre of the longest run of the belt.
4 Make periodic inspections of the belt and renew it when any sign of fraying is evident.

7 Alternator - fault finding and repair

Due to the specialist knowledge and equipment required to test or service an alternator it is recommended that if the performance is suspect, the car be taken to an auto electrician who will have the facilities for such work. Because of this recommendation, information is limited to the inspection and renewal of the brushes. Should the alternator not charge or the system be suspect the following points may be checked before seeking further assistance.
1 Check the fan belt tension.
2 Check the battery.
3 Check all electrical cable connections for cleanliness and security.

8 Alternator - removal and refitting

1 Disconnect the leads from the battery terminals.
2 Remove the drive belt protective shield.
3 Slacken the alternator mounting bolts and adjustment strap bolts.
4 Push the alternator in towards the engine and slip the driving belt from the crankshaft, water pump and alternator pulleys.
5 Disconnect the four leads from the rear end of the alternator (photo).
6 Disconnect the alternator from its mounting bracket and adjustment strap, according to type. Fig.11.3.
7 Refitting is a reversal of removal but where early type mounting and adjustment brackets are used, ensure that the rectangular spacer is correctly located in the adjustment strap.
8 Adjust the belt tension as described in Section 6 and check that the leads are correctly reconnected to the alternator — black to earth (−) red/green to AUX red/yellow to EXC red to + (Bat).

9 Alternator (Ducellier) - servicing

1 Unscrew and remove the two screws (1) which secure the brush holder (2) to the alternator rear casing and extract the brush holder, Fig.11.4.
2 Withdraw the earth brush from its holder.
3 Withdraw the second brush after removal of the securing screw.
4 Clean the brushes and brush holder with a rag soaked in clean fuel and check that they slide easily in their holders.
5 If the brushes are well worn, they should be renewed.
6 This should be the limit of servicing. If the rotor or stator are damaged or the front or rear bearings are worn then it is quite uneconomical to consider a repair even if the individual components were obtainable and it is recommended that a factory reconditioned unit is obtained.
7 Refitting of the brushes and brush holder is a reversal of removal.

10 Alternator (Paris-Rhone) - servicing

1 The procedure for brush removal is similar to that described in the preceding Section. An exploded view of the alternator is shown in Fig.11.5.
2 The screws which secure the brush holder are shown as (C) in Fig.11.6.

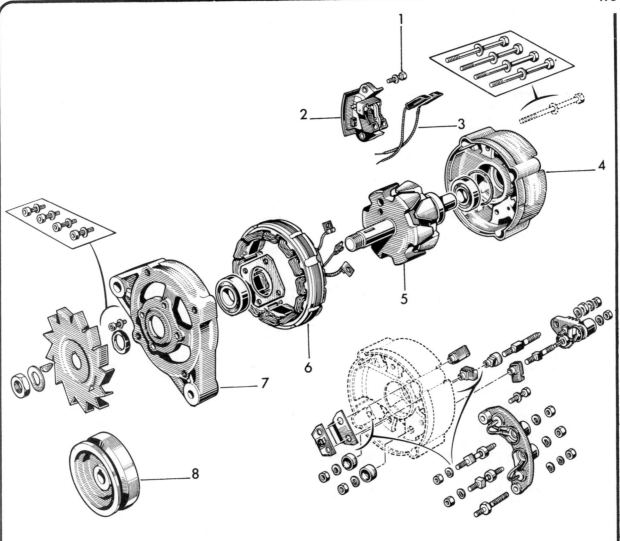

FIG. 11.5. ALTERNATOR – PARIS RHONE (SEC. 10)

| 1 | Brush holder screw | 3 | Brush | 5 | Rotor | 7 | Front housing |
| 2 | Brush holder | 4 | Rear housing | 6 | Stator | 8 | Drive pulley |

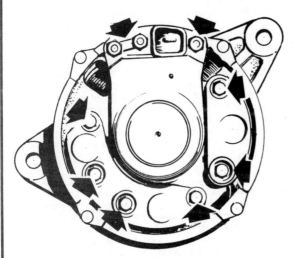

Fig. 11.6. Brush securing screws (PARIS–RHONE ALTERNA-TOR) (C) (Sec. 10.2)

18.2 Removing a windscreen wiper arm

3 Pull the brushes from their spring holders.
4 Refer to paragraphs 4,5,6 and 7 of the preceding Section.

11 Starter motor - general description

1 The starter motor is of pre-engaged type which is designed to ensure that the pinion is engaged with the ring gear on the flywheel (torque convertor-automatic) before the starter motor is energised.
2 Conversely, the drive does not disengage, until the starter motor is de-energised.
3 The starter motor may be of Ducellier make, Fig.11.7 or Paris-Rhone, Fig.11.8.

12 Starter motor - testing in vehicle

1 If unsatisfactory operation of the starter motor is experienced, check that the battery connections are tight and that the battery is charged.
2 Check the security of cable terminals at the starter motor solenoid and the leads at the combined ignition starter switch.
3 Do not confuse a jammed starter drive with an inoperative motor. If a distinct click is heard when the starter switch is operated but the motor will not turn then it is certain to be due to a jammed starter drive and the vehicle should be rocked in gear to release it.
4 Where the foregoing possibilities have been eliminated, proceed to test the starter but first disconnect the LT lead from the distributor to prevent the engine from firing.
5 Connect a 0-20 voltmeter between the starter terminal and earth, operate the starter switch and with the engine cranking, note the reading. A minimum voltage (indicated) of 4.5 volts proves satisfactory cable and switch connections. Slow cranking speed of the starter motor at this voltage indicates a fault in the motor.
6 Connect the voltmeter between the battery and the starter motor terminal and with the starter motor actuated, the voltage drop should not exceed more than half the indicated battery voltage (12 volts). Where this is exceeded it indicates excessive resistance in the starter circuit.

13 Starter motor - removal and refitting

1 Disconnect the battery leads.
2 Disconnect the leads from the starter motor terminals.
3 Unscrew the securing bolts which hold the starter motor to the clutch bell housing or (automatic transmission) converter housing.
4 Withdraw the starter motor from beneath the vehicle.
5 Refitting is a reversal of removal.

14 Starter (Ducellier) - dismantling, servicing, reassembly

1 Remove the end cover (2) Fig.11.7.
2 Unscrew and remove the armature end bolt (12) and withdraw the various armature shaft end components and the brush holders and plate.
3 Unscrew the nuts from the two tie bolts (7) and pull off the body (9). Remove the circlips from the fork bearing pin (location arrowed) and drift out the pin.
4 Withdraw the armature and lift the solenoid connecting fork out of engagement with the pinion drive assembly (5).
5 The pinion drive assembly may be dismantled by compressing the end collar (13) and detaching the circlip (14).
6 Dismantling beyond this stage should not be undertaken as if bearings or field coils require attention it will be more economical to exchange the unit for a factory reconditioned one, apart from the fact that special tools are needed to release the pole screws and to remove and install new bearings.

7 Check for wear in the starter brushes and renew them if their overall length is less than 9/16 in. The brushes must be unsoldered and the new ones soldered into position. Take care to localise the heat during the operation and do not damage the insulation of the field coils.
8 Clean the commutator on the armature with a fuel soaked cloth. Any pitting or burning may be removed with fine glass-paper, not emery. If the commutator is so badly pitted that it would require skimming on a lathe to remove it, renew the complete starter.
9 Checking of suspect field coils for continuity should be carried out by connecting a battery and bulb between the starter terminal and each brush in turn.
10 Reassembly is largely a reversal of dismantling but use a new collar (13) and circlip (14) and stake the collar rim in several places to retain the circlip.
11 Ensure that all starter drive components are clean and lightly oil them with thin oil when assembled.
12 Check the starter drive pinion end-float as described in Section 16.

15 Starter (Paris-Rhone) - dismantling, servicing, reassembly

1 Refer to the previous Section and carry out the operations described but in conjunction with Fig.11.8.

16 Starter motor drive pinion end-float - checking and adjusting

1 Disconnect the field coil wire from the solenoid terminal.
2 Using a 6 volt dry battery, energise the solenoid which will cause the pinion drive assembly to move forward into its engaged position. Press the pinion towards the motor to take up any end-float and using feeler gauges, check the clearance between the end of the pinion and the face of the thrust collar. The clearance should be between 0.020 and 0.090 in. If adjustment is required, screw the nut in or out as necessary.

17 Flasher circuit - fault tracing and rectification

1 The actual flasher unit consists of a small alloy container positioned at the sides of the steering column.
2 If the flasher unit works twice as fast as usual when indicating either right or left turns, this is an indication that there is a broken filament in the front or rear indicator bulb on the side operating quickly.
3 If the external flashers are working but the internal flasher warning light has ceased to function, check the filament of the warning bulb and replace as necessary.
4 With the aid of the wiring diagram check all the flasher circuit connections if a flasher bulb is sound but does not work.
5 With the ignition switched on check that the current is reaching the flasher unit by connecting a voltmeter between the 'plus' terminal and earth. If it is found that current is reaching the unit, connect the two flasher unit terminals together and operate the direction indicator switch. If one of the flasher warning lights comes on this proves that the flasher unit itself is at fault and must be renewed as it is not possible to dismantle and repair it.

18 Windscreen wiper arms and blades - removal and refitting

1 Before removing a wiper arm, turn the windscreen wiper switch on and off to ensure the arms are in their normal parked position parallel with the bottom of the windscreen.
2 To remove the arm, pivot the arm back and pull the wiper arm head off the splined drive. If the arm proves difficult to remove a screwdriver with a long blade can be used to lever the wiper arm head off the spline. Care must be taken not to damage the splines (photo).

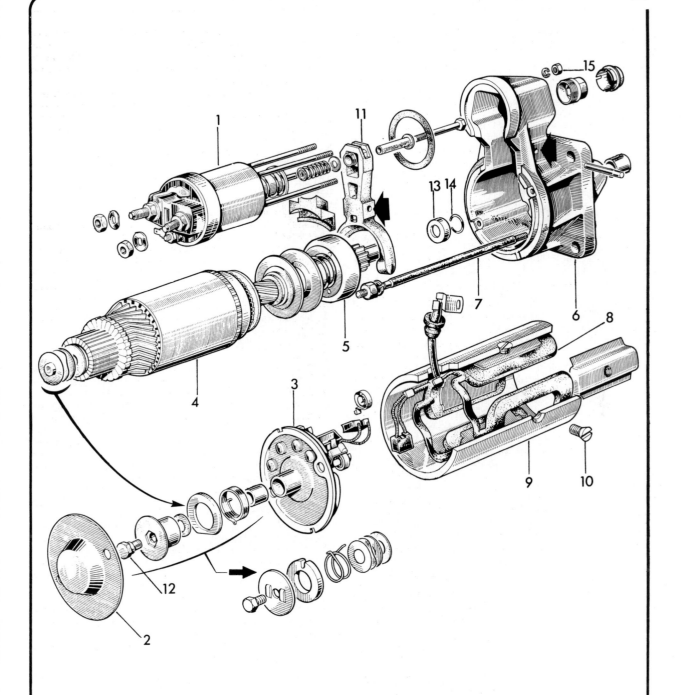

FIG. 11.7. STARTER MOTOR — DUCELLIER (SEC. 11.3)

1 Solenoid body	5 Pinion drive	9 Body	13 Collar
2 End cover	6 Bearing cover	10 Pole screw	14 Circlip
3 Brush holders	7 Tie bolt	11 Engagement fork	15 Adjuster nut
4 Armature	8 Field coil	12 Bolt	

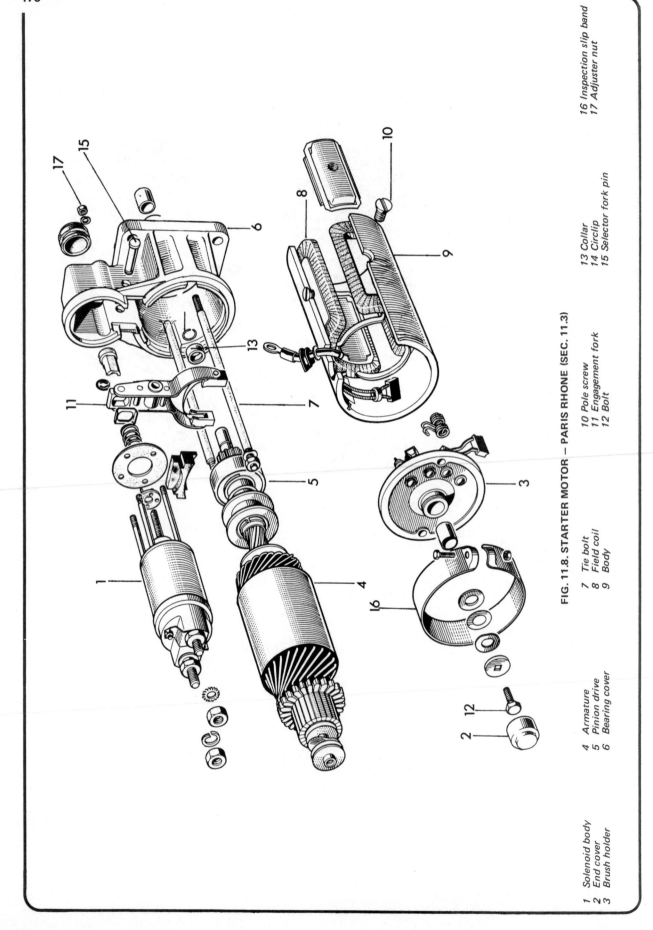

FIG. 11.8. STARTER MOTOR – PARIS RHONE (SEC. 11.3)

1 Solenoid body
2 End cover
3 Brush holder

4 Armature
5 Pinion drive
6 Bearing cover

7 Tie bolt
8 Field coil
9 Body

10 Pole screw
11 Engagement fork
12 Bolt

13 Collar
14 Circlip
15 Selector fork pin

16 Inspection slip band
17 Adjuster nut

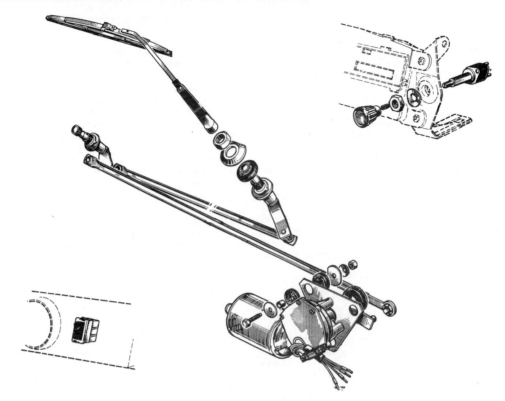

Fig. 11.9. WINDSCREEN WIPERS (BOSCH) Sec. 20

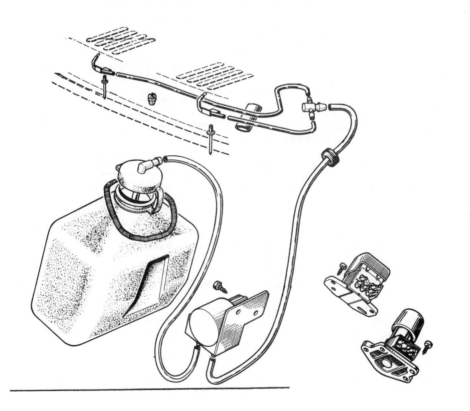

Fig. 11.10. WINDSCREEN WASHER 'ONE WIPE' FOOT OPERATED PEDAL SWITCH (SEC. 21)

3 When replacing an arm position it so it is in the correct relative parked position and then press the arm head onto the splined drive until it is fully home on the splines.

4 Renew the windscreen wiper blades at intervals of 12000 miles or annually or whenever they cease to wipe the screen effectively.

19 Windscreen wiper mechanism - fault diagnosis and rectification

1 Should the windscreen wipers fail, or work very slowly, then check the terminals on the motor for loose connections and make sure the insulation of all wiring has not been damaged thus causing a short circuit. If this is in order then check the current the motor is taking by connecting an ammeter in the circuit and turning on the wiper switch. Consumption should be between 2.3 and 3.1 amps.

2 If no current is passing through the motor, check that the switch is operating correctly.

3 If the wiper motor takes a very high current check the wiper blades for freedom of movement. If this is satisfactory check the gearbox cover and gear assembly for damage.

4 If the motor takes a very low current ensure that the battery is fully charged. Check the brush gear and ensure the brushes are bearing on the commutator. If not, check the brushes for freedom of movement and, if necessary, renew the tension springs. If the brushes are very worn they should be replaced with new ones. Check the armature by substitution if this part is suspect.

20 Windscreen wiper motor - removal and refitting

1 The wiper motor may be one of three makes, Marchal, Bosch or Seim. All three are similar in design and construction and the Bosch type with alternative facia mounted switches is shown in Fig.11.9.

2 Disconnect the battery leads.

3 Remove the wiper arm assemblies from the splined driving shafts.

4 Unscrew and remove the six screws which retain the cowl and grille. Pull the cowl horizontally to detach it from its clips.

5 Disconnect the washer supply tube from the three way union (Section 21).

6 Identify the wiper motor leads and then disconnect them.

7 Disconnect the snap joint (linkage to motor operating arm).

8 Unscrew and remove the nut which secures the operating arm to the wiper motor shaft. Detach the arm.

9 Unscrew and remove the three nuts which secure the wiper motor to its mountings and lift the motor away.

10 Refitting is a reversal of removal but check the correct connection of the motor leads.

11 Any servicing of the motor should be limited to the operations described in Section 19 otherwise the motor should be exchanged for a factory reconditioned unit. Any wear in the linkage should be rectified by renewal of the components concerned.

21 Windscreen washer - description and servicing

1 After 1970, an electric windscreen washer is fitted to all models including the 1100 LS which has an additional 'one wipe' foot operated washer and wiper switch, Fig.11.10.

2 The washer assembly of other types is similar to the illustration with the omission of the foot switch.

3 Servicing should be limited to occasionally checking the security of the tubes and connectors and the security of the electrical leads to the switch and pump motor. Keep the washer fluid container topped up as described in the Routine Maintenance Section at the front of this manual.

22 Horns - description, fault tracing and rectification

1 Twin electric horns are fitted and are actuated, according to model and year of vehicle manufacture, by a horn ring, a stalk type control or the central spokes of the steering wheel. Components of the latter are shown in Fig.11.11.

2 Failure of a horn to sound may be due to broken, loose or disconnected leads or the horn mounting bolts having worked loose. Tighten and reconnect as appropriate.

3 A continuously sounding horn will probably be due to breakage of the coil spring in the steering wheel boss. Remove the steering wheel name plate and boss cover plate and renew as appropriate.

23 Headlights (Marchal) - bulb renewal

1 Insert a screwdriver at the bottom of the bezel, Fig.11.12.

2 Lever the bezel upwards and then lift the top part so that the tongue of the bezel disengages.

3 Place a finger in the ring now exposed and pull it in an upward direction, the lamp unit can now be released (photo).

4 Press the bulb holder springs aside (photo).

5 Withdraw the bulb holder (photo).

6 Renew the bulb with one of the specified type and wattage.

7 Refitting of the lamp unit is a reversal of removal.

24 Headlights (Ducellier) - bulb renewal

1 Renewal of a bulb is similar to the procedure described for Marchal headlamps except that after removal of the bezel, the lamp unit must be turned in an anti-clockwise direction and pulled out.

25 Headlights (Iodine) - bulb renewal

1 Square type iodine headlamps may be fitted of SIEM or CIBIE manufacture, Fig.11.12A.

2 Access to the bulbs is obtained by withdrawing the two securing screws from the headlamp unit rim.

26 Headlights (sealed beam) - renewal

1 In the event of failure of one of these headlamp units fitted to vehicles operated in certain territories, the complete unit must be renewed.

2 Access to the sealed beam unit is obtained in a similar manner to that described in Sections 23 or 24 according to manufacturer.

27 Headlights - alignment

1 It is always advisable to have the headlamps aligned on proper optical beam setting equipment but if this is not available the following procedure may be used.

2 Position the car on level ground 30 feet in front of a dark wall or board. The wall or board must be at right angles to the centre line of the car.

3 Draw a vertical line on the board in line with the centre line of the car.

4 Bounce the car on its suspension to ensure correct settlement and then measure the height between the ground and the centre of the headlamps.

5 Draw a horizontal line across the board at this measured height. On this horizontal line mark a cross at a point equal to half the distance between the headlamps centres either side of the vertical centre line.

6 Remove the two headlamp bezels on either side and switch

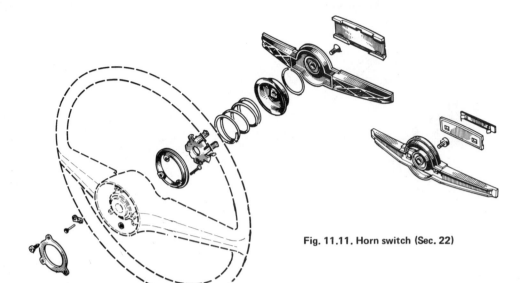

Fig. 11.11. Horn switch (Sec. 22)

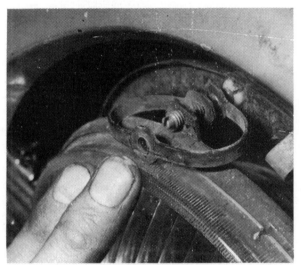

23.3 Withdrawing a Marchal type light unit

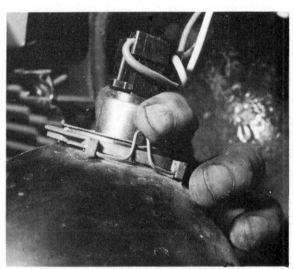

23.4 Pressing the bulb holder springs aside (Marchal)

23.5 Withdrawing the bulb holder (Marchal)

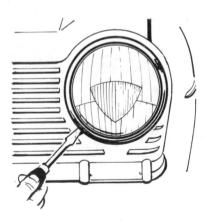

Fig. 11.12. Prising the bezel from a Marchal type headlamp (Sec. 23)

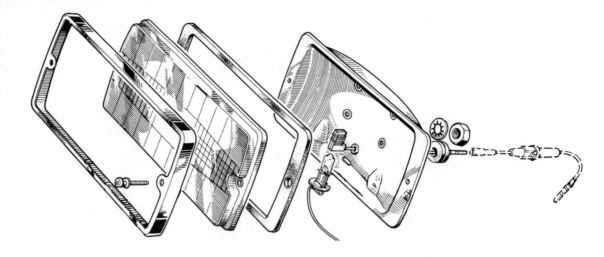

Fig. 11.12A. RECTANGULAR HEADLAMP (IODINE TYPE) (SEC. 25)

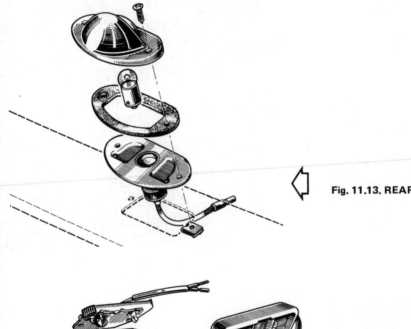

Fig. 11.13. REAR NUMBER PLATE LAMP (SEC. 30)

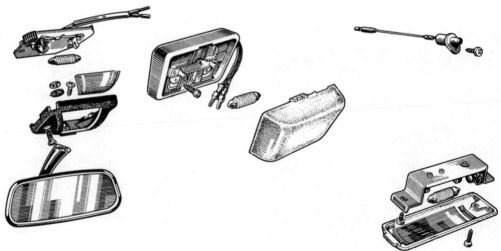

Fig. 11.14. INTERIOR LIGHTS, FRONT AND REAR (SEC. 31)

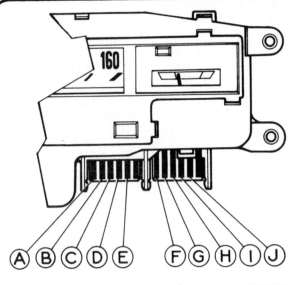

FIG. 11.15. INSTRUMENT PANEL PRINTED CIRCUIT CONNECTIONS (SEC. 32.8)

A   Earth
B   Panel lights
C   Charging indicator circuit
D   (+) input
E   Indicator lamp input
F   Fuel gauge input
G   Low fuel level indicator lamp input
H   Radiator temperature input
I   Flasher indicator input
J   Main headlamp beam indicator lamp

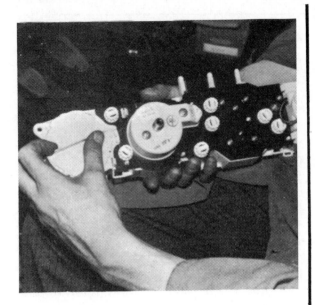

Fig. 11.16. Withdrawing the Instrument Panel (Sec. 33.5)

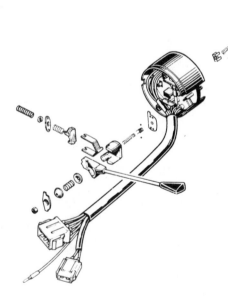

Fig. 11.17. Flasher/lighting switch L.M.P. Type (Sec. 34.1)

Fig. 11.18. Flasher/lighting switch VITALONI Type (Sec. 34.2)

the headlamps onto full beam;

7 By carefully adjusting the horizontal and vertical adjusting screws on each lamp, align the centres of each beam onto the crosses which you have previously marked on the horizontal line.

8 Bounce the car on its suspension again and check that the beams return to the correct positions. At the same time check the operation of the dip switch, replace the bezel.

28 Sidelamp and front flasher - bulb renewal

1 Access is obtained simply by removing the two lens securing screws (photo).

2 Renew the bulbs with ones of the same type and wattage. Do not overtighten the lens securing screws.

29 Rear lamp, stop light, rear flasher - bulb renewal

1 Access is obtained by removing the two lens securing screws (photo).

2 Renew the bulbs with ones of the same type and wattage, do not overtighten the lens securing screws.

30 Index plate lamp - bulb renewal

1 Access to the bulb is obtained by removing the two lens securing screws, Fig.11.13.

2 Renew the bulb with one of the same type and wattage and do not overtighten the lens securing screws when refitting.

31 Interior lamps - bulb renewal

1 A front and a rear compartment interior lamp is fitted.

2 The lamp located above the driver's mirror has a screw visible just below the switch. Remove this for access to the festoon type bulb, Fig.11.14.

3 Access to the bulb in the rear compartment lamp is obtained by pressing down on the top of the lens to disengage the securing lug and then withdrawing it.

32 Instruments - removal and refitting (1968 - 1969 models)

1 Disconnect the leads from the battery terminals.

2 Pull off the windscreen wiper control knob.

3 Remove the socket headscrew from the light switch knob and withdraw the switch knob.

4 Unscrew and remove the nuts which secure the lighting and windscreen wiper switches to the instrument cluster embellisher, retain the washer fitted beneath each switch.

5 Remove the instrument cluster embellisher.

6 Disconnect the speedometer cable and then disconnect the junction boxes from the instrument cluster.

7 Unscrew and remove the four self-tapping screws which secure the instrument cluster to the instrument panel (dashboard). Remove the instrument cluster.

8 The printed circuit at the rear of the cluster may be removed (six self-tapping screws) Fig.11.15.

9 The various gauges and speedometer may now be removed and renewed as required. The indicator lamp holders are retained by a key which should be pressed in and turned in an anti-clockwise direction to gain access to the bulbs for renewal.

10 Refitting the instrument cluster is a reversal of removal.

33 Instruments - removal and refitting (1970 on)

1 Disconnect the leads from the battery terminals.

2 Unscrew and remove the wiper and lighting switches.

3 Unscrew and remove the two screws which retain the facia to the instrument panel (dashboard).

4 Withdraw the facia and then unscrew and remove the four instrument cluster securing setscrews.

5 Disconnect the two plugs from the printed circuit and disconnect the speedometer cable. The instrument cluster may now be withdrawn for renewal of instruments or indicator bulbs, Fig.11.16.

6 Refitting is a reversal of removal.

34 Combined steering column switch

1 Vehicles built up until 1969 are fitted with an LMP type combined flasher, and lighting switch, Fig.11.17.

2 Vehicles built after this date are fitted with a VITALONI type switch, Fig.11.18 up until 1970.

3 Access to both switches is obtainable after removal of the steering wheel.

4 The switches fitted to 1969 and 1970 models are interchangeable provided new upper steering shaft components are fitted at the same time. The latest type switch is not interchangeable with the earlier patterns as it incorporates a horn control on the dip stalk switch (not USA and Sweden).

35 Fuses

1 The fuse block is shown in Fig.11.19.

2 No. 1 protects the front side lights, rear lamps, index plate lamp, instrument cluster lamp and the side and rear lamp warning light.

3 No. 2 protects the electric clock (if fitted) and the interior lamps.

4 No. 3 protects the heater and the flasher circuit.

5 No. 4 protects the windscreen wiper motor.

6 Additional 10 amp fuses protect the cigar lighter and the heated rear window, where fitted.

7 Always renew fuses with ones of similar rating and establish the cause of the fuse blowing as quickly as possible.

36 Alternator control unit - testing, removal, refitting

1 The control unit is located on the wheel housing within the engine compartment.

2 If the unit is suspect after reference to the fault finding chart it will require special meters and a rev counter to test it and it is therefore recommended that the work should be left to an auto. electrical company or a new unit substituted.

3 Removal is carried out by first disconnecting both leads from the battery terminals and the two leads from the control unit.

4 Remove the two control unit securing screws noting that the lower screw retains the condenser, and lift the unit from its location.

5 Refitting is a reversal of removal.

37 Modifications

1 Details of component modifications are listed in the Specifications Section of this Chapter.

2 From 1970 onwards, F series vehicles were fitted with a modified alternator mounting bracket requiring a longer alternator/water pump driving belt.

3 From 1972 onwards, H series vehicles have a rubber anti-vibration pad fitted between the starter motor and the sump.

4 From 1970 onwards, F series vehicles are fitted with a different type wiper motor compared with earlier models. The two types are not interchangeable.

FUSES

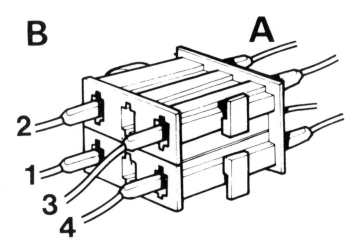

FIG. 11.19. THE FUSE LINK (A — INPUT) (B — OUTPUT) (SEC. 35.1)

A1	Green	B1	Green
A2	Red	B2	White/red
A3	Red/grey	B3	Grey
A4	Red/brown	B4	Grey/brown

28.1 Removing side lamp/flasher lens

29.1 Removing rear lamp/flasher lens

Fault diagnosis - Electrical system

Symptom	Reason/s	Remedy
No electricity at starter motor	Battery discharged	Charge battery.
	Battery defective internally	Fit new battery.
	Battery terminal leads loose or earth lead not securely attached to body	Check and tighten leads.
	Loose or broken connections in starter motor circuit	Check all connections and tighten any that are loose.
	Starter motor switch or solenoid faulty	Test and replace faulty components with new.
Electricity at starter motor: faulty motor	Starter brushes badly worn, sticking, or brush wires loose	Examine brushes, replace as necessary, tighten down brush wires.
	Commutator dirty, worn or burnt	Clean commutator, recut if badly burnt.
	Starter motor armature faulty	Overhaul starter motor, fit new armature.
	Field coils earthed	Overhaul starter motor.
Electrical defects	Battery in discharged condition	Charge battery.
	Starter brushes badly worn, sticking, or brush wires loose	Examine brushes, replace as necessary, tighten down brush wires.
	Loose wires in starter motor circuit	Check wiring and tighten as necessary.
Dirt or oil on drive gear	Starter motor pinion sticking on the screwed sleeve	Remove starter motor, clean starter motor drive.
Mechanical damage	Pinion or flywheel gear teeth broken or worn	Fit new gear ring to flywheel, and new pinion to starter motor drive.
Lack of attention or mechanical damage	Pinion or flywheel gear teeth broken or worn	Fit new gear teeth to flywheel, or new pinion to starter motor drive.
	Starter drive main spring broken	Dismantle and fit new main spring.
	Starter motor retaining bolts loose	Tighten starter motor securing bolts. Fit new spring washer if necessary.
Wear or damage	Battery defective internally	Remove and fit new battery.
	Electrolyte level too low or electrolyte too weak due to leakage	Top up electrolyte level to just above plates.
	Plate separators no longer fully effective	Remove and fit new battery.
	Battery plates severely sulphated	Remove and fit new battery.
Insufficient current flow to keep battery charged	Alternator belt slipping	Check belt for wear, replace if necessary, and tighten.
	Battery terminal connections loose or corroded	Check terminals for tightness, and remove all corrosion.
	Alternator not charging properly	Remove and overhaul alternator.
	Short in lighting circuit causing continual battery drain	Trace and rectify.
	Alternator control unit not working correctly	Renew control unit.
Alternator not charging	Drive belt loose and slipping, or broken	Check, replace and tighten as necessary.
	Brushes worn, sticking, broken or dirty	Examine, clean or replace brushes as necessary.
	Brush springs weak or broken	Examine and test. Replace as necessary.
	Commutator dirty, greasy, worn, or burnt	Clean commutator and undercut segment separators.
	Armature badly worn or armature shaft bent	Fit new or reconditioned armature.
	Commutator bars shorting	Undercut segment separations.
	Alternator bearings badly worn	Fit exchange unit.
	Alternator field coils burnt, open, or shorted	Remove and fit rebuilt unit.
	Commutator no longer circular	Recut commutator and undercut segment separators.
	Open circuit in wiring of cut-out and regulator unit	Remove, examine and renew as necessary. Take car to specialist Auto-Electrician.

Fault Diagnosis - Electrical System

Symptom	Reason/s	Remedy
FUEL GAUGE		
Fuel gauge gives no reading	Fuel tank empty!	Fill fuel tank.
	Electric cable between tank sender unit and gauge earthed or loose	Check cable for earthing and joints for tightness.
	Fuel gauge case not earthed	Ensure case is well earthed.
	Fuel gauge supply cable interrupted	Check and replace cable if necessary.
	Fuel gauge unit broken	Replace fuel gauge.
Fuel gauge registers full all the time	Electric cable between tank unit and gauge broken or disconnected	Check over cable and repair as necessary.
HORN		
Horn operates all the time	Horn push either earthed or stuck down	Disconnect battery earth. Check and rectify source of trouble.
	Horn cable to horn push earthed	Disconnect battery earth. Check and rectify source of trouble.
Horn fails to operate	Blown fuse	Check and renew if broken. Ascertain cause.
	Cable or cable connection loose, broken or disconnected	Check all connections for tightness and cables for breaks.
	Horn has an internal fault	Remove and overhaul horn.
Horn emits intermittent or unsatisfactory noise	Horn incorrectly adjusted	Adjust horn until best note obtained.
LIGHTS		
Lights do not come on	If engine not running, battery discharged	Push-start car, charge battery.
	Light bulb filament burnt out or bulbs broken	Test bulbs in live bulb holder.
	Wire connections loose, disconnected or broken	Check all connections for tightness and wire cable for breaks.
	Light switch shorting or otherwise faulty	By-pass light switch to ascertain if fault is in switch and fit new switch as appropriate.
Lights come on but fade out	If engine not running battery discharged	Push-start car, and charge battery.
Lights give very poor illumination	Lamp glasses dirty	Clean glasses.
	Reflector tarnished or dirty	Fit new reflectors.
	Lamps badly out of adjustment	Adjust lamps correctly.
	Incorrect bulb with too low wattage fitted	Remove bulb and replace with correct grade.
	Existing bulbs old and badly discoloured	Renew bulb units.
	Electrical wiring too thin not allowing full current to pass	Re-wire lighting system.
Lights work erratically - flashing on and off, especially over bumps	Battery terminals or earth connection loose	Tighten battery terminals and earth connection.
	Lights not earthing properly	Examine and rectify.

WIRING DIAGRAMS

There are at least 2 U.S.A. and 5 European Basic Wiring diagrams depending upon the year of the model. There are "19" partial wiring diagrams for European countries, again depending upon the year of the model and the country in which it operates. Italy (4) Austria (3) Switzerland (2) Finland (2) Germany (3) Sweden (4) and Norway (2) have partial diagrams and there are doubtless many more.

The manual supplies one basic U.S.A. and one basic European diagram for there is little point in supplying 26 diagrams to an owner who requires only one. If either of the basic diagrams supplied does not provide enough information your local SIMCA dealer will, we are sure, produce the extra information required.

WIRE COLOUR

Wire No.		Main	Secondary	Additional	Section in mm²	Wire No.		Main	Secondary	Additional	Section in mm²
1		Red			7	22		Blue			2
1	A	Red			3	22	A	Blue			1
1	B	Red			2	22	T	Blue			0.6
1	C	Red			2	23		Blue	Yellow		2
1	D	Red			1.4	23	A	Blue	Yellow		1
1	F	Red			2	24		Blue	Blue	Yellow	2
1	L	Red			0.6	33		Blue	Grey		1
1	R	Red			2	40		Green			1
1	V	Red	Purple		2	41		Green			0.6
3		Red			1.4	41	F	Green			1
3	A	Red			1	44		Black			0.6
3	P	White	Red		0.6	70		White	Brown		1
4		Red			0.6	70	C	White	Brown		1.4
8		Red	Yellow		1	70	T	White			0.6
9		Red	Green		1	71		White	Purple		1
9	T	Red	Green		0.6	71	A	White	Purple		0.6
10		Red	Grey		3	72		White	White	Green	1
10	B	Red	Grey		1	72	A	White			0.6
10	E	Red	Grey		0.6	73		White	White	Red	1
10	F	Red	Grey		2	73	A	White			0.6
10	T	Red	Grey		0.6	80		White	Blue		1
11		Grey			2	90	T	Yellow	Black		1
11	B	Grey			0.6	92		Yellow	Red		0.6
11	C	Grey			1	93	T	Yellow			0.6
11	E	Grey			1	94		Yellow	White		1
11	L	Grey			1	110		Black			5
11	M	Red	Red		1	110 A		Black			1
11	R	Red	Red		1	110 B		Black			0.6
11	S	Red			1	110 C		Black			1
12		Red	White		1	110 D		Black			1.4
12	A	Red	Blue		1	110 F		Black			0.6
12	B	Black			1	110 L		Black			3
12	C	Grey	Yellow		1	110 M		Black			1
14		Grey	Black		2	110 T		Black			0.6
16		Green	White		0.6	110 V		Black			2
17		Black	Green		0.6	132		Black			0.6
20		Blue	Red		2	133		Black			0.6

Key to representative wiring diagram (USA)

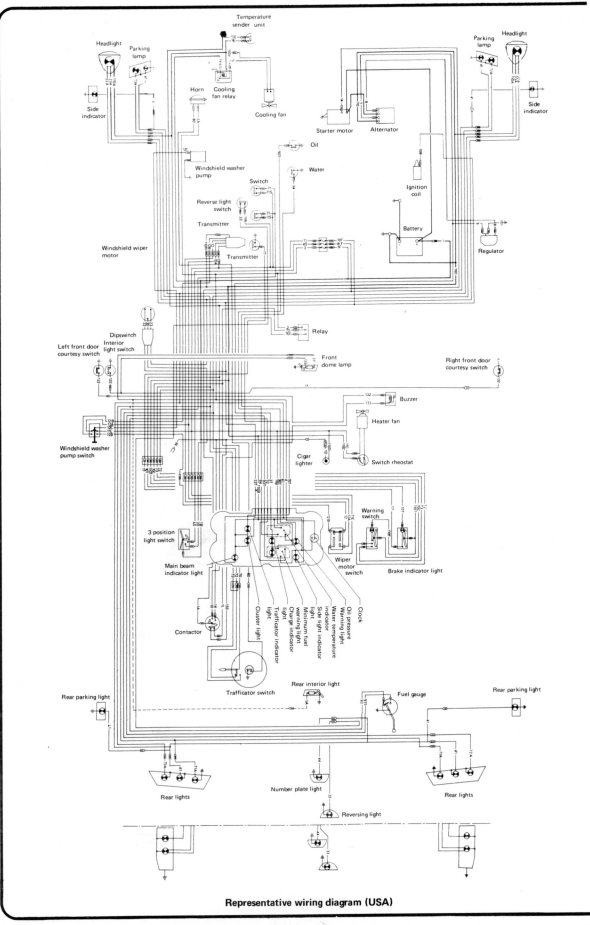

Representative wiring diagram (USA)

WIRE COLOUR

Wire No.		Main	Secondary (COLOUR)	Additional	Section in mm^2	Wire No.		Main	Secondary (COLOUR)	Additional	Section in mm^2
1		Red	White		7	20		Blue	Red		2
1	A	Red			3	22		Blue			2
1	B	Red			2	22	A	Blue			1
1	C	Red			2	22	B	Blue	Green		1
1	D	Red			1.4	22	D	Blue	Green		2
1	F	Red			2	22	R	Blue	Green		0.6
1	H	Red			2	22	T	Blue	Green		0.6
1	R	Red			2	23		Blue	Yellow		2
1	V	Red	Purple		2	23	A	Blue	Yellow		1
3	F	White	Red		0.6	24		Blue	Blue	Yellow	2
3	P	White	Red		0.6	40		Green			0.6
4		Red			0.6	41		Green			0.6
8		Red	Yellow		1	44		Black			0.6
9		Red	Green		1	70		White	Brown		1.4
9	T	Red	Green		0.6	70	T	White			0.6
10		Red	Grey		3	71		White	Purple		1
10	B	Red	Grey		1	71	A	White	Purple		0.6
10	C	Red	Grey		0.6	72		White	White	Green	1
10	F	Red	Grey		2	72	A	White			0.6
10	M	Red	Brown		1	73		White	White	Red	1
10	S	Red	Grey		1	73	A	White			0.6
10	V	Red	Grey		0.6	80		White	Blue		2
11		Grey			2	81		White	Blue		1
11	A	Grey	Brown		1	90	T	Yellow	Black		1
11	C	Grey			1	92		Yellow	Red		0.6
11	E	Grey			1	93	T	Yellow			0.6
11	F	Grey			1	94		Yellow	White		1
11	L	Grey			1	110		Black			5
11	M	Grey	Red		1	110	A	Black			1
12		Grey	White		1	110	B	Black			0.6
12	A	Grey	Blue		1	110	C	Black			1
12	B	Black			1	110	D	Black			1.4
12	C	Grey	Yellow		0.6	110	I	Black			3
14		Grey	Black		2	110	M	Black			1
15		Black	Yellow		0.6	110	R	Black			1
15	A	Black			1	110	V	Black			2
16		Green	White		0.6	132		Black			0.6

Key to representative wiring diagram (UK)

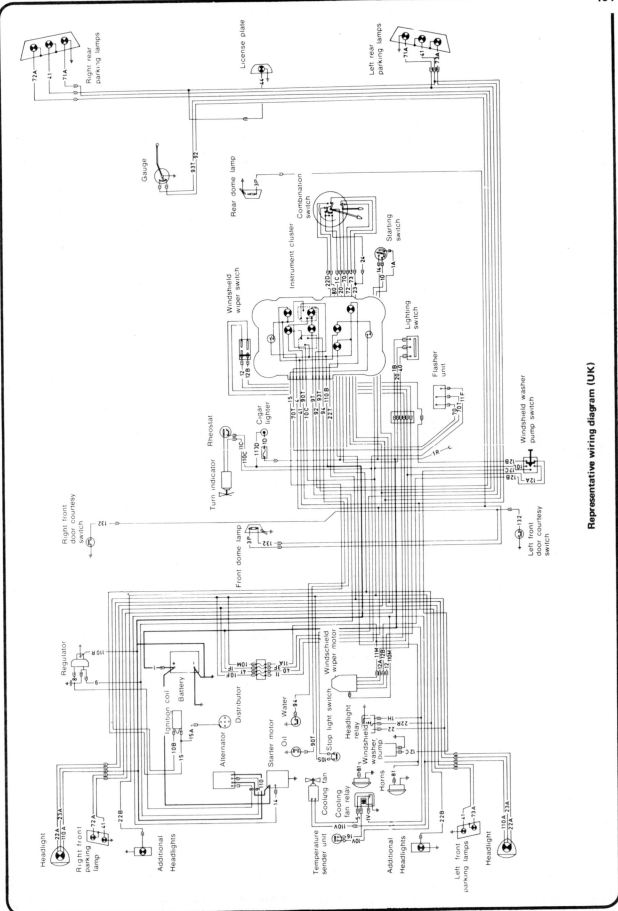

Representative wiring diagram (UK)

Chapter 12 Bodywork and underframe

Contents

1 General description

1 The body and underframe is a unitary, all steel, welded structure. The doors, front and rear wings are renewable in the event of damage simply by removal of the hinge or securing bolts. The main shell with the doors and wings and other panels removed is shown in Fig.12.1.

2 Fresh air ventilators are fitted, one either side of the instrument panel and all models are fitted with a heater. Many optional extras are available and may be specified for fitting to all models in the range.

3 The bonnet is hinged at its forward edge and is released from the vehicle interior.

2 Maintenance - bodywork and underframe

1 The condition of your car's bodywork is of considerable importance as it is on this that the second hand value of the car will mainly depend. It is much more difficult to repair neglected bodywork than to renew mechanical assemblies. The hidden portions of the body, such as the wheel arches, the underframe and the engine compartment are equally important, although obviously not requiring such frequent attention as the immediately visible paintwork.

2 Once a year or every 12000 miles (20,000 km) it is sound to visit your local main agent and have the underside of the body steam cleaned. This will take about 1½ hours. All traces of dirt and oil will be removed and the underside can then be inspected carefully for rust, damaged hydraulic pipes, frayed electrical wiring and similar maladies. The car should be greased on completion of this job.

3 At the same time the engine compartment should be cleaned in a similar manner. If steam cleaning facilities are not available then brush a water soluble cleanser over the whole engine compartment with a stiff paint brush, working it well in where there is an accumulation of oil and dirt. Do not paint the ignition system, and protect it with oily rags when the cleanser is washed off. As the cleanser is washed away it will take with it all traces of oil and dirt, leaving the engine looking clean and bright.

4 The wheel arches should be given particular attention as under sealing can easily come away here and stones and dirt thrown up from the road wheels can soon cause the paint to chip and flake, and so allow rust to set in. If rust is found, clean down the bare metal with wet and dry paper, paint on an anti-corrosive coating, or if preferred, red lead, and renew the paintwork and undercoating.

5 The bodywork should be washed once a week or when dirty. Thoroughly wet the car to soften the dirt and then wash the car down with a soft sponge and plenty of clean water. If the surplus dirt is not washed off gently, in time it will wear the paint down as surely as wet and dry paper. It is best to use a hose if this is available. Give the car a final wash down and then dry with a soft chamois leather to prevent the formation of spots.

6 Spots of tar and grease thrown up from the road can be removed by a rag dampened with petrol.

7 Once every six months, or every three months if wished, give the bodywork and chromium trim a thoroughly good wax polish. If a chromium cleaner is used to remove rust on any of the car's plated parts remember that the cleaner also removes part of the chromium, so use sparingly.

3 Maintenance - upholstery and carpets

1 Mats and carpets should be brushed or vacuum cleaned regularly to keep them free of grit. If they are badly stained remove them from the car for scrubbing or sponging and make quite sure they are dry before replacement. Seats and interior trim panels can be kept clean by a wipe over with a damp cloth. If they do become stained (which can be more apparent on light coloured upholstery) use a little liquid detergent and a soft nail brush to scour the grime out of the grain of the material. Do not forget to keep the head lining clean in the same way as the upholstery. When using liquid cleaners inside the car do not over-wet the surfaces being cleaned. Excessive damp will cause odours or even rot. If the inside of the car gets wet accidently it is worthwhile taking some trouble to dry it out properly, particularly where carpets are involved. Do NOT leave oil or electric heaters inside the car for this purpose.

4 Minor body repairs

See photo sequences on pages 198 and 199.

1 A car which does not suffer some minor damage to the bodywork from time to time is the exception rather than the rule. Even presuming the gate post is never scraped or the door opened against a wall or high kerb there is always the likelihood

193

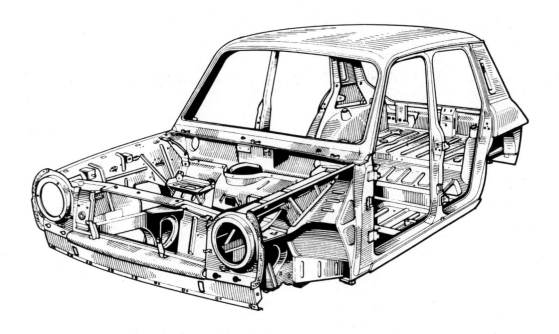

Fig. 12.1. Body shell construction (Sec. 1.1)

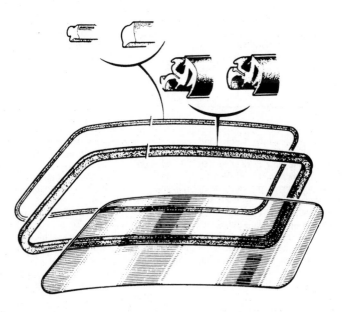

Fig. 12.2. Windscreen, rubber surround and embellisher (Sec. 9.3)

of gravel and grit being thrown up and chipping the surface, particularly at the lower edges of the doors and sills.

2 If the damage is merely a paint scrape which has not reached the metal base, delay is not critical but where bare metal is exposed action must be taken immediately before rust sets in.

3 The average owner will normally keep the following 'first aid' materials available which can give a professional finish for minor jobs:

a) A resin based filler paste
b) Matched paint either for spraying by gun or in an aerosol can
c) Fine cutting paste
d) Medium and fine grade wet and dry abrasive paper.

4 Where the damage is superficial (ie not down to the bare metal and not dented) fill the scratch or chip with sufficient filler to smooth the area, rub down with paper and apply the matching paint.

5 Where the bodywork is scratched down to the metal, but not dented, clean the metal surface thoroughly and apply a suitable metal primer first - such as red lead or zinc chromate. Fill up the scratch as necessary with filler and rub down with wet and dry paper. Apply the matching colour paint.

6 If more than one coat of colour is required rub down each coat with cutting paste before applying the next.

7 If the bodywork is dented, first beat out the dent to conform as near as possible to the original contour. Avoid using steel faced hammers - use hard wood mallets or similar and always support the panel being beaten with a hardwood or metal 'dolly'. In areas where severe creasing and buckling has occurred it will be virtually impossible to reform the metal to the original shape. In such instances a decision should be made whether or not to cut out the damaged piece or attempt to recontour over it with filler paste. In large areas where the metal panel is seriously damaged or rusted the repair is to be considered major and it is often better to replace a panel or sill section with the appropriate piece supplied as a spare. When using filler paste in largish quantities make sure that the directions are carefully followed. It is false economy to rush the job as the correct hardening time must be allowed between stages and before finishing. With thick applications the filler usually has to be applied in layers - allowing time for each layer to harden. Sometimes the original paint colour will have faded and it will be difficult to obtain an exact colour match. In such instances it is a good scheme to select a complete panel - such as a door or boot lid - and spray the whole panel. Differences will be less apparent where there are obvious divisions between the original and resprayed areas.

5 Major body repairs

Where serious damage has occurred or large areas need renewal due to neglect, it means certainly that completely new sections or panels will need welding in and this is best left to professionals. If the damage is due to impact it will also be necessary to completely check the alignment of the body shell structure. Due to the principle of contruction the strength and shape of the whole can be affected by damage to a part. In such instances the services of a Simca agent with specialist checking jigs are essential. If a body is left misaligned it is first of all dangerous as the car will not handle properly and secondly uneven stresses will be imposed on the steering, engine and transmission, causing abnormal wear or complete failure. Tyre wear may also be excessive.

6 Maintenance - hinges and locks

1 Oil the hinges of the bonnet, boot and doors with a drop or two of light oil periodically. A good time is after the car has been washed.

2 Oil the bonnet release catch pivot pin and the safety catch pivot pin periodically.

3 Do not over lubricate door latches and strikers. Normally a little oil on the rotary cam spindle alone is sufficient.

7 Doors - (racing rattles and their rectification)

1 Check first that the door is not loose at the hinges and that the latch is holding the door firmly in position. Check also that the door lines up with the aperture in the body.

2 If the hinges are loose or the door is out of alignment it will be necessary to reset the hinge positions.

3 If the latch is holding the door properly it should hold the door tightly when fully latched and the door should line up with the body. If it is out of alignment it needs adjustment. If loose, some part of the lock mechanism must be worn out and requiring renewal.

4 Other rattles from the door would be caused by wear or looseness in the window winder, the glass channels and sill strips or the door buttons and interior latch release mechanism.

8 Wings - removal and refitting

1 The front and rear wings are retained in position by bolts. For a front wing removal, first detach the headlamp surround.

2 Brush the heads of the bolts clean of mud and apply freeing fluid. Unscrew the retaining bolts and remove the wing. It may be necessary to cut along the wing to body sealing strip before the wing can be detached.

3 Clean all trace of sealing mastic from the body mating flanges.

4 Place a bead of sealing compound on the whole length of the body to wing mating flange and then locate the front wing in position. Screw in the securing bolts, with their threads well greased, finger tight. Note that the front of the wing is secured to the deflector by plastic rivets.

5 Move the wing slightly as required to obtain an exact and flush fit with adjacent body panels and then tighten the securing bolts.

6 Refit the headlamp surround and apply a coat of underbody sealer to the undersurface of the new wing.

7 As new wings are supplied in primer, the external surface will now have to be sprayed in cellulose to match the body. If the vehicle is reasonably new this can be carried out using a colour matched aerosol spray but if the body paint is badly faded it is advisable to leave the refinishing to a professional bodyshop.

8 The procedure for a rear wing is similar but before the damaged wing can be removed, the rear lamp cluster, the rear bumper and the fuel filler cap cover must be removed.

9 Windscreen glass - removal and refitting

1 Where a windscreen is to be replaced then if it is due to shattering, the facia air vents should be covered before attempting removal. Adhesive sheeting is useful to stick to the outside of the glass to enable large areas of crystallised glass to be removed.

2 Where the screen is to be removed intact then an assistant will be required. First release the rubber surround from the bodywork by running a blunt, small screwdriver around and under the rubber weatherstrip both inside and outside the car. This operation will break the adhesion of the sealer originally used. Take care not to damage the paintwork or cut the rubber surround with the screwdriver.

3 Have your assistant push the inner lip of the rubber surround off the flange of the windscreen body aperture. Once the rubber surround starts to peel off the flange, the screen may be forced gently outwards by careful hand pressure. The second person should support and remove the screen complete with rubber surround and metal beading as it comes out, Fig.12.2.

4 If you are having to replace your windscreen due to a shattered screen, remove all traces of sealing compound and broken glass from the weatherstrip and body flange.

5 Now is the time to remove all pieces of glass if the screen has shattered. Use a vacuum cleaner to extract as much as possible.

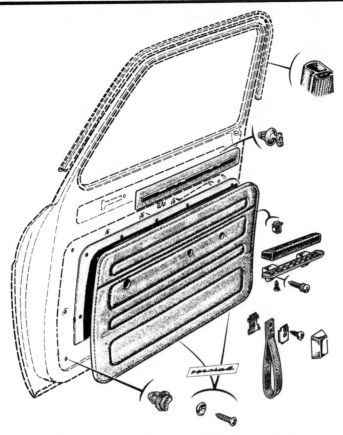

Fig. 12.3. Exploded view of a door interior panel and attachments (Sec. 10.1)

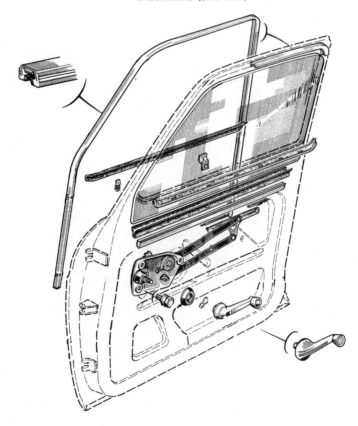

Fig. 12.4. Exploded view of the window winder assembly (Sec. 10.2)

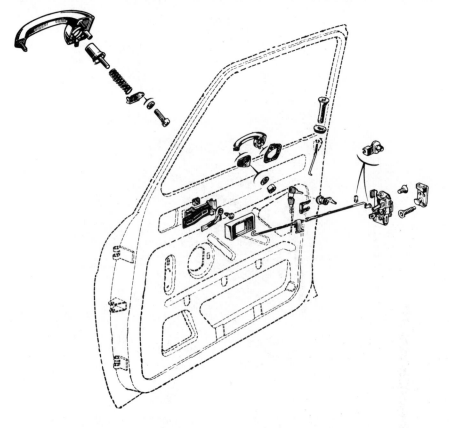

Fig. 12.5. Exploded view of a door lock and operating handles (Sec. 10.5)

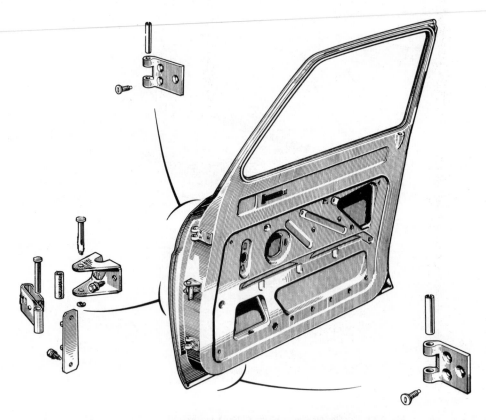

Fig. 12.6. Details of door hinges and check strap (Sec. 12.1)

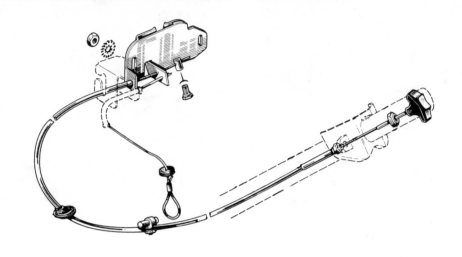

Fig. 12.7. The bonnet interior release and emergency release cord (Sec. 13.3)

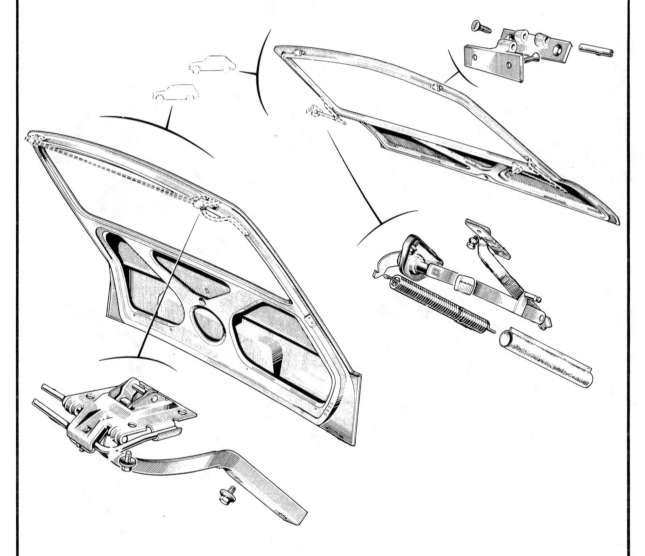

Fig. 12.8. The two types of rear tailgate counterbalance assemblies (Sec. 14.2)

This sequence of photographs deals with the repair of the dent and scratch (above rear lamp) shown in this photo. The procedure will be similar for the repair of a hole. It should be noted that the procedures given here are simplified - more explicit instructions will be found in the text

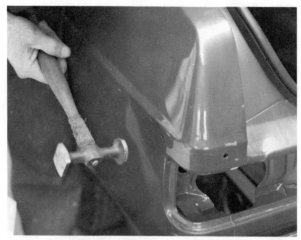

In the case of a dent the first job - after removing surrounding trim - is to hammer out the dent where access is possible. This will minimise filling. Here, the large dent having been hammered out, the damaged area is being made slightly concave

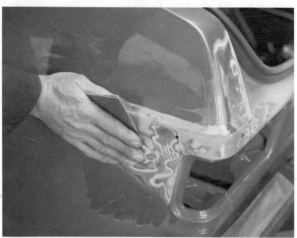

Now all paint must be removed from the damaged area, by rubbing with coarse abrasive paper. Alternatively, a wire brush or abrasive pad can be used in a power drill. Where the repair area meets good paintwork, the edge of the paintwork should be 'feathered', using a finer grade of abrasive paper

In the case of a hole caused by rusting, all damaged sheet-metal should be cut away before proceeding to this stage. Here, the damaged area is being treated with rust remover and inhibitor before being filled

Mix the body filler according to its manufacturer's instructions. In the case of corrosion damage, it will be necessary to block off any large holes before filling - this can be done with zinc gauze or aluminium tape. Make sure the area is absolutely clean before ...

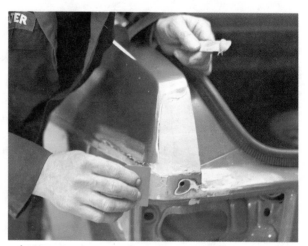

... applying the filler. Filler should be applied with a flexible applicator, as shown, for best results: the wooden spatula being used for confined areas. Apply thin layers of filler at 20-minute intervals, until the surface of the filler is slightly proud of the surrounding bodywork

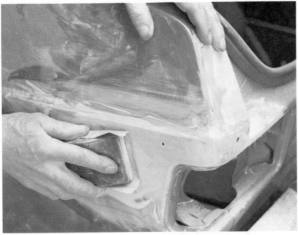

Initial shaping can be done with a Surform plane or Dreadnought file. Then, using progressively finer grades of wet-and-dry paper, wrapped around a sanding block, and copious amounts of clean water, rub-down the filler until really smooth and flat. Again, feather the edges of adjoining paintwork

The whole repair area can now be sprayed or brush-painted with primer. If spraying, ensure adjoining areas are protected from over-spray. Note that at least one-inch of the surrounding sound paintwork should be coated with primer. Primer has a 'thick' consistency, so will fill small imperfections

Again, using plenty of water, rub down the primer with a fine grade of wet-and-dry paper (400 grade is probably best) until it is really smooth and well blended into the surrounding paint-work. Any remaining imperfections can now be filled by carefully applied knifing stopper paste

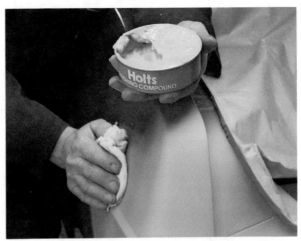

When the stopper has hardened, rub-down the repair area again before applying the final coat of primer. Before rubbing-down this last coat of primer, ensure the repair area is blemish-free - use more stopper if necessary. To ensure that the surface of the primer is really smooth use some finishing compound

The top coat can now be applied. When working out of doors, pick a dry, warm and wind-free day. Ensure surrounding areas are protected from over-spray. Agitate the aerosol thoroughly, then spray the centre of the repair area, working outwards with a circular motion. Apply the paint as several thin coats.

After a period of about two-weeks, which the paint needs to harden fully, the surface of the repaired area can be 'cut' with a mild cutting compound prior to wax polishing. When carrying out bodywork repairs, remember that the quality of the finished job is proportional to the time and effort expended

Switch on the heater boost motor and adjust the screen controls to screen defrost' but watch out for flying pieces of glass which might have blown out of the ducting.

6 Carefully inspect the rubber moulding for signs of splitting or deterioration.

7 To refit the glass, first fit the weatherstrip onto the glass with the joint at the lower edge.

8 Insert a piece of thick cord into the channel of the weatherstrip with the two ends protruding by at least 12 in at the top centre of the weatherstrip.

9 Mix a concentrated soap and water solution and apply to the flange of the windscreen aperture.

10 Offer the screen up to the aperture and with an assistant to press the rubber surround hard against one end of the cord, move round the windscreen, so drawing the lip over the windscreen flange of the body. Keep the draw cord parallel to the windscreen. Using the palms of the hands, thump on the glass from the outside to assist the lip in passing over the flange and to seat the screen correctly onto the aperture.

11 To ensure a good watertight joint apply some Seelastik SR51 between the weatherstrip and the body and press the weatherstrip against the body to give a good seal.

12 Any excess Seelastik may be removed with a petrol moistened cloth.

10 Door locks - removal, refitting, adjustment

1 Remove the arm rests and door pulls which are secured to the interior panels of the doors by self-tapping screws, Fig.12.3.

2 Press the window winder handle escutcheon plate inwards and remove the spring clip which retains the handle to the winder mechanism shaft, Fig. 12.4.

3 Insert a screwdriver between the door interior panel and the door and lever the panel clips from their locations. Once the first securing clip has been displaced, use the fingers instead of the screwdriver and by giving the panel a sharp jerk, the remaining clips can be removed in succession.

4 Carefully remove the polythene sheet water barrier now exposed. The upper, narrow, door panel is removed in similar manner.

5 Front and rear door lock assemblies are similar, Fig.12.5.

6 Disconnect the remote control lever (one screw) and disconnect the operating rod. Remove the lock securing screws and remove the assembly from the door interior.

7 The exterior door handle, push button and cylinder lock are retained by a nut, screw and clip all accessible through one of the door interior apertures.

8 It is seldom worthwhile to attempt to repair a door lock or remote control mechanism, renew as an assembly.

9 Refitting is a reversal of removal but take care to adjust the stroke of the external push button in relation to the lock operating plate. Ensure that the polythene sheet beneath the interior trim panel is replaced.

10 Check the door closure. Adjust the position of the striker plate on the door pillar if necessary, so that the door closure is firm and rattle free and the edge of the door is flush with the surrounding body panel surfaces when fully closed.

11 Window winder mechanism and glass - removal and refitting

1 Carry out operations as described in the preceding Section, paragraphs 1 to 4.

2 Raise the glass to its fullest extent by temporarily refitting the winder handle.

3 Unscrew and remove the three screws which secure the triangular baseplate of the winder mechanism to the door interior panel, Fig.12.4.

4 Slide the winder mechanism aside to disengage the operating arm rollers from the window channel. Hold the window in its upper position as the mechanism is withdrawn.

5 Loosen the screws which secure and also provide adjustment

of the two glass sliding side channels. Lower the glass, turn it through an angle of about 45° and then remove it upwards from the aperture.

6 Renew the winder mechanism as an assembly if the spring is broken or other components are worn or damaged.

7 Refitting is a reversal of removal but lightly grease the channel at the bottom of the glass before engaging the operating arm rollers.

8 Wind the window up and down to the fullest extent of its travel and adjust the side channel bottom securing screws so that the window glass slides squarely and smoothly and yet the channels exert a slight grip to prevent the glass dropping sharply when the regulator handle is first moved to wind the window down.

12 Doors - removal and refitting

1 The door hinges are secured to the body pillars by welding but held to the door frame by screws.

2 A metal type of check strap is fitted.

3 Remove the circlips from the base of one or both of the check strap clevis pins.

4 Open the door wide and support it at its lower edge on blocks or jacks. Use cloth to protect the paintwork.

5 Using a suitable drift, drive each of the hinge tension pins from their locations and remove the door.

6 If the hinges are to be removed for any reason, carefully mark round their outside edges so that they can be refitted to their original positions on the door edge.

7 Refitting is a reversal of removal but use new tension pins in the hinges and adjust the door lock striker plate if necessary to provide smooth and flush closure.

13 Bonnet - removal and refitting

1 The bonnet lid (hood) is hinged at its forward edge and is locked from inside the vehicle.

2 Occasional oiling of the hinges and the lock mechanism is all that is normally required.

3 In the event of the lock release cable breaking or seizing then an emergency cord, located behind the facia should be pulled, Fig.12.7.

4 The bonnet lid is not normally required to be removed as the power and transmission units are removed from below the vehicle. Where it is required to remove this component, unscrew and remove completely the hinge and support stay fixings.

14 Tailgate - removal and refitting

1 The rear tailgate (or fifth door) may be one of two types according to model.

2 One type is fitted with conventional hinges at its upper edge and side mounted coil spring support struts and the other has combined hinges and torsion rods to retain the tailgate in the open position, Fig.12.8.

3 To remove the torsion rod type hinges, support the tailgate in the fully open position using a length of wood.

4 Using a suitable tool, lever the torsion rod from the forked shaped cut-out of the hinge arm. Release the tension gently, repeat on the opposite hinge assembly and then unbolt the hinges from the tailgate.

5 With the coil spring type of supports, open the tailgate fully and remove the bolts from the side arms.

6 Both types of tailgate have securing locks at their lower edges and the two patterns of lock are shown in exploded form in Fig.12.9.

7 Refitting is a reversal of removal and dismantling.

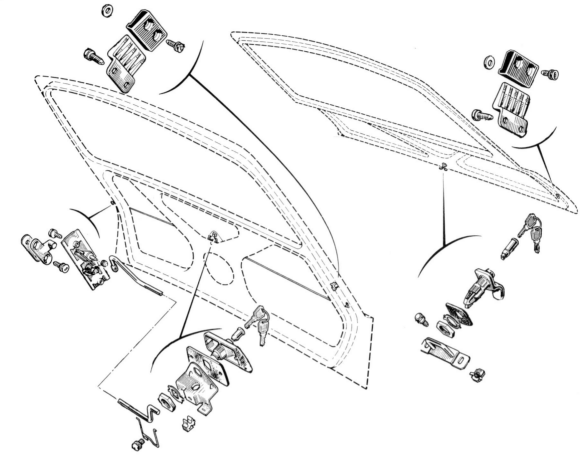

Fig. 12.9. The two types of tailgate locks (Sec. 14.6)

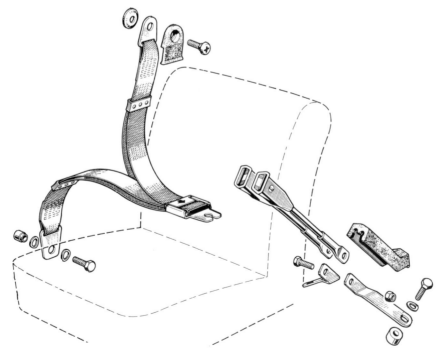

Fig. 12.10. Components of a front seat belt (Sec. 15.2)

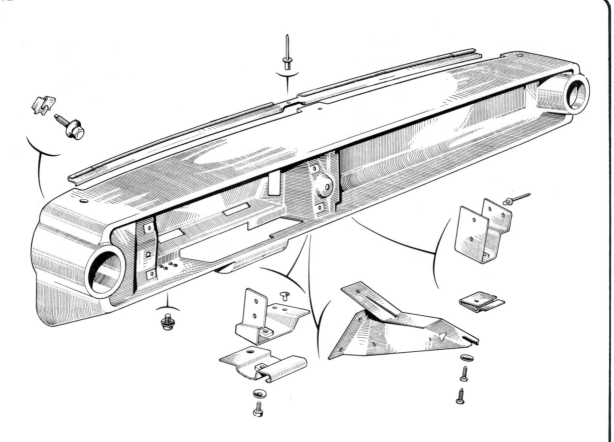

Fig. 12.11. The fascia panel and attachment brackets (Sec. 16.1)

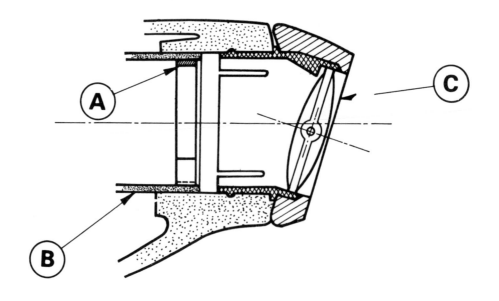

FIG. 12.12. CROSS SECTIONAL VIEW OF A FACIA PANEL FRESH AIR VENTILATOR (SEC. 16.4)

| A | Circlip | B | Duct | C | Adjustable outlet |

Fig. 12.13. Removal point for ventilator duct (Sec. 16.5)

Fig. 12.14. Retaining screws at one side of the facia panel (Sec. 16.6)

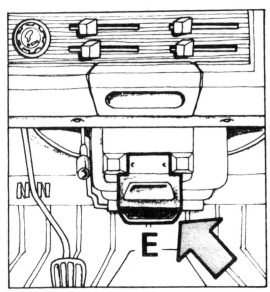

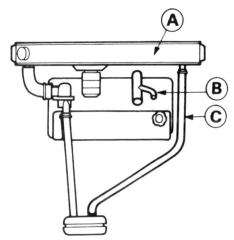

Fig. 12.16. The heater unit control panel (Sec. 17.4)

Fig. 12.15. Flap (E) to deflect warm air from interior heater to rear passenger compartment (Sec. 17.3)

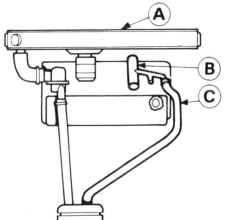

Fig. 12.19a. Heater return pipe (F series) (early) (Sec. 21.1)
A Radiator   B Union   C Return hose

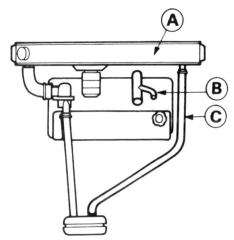

Fig. 12.19b. Heater return pipe (F series) (late) (Sec. 21.1)
A Radiator   B Union   C Return hose

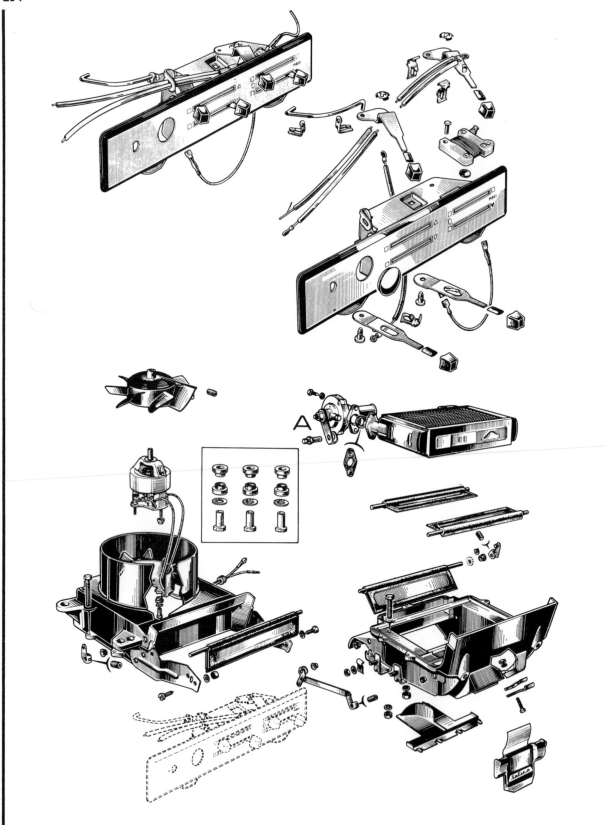

Fig. 12.17. Exploded view of the heater unit (lower) and control panel (upper) (2 parts) A is water control valve (Sec. 17.6)

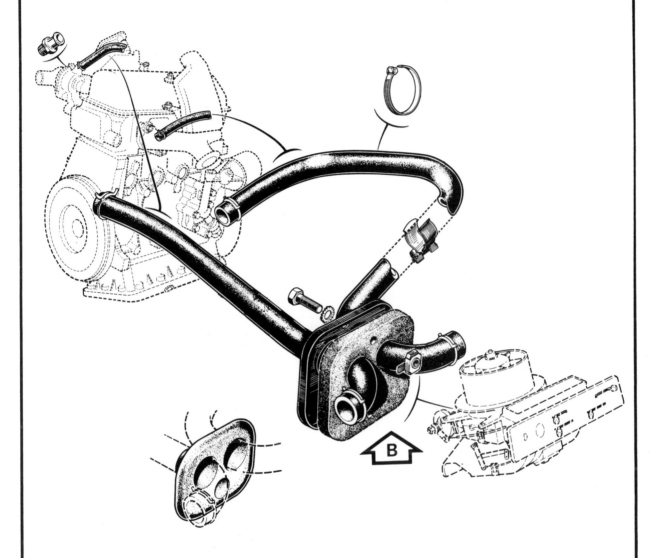

Fig. 12.18. The heater unit water flow and return hoses, bulkhead plate and rubber seal (B) (Sec. 18.2)

15 Seat belts

1 Seat belts of the three point fixing type are installed.
2 Components of the belts and anchorages are shown in Fig. 12.10.
3 On no account must the sequence of fitting of the anchorage plates, distance pieces or washers be changed nor the location of the fixing points be moved.
4 Periodically, inspect the straps for fraying or general deterioration and renew if necessary with ones of identical type.

16 Facia panel - removal and refitting

1 Components of the facia are shown in Fig.12.11.
2 Disconnect the battery leads.
3 On GLS models, remove the right hand glove box.
4 Remove the side fresh air ducts, these can be jerked from their locations as they snap into position, Fig.12.12.
5 Remove the side ventilator rubber ducts, Fig.12.13.
6 Remove the four screws (two at each end) which secure the facia panel in position (arrowed, Fig.12.14).
7 Disconnect the two junction boxes which are located beneath the facia panel just above the ignition/starter switch. Note the colour coding of these junction boxes for exact replacement.
8 Disconnect the junction box located directly behind the instrument cluster.
9 Disconnect the speedometer cable, withdraw the facia/instrument panel assembly and remove it through the left hand door. Removal of the instrument cluster independently from the facia panel is fully described in Chapter 11 of this manual.
10 Refitting is a reversal of removal.

17 Heater unit - general description

1 The heater unit is mounted in the vehicle interior below the facia panel. The unit combines the facilities of fresh air ventilation (air being drawn in through the grille just below the base of the windscreen) and warmed air which is heated by the engine cooling system.
2 A booster fan is incorporated to increase the air flow to the vehicle interior when the vehicle is moving slowly or stationary.
3 The heater unit controls are of the sliding type and provide settings for every heating, demisting or defrosting requirement. A flap (E) at the base of the heater, controls the air flow to the rear compartment, Fig.12.15.
4 To defrost and demist, shut the flap E, place the levers A and D in the 'maximum' position. Push lever C fully to the left to deflect all air stream to the screen and move blower speed lever B as required, Fig.12.16.
5 To heat the interior of the vehicle, move lever C fully to the right of its slot, regulate lever B to obtain the desired blower speed, place lever D centrally in its slot (to provide a reduced demisting airflow) and open flap E if required.
6 One of two different makes of heater unit may be encountered (IPRA or SOFICA). The assemblies differ in detail but the operating and servicing procedure is identical. The SOFICA type of heater and controls are shown in Fig.12.17.

18 Heater - removal and refitting

1 Disconnect the battery leads, drain the cooling system (Chapter 2), keeping the heater control valve lever to 'maximum'.

2 Disconnect the two heater water hoses from the engine, Fig.12.18.
3 Unscrew and remove the bulkhead blanking panel and rubber seal (B) through which the hoses pass. Slide these components over the hoses and withdraw them.
4 Remove the choke control knob on the facia panel, unscrew the assembly from the rear of the facia panel.
5 Unscrew and remove the four screws which secure the heater unit to the facia panel. Lower the unit from its location, disconnect the three electric leads (mark them for exact replacement) and withdraw the heater assembly complete with hoses.
6 Refitting is a reversal of removal but check the correct connection of the electrical leads. Refill the cooling system as described in Chapter 2 and reconnect the battery leads.
7 Check that the heater hoses do not rub or impinge upon any part of the engine or mountings. Where this is the case, release the hose clip and twist the hose so that it will support itself away from contact with the adjacent component, or use insulating tape to tie it out of the way. Where any of the Corbin type hose clips are suspect renew with worm drive types.

19 Heater motor - servicing

1 The motor is secured to the heater casing by two screws of different lengths. Separate the casing as described in the next Section. Mark the location of the longer screw and then withdraw both screws.
2 Where other than renewal of the carbon brush assembly is required, it is recommended that a new motor is fitted complete. The time involved in obtaining access to an unreliable motor on frequent occasions is not worthwhile considering that the cooling system must be drained each time.
3 Refitting of the motor is a reversal of removal.

20 Heater matrix - servicing

1 Remove the water valve (A) and rubber hoses, Fig. 12.17.
2 Remove the control panel.
3 Separate the two halves of the heater casing which is held together by four bolts and a screw.
4 Remove the matrix. Where there is evidence of water leakage from this component, renew it, attempts to solder it are seldom satisfactory. It is possible to unblock the matrix by reverse flushing with a cold water hose but the use of descaling or cleansing compounds is not recommended as the water tubes are so narrow that any sediment resulting from such treatment will probably only clog the matrix in another position.
5 Refitting is a reversal of dismantling but check that the controls are correctly connected and adjusted. Renew the rubber gasket located within the heater valve assembly.

21 Modifications

1 To improve the efficiency of the heater matrix water flow on units fitted to 1970 F series vehicles, the water return hose from the heater matrix connects directly into the vehicle cooling system radiator instead of a multi-point union adjacent to the water pump. Both the old and new circuits are shown in Fig.12.19.
2 The old and new type radiators are interchangeable.
3 A blower fan of higher output is also fitted to 1970 and later vehicles.

Chapter 13 Supplement

Contents

and high top vans and Pick-up are also covered in this manual.

1 Introduction

General

1 This supplement includes details of changes to specifications, and revised or new repair and servicing procedures, which have been introduced since 1973/74 (commencing with 4 Series vehicles).

2 Although basically the Simca 1100 range has remained unchanged over the years of production, detail modifications have been numerous and mostly concern minor re-design of small components. It is essential therefore to quote precise vehicle details when ordering spare parts.

3 The Simca 1100 (later redesignated Dodge 1100) standard

Jacking and towing

1 The car should only be raised by placing a jack under the sill jacking points or under the centre of the front crossmember. When working under the car, always supplement the jack with axle stands and chock the roadwheels on both sides.

2 The front and rear towing eyes may be used in an emergency, but if a trailer is to be towed then a specially designed towbar must be obtained.

Spanner sizes and thread locking

1 Nuts and bolts on the Simca range are all to metric standards and in the interest of economy obviously only metric spanners

and sockets need be purchased initially.

2 The following threads have thread locking compound applied to them during production and it is recommended that, whenever these nuts and bolts are disturbed, the threads are thoroughly cleaned by wire brushing and new thread locking compound applied:

Sump setscrews
Flywheel retaining bolts
Driveplate retaining bolts
Inlet manifold vacuum pipe adaptor
Gauze oil filter to crankcase
Differential carrier to crownwheel
Gearbox and differential housing covers
Locking bolts on selector forks and gear lever

2 Routine maintenance

In view of improvements which have taken place in the materials used and lubricants specified, the following maintenance programme is recommended for vehicles produced from 1974 on.

Every 250 miles (400 km) or weekly
Check and top up the engine oil
Check and top up the cooling system reservoir
Check the tyre pressures
Check the operation of all lights, wipers, washers and the horn

Every 1000 miles (1600 km) or monthly
Check and top up the battery electrolyte
Check and top up the brake and clutch fluid reservoirs

Every 5000 miles (8000 km) or at six-monthly intervals
Clean, lubricate and reset distributor points (Paris-Rhone and Ducellier distributors)
Examine and renew if necessary cassette points (SEV distributor) and adjust dwell angle
Clean and re-gap spark plugs
Check ignition timing

Renew engine oil
Check front brake disc pad wear
Examine all components for wear or slackness and check condition of rubber dust excluders and gaiters

Every 10 000 miles (16 000 km) or at twelve-monthly intervals
Check and adjust drivebelt tension
Clean flame trap in crankcase ventilation system
Clean fuel pump
Adjust valve clearances
Check carburettor settings
Renew engine oil filter
Check and top up gearbox and final drive oil levels
Check hydraulic system for leaks
Check drum linings for wear
Adjust rear brakes
Check handbrake adjustment
Check driveshaft gaiters for condition
Check tyre wear
Check security of roadwheel bolts
Clean battery terminals and apply petroleum jelly
Check exhaust system for corrosion and condition of supports
Clear body and door drain holes
Lubricate all controls, door locks and hinges
Check condition of safety belts
Check strength of antifreeze mixture

Every 15 000 miles (24 000 km) or at eighteen month intervals
Renew air cleaner element
Renew fuel filter (where fitted)
Check and adjust rear hub endfloat
Renew hydraulic brake fluid by bleeding out old fluid

Every two years
Renew antifreeze mixture

Every 30 000 miles (48 000 km) or at three-yearly intervals
Dismantle rear hubs, repack with specified grease and adjust
Renew all rubber components in brake hydraulic system

3 Specifications

The specifications listed here are revised or additional to those given in the earlier chapters of this manual. The original specifications apply unless modified in this Section.

Engine
Application chart

Year and model	Engine capacity (cc)	Engine code	Compression ratio
1967–68 (D Series)	1118	350	8.2 : 1
		350S	9.6 : 1
1968–69 (E Series)	1118 (Estate)	350	8.2 : 1
	1118 (GL, GLS)	350S	9.6 : 1
1969–70 (F Series)	1118 (LS, Estate, Auto)	350	8.2 : 1
	1118 (GL, GLS, Auto)	350S	9.6 : 1
1970–71 (G Series)	1118 (LS, Van, Auto)	350	8.2 : 1
	1118 (GLS, Estate, Auto)	350	9.6 : 1
	1204 (1100S, Auto)	353S	9.5 : 1
1971–72 (H Series)	1118 (LS, GLS, Van, Estate)	350	8.2 : 1
	1118 (LS, GLS, Auto)	350	9.6 : 1
	1294 (1100S and Auto)	366	9.6 : 1
1972–73 (J Series)	1118 (GLS, Van, Estate, Auto)	350S	9.6 : 1
	1118 (1100S, GLS and Auto)	350S	9.6 : 1
	1294 (1100S and Auto)	366	9.6 : 1
1973–74 (4 Series)	1118 (Van, Estate)	350	8.2 : 1
	1118 (TT and Auto)	350	9.6 : 1
	1294 (1100S and Auto)	366	9.6 : 1
	1294 (1100TI)	3G4	9.8 : 1

Year and model	Engine capacity (cc)	Engine code	Compression ratio
1974–75 (5 Series)	1118 (ES, GLS)	3E1	9.6 : 1
	1118 (LX, LS)	3E1	8.2 : 1
	1294 (Special)	3G2	9.8 : 1
	1294 (TI)	3G4	9.8 : 1
	1118 (Estate, LS, GLS)	3E1	9.6 : 1
	1294 (Special, Estate)	3G2	9.8 : 1
	1118 (Van)	3E1	8.2 : 1
1975 on (6 and 7 Series)	1118 (Manual and Auto)	3E1A	9.6 : 1
	1294 (1100TI)	3G4	9.5 : 1

Standard piston diameters

As from December 1975, the piston-to-bore clearance is reduced to between 0.022 and 0.037 mm. At the same time, the number of piston grades is increased to four in increments of 0.0075 mm.

	1118 cc	1294 cc
Grade A	73.9625 to 73.9700 mm	76.6575 to 76.6650 mm
Grade B	73.9700 to 73.9775 mm	76.6650 to 76.6725 mm
Grade C	73.9775 to 73.9850 mm	76.6725 to 76.6800 mm
Grade D	73.9850 to 73.9925 mm	76.6800 to 76.6875 mm

Cylinder bore sizes (1975 on)

	1118 cc	1294 cc
Grade A	73.9920 to 73.9995 mm	76.6870 to 76.6945 mm
Grade B	73.9995 to 74.0070 mm	76.6945 to 76.7020 mm
Grade C	74.0070 to 74.0145 mm	76.7020 to 76.7095 mm
Grade D	74.1045 to 74.0220 mm	76.7095 to 76.7170 mm

Gudgeon pin length

1294cc engine	2.62 in (66.7 mm)

Camshaft and valvegear

Camshaft bearing journal diameters (numbered from flywheel end):

No. 1	1.395 to 1.396 in (35.439 to 35.459 mm)
No. 2	1.611 to 1.612 in (40.939 to 40.959 mm)
No. 3	1.631 to 1.632 in (41.439 to 41.459 mm)
Camshaft running clearance	0.0010 to 0.0032 in (0.025 to 0.081 mm)
Tappets (cam followers):	
Diameter	0.904 to 0.905 mm (22.974 to 23.000 mm)
Inlet valve lift (commencing Series 6):	
1118cc engine	0.319 in (8.1 mm)
1294cc engine	0.354 in (9.0 mm)
Exhaust valve lift (commencing Series 6):	
Single carburettor engines	0.334 in (8.5 mm)
Other engines	0.354 in (9.0 mm)
Timing chain:	
Number of links	50
Pitch	0.375 in (9.525 mm)
Valve clearances (commencing Series 6):	
Inlet (cold)	0.010 in (0.25 mm)
Exhaust (cold)	0.012 in (0.30 mm)

Oil pressure

At normal operating temperature	57 to 85 lbf/in^2 (4 to 6 kgf/cm^2) at 3000 rev/min.

Torque wrench settings

	lbf ft	Nm
Cylinder head bolts (cold)	50	68
Crankshaft pulley bolt	110	150
Oil pressure switch	14	19

Carburettor specifications — 1975 on, 3E1 (1118cc) engine

Solex BISA5

	High Compression	Low Compression
Venturi	25	25
Secondary venturi	1.8 mm	2.0 mm
Main jet	132.5 ± 2.5	127.5 ± 2.5
Air correction jet	200 ± 5	180 ± 5
Emulsion tube	E7	E2
Econostat	50	50
Idler jet	39 to 45	35 to 45 (with damper)
Pump jet	45	45
Pump stroke	3 mm	—
Needle valve	1.5	1.5
Float level	4.9 mm dia. rod	—
Fast idle gap	0.95 ± 0.05 mm	—

		High Compression	Low Compression
Constant CO air feed		500	500
Constant CO fuel jet		30	30
Constant CO air jet		100	100

Bressel 32 IBS 7 for 3E1 (1118cc) low compression engine

Main venturi	24.5
Secondary venturi	4.5
Main jet	130 ± 2.5
Air correction jet	165 ± 5
Emulsion tube	F6
Fuel enrichment jet	120
Air enrichment jet	70
Mixture enrichment jet	200
Idle jet with damper	42 ± 2.5
Idler air jet	195
Progression holes	100—100—70
Pump jet	45
Pump discharge	40
Needle valve	150
Float level	6 mm ± 0.25
Idle discharge hole	140
Fast idle gap	0.75 ± 0.05 mm
Mechanical opening	5.25 mm

Weber with 1294cc engine

	Weber 36DCNV1 with 3G2 engine	Weber 36DCNF with 3G4 engine
Venturi	28	29
Secondary venturi	4.5	3.5
Main jet	127.5 ± 2.5	125
Air correction jet	160 ± 5	200 ± 15
Emulsion tube	F36	F36
Idle jet	40 to 42	45
Idler air jet	135 ± 5	135 ± 15
Progression holes	90—90—90—100	80—90—90—105
Pump jet	45	40
Pump discharge	—	40
Needle valve	175	175
Float level	52 ± 0.25	52 ± 0.25
Fast idle gap	0.40	—
Vacuum gap	5 to 5.5 mm	—
Mechanical gap	8 to 8.5 mm	—
Air jet	—	250
Fuel jet	—	70
Emulsion tube	—	F5

Idle speeds (1975 on)

Engine		Transmission	Idle speed (rev/min)
3E1 (1118cc)		Manual	850 ± 50
3E1 (1118cc)		Automatic	900 ± 50
3G2 (1294cc)		Manual	950 ± 50
3G2 (1294cc)		Automatic	950 ± 50
3G4 (1294cc)		Manual	950 ± 50

CO content of exhaust gas (tamperproof carburettors) not to exceed 4.5% at idle speed

Ignition system
Distributor applications and static timing

Year	Engine	Distributor make	Distributor No.	Static Timing (BTDC)
1968	350 from No. 6 002 416	Ducellier	4199	9°
	350 from No. 6 002 417	Ducellier	4214—4222	12°
1969	350S	Ducellier	4286	12°
1970 on	350S, 3E1	Ducellier	4287	10°
	353S	Ducellier	4342	12°
1972	366	Ducellier	4332	12° (anti-pollution)
1972	366	Ducellier	4389	12° (non anti-pollution)
1973	350, 350S	Ducellier	4287	
		Paris-Rhone	DA 4CS1	10°
		SEV-Marchal	41 102 402	
1973	366	Ducellier	4425	4°
	366 from No. 3 332 681	Ducellier	4389	12°

Year	Engine	Distributor make	Distributor No.	Static Timing (BTDC)
1974 on	366 (manual only)	Ducellier	4479 }	12°
		SEV-Marchal	41 101 802 }	
	366 (auto only)	Ducellier	4389 }	12°
		SEV-Marchal	41 102 302 }	
	3G4	Ducellier	4426 }	4°
		Paris-Rhone	DA 4CS6 }	
		SEV-Marchal	41 102 202 }	
1975 on	3G2	Ducellier	4522 }	12°
		Paris-Rhone	DA 4CS8 }	
		SEV-Marchal	41 102 502 }	
1976 on	3E1 and 3E1A*	Ducellier	6610 }	6° to 8°
		SEV-Marchal	41 102 802 }	
		Paris-Rhone	DA4 CS9 }	
	3G2*	Ducellier	6621 or }	10° to 12°
		SEV-Marchal	41 103 002 }	
		Paris-Rhone	DA4 CS10 }	
	3G4*	Ducellier	6618 }	6° to 8°
		SEV-Marchal	41 102 902 }	
		Paris-Rhone	DA4 CS11 }	

Dynamic timing is recommended for these engines. The static timing settings shown are valid for this method provided engine speed is kept below 1000 rpm.

Clutch

Torque wrench settings:	lbf ft	Nm
Clutch housing to engine	36	49
Clutch housing to gearbox	19	26

Manual gearbox

Primary shaft roller bearings shim availability   ...   ...   0.0039 in (0.01 mm) 0.0196 in (0.025 mm)
0.0078 in (0.015 mm) 0.0393 in (0.03 mm)

Input shaft roller bearing shim availability   ...   .   0.004 in (0.1 mm) 0.020 in (0.5 mm)
0.008 in (0.2 mm) 0.040 in (1.0 mm)

Torque wrench settings:	lbf ft	Nm
Output shaft locknut (left-hand thread)	107	146
Shift forks to shafts	12	16
Shift fork control lever to shaft	19	26
Reversing lamp switch bolts	19	26
Clutch or differential housing to gearbox	19	26
Relay bracket to differential housing	24	33
Relay support to brackets	33	45
Swivel lever bearing to body	33	45

Driveshafts

Diameter (all later models 1974 on)	1.574 in (40.0 mm)
Shaft length (right-hand)	24.7/16 in (621.0 mm)
Shaft length (left-hand)	17.13/16 in (451.5 mm)

Front suspension

Torque wrench settings:	lbf ft	Nm
Shock absorber upper mounting	11	15
Shock absorber lower mounting	18	25
Hub bearing screwed sleeve to stub axle carrier	240	326

Rear suspension

Track (not adjustable) ...   .   0.078 in (2.0 mm) toe-in to 0.078 in (2.0 mm) toe-out

Torsion bar diameter:

Saloons	53/64 in (20.9 mm)
Vans, Estates, Pick-ups	7/8 in (22.2 mm)

Torque wrench settings:	lbf ft	Nm
Shock absorber upper mounting	11	15
Shock absorber lower mounting	18	25

Steering

Overall turning circle (between kerbs):

All models up to and including Series 6, right-hand drive
VF1 and VF2, Pick-up, Series 7   ...   .   35 ft 5 in (10.80 m)

All models commencing Series 7 except right-hand drive
VF1, VF2 and Pick-up   ...   .   34 ft 1½ in (10.40 m)

Steering ratio:
    Models with turning circle of 35 ft 5 in (10.80 m) ... 15.6 : 1
    Models with turning circle of 34 ft 1½ in (10.40 m) ... 21.46 : 1
Steering rack grease capacity (refill after overhaul) ... ... 2.5 oz (72 g)
Steering adjustment up to chassis E2 1 110 563:
    Track ... ... 0.040 in (1.0 mm) toe-in to 0.118 in (3.0 mm) toe-out
    Camber (Saloon) ... ... 0° 15' ± 30'
    Camber (Estate) ... ... −30' ± 30'
    Castor (Saloon) ... ... 1° 15' ± 30'
    Castor (Estate) ... ... 2° 15' ± 30'
Steering adjustment from chassis E2 111 0564:
    Track ... ... 0.040 in (1.0 mm) toe-in to 0.118 in (3.0 mm) toe-out
    Camber (Saloon) ... ... -0° 15' ± 0° 30'
    Camber (Estate, Van, Pick-up) ... ... -1° ± 0° 30'
    Castor (all models) ... ... 2° ± 0° 30'
Torque wrench settings:

	lbf ft	Nm
Steering wheel nut	41	56
Rack ball end fitting nuts	33	45
Track rod end locknuts	44	60

Roadwheels and tyres

Wheel type:
    Up to 1972 ... ... Pressed steel
    Special and TI 1973 on ... ... Light alloy
Size:
    1100 cars and all vans ... ... 4½J x 13
    Specials and TI ... ... 5J x 13
Tyre size:
    1100 saloon 145 SR13
    Estate and van 155 SR13
    Special and TI (1973 on) 145 HR13
Tyre pressures (normal speeds and loads):

	Front lbf/in^2	kgf/cm^2	Rear lbf/in^2	kgf/cm^2
Saloon (1118cc)	25	1.75	26	1.82
Saloon (1294cc)	26	1.82	26	1.82
Estate, Van, Pick-up	23	1.61	26	1.82

Tyre pressures (sustained high speeds or fully laden):

	Front lbf/in^2	kgf/cm^2	Rear lbf/in^2	kgf/cm^2
Saloon (1118cc)	26	1.82	30	2.10
Saloon (1294cc)	28	1.96	30	2.10
Estate, Van, Pick-up	23	1.61	32	2.24

Braking systems
Dimensions
Disc caliper cylinder diameter:
    1100 TI 1973 on ... ... 1.889 in (48.0 mm)
    Other models ... ... 1.732 in (44.0 mm)
Rear wheel cylinder diameter:
    TI models 1975/1976 ... ... 0.866 in (22.0 mm)
    Series 7 models except 1100 TI ... ... 0.687 in (17.5 mm)
    Series 7 TI models ... ... 0.811 in (20.6 mm)
Discs — models from 1973 (except TI models 1975 on):
    Outside diameter ... ... 9.231 in (234.5 mm)
    Thickness ... ... 0.429 in (10.9 mm)
    Minimum thickness after regrinding ... ... 0.389 in (9.9 mm)
Discs — TI models 1975 on:
    Outside diameter ... ... 9.389 in (238.5 mm)
    Thickness ... ... 0.429 in (10.9 mm)
    Minimum thickness after regrinding ... ... 0.389 in (9.9 mm)
Drums — models from 1973 (except TI models from 1975):
    Internal diameter ... ... 8.511 in (216.2 mm)
    Maximum internal diameter after regrinding ... ... 8.551 in (217.2 mm)
Drums on TI models 1975 on:
    Internal diameter ... ... 8.999 in (228.6 mm)
    Maximum internal diameter after regrinding ... ... 9.038 in (229.6 mm)
Torque wrench settings

	lbf ft	Nm
Brake disc to hub	35	48
Reservoir to master cylinder	24	33

Electrical system

Bulbs: *Wattage*
    Headlamps (Halogen) 60/65
    Driving lamps (Halogen) 55
    Fog lamps (Halogen)   55
    Rear fog lamps   21

Bodywork
General dimensions

Saloon:
    Overall length ... ...   155.3 in (3944 mm)
    Overall width ... ...   62.5 in (1588 mm)
    Overall height ... ...   57.4 in (1458 mm)
    Wheelbase ... ...   99.2 in (2520 mm)

Estate:
    Overall length ... ...   154.7 in (3929 mm)
    Overall width ... ...   62.5 in (1588 mm)
    Overall height ... ...   58.3 in (1480 mm)
    Wheelbase ... ...   99.2 in (2520 mm)

Van:
    Overall length ... ...   as Estate version
    Overall width ... ...   as Estate version
    Overall height (Standard van) ... ... 58.3 in (1480 mm)
    (High-top van) ... ...   73.3 in (1863 mm)
    (Pick-up) ... ...   64.6 in (1640 mm)
    Wheelbase ... ...   as Estate version

Weights

Unladen weight:
    3-door Saloon ... ...   1990 lb (903 kg)
    5-door Saloon ... ...   2051 lb (930 kg)
    Special ... ...   2117 lb (960 kg)
    Estate ... ...   2035 lb (923 kg)
    Standard Van ... ...   1962 lb (890 kg)
    High-top Van ... ...   2028 lb (920 kg)
    Pick-up ... ...   1951 lb (885 kg)
Nominal pay load (all vans) ... ...   10 cwt (500 kg)
Gross Vehicle Weight:
    Standard Van ... ...   3086 lb (1400 kg)
    High-top Van ... ...   3131 lb (1420 kg)
    Pick-up ... ...   3131 lb (1420 kg)

4 Engine

The engines fitted to later models are basically the same as described in Chapter 1 but incorporate the following modifications.

Lubrication system

1 On the 1100 TI models the engine oil pressure is indicated by a pressure gauge on the instrument panel; the gauge is electrically operated by a sender unit in the cylinder block. With the engine at normal operating temperature the indicated pressure should be within the range quoted in the Specifications (Section 3).

2 On the 350 and 350S type engines from engine numbers 6 003 815 and 6 422 798 respectively, the overall size of the oil pump cover and the pressure relief valve body and plug have been reduced. Should it be necessary to replace the old type oil pump cover with one of the new type, a new pressure relief valve body and plug must also be fitted. Similarly, the new valve body cannot be fitted to the old type cover although the new plug will fit either the new or old type valve body. **Note:** *On some of the later type pumps the use of a pressure relief valve spring has been discontinued.*

Modified cylinder head gasket (1100cc)

3 On engines produced from September 1977 the cylinder head gasket incorporates triangular coolant passage holes instead of the earlier round type. This later type of gasket may be used on earlier engines but the earlier, round hole gasket must not be used on the later engines.

Connecting rod/piston assemblies — refitting to crankshaft

4 On the later type 1118cc and 1294cc engines the side faces of the connecting rod bearings and caps have oil grooves machined into them. When refitting these rods into the cylinder block, always ensure that the grooves are towards the camshaft side of the engine (see Fig. 13.1).

5 Pistons used in 1100 S and 1100 TI engines have two cut-outs in the crown. Correct assembly of the piston to the connecting rod is most important. The locating mark (C) at the bottom of the skirt is to be towards the timing gear and the numbers and lubrication grooves on the connecting rod are to be on the camshaft side.

6 When refitting the piston rings, ensure that they are located the right way up in the correct piston groove (see Fig. 13.3). The ring gaps must be positioned 120° from each other around the piston (see Fig. 13.4).

Crankcase ventilation systems

7 The crankcase ventilation system on the type 3G4 engine fitted to the 1100 TI comprises a short hose connected between the oil filler cap on the rocker cover and the hose between the air filter and carburettors (see Fig. 13.5).

5 Cooling system

The cooling system on later Simca models is basically unchanged with the following exceptions:

1 The upper radiator support bracket has been deleted on all models manufactured after April 1972, and Chrysler recommend

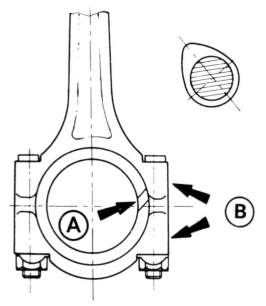

Fig. 13.1 Connecting rod installation in relation to camshaft

A   *Oil groove*   B   *Rod and cap numbers*

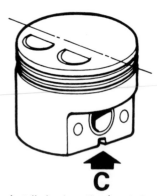

Fig. 13.2 Piston installation in engine (notch C towards timing gear)

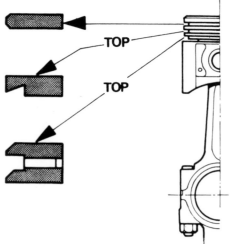

Fig. 13.3 Piston ring installation diagram

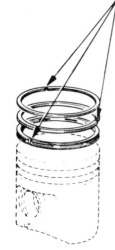

Fig. 13.4 Staggering of piston ring end gaps

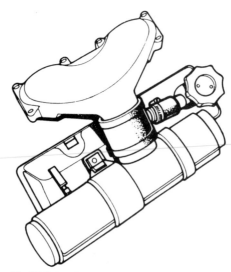

Fig. 13.5 Crankcase ventilation system (1100 TI)

that if working on a car built prior to this date the upper attachment lug should be removed. This will avoid the possibility of the lug subjecting the radiator to stress and causing leakage.

2 From June 1971 the thermostat on all models has been replaced with one that starts to open at 83°C (181°F) and is fully open at 96°C (202°F). When working on the cooling system on older models it is recommended that the original thermostat is discarded and replaced with the latest type.

---

6   Fuel system and carburation

1 Apart from certain carburettor data changes (see Specifications) and the deletion of the fuel tank drain plug, no major changes have been made to the fuel system. On some models a fuel return pipe is fitted between the pump and tank and a disposable filter is fitted between the pump and carburettor (see Fig. 13.6).

Solex 32 BISA carburettor
2 Later vehicles are fitted with a modified carburettor to meet the more stringent anti-pollution regulations. The main difference between this type of carburettor and earlier versions is

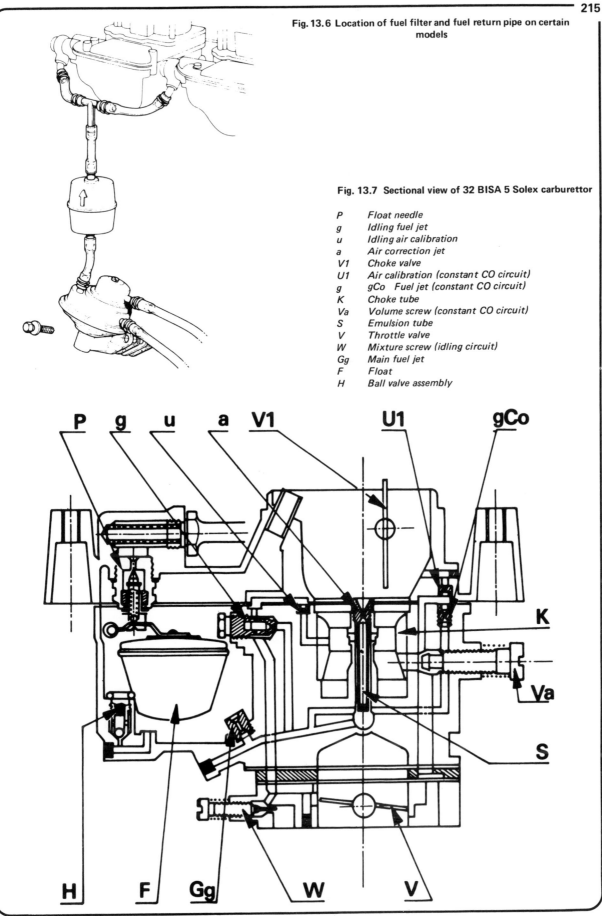

Fig. 13.6 Location of fuel filter and fuel return pipe on certain models

Fig. 13.7 Sectional view of 32 BISA 5 Solex carburettor

P — Float needle
g — Idling fuel jet
u — Idling air calibration
a — Air correction jet
V1 — Choke valve
U1 — Air calibration (constant CO circuit)
g gCo — Fuel jet (constant CO circuit)
K — Choke tube
Va — Volume screw (constant CO circuit)
S — Emulsion tube
V — Throttle valve
W — Mixture screw (idling circuit)
Gg — Main fuel jet
F — Float
H — Ball valve assembly

the inclusion of an independent, additional idling system.

3 The throttle stop screw is pre-set and should not be tampered with.

4 The mixture control screw is pre-set during production and is fitted with a tamperproof cap and sleeve. Normally, this screw should not be altered, any variation in engine idling speed being carried out by screwing the volume screw in or out.

5 It has been found from experience however that the factory setting on some carburettors is so lean that the engine tends to stall when the clutch is depressed as the vehicle comes to a standstill. Also cold starting and warm-up requires more than a reasonable amount of choke operation. In these instances, or when a major overhaul is to be carried out, break off the plastic cap and carry out the following adjustment using the mixture control screw.

6 Have the engine at normal operating temperature and idling at a slightly higher speed than normal. Use a tuning device such as 'Colortune' or attach a vacuum gauge to the brake servo hose connection on the intake manifold.

7 Turn the mixture control screw B (Fig.13.9) in or out until

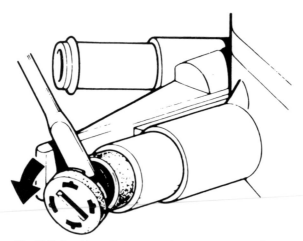

Fig. 13.8 Breaking off plastic cap from mixture screw (Solex tamperproof carburettor)

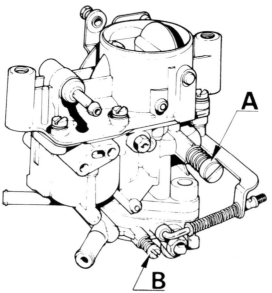

Fig. 13.9 Solex adjusting screws

A Volume screw   B Mixture screw

the combustion flame is of the correct colour in accordance with the manufacturer's recommendations (Colortune) or, if a vacuum gauge is being used, turn the screw until the reading on the gauge is at its highest point.

8 Adjust the engine idling speed to the specified level by turning the volume screw (A).

9 Switch off the engine and remove the tuning device or vacuum gauge.

10 A new plastic sealing cap should be fitted once the adjustment has been completed.

Bressel 32 1BS 7 carburettor

11 This type of carburettor is fitted to low compression engines as an alternative to the Solex type after April 1976. The carburettors are interchangeable and similar except that limiter caps are fitted to the adjustment screws on the Bressel to prevent the idle mixture from being enriched.

Weber 36 DCNF carburettors (to 1975)

12 A revised slow-running adjustment procedure is recommended for vehicles equipped with these carburettors.

1294cc special with 3G2 engine

13 A tachometer should be attached to the engine in accordance with the makers' instructions. A carburettor synchroniser (balancer) should also be available.

14 Tighten the mixture screws 1 and 2 (Fig.13.10) until they seat and then loosen them by 3 turns.

15 Unscrew the stop screw (5) until the throttle butterflies are fully closed. Now turn the stop screw until it contacts the control lever and then give it a further complete turn.

16 Screw in the compensator screws (3) and (4) lightly.

17 Start the engine and adjust the idle speed to 950 rev/min.

18 Using the balancing device, balance the readings by unscrewing the compensator screw on the side which is indicating the highest reading. The other compensator screw is to remain tightened.

19 When balance is achieved, tighten the compensator screw locknuts.

20 Set the idle speed to 950 rev/min using the stop screw (5).

21 Now obtain the highest idling speed using the mixture screws (1) and (2).

22 Reset the engine idle speed to 950 rev/min using screw (5).

23 Turn screw (1) inward to achieve a speed drop of 25 rev/min. Turn screw (2) inwards to achieve a similar drop.

24 Reset the idle speed to 950 rev/min using the stop screw (5).

1294cc TI with 3G4 engine

25 A tachometer should be connected to the engine in accordance with the makers' instructions. A carburettor synchroniser (balancer) should also be available.

26 Release the locknuts and screw the four compensator screws (A) fully in (Fig.13.11).

27 Screw in the four mixture screws (B) until they seat and then unscrew them two complete turns.

28 Unscrew the stop screw (C) until the throttle butterfly is closed on the carburettor nearer the flywheel end of the engine.

29 Loosen the synchroniser screw (D).

30 Depress the lever (E) to compress the spring on the stud (F) and so close all four butterfly valves.

31 Holding the lever depressed, screw in the screw (D) until it just contacts the lever (E) but without opening the throttle butterfly valves on the right-hand carburettor.

32 Now turn screw (C) until it just contacts the idle speed stop and then give it one more complete turn.

33 Start the engine and adjust the idle speed to 950 rev/min using the stop screw.

34 Using the screw (D) balance the vacuum readings on the synchroniser between barrels 2 and 3.

35 Readjust the idle speed to 950 rev/min.

36 Now check the vacuum readings between the two barrels

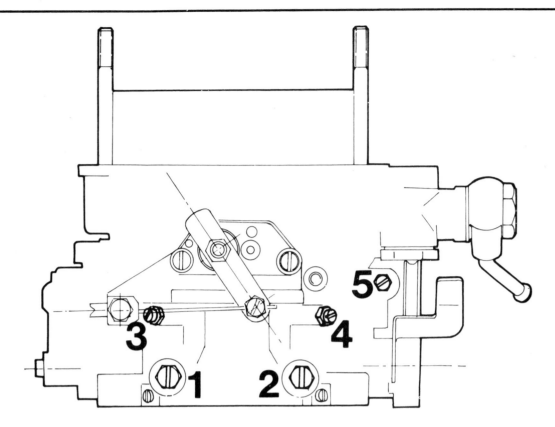

Fig. 13.10 Adjusting screws (Weber 36 DCNF carburettor to 1975) — 1294 cc Special with 3G2 engine

1 and 2 Mixture screws   3 and 4 Compensator screws   5 Stop screw

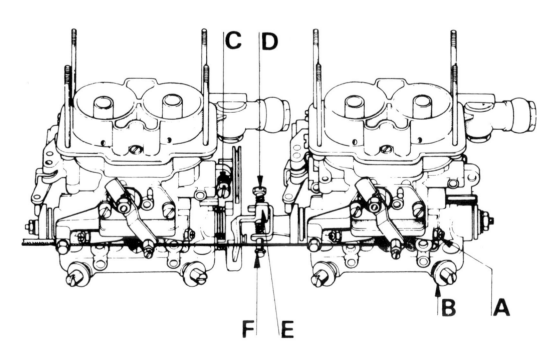

Fig 13.11 Adjusting screws (Weber 36 DCNF carburettor to 1975) — 1294 cc TI with 3G4 engine

A Compensator screws   C Stop screw   E Lever
B Mixture screws   D Synchroniser screw   F Stud

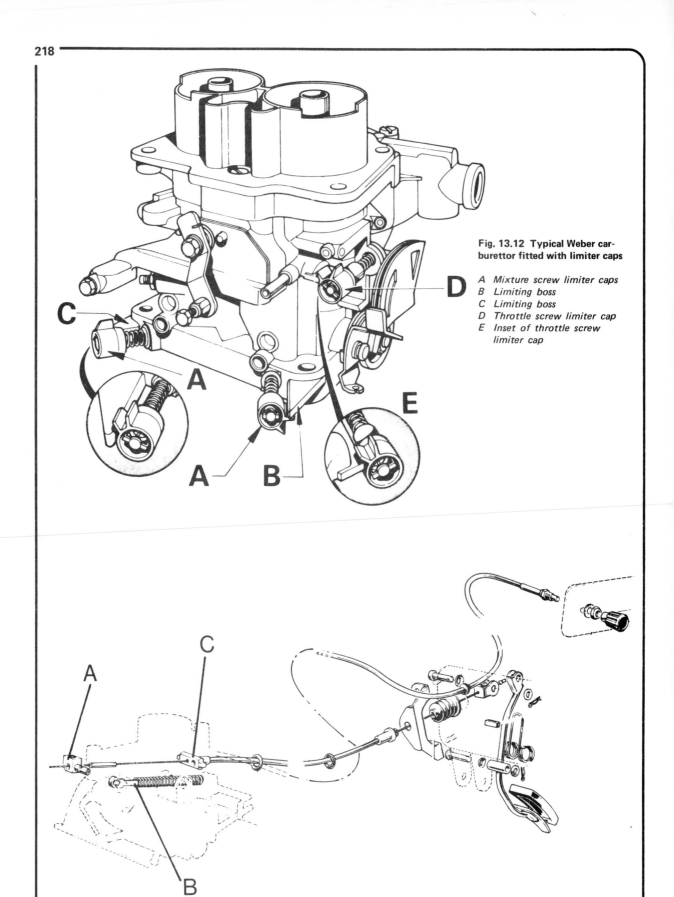

Fig. 13.12 Typical Weber carburettor fitted with limiter caps

A Mixture screw limiter caps
B Limiting boss
C Limiting boss
D Throttle screw limiter cap
E Inset of throttle screw
   limiter cap

Fig. 13.13 Later type throttle cable control

A Brass trunnion block   B Tension rod   C Nylon pivot block

of each carburettor in sequence. Balance out any differences by means of the compensator screws (A). Always unscrew the screw on the barrel which has the greatest vacuum leaving the other screw tight. Tighten the compensator locknuts on completion.

Weber DCNF carburettors with limiter cap screws
37 These carburettors are fitted with plastic caps on the adjustment screws to limit the amount of travel of the screws.
38 Any adjustment should normally be confined to turning the screws within the limit of travel of the ears of the screw caps in order to achieve smooth idling at the specified speed.
39 Adjusting after major overhaul or to correct grossly bad running should be carried out in one of the two following ways.

With CO meter (connected in accordance with the makers' instructions)
40 Have the engine at normal operating temperature and adjust to 950 rev/min using the stop screw (C) (Fig.13.11).
41 Break off the limiter caps and adjust the mixture screws (B) to achieve a CO reading less than 4.5%. Reset the idle speed if necessary.

Without CO meter
42 Have the engine at normal operating temperature and adjust the idle speed to 950 rev/min using the stop screw (C).
43 Attain the highest engine speed by turning each of the mixture screws (B) in sequence. Readjust the idle speed if necessary.
44 Now turn each of the mixture screws (B) to give a speed drop of between 15 and 20 rev/min.
45 Reset the engine speed to 950 rev/min.
46 Once adjustment is completed, new limiter caps should be fitted with their ears against the stops to prevent any future anti-clockwise rotation.

Weber type DCNV carburettor — adjustment
47 These carburettors fitted to Series 7 vehicles have tamper-proof caps fitted to the mixture screws to prevent any alteration to the factory setting.
48 The only adjustment which should be necessary is to the throttle stop screw to bring the idle speed within specification.
49 If, due to major overhaul, the mixture screws have to be altered, then adjustment must be carried out using a CO meter as described in the preceding Section, and on completion new caps must be installed.

Revised throttle control mechanism
50 The rod type control fitted to early models has been replaced by a cable type.
51 Disconnection from the carburettor lever should be carried out in the following way.
52 Release the pinch screw and remove the cable from the brass trunnion block (A) (Fig.13.13).
53 Turn the trunnion block through 90° and pull the tension rod (B) towards the rear of the car against the pressure of the coil spring. Withdraw the tension rod and spring.
54 Tilt the nylon pivot block (C) forward and down to release its lugs from the support bracket on the rocker cover. The cable assembly can then be lifted free from its attachment to the engine, ready for disconnection from the bulkhead and from the accelerator pedal.
55 On 1294cc engines, the cable outer conduit incorporates an adjustment sleeve.

---

7 Ignition system

SEV-Marchal distributors — general description
1 Later vehicles may be fitted with the SEV-Marchal type distributor. This differs from other units by having cassette type breaker points. Renewal of the cassette will entail the use of a

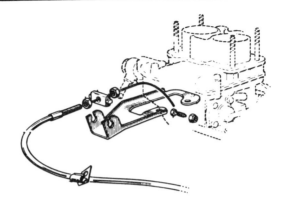

Fig. 13.14 Throttle cable adjuster sleeve (1294 cc engines only)

dwell meter as the points cannot be set satisfactorily using a feeler gauge.

SEV-Marchal cassette points — removal and refitting
2 It is recommended that the air cleaner is removed to provide better access to the distributor.
3 Prise off the distributor cap securing clips, remove the anti-splash shield, and lift away the cap complete with HT leads and place it to one side.
4 Pull off the rotor arm.
5 Pull the earth tag from the base of the condenser.
6 Carefully pull the complete vacuum diaphragm/cassette assembly upwards from the distributor body. Do not strain the LT lead to the condenser (Fig.13.16).
7 Push the condenser partially out of the plastic housing and disconnect the plug from its upper terminals.
8 Separate the cassette from the crosspiece of the vacuum diaphragm operating arm.
9 The new cassette will be supplied with the notch central in the triangular cut-out to give an approximate contact points setting.
10 Engage the cassette with the crosspiece of the vacuum diaphragm capsule operating arm so that the red pivots of the crosspiece engage in the cut-outs in the upper and lower plates of the cassette.
11 Check that the cam follower (A) (Fig.13.17) in the centre hole in the cassette will not foul the rotor arm positioning notch (B) when the cassette is installed. If it will, turn the engine over to reposition the notch.

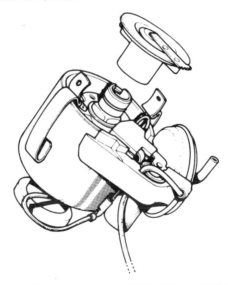

Fig. 13.15 Removing rotor arm (SEV—Marchal distributor)

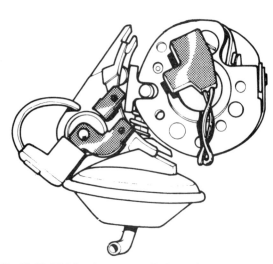

Fig. 13.16 Withdrawing vacuum diaphragm/cassette assembly
from SEV—Marchal distributor

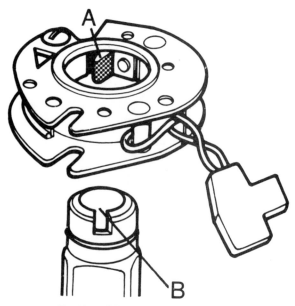

Fig. 13. 17 SEV—Marchal cassette points

A Cam follower   B Rotor arm positioning notch

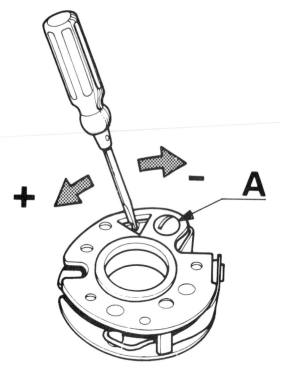

Fig. 13. 18 SEV—Marchal cassette points adjustment

A Clamp screw not to be disturbed

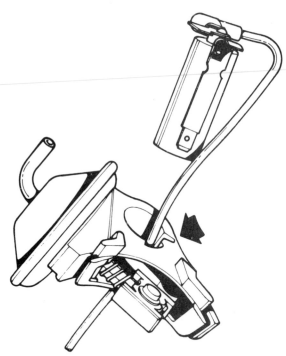

Fig. 13. 19 SEV—Marchal condenser. LT wire slot arrowed

12 Push the complete vacuum unit/cassette down into the
distributor making sure that the securing claws (one at each end
of the vacuum capsule unit) engage correctly with the distributor body.
13 Before pushing the condensor downwards, connect the plug
to the terminal tags on the top of the condenser.
14 Push the condenser fully down, making sure that the
plastic connecting plug does not stand proud of the recess in
the distributor body rim.
15 Push the earth lead on to the tag at the base of the
condenser.

16 Install the rotor arm and the cap but not the splash shield at
this stage.

SEV-Marchal cassette points — adjustment
17 Connect a dwell meter in accordance with the makers'
instructions, start the engine and check the dwell angle on the
meter. If it is outside the specified angle, adjust in the following
way.
18 Stop the engine, remove the distributor cap and insert a
screwdriver into the triangular cut-out in the cassette upper
plate, engaging it with the notch. If the dwell angle is too

small, twist the screwdriver blade to move the notch in the fixed contact towards the domed head of the clamp screw. This will have the effect of closing the points gap and increasing the dwell angle.

19 If the dwell angle is too large, twist the screwdriver blade to move the notch in the fixed contact towards the vacuum capsule operating rod crosspiece slot in the cassette upper plate. This will open the points gap and reduce the dwell angle.

20 Two factors are very important when adjusting this assembly:

(i) never tamper with the clamp screw (A) (Fig.13.18)

(ii) make only fractional adjustments, re-checking the dwell angle between adjustments. Too great a movement of the notch may prevent the engine firing at all.

21 Refit the distributor cap and the splash shield and remove the dwell meter.

SEV-Marchal distributor — condenser renewal

22 The condenser can be renewed by first detaching the earth lead from its base, removing the distributor cap and then partially pushing the condenser upwards until the leads can be disconnected from its upper terminal tags. Keep the cassette/vacuum capsule pushed well down during the time when upward pressure is applied to the condenser.

23 Pull the condenser out of its housing and note the cut-out in the housing through which the LT lead slides.

Ignition timing — modified settings

24 Refer to the Specifications in Section 3 of this Chapter for details of revised ignition timing for all models.

Modified distributor cap

25 Distributors from 1974 are fitted with a 'Norsomix' type cap which is interchangeable with distributor caps fitted from 1972. However, if replacing the earlier type cap fitted prior to 1972 with a 'Norsomix' cap it will be necessary to increase the depth of the locating slot in the top of the distributor body by carefully filing it down to a depth of 9/64 inch (3.5 mm). Protect the interior of the distributor with a piece of cloth to prevent the entry of filings.

8 Clutch

Modification to components

1 A number of modifications and changes have been carried out to the clutch components over the years of production and it is essential that precise details of the vehicle are given when obtaining spare parts.

2 In January 1973, a self-centering release bearing was fitted which bears directly on the diaphragm spring. This necessitated a change in supporting components including the release fork and spring and the ball stud.

3 Commencing with Series 7 models (1976 on) the clutch slave cylinder is of the non-adjustable type, no pedal free movement being required. This necessitated a change in the design of the master cylinder, the slave cylinder, the flywheel and the clutch pedal components.

Alternative manufacture

4 On some later models, a Borg and Beck clutch driven plate and pressure plate assembly is used as an alternative to the Verto-Brevet components. It is important that only the correct type of clutch driven plate is used in conjunction with the same make of pressure plate. If both the driven plate and the pressure plate are being renewed then both components of either make can be fitted as a matching pair.

9 Manual gearbox

General

1 On all vehicles from March 1975, all the gears with the exception of reverse have deeper teeth and a different tooth form. These later type gears are *not* interchangeable with the earlier type and if a replacement is required the old gear(s) should be taken to your Simca dealer to ensure that the correct part is obtained. As a further check, the later type gears have a larger diameter than the earlier type as shown in the following chart:

	Diameter (early type)		Diameter (late type)	
Input shaft	mm	in	mm	in
1st gear	33.5	1.319	34.6	1.362
2nd gear	44.9	1.768	45.64	1.797
3rd gear	56.9	2.240	58.6	2.307
4th gear	67.6	2.661	69.5	2.736
Output shaft				
1st gear	107.0	4.212	108.4	4.251
2nd gear	95.2	3.748	96.36	3.794
3rd gear	83.1	3.272	84.6	3.331
4th gear	72.5	2.854	74.28	2.924

Output shaft thrust bearing

2 Later type gearboxes are fitted with a needle roller thrust bearing in front of the 1st speed gear on the output shaft, to improve gear engagement. The bearing front track replaces the oil seal previously fitted (see Fig. 13.20).

Input shaft clutch splines

3 The clutch splines on the input shaft have been strengthened and reduced in number from 21 to 18. If the later type gearbox is fitted, the 180 DBR type clutch disc with 18 splines must also be obtained.

Input shaft oil seal

4 On the later type gearboxes, the input shaft oil seal is located in front of the roller bearing in the gearbox casing

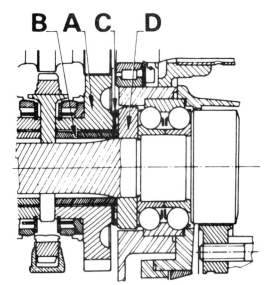

Fig. 13.20 Gearbox output shaft needle roller thrust bearing

A First gear pinion   C Needle roller bearing
B First gear bush   D Bearing front track

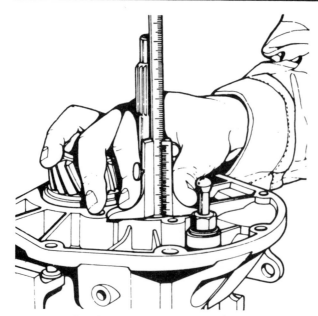

Fig. 13.21 Measuring the gearcase recess

instead of in the clutch release bearing support as on earlier type boxes. The procedure for calculating the thickness of the bearing shims differs from that described for the earlier type gearboxes (see Chapter 1, Section 5). For the later type gearboxes the following method must be used when refitting the clutch release bearing support tube.

5 First measure the distance from the face of the gearbox casing to the front face of the roller bearing outer track using a depth gauge (see Fig. 13.21).

6 Using the depth gauge, measure the depth of the spigot ('A' Fig. 13.22) on the clutch release bearing support tube.

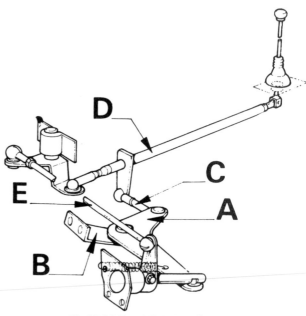

Fig. 13.24 Gearshift linkage (1975 on)

A   Relay lever   D   Control tube
B   Support bracket   E   Transverse rod
C   Lateral rod

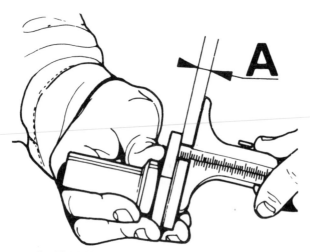

Fig. 13.22 Measuring the clutch release bearing spigot

A = depth of spigot

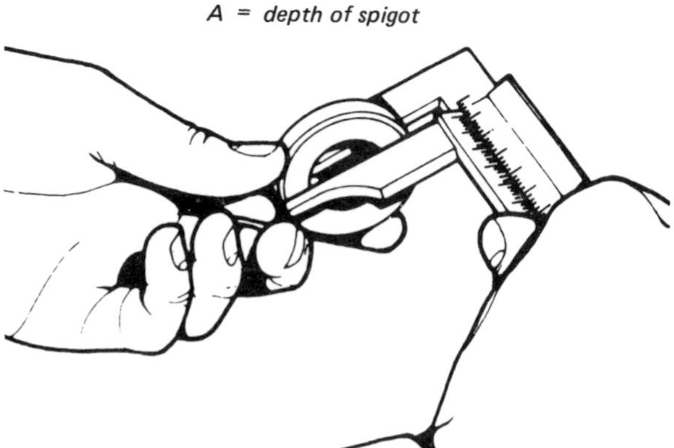

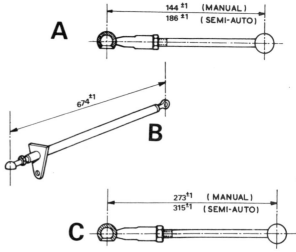

Fig. 13.25 Setting dimensions of gearshift control rods (1975 on)

A   Gear selection rod   C   Gear engagement rod
B   Control tube

Fig. 13.23 Measuring thickness of gearbox input shaft oil seal

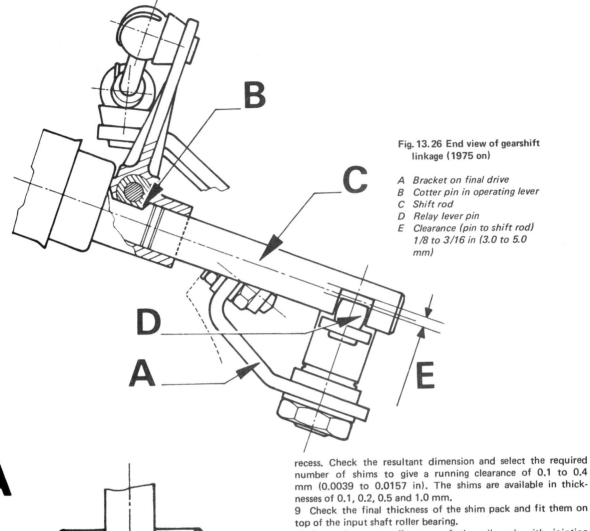

Fig. 13.26 End view of gearshift
linkage (1975 on)

A Bracket on final drive
B Cotter pin in operating lever
C Shift rod
D Relay lever pin
E Clearance (pin to shift rod)
    1/8 to 3/16 in (3.0 to 5.0
    mm)

recess. Check the resultant dimension and select the required
number of shims to give a running clearance of 0.1 to 0.4
mm (0.0039 to 0.0157 in). The shims are available in thicknesses of 0.1, 0.2, 0.5 and 1.0 mm.
9 Check the final thickness of the shim pack and fit them on
top of the input shaft roller bearing.
10 Coat the outer diameter of the oil seal with jointing
compound, position it in the casing recess with the lip towards
the bearing and carefully drive it into position using a piece of
tube of suitable diameter.
11 Refit the clutch release bearing support tube over the input
shaft and tighten the bolt to the specified torque setting.

Gearshift linkage

12 From April 1975 the gearshift linkage was improved by
attaching the relay lever to the final drive unit, thus enabling
the shift control shaft to be operated directly (see Fig. 13.24).
13 If difficulty is experienced in changing gear and the linkage
is thought to be faulty, check the length of the gear selection
rod, control tube and gear engagement rod and if necessary
adjust them to the dimensions shown in Fig. 13.25.
14 When refitting the gearshift linkage to the gearbox shift
rod, ensure that the cotter pin sits correctly on the flat on the
rod and holds the lever securely without free movement (see
'B', Fig. 13.26).
15 Also check that with the gearbox in neutral a free movement
of 3 to 5 mm (1/8 to 3/16 in) exists between the slot in the
shift rod and the pin on the relay lever ('E', Fig. 13.26). If
necessary, adjust the clearance by altering the thickness of the
spacers under the relay support on the final drive ('A', Fig.
13.26).
16 Note that from April 1975 the gear lever ball and spring
housing assembly is inverted in relation to the earlier type (see
Fig. 13.27).

Fig. 13.27 Gear lever ball and spring housing (1975 on)

A Automatic transmission only

7 Next measure the thickness of the new input shaft oil
seal using a vernier caliper or micrometer (see Fig. 13.23).
8 Now subtract the release bearing spigot and oil seal dimensions from the initial dimension obtained from the gear casing

10 Automatic transmission

Primary shaft roller bearing shims

1 The following operation must always be carried out if the gearbox or torque converter have been removed or the primary shaft oil seal or bearings disturbed or renewed.

2 With the oil seal removed, measure the distance (A) between the face of the gasket on the gearbox and the surface of the roller bearing outer track. Use a depth gauge for this (Fig.13.28).

3 Again using the gauge, measure the distance (B) between the face of the gasket on the converter housing and the locating ring (Fig.13.29).

4 Using a vernier gauge, measure the thickness (C) of the oil seal (Fig.13.30).

5 By simple calculation add dimensions B and C together, then add the necessary free play which is between 0.004 and 0.016 in (0.1 and 0.4 mm). Subtract this resultant figure from dimension (A) to give the required thickness of the shim pack which must be located on the roller bearing.

6 Install the oil seal so that its flat face is against the shims.

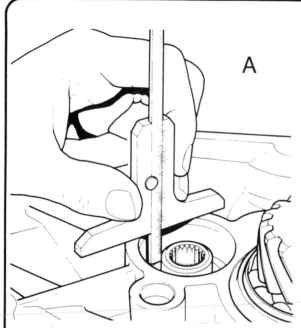

Fig. 13. 28 Measuring distance between gasket and bearing track (automatic transmission)

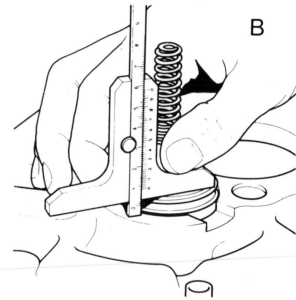

Fig. 13. 29 Measuring distance between converter housing gasket and locating ring (automatic transmission)

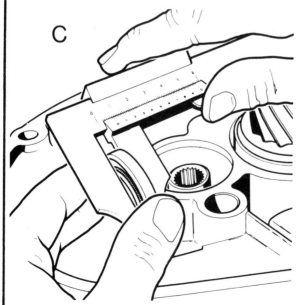

Fig. 13. 30 Measuring thickness of oil seal (primary shaft oil seal — automatic transmission)

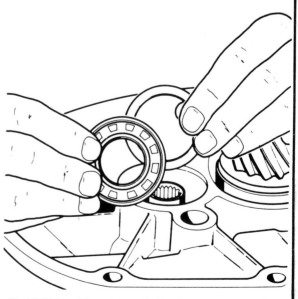

Fig. 13. 31 Installing primary shaft roller bearing shims (automatic transmission)

11 Front suspension

Driveshafts

1 Since the introduction of the Simca 1100 TI and all subsequent models (1974 on) the diameter of the driveshafts has been increased to 1.574 in (40 mm). Additionally the inner splined section of the shaft has been increased in length by 0.118 in (3 mm). Resulting from this a cut-out has been made in the planet wheel shaft retaining spacer to prevent it fouling the universal joint yoke.

2 Before fitting the later type shafts, first check that the shaft retaining spacer has a cut-out by looking through the driveshaft locating aperture in the differential. If the modified spacer is not fitted, the earlier type shafts must be obtained or the spacers changed.

12 Steering

Steering rack couplings

1 On all models from April 1972 the flexible couplings on each end of the steering rack have been replaced with balljoints. New type rubber bellows have also been fitted (see Fig. 13.33).

2 The old type couplings are interchangeable with the new balljoints providing both are renewed at the same time. Screw

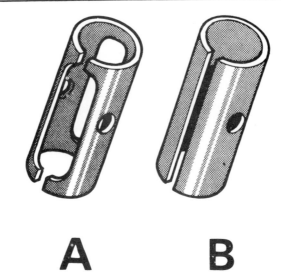

Fig. 13.32 Two types of driveshaft retaining spacers

A New type   B Old type

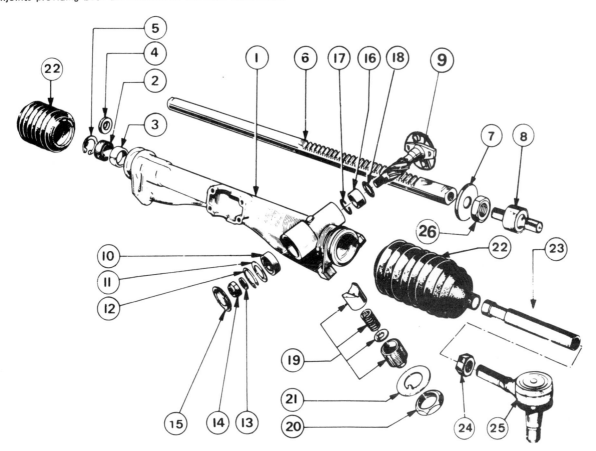

Fig. 13.33 Exploded view of later type steering assembly

1 Housing	8 Rack end balljoint	15 Cap	21 Washer
2 Flexible bush	9 Pinion/flexible coupling	16 White metal bush	22 Flexible bellows
3 Steel ring	10 Bearing	17 Snap ring	23 Track rod
4 Washer	11 Washer	18 'O' ring	24 Locknut
5 Circlip	12 Circlip	19 Slipper/spring	25 Track rod end
6 Rack	13 Washer	assembly	balljoint
7 Thrust washer	14 Nyloc nut	20 Nut	26 Locknut

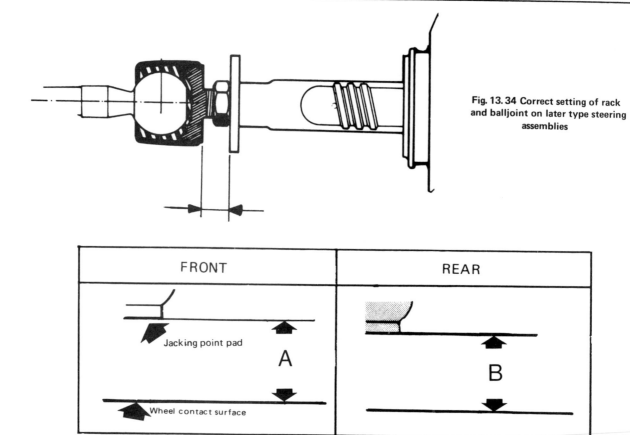

Fig. 13.34 Correct setting of rack and balljoint on later type steering assemblies

FRONT	REAR

Jacking point pad

A

Wheel contact surface

B

Fig. 13.35 Body height setting diagrams (1974 on)

	A	B
Saloon	215 mm	240 to 250 mm
Saloon (high ground clearance)	215 mm	255 mm
Estate and VF1 van		
VF2 Pick-up	235 mm	260 to 270 mm
High top van from S3 JD16P-506621	235 mm	275 mm

the joint into the rack until the distance between the spacer and the end of the balljoint is 0.433 in (11 mm) (see Fig. 13.34).

Front wheel toe-in adjustment (balljoint end fittings)
3 To adjust the front wheel toe-in on later models which have balljoint end fittings on the steering rack, release the locknut which holds the track rod end to the track rod link and then, by means of the flats provided, turn the link to reduce or increase the effective length of the link by screwing it on or off the threaded part of the track rod end. This will increase or decrease the toe-in. The links should be rotated in opposite directions (when viewed from the centre of the vehicle) in order to adjust the track equally on both sides.

Body height adjustment — revised procedure
4 The body height adjustment is now carried out by measuring directly to the lower surface of the jacking points and working to the revised dimensions shown in the illustration (Fig. 13.35).

Castor and camber angles
5 These angles are adjusted by increasing or decreasing the number of shims located between the suspension upper cross-member and the suspension arm pivot pins.
6 Moving the shims between the front and the rear bolts will alter the castor angle. Varying the thickness of the shim packs equally will alter the camber.

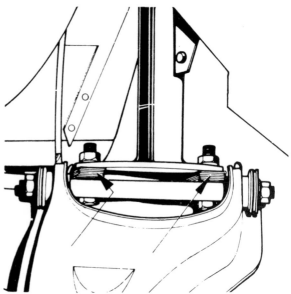

Fig. 13.36 Location of castor and camber adjustment shims on front suspension arm

13 Braking system

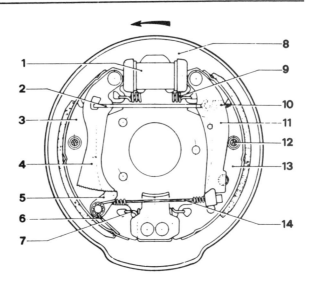

Self-adjusting rear drum brakes

1 On some models from 1973 the rear drum brakes are self-adjusting. The adjusting mechanism comprises an adjusting lever pivoted on the leading shoe, a serrated adjusting pawl and a return spring (see Fig. 13.37).

2 When the shoes move relative to each other on application of the footbrake, the adjusting lever turns on its pin and causes the pawl to rotate. This continues until the relative movement of the two levers is sufficient to permit the pawl and lever to jump one serration and thus compensate for lining wear.

Self-adjusting drum brakes — removal and refitting

3 The method of removing and refitting the self-adjusting brake shoes is basically the same as for the conventional type, with the exception that the shoes are held against the backplate by spring retainers. To remove them, push down and rotate them with a screwdriver.

4 If the adjusting lever and pawl are to be removed from the shoes, make a careful note of their positions before removing the retaining clips and springs.

5 When refitting the shoes, ensure that the adjusting lever is correctly engaged with the pawl and positioned near the lining. Fit the brake drum and press the brake pedal several times to enable the adjusting mechanism to seat the linings against the drum.

Metric hydraulic components

6 Commencing with 7 Series vehicles (1976 on) the threads used on all hydraulic components are to metric standards

Fig. 13.37 Self adjusting type of drum brake

1 Wheel cylinder	8 Backplate
2 Handbrake link	9 Shoe return spring
3 Leading shoe	10 Handbrake link springs
4 Adjusting lever	11 Handbrake lever
5 Adjusting pawl	12 Shoe steady spring
6 Pawl spring	13 Trailing shoe
7 Shoe return spring	14 Handbrake cable

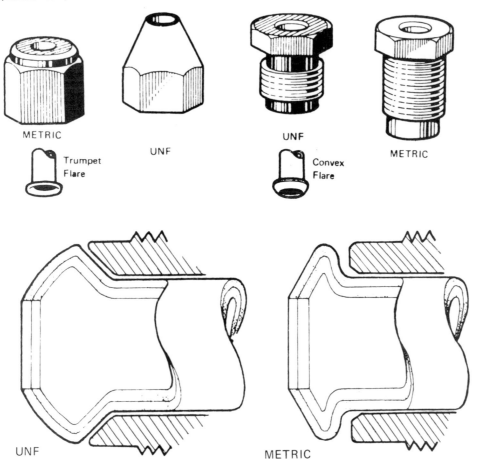

METRIC   UNF   UNF   METRIC

Trumpet Flare   Convex Flare

UNF   METRIC

Fig. 13.38 Comparison of metric and UNF hydraulic fittings

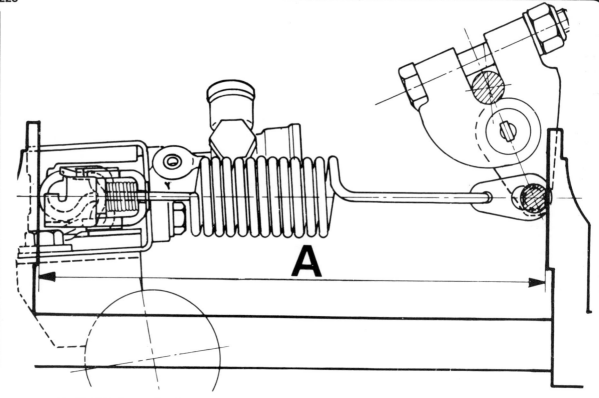

Fig. 13.39 Brake equaliser (compensator valve) adjustment diagram (up to 1975). For dimension A see text

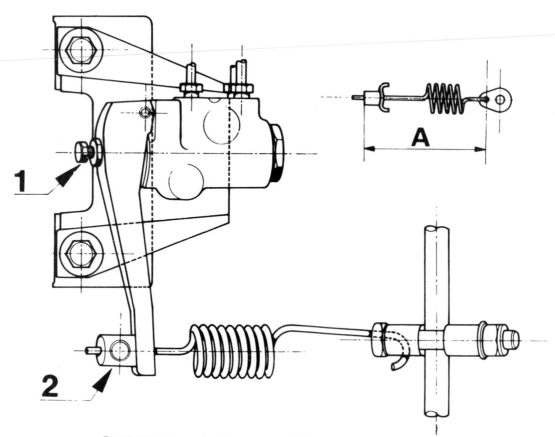

Fig. 13.40 Brake equaliser (compensator valve) adjustment diagram (1976 on)

1 Adjuster screw   2 Lock screw (do not alter)   A Setting dimension

instead of the previously used UNF threaded components.

7 Ensure that any replacements are to the correct thread pattern. Always check compatibility by screwing in the component with the fingers first.

Brake equaliser (compensator) valve up to and including Series 6 vehicles — revised adjustment procedure

8 Disconnect the lower ends of the rear shock absorbers. Do not disconnect the anti-roll bar.

9 Detach the rubber suspension ring on the right-hand side of the exhaust silencer.

10 Using a vernier gauge, measure dimension A as shown in Fig. 13.39. For models built before 1970 this should be 7.756 in (197.0 mm). For later models 7.992 in (203.0 mm).

11 If necessary, release the pinch bolt on the lever (1) and alter the position of the lever.

12 Reconnect the shock absorbers and exhaust ring.

Brake equaliser (compensator valve) commencing Series 7 vehicles (1976 on) — adjustment procedure

13 This operation should be carried out if it is suspected that there is insufficient rear wheel braking, or after removal and re-fitting of the valve assembly, the rear anti-roll bar, or the rear suspension crossmember.

14 Set the vehicle on level ground with a full fuel tank. If the tank is not full, weight the luggage area as follows:
Tank nearly empty: load with 66 lbs (30 kg)
Tank half full: load with 33 lbs (15 kg).

15 Release the handbrake and bounce the vehicle to settle the suspension.

16 Load the luggage area with a further 176 lbs (80 kg) as near to the rear panel as possible.

17 Disconnect the exhaust silencer rear right-hand suspension ring.

18 Now measure the length of the valve sensing spring as shown in Fig.13.40. The dimension must be in accordance with the following:

All models except TI and those for Sweden: 6.46 to 6.57 in (164 to 167 mm).
TI and Swedish models: 6.70 to 6.81 in (170 to 173 mm).

19 If adjustment is necessary, slacken the nut on the operating arm and move the adjusting screw (1) in or out as necessary. On no account disturb the setting of the spring stop lock screw (2).

20 Reconnect the exhaust silencer suspension ring and remove the weights from the luggage area.

Single circuit hydraulic system — revised bleeding procedure

21 It has been found that, due to the routeing of the hydraulic lines on vehicles equipped with a servo unit, satisfactory bleeding cannot be carried out without using a pressure bleed kit. These kits are readily available and usually operate from the spare wheel.

22 Depress the brake pedal several times in rapid succession in order to destroy the servo vacuum.

23 Connect the bleed kit in accordance with the makers' instructions and pressurize (usually by air pressure from the spare wheel) at between 20 and 28 lbf/in^2.

24 Open each bleed screw in turn (one on each caliper and wheel cylinder plus one screw on the cylinder attached to the servo unit).

25 As the bleeding is being carried out, have an assistant depress the brake pedal very slowly several times and control the return of the pedal so that it does not fly back under its own force.

26 Close each bleed nipple as soon as there is no longer any sign of air bubbles in the fluid being ejected, with the assistant holding the foot pedal depressed.

27 Remove the pressure bleed equipment, discard the fluid which has been bled from the system and top up the fluid reservoir with fresh fluid which has been stored in a sealed container and which has remained unshaken for 24 hours.

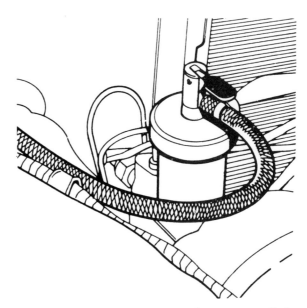

Fig. 13.41 Typical brake bleed connection to master cylinder reservoir ready for pressure bleeding

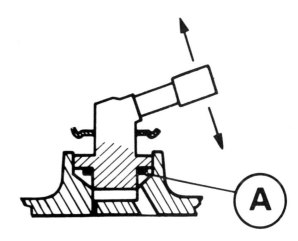

Fig. 13.42 Master cylinder inlet union seal (A)

Dual-circuit hydraulic system — revised bleeding procedure

28 The operations are similar to those described for single-circuit systems, except that only if the master cylinder has been disturbed need the complete system be bled. Otherwise, only the front or rear circuit need be bled dependent upon which circuit has been 'broken'.

Master cylinder plastic fluid inlet unions — renewal

29 If the plastic type inlet unions are to be renewed, it is imperative that the following points are observed:
  (a) Before removing a union, mark its relative position with respect to the centre line of the cylinder
  (b) Always use a new seal (A) (Fig.13.42)
  (c) Install the new Truarc ring with a tubular tool so that (i) the union is in the original marked position and (ii) the tabs on the new ring do not coincide with the original staking marks on the master cylinder body
  (d) Never attempt to reposition the inlet union once the Truarc ring has been fitted

14 Electrical system

Starter motor

1 From 1973 onwards a starter motor with a nine-tooth pinion is fitted in place of the ten-tooth pinion used previously. A larger diameter starter ring is also used in conjunction with the new pinion and if a new starter motor/pinion is being fitted ensure the correct type is obtained from your Simca dealer.

2 The pinion end-float on these later starter motors should be adjusted in the following way.

3 Remove the cap from the solenoid core to gain access to the adjusting screw.

4 Press down on the starter solenoid to bring the pinion into its operating position.

5 The clearance (H) (Fig.13.43) should be between 0.019 and 0.059 in (0.5 and 1.5 mm). Adjust if necessary by turning the solenoid core screw with a 12 mm spanner.

Instrument panel (1100 TI models) — removal and re-fitting

6 The Simca 1100 TI models are fitted with a six-dial instrument panel.

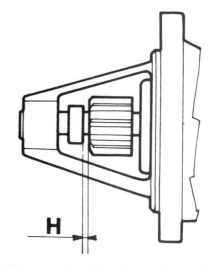

Fig. 13.43 Starter motor pinion clearance diagram for (H) see text

Fig. 13.44 Instrument panel (1100 TI)

1 Main lighting switch	9 Direction indicator lamp	17 Wiper switch
2 Securing screw	10 Tachometer	18 Fog or auxiliary lamp
3 Fuel gauge	11 Trip recorder knob	switch
4 Low fuel warning lamp	12 Ignition warning lamp	19 Heated rear window
5 Oil pressure gauge	13 Water temperature gauge	switch
6 Oil pressure warning lamp	14 Parking lamp warning indicator	20 Brake hydraulic system
7 Headlamp warning lamp	15 Clock	leakage warning lamp
8 Speedometer	16 Securing screw	21 Hazard warning switch

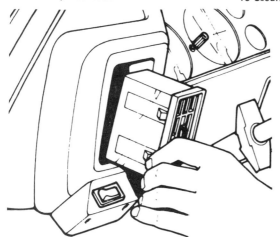

Fig. 13.45 Withdrawing a fresh air vent (1975 on)

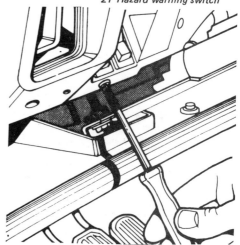

Fig. 13.46 Removing switch panel lower screws (1975 on)

7 To remove the panel, first undo the two facia securing screws (items 2 and 16 in Fig. 13.44).

8 Remove the two securing screws from beneath the dashboard.

9 Disconnect the speedometer cable from the gearbox.

10 Disconnect the battery earth terminal.

11 Carefully pull the facia panel forward just enough to disconnect the wiring connectors, and lift away the panel.

12 Refit the panel using the reverse procedure to removal.

Instrument panel (LS, GLS, Special) 1975 on — removal and refitting

13 To remove the instrument panel on these later LS, GLS and Special models it is first necessary to remove the surrounding crash padding.

14 For safety reasons, disconnect the battery earth terminal.

15 Remove the two steering column upper mounting bolts and lower the upper column and steering wheel.

16 Remove the screw from each end of the crash roll and withdraw the fresh air vent (Fig. 13.45).

17 Remove the two screws securing the ashtray and withdraw the ashtray assembly.

18 If a radio is fitted, remove the control knobs and the radio finisher screws.

19 Remove the two screws securing the heater control surround and withdraw the surround.

20 Remove the bottom screws from the switch panels (Fig. 13.46).

21 Remove the seven screws securing the crash roll (see Fig. 13.47).

22 Lift the crash roll assembly upwards to release it from the clips on the upper edge of the facia (see Fig. 13.48).

23 Pass the switches through the crash roll assembly, disconnect the cigar lighter, clock and map light if fitted and lift the crash roll away from the vehicle.

24 To remove the instrument panel, undo the four screws retaining the panel to the facia ('B' in Fig. 13.49).

25 Carefully withdraw the instrument panel away from the facia and disconnect the speedometer cable and electrical plug from behind the panel.

26 Withdraw the instrument panel from the vehicle.

27 Access to the instruments is gained by releasing the six clips securing the front glass to the instrument panel.

28 Refit the instrument panel and crash roll assembly using the reverse procedure to removal.

Steering column combination switch (1100 TI) — removal and installation

29 Disconnect the battery.

30 Remove the cap from the centre of the steering wheel hub, unscrew the securing nut and withdraw the steering wheel.

31 Extract the two screws which retain the combination switch plate.

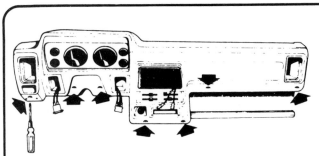

Fig. 13.47 Crash roll securing screws (1975 on — left-hand drive shown)

Fig. 13.48 Releasing crash roll from upper clips (1975 on)

Fig. 13.49 Releasing instrument panel screws (A and B) 1975 on

Fig. 13.50 Steering column switch (1100 TI). Extracting switch plate screws

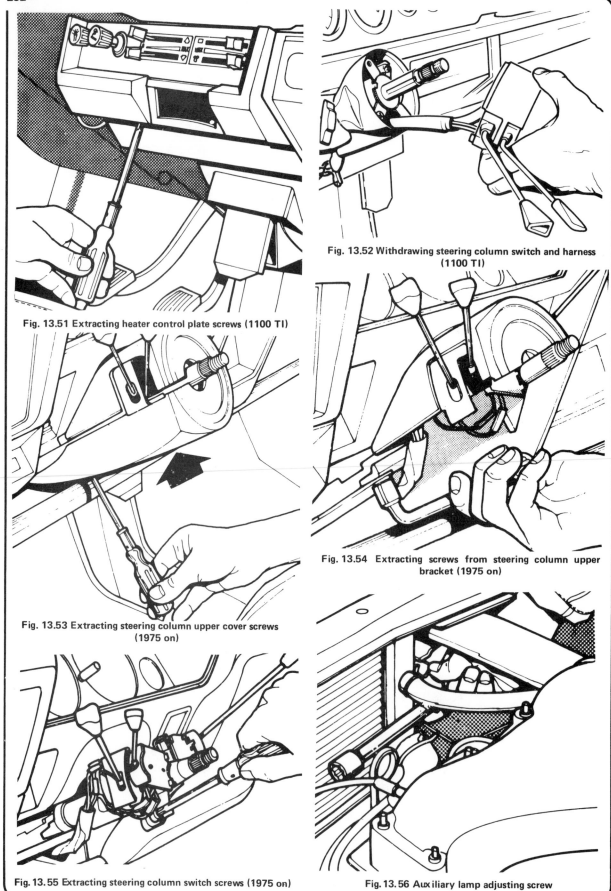

Fig. 13.51 Extracting heater control plate screws (1100 TI)

Fig. 13.52 Withdrawing steering column switch and harness (1100 TI)

Fig. 13.53 Extracting steering column upper cover screws (1975 on)

Fig. 13.54 Extracting screws from steering column upper bracket (1975 on)

Fig. 13.55 Extracting steering column switch screws (1975 on)

Fig. 13.56 Auxiliary lamp adjusting screw

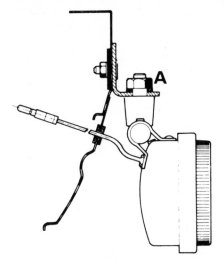

Fig. 13.57 Fog lamp adjusting screw (1100 TI)

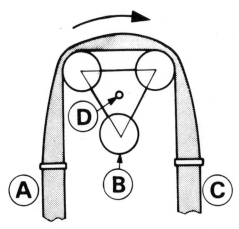

Fig. 13.58 Diagrammatic view of windscreen washer pump

A Inlet tube   C Outlet tube
B Rollers   D Motor shaft

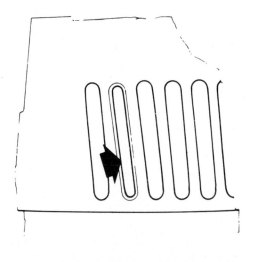

Fig. 13.59 Location of windscreen washer jets on all later models

32 Extract the four screws which retain the heater control surround, and pull the surround away to provide access to the switch wiring harness junction box.
33 Disconnect the leads and junction box and withdraw the switch with wiring harness.
34 Install the switch by reversing the removal operation.

Steering column combination switch (1975 on) — removal and installation
35 Disconnect the battery.
36 Prise out the motif from the centre of the steering wheel hub, unscrew the retaining nut and withdraw the steering wheel.
37 Extract the three screws which hold both halves of the steering column upper covers together and remove the lower cover.
38 Extract the two screws which hold the steering column upper bracket in position and lower the steering column carefully. Remove the upper cover.
39 Extract the three screws and withdraw the combination switch until the multi-plug connectors can be disconnected.
40 Installation is a reversal of removal.

Auxiliary lamp adjustment
41 The lamp adjusting nuts are accessible from within the engine compartment.
42 The fog lamps on 1100 TI vehicles have their combined fixing and adjusting nuts located behind the bumpers.

Windscreen washer/wiper switch
43 Later types have a stalk switch mounted on the steering column which gives continuous (two-speed) operation, single wipe, and washer control.
44 The electrically-operated washer pump is mounted on the engine compartment valance and is of a roller type which squeezes a rubber tube flat to create the pumping action.
45 The washer jets on all later models are located within one of the slots in the cowl grille.

15 Bodywork and underframe

Heater controls (up to 1975) — removal and refitting
1 Extract the four screws which hold the padding round the heater control plate.

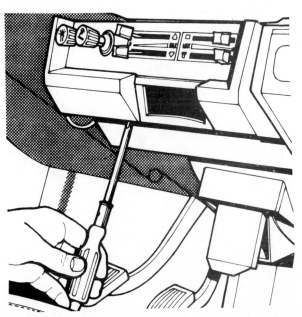

Fig. 13.60 Extracting heater control panel surround (to 1975)

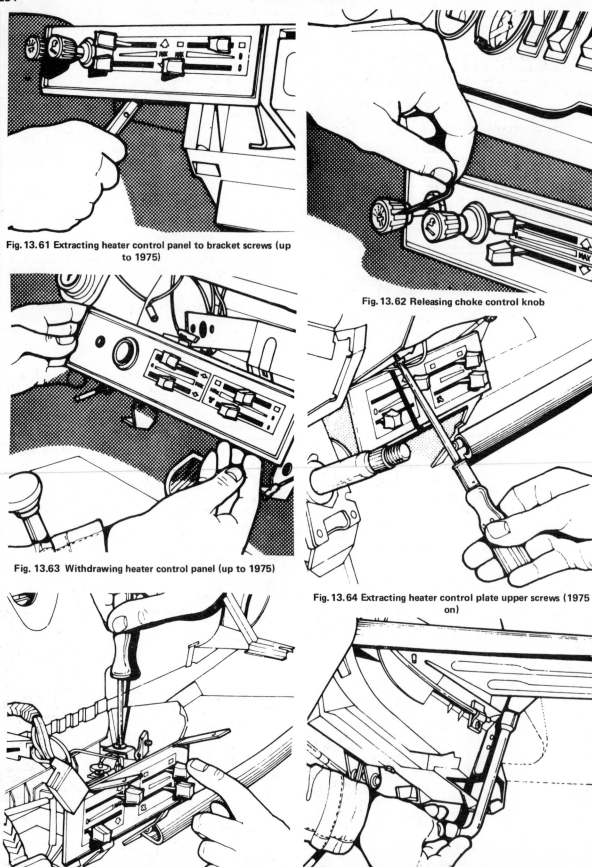

Fig. 13.61 Extracting heater control panel to bracket screws (up to 1975)

Fig. 13.62 Releasing choke control knob

Fig. 13.63 Withdrawing heater control panel (up to 1975)

Fig. 13.64 Extracting heater control plate upper screws (1975 on)

Fig. 13.65 Heater control plate lower screws (1975 on)

Fig. 13.66 Removing heater mounting screws (1975 on)

2 Extract the three screws which hold the control plate to its brackets.

3 Using an Allen key, loosen the grub screw and pull off the choke knob. Release the choke cable nut.

4 Release all the heater control cable positioning clips and disconnect the cigar lighter leads (if fitted).

5 Disconnect the heater rheostat leads and withdraw the heater control panel.

6 Refitting is a reversal of removal.

Heater controls (1975 on) — removal and refitting

7 Disconnect the battery and remove the crash roll (see Section 14, paragraphs 13 to 28 of this Chapter).

8 Extract the two upper screws which hold the heater control plate to the facia, followed by the two lower screws.

9 Disconnect the heater control cables and the leads from the

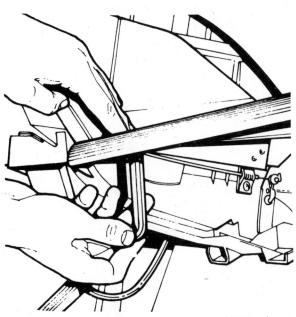

Fig. 13.67 Removing parcels shelves screws (1975 on)

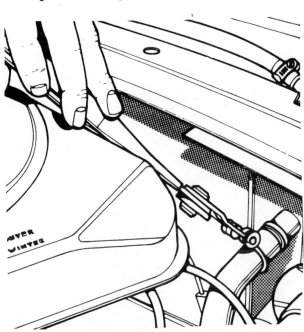

Fig. 13.68 Disconnecting heater hose from radiator (1975 on)

rheostat and withdraw the control panel.

Heater (1975 on) — removal and refitting

10 Disconnect the battery and remove the crash roll.

11 Drain the cooling system.

12 Remove the centre console (if fitted).

13 Remove the four screws which hold the heater assembly to the bulkhead.

14 Extract the two bolts which hold the left-hand and right-hand parcel shelves, also the screw which holds the heater control panel.

15 Disconnect the heater hoses from the radiator and also from the inlet manifold.

16 Push the heater hose insulating piece, with hoses, through the engine compartment rear bulkhead and withdraw the heater from the vehicle interior.

17 Refitting is a reversal of removal.

Front door handle (1975 on) — removal and refitting

18 Remove the door interior panel as described for earlier models (Chapter 12, Section 10).

19 Disconnect the locking rod (A) (Fig.13.70) at the lock end, withdraw the clip and locking plunger (D).

20 Disconnect the external handle rod (B) from the lock and remove the lock assembly.

21 Release the fixings from the external handle mounting studs and remove the handle.

22 Refitting is a reversal of removal.

Rear door handle (1975 on) — removal and refitting

23 To remove the interior locking mechanism, take off the door trim panel as described for earlier models (Chapter 12, Section 10).

24 Disconnect the interior locking rod (C) (Fig.13.71) from the lock and the intermediate control.

25 Withdraw the bush which retains the locking rod to the door inner panel and remove the rod.

26 Release the intermediate control from the door inner panel.

27 Prise off the remote control embellisher (Fig.13.72).

28 Extract the remote control fixing screw (Fig.13.73).

29 Slide the remote control handle to release its front locating tab (Fig.13.74).

30 Disconnect the remote control rod from the handle.

31 Remove the exterior handle by inserting a screwdriver and extracting the securing screws as shown in Fig.13.75.

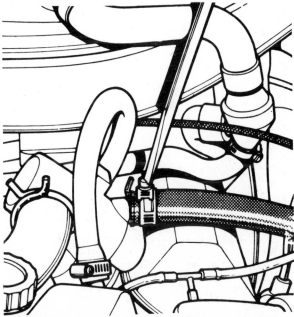

Fig. 13.69 Disconnecting heater hose from inlet manifold

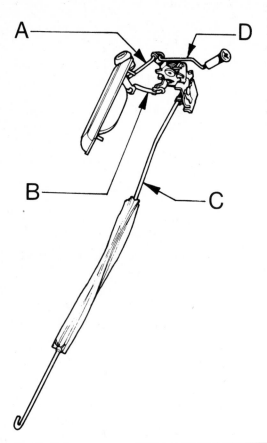

Fig. 13.70 Front door handle connections (1975 on)

A Locking rod   C Interior locking rod
B External handle link rod D Locking plunger

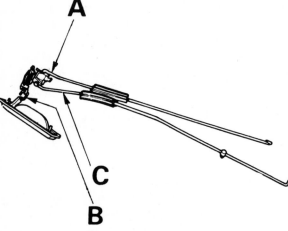

Fig. 13.71 Rear door handle connections (1975 on)

A Locking rod   C Interior locking rod
B External handle link rod

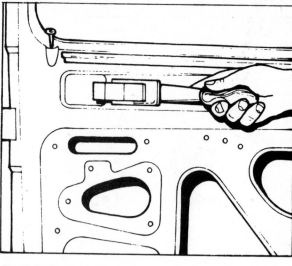

Fig. 13.72 Removing door remote control embellisher (1975 on)

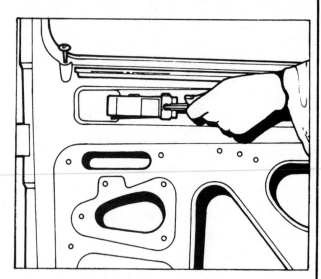

Fig. 13.73 Extracting remote control fixing screw (1975 on)

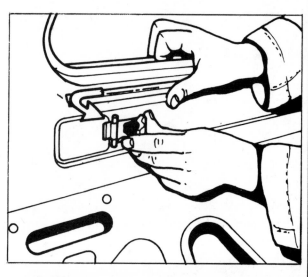

Fig. 13.74 Sliding remote control from its locating tag

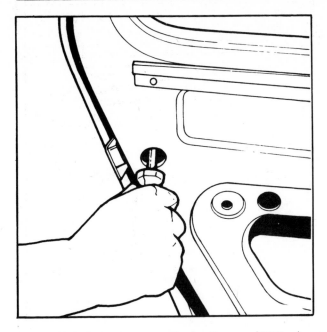

Fig. 13.75 Extracting an exterior handle screw (1975 on)

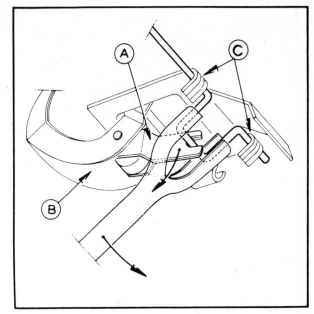

Fig. 13.76 Tool for releasing tailgate counterbalance rods on estate car

A Notched link   B Swan neck   C Lugs

32 Extract the door lock mounting screws.
33 Remove the striker backplate.
34 Disconnect the remote control rod (A) and the link (B) in Fig.13.71. Remove the lock and exterior handle.

Estate tailgate counterbalance rods — removal and refitting
35 Open the tailgate fully, and support it with a strut or have an assistant hold it in this position.
36 A long bar should now be made up with a fork at one end so that the counterbalance rod can be tensioned by prising it to-

wards the front of the vehicle until the bottom of the serrated link (A) (Fig.13.76) which is hinged to the swan neck (B) can be released.
neck as a fulcrum point, release the counterbalance rod from the lugs (C).
38 Free the counterbalance rod in a similar way from the opposite end.
39 Refitting is a reversal of removal, but fit the right-hand rod first. This is the rod which has an extra crank at the end opposite to the large crank. Both rods incorporate these large cranks.

See overleaf for wiring diagrams

238

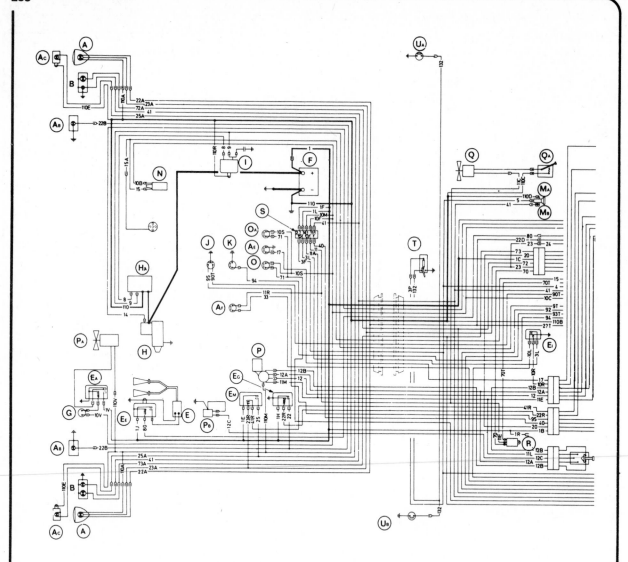

Fig. 13.77 Wiring diagram for 1974 models
See key on Pages 244 and 245

Wire No.	Colour		Sectional area in mm²
	Main	Secondary	
1	Red	White	7
1 A	Red		3
1 B	Red		2
1 C	Red		2
1 E	Red		2
1 F	Red		2
1 H	Red		2
1 R	Red		2
1 J	Red		3
1 L	Red		2
1 V	Red	Violet	2
3 F	White	Red	2
3 L	White	Red	2
3 P	White	Red	0.6
4	Red		0.6
5	White	Red	1.4

Wire No.	Colour		Sectional area in mm²
	Main	Secondary	
8	Red	Yellow	1
9	Red	Green	1
9 T	Red	Green	0.6
10	Red	Grey	3
10 B	Red	Grey	1
10 C	Red	Grey	0.6
10 F	Red	Grey	2
10 L	Black	Blue at relay end / Black harness end	2
10 M	Red	Brown	1
10 R	Red	Green	0.6
10 S	Red	Grey	1
10 V	Red	Grey	0.6
11	Grey		2
11 A	Grey	Brown	1
11 C	Grey		1

Wire No.	Colour		Sectional area in mm²
	Main	Secondary	
11 E	Grey		1
11 F	Grey		1
11 L	Grey		1
11 M	Grey	Red	1
11 R	Grey	Brown	1
12	Grey	White	1
12 A	Grey	Blue	1
12 B	Black		1
12 C	Grey	Yellow	0.6
14	Grey	Black	2
15	Black	Yellow	0.6
15 A	Black		1
17	Black	Green	0.6
20	Blue	Red	2
22	Blue		2
22 A	Blue		1

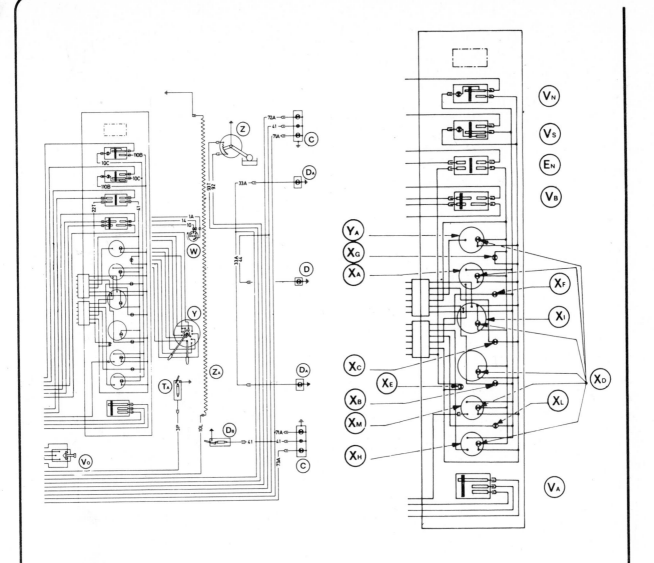

239

Fig. 13.77 Wiring diagram for 1974 models (continued)

Wire No.	Colour			Sectional area in mm²
	Main	Secondary	Additional	
22 B	Blue	Green		1
22 D	Blue	Green		2
22 R	Blue	Green		0.6
22 T	Blue			0.6
23	Blue	Yellow		2
23 A	Blue	Yellow		1
23 R	Blue	Yellow		0.6
24	Blue	Blue	Yellow	2
25	Blue			2
25 A	Blue	Brown		1
33	Blue	Grey		1
33 A	Blue	Grey		0.6
40	Green			0.6
41	Green			0.6
41 R	Green	White		0.6
44	Black			
70	White	Brown		1.4

Wire No.	Colour			Sectional area in mm²
	Main	Secondary	Additional	
70 T	White	Violet		0.6
71	White	Violet		1
71 A	White	Violet		0.6
72	White	White	Green	1
72 A	White			0.6
73	White	White	Red	1
73 A	White			0.6
80	White	Green at relay end Blue harness end		0.6
90 T	Yellow	Black		1
92	Yellow	Red		0.6
93 T	Yellow			0.6
94	Yellow	White		1
95	Yellow	Brown		1

Wire No.	Colour	Sectional area in mm²
	Main	
110	Black	5
110 A	Black	1
110 B	Black	0.6
110 C	Black	1
110 D	Black	1.4
110 E	Black	1
110 M	Black	1
110 P	Black	0.6
110 R	Black	1
110 V	Black	2
132	Black	0.6

WIRING AND TERMINAL COLOUR CODE

Code	Colour	Code	Colour
BA	White	MR	Brown
BE	Blue	RG	Red
GR	Slate	VE	Green
JN	Yellow	VI	Purple
NO	Black		

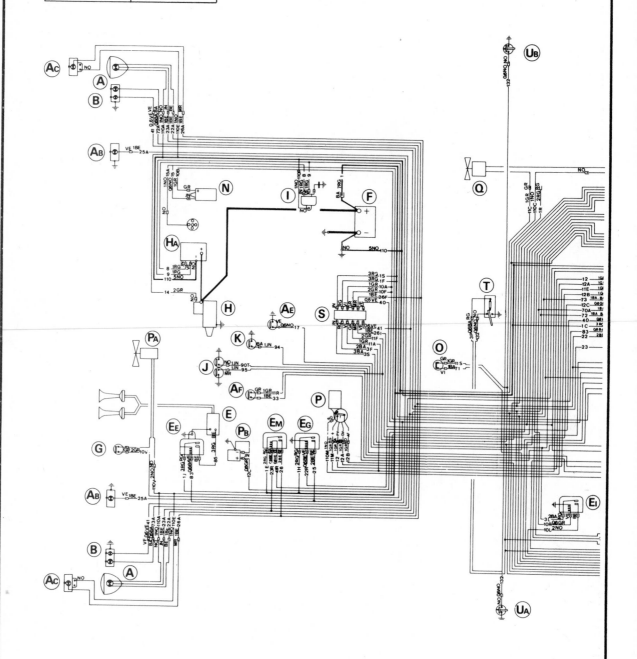

Fig. 13.78 Wiring diagram for 1975 and 1976 models
See key on Pages 244 and 245

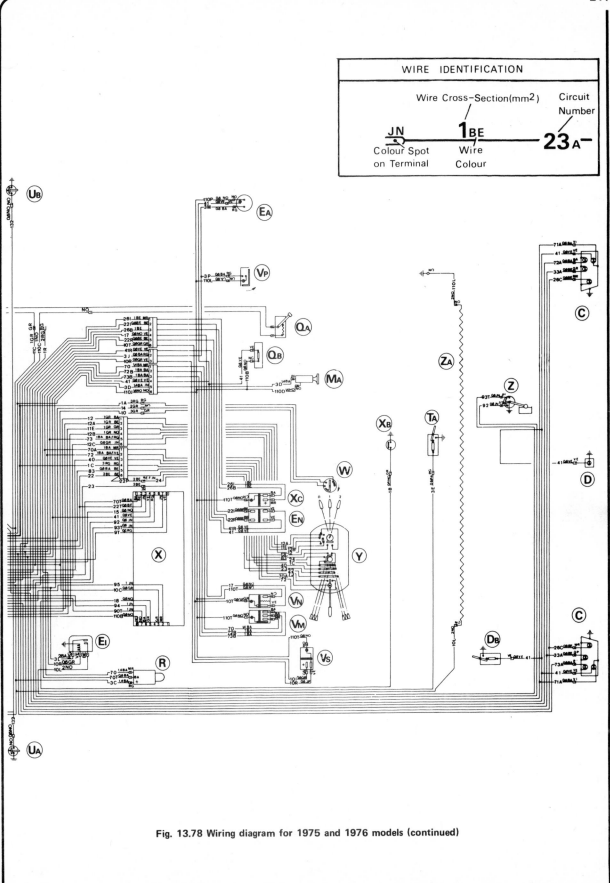

Fig. 13.78 Wiring diagram for 1975 and 1976 models (continued)

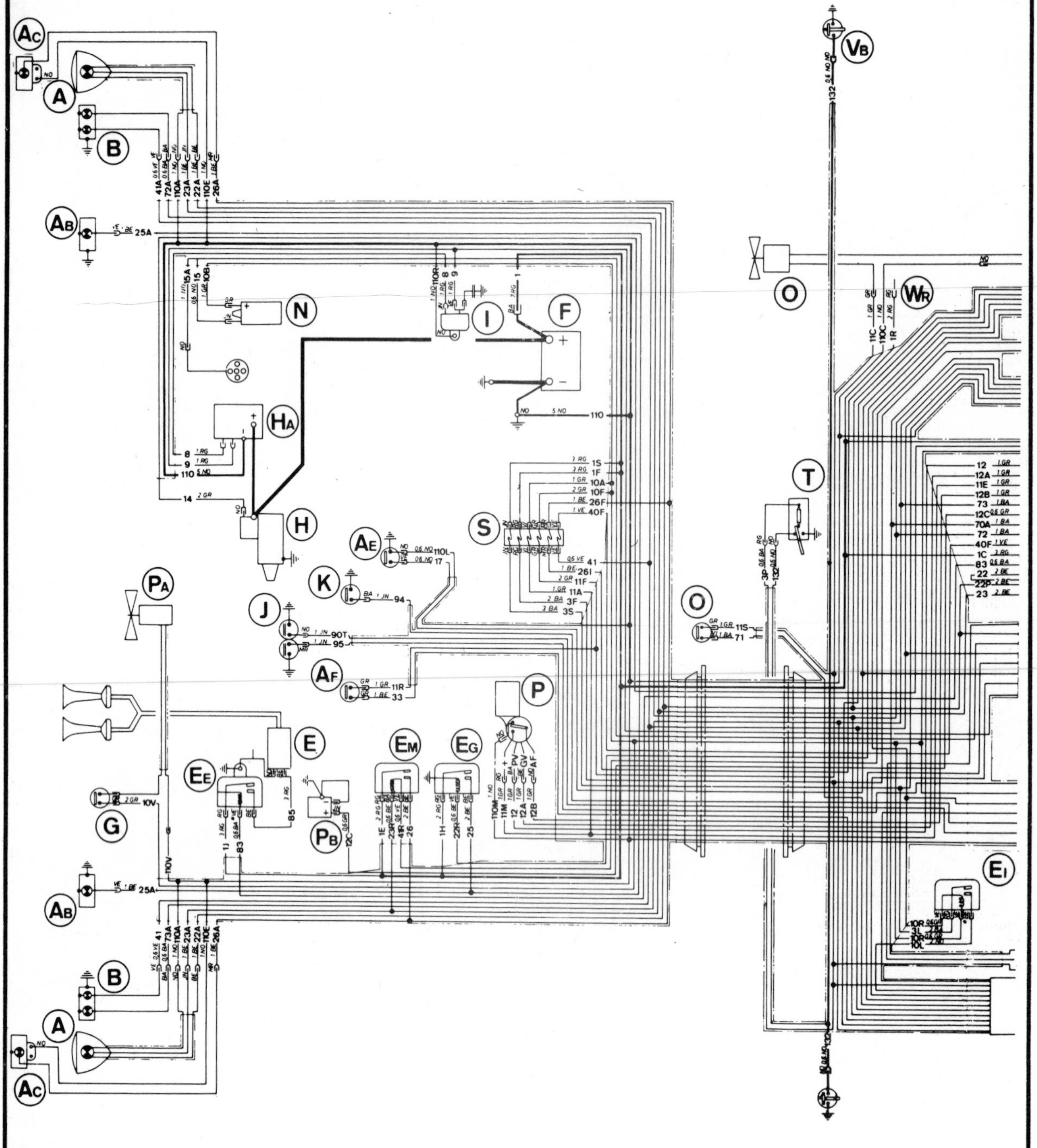

Fig. 13.79 Wiring diagram for 1977 models
See key on Pages 244 and 245

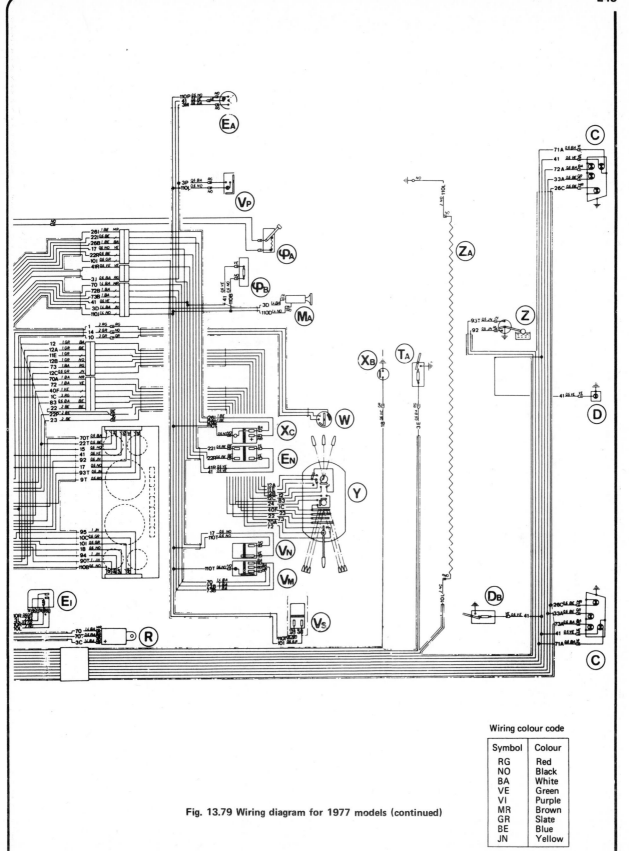

Fig. 13.79 Wiring diagram for 1977 models (continued)

Wiring colour code

Symbol	Colour
RG	Red
NO	Black
BA	White
VE	Green
VI	Purple
MR	Brown
GR	Slate
BE	Blue
JN	Yellow

Key to wiring diagrams for 1974 to 1977 models

FUNCTION	QUANTITY	POSITION		POWER
Battery	1	on scuttle	F	12V - 40AH
Dipped headlights	2	on front end panel	A	40W or 55W iodine vapour
Main beam headlights	2	on front end panel	A	45W or 60W iodine vapour
Long-range headlights (S, TI)	2	recessed into radiator grille	A_B	55W iodine vapour
Long-range headlights relay (S, TI)	1	on front LH wheel arch	E_G	
Sidelights	2	under headlight	B	5W
Rear lights	2	on rear end panel	C	5W
Instrument panel light	3	in instrument panel X		2W
Number plate light	1	on rear bumpers	D	5W
Side light warning light	1	in instrument panel X	X_G	as instrument panel light
Direction indicators (front)	2	under headlights	B	21W
Direction indicators (rear)	2	on rear end panel	C	21W
Flasher unit	1	on bracket of glove box	R	42W/84W
Flasher indicator light	1	in instrument panel X		2W
Headlight warning light	1	in instrument panel X		2W
'No charge' warning light	1	in instrument panel X		3W/24V
Oil pressure warning light	1	in instrument panel X		2W
Coolant temperature gauge	1	in instrument panel X		
Fuel warning light	1	in instrument panel X		
Fuel gauge	1	in instrument panel X		
Clock (GLS, S)	1	in instrument panel X		
Tachometer (S, TI)	1	in instrument panel X		
Cigar lighter (GLS, S, TI)	1	on facia	M_A	
Front interior light	1	on the centreline of the vehicle above the windscreen	T	4W
Rear interior light (Estate, GLS, S, TI)	1	on the centreline of the vehicle above the rear window	T_A	4W
Heater motor	1	in the centre under the facia	O	
Windscreen wiper motor	1	on the left, under the scuttle panel	P	
Fan motor	1	in the radiator casing	P_A	
Clock (TI)	1	right hand of facia	E_A	
Horn compressor (TI)	1	on the front LH wheel arch	E	
Horn compressor relay (TI)	1	on the front LH wheel arch	E_E	
Windscreen washer electric pump	1	on the scuttle	P_B	
Stop lights	2	on the rear panel	C	21W
Starter motor	1	on the clutch housing	H	
Alternator	1	at the right behind the lower front flap	H_A	
Regulator	1	alongside the battery	I	
Coil	1	on the front RH wheel arch	N	
Brake warning light (TI)	1	in instrument panel X		2W
Headlight flasher	2	on the front end panel	A	40W or 60W iodine vapour
Fog lights (TI)	2	on the front flap	A_C	55W iodine vapour
Fog light relay (TI)	1	on the front LH wheel arch	E_M	
Rear window heater element	1	in the rear window	Z_A	110W
Heated rear window relay	1	on the steering column support	E_I	
Rear window warning light	1	in instrument panel X		2W
Oil pressure gauge (TI)	1	in the instrument panel X		
Reversing light (GLS, S and TI)	2	on the rear end panel	C	21W
Boot light (GLS, S and TI)	1	on the rear panel LH stiffener	D_B	4W
Map reading light (TI)	1	on facia	V_P	4W
Diaphragm horn (S)	2	on the LH and RH bumper ties	—	
HF horn (LS, GLS)	2	on the front LH side member	—	
Hazard warning	4	as flasher unit	B and C	21W
Hazard warning light	1	in hazard warning switch	in MM	2W
Handbrake warning light (S and TI)	1	in instrument panel X		2W
Heater control illumination	1	on facia	OB	5W/24V
Rear fog lamps	2	on rear panel	C	21W
Fuse box	1	on bulkhead		
Accessory socket	1	behind heater panel		

Key to wiring diagrams for 1974 to 1977 models

WIRE NUMBERS	CONTROLS	PROTECTION
23A, 110A	on the combination switch Y under the steering column	
22A, 110A	on the combination switch Y under the steering column	
25A	on the combination switch Y under the steering column + relay E_G	
25, 22R, 1H	on the combination switch Y under the steering column + 2-way switch E_N	
41	on combination switch	fuse 1
41	on combination switch	fuse 1
41, 110B	on combination switch	fuse 1
41	on combination switch	fuse 1
41, 110B	combination switch	fuse 1
72A, 73A	control on combination switch)	fuse 5
72A, 73A	control on combination switch)	fuse 5
3C, 70, 70T	control on combination switch) simultaneously controlled	fuse 5
70T, 110B	control on combination switch)	fuse 5
22T, 110B	in common with headlight control	
9T, 10C	in common with alternator	
90T, 10C	pressure switch J on engine	
10G, 94, 110B	temperature switch K on engine	
10C, 93T	tank unit Z	
10C, 92, 110B	tank unit Z	
4, 110B	from + battery before ignition switch	fuse 5
15, 110B	by contact breaker and distributor	
3D, 110D	by button	fuse 6
3P, 132	manual or by door switch U_A and U_B	fuse 5
3P	manual	fuse 5
11C, 110C	by rheostat switch Q_A	fuse 3
11M, 12, 12A, 12B, 110M	on combination switch	fuse 4
110P, 3M	by temperature switch on radiator	
110P, 3M	from + battery before ignition switch	fuse 5
	by horn relay E_E	
1J, 83	at the end of the dipswitch control	
12G	combination switch	fuse 4
71A	by switch O on brake pedal	fuse 3
14, cable +	stg. column switch W in starting position	
8, 9, 110	by engine	
8, 9	by charging voltage	
10B, 15		
17, 110B	by brake warning light V_N or transmitter A_E	
22A, 110B	on combination switch under steering column	
26A, 110E	by fog light relay E_M	
1E, 23R, 41R, 26	on combination switch under steering column + 2-way switch E_N	
110L, 10L	by switch with built-in warning light V_S + relay E_I	fuse 6
10B, 10L, 3L	by switch with built-in warning light V_S	
10C, 110B	by brake warning light switch V_S	
95, 110B, 10C	by oil pressure transmitter J on engine	
33A	by switch on gearbox A_F	fuse 3
41	by manual switch + main switch V_A	fuse 1
3P, 110L	by switch on the light unit	fuse 5
80	at the end of the dipswitch control	
80	at the end of the dipswitch control	
72A, 73A	by hazard warning switch M_M	fuse 5
110T, 70	common with hazard warning	fuse 5
18, 10C	by switch Xb on handbrake	
110B, 41	on the combination switch under steering column	
26C	by fog lamp switch XO	fuse 2

Index

Printed by
Haynes Publishing Group
Sparkford Yeovil Somerset
England